PRINCIPLES OF EUROPEAN FAMILY LAW REGARDING PARENTAL RESPONSIBILITIES

EUROPEAN FAMILY LAW SERIES

PRINCIPLES OF EUROPEAN FAMILY LAW REGARDING PARENTAL RESPONSIBILITIES

Katharina Boele-Woelki
Frédérique Ferrand
Cristina González Beilfuss
Maarit Jänterä-Jareborg
Nigel Lowe
Dieter Martiny
Walter Pintens

in collaboration with

Masha Antokolskaia, Nina Dethloff, Heinz Hausheer,
Milana Hrusaková, Achilles Koutsouradis, Kirsti Kurki-Suonio,
Ingrid Lund-Andersen, Andrzej Mączyński, Miguel Martín-Casals,
Valentinas Mikelenas, Guilherme De Oliveira, Salvatore Patti,
Marianne Roth, Ingeborg Schwenzer, Geoffrey Shannon,
Tone Sverdrup, Velina Todorova, Emilia Weiss

intersentia
Antwerpen – Oxford

Distribution for the UK:
Hart Publishing Ltd.
16C Worcester Place
Oxford OX1 2JW
UK
Tel: + 44 1865 51 75 30
Fax: + 44 1865 51 07 10

Distribution for Switzerland and Germany:
Stämpfli Verlag AG
Wölflistrasse 1
CH-3001 Bern
Switzerland
Tel: + 41 (0)31 300 63 18
Fax: + 41 (0)31 300 66 88

Distribution for North America:
Gaunt Inc.
Gaunt Building
3011 Gulf Drive
Holmes Beach
Florida 34217-2199
USA
Tel: + 1 941 778 5211
Fax: + 1 941 778 5252

Distribution for other countries:
Intersentia Publishers
Groenstraat 31
BE-2640 Mortsel
Belgium
Tel: + 32 3 680 15 50
Fax: + 32 3 658 71 21

Principles of European Family Law Regarding Parental Responsibilities
Katharina Boele-Woelki, Frédérique Ferrand, Cristina González Beilfuss, Maarit Jänterä-Jareborg, Nigel Lowe, Dieter Martiny, Walter Pintens

ISBN 978-90-5095-645-1
D/2007/7849/36
NUR 822 and 828

PREFACE

The Commission on European Family Law

The Commission on European Family Law (CEFL), which was established in September 2001, drafts common principles that are thought to be the most suitable for the harmonisation of family law in Europe. The first set of Principles was published in 2004 (BOELE-WOELKI/FERRAND/GONZÁLEZ BEILFUSS/JÄNTERÄ-JAREBORG/LOWE/MARTINY/PINTENS, *Principles of European Family Law Regarding Divorce and Maintenance Between Former Spouses*, European Family Law Series No. 7). This book contains the second set.

Organisation

The CEFL consists of the *Organising Committee* (Katharina Boele-Woelki (chair), Frédérique Ferrand, Cristina González Beilfuss, Maarit Jänterä-Jareborg, Nigel Lowe, Dieter Martiny and Walter Pintens) and the *Expert Group* which at present has 26 members. The Organising Committee prepares and co-ordinates the work of the CEFL as a whole. The members of the Organising Committee are at the same time members of the Expert Group. The Expert Group comprises specialists in the field of family and comparative law from most of the Member States of the European Union with the involvement of experts from other European countries, such as Norway, Russia and Switzerland.

The CEFL is a foundation according to Dutch law. It has its seat at Utrecht University's Molengraaff Institute for Private Law, Nobelstraat 2a, 3512 EN Utrecht, www.law.uu.nl/priv/cefl. Dr. Bente Braat heads CEFL's secretariat, its Webmaster is Dr. Ian Curry-Sumner. They are both researchers at the Utrecht Centre for European Research into Family Law (UCEFF) of the Molengraaff Institute for Private Law at Utrecht University's School of Law.

Aims and objectives

CEFL's activities are intended to produce results that may be used for specific practical and academic purposes. First and foremost, the Principles are addressed to national legislators in their quest to modernise their national family law. They also function as a source of inspiration for both the European and international legislatures. The

Principles are spelt out in provisions but these must be read in conjunction with comments, which elucidate the rules and offer comparative information. These comments are part and parcel of the Principles. The Principles could considerably facilitate the task of legislators due to the reason that, on the one hand, CEFL's in-depth and comprehensive comparative research is easily accessible and, on the other hand, many of the rules have been drafted: in a manner that legislators often consider to be appropriate. Some of the Principles, but not all, have been drafted so that they could be implemented in a national system. Second, research into the effectiveness of national solutions in the field of family law can largely profit from CEFL's results. The drafting of the Principles is based on an evaluation of the legal institutions, legal solutions and norms of the various legal orders, which express the hierarchy of values inherent in every legal order, although to different degrees. It is to be expected that future scientific research in the field of the harmonisation of family law in Europe to be carried out by individual researchers or eventually research teams will necessarily refer to and compare national solutions with the CEFL Principles. Third, CEFL's comparative material contains comprehensive information about twenty-two family law systems in Europe and it has been regularly consulted by practitioners. Specific information about, for instance, the divorce grounds in GREECE or the position of the new partner of the parent who holds parental responsibilities in respect of the child under HUNGARIAN law is easily accessible and may help in those cases where lawyers seek information about the precise content of foreign family law. In addition, all national reports are written in English, which in most cases facilitates access to those national systems where the official language is not English, French or German. The often difficult legal translations have thus already been done by national experts.

Experts

The following persons contributed to the drafting of the Principles regarding Parental Responsibilities through the writing of a national report and/or taking part in the discussions at the CEFL meetings. Several experts wrote their national reports together with co-authors. Their names are both mentioned on CEFL's website (www2.law.uu.nl/priv/cefl) and listed in the integrated version of all national reports (BOELE-WOELKI/BRAAT/CURRY-SUMNER, *European Family Law in Action, Volume III: Parental Responsibilities*, European Family Law series No. 9, pp. vii-x).

AUSTRIA	*Professor Marianne Roth* University of Salzburg
BELGIUM	*Professor Walter Pintens* Catholic University Leuven
BULGARIA	*Dr. Velina Todorova* Plovdiv University, Sofia
CZECH REPUBLIC	*Professor Milana Hrusaková* Masarykovy University, Brno
DENMARK	*Professor Ingrid Lund-Andersen* Department of Private Law, University of Århus
ENGLAND AND WALES	*Professor Nigel Lowe* Law Department, University of Cardiff, Wales
FINLAND	*Dr. Kirsti Kurki-Suonio* Office of the Parliamentary Ombudsman, Helsinki
FRANCE	*Professor Frédérique Ferrand* University of Lyon
GERMANY	Professor *Nina Dethloff* University of Bonn *Professor Dieter Martiny* European University Viadrina, Frankfurt (Oder)
GREECE	*Professor Achilles G. Koutsouradis* Faculty of Law, University of Thessaloniki
HUNGARY	*Professor Emila Weiss* Civil Law Department, University of Eötvös Loránd

REPUBLIC OF IRELAND	*Professor Geoffrey Shannon* Law Society of Ireland, Dublin
ITALY	*Professor Salvatore Patti* Department of Private Law, La Sapienza University, Rome
LITHUANIA	*Professor Valentinas Mikelenas* Supreme Court of Lithuania
THE NETHERLANDS	*Professor Katharina Boele-Woelki* UCERF, Molengraaff Institute for Private Law, University of Utrecht
NORWAY	*Professor Tone Sverdrup* Department of Private Law, Faculty of Law, University of Oslo
POLAND	*Professor Andrzej Mączyñski* Jagiellonian University of Kraków *Dr. Tomasz Sokołowski* University of Poznañ University of Gdañsk
PORTUGAL	*Professor Guilherme De Oliveira* University of Coimbra
RUSSIA	*Professor Masha Antokolskaia* Free University of Amsterdam
SPAIN	*Professor Cristina González Beilfuss* University of Barcelona *Professor Miquel Martín-Casals* University of Girona

SWEDEN	*Professor Maarit Jänterä-Jareborg* University of Uppsala
SWITZERLAND	*Professor Heinz Hausheer* University of Bern *Professor Ingeborg Schwenzer* University of Basel

Meetings

The meetings of the *Organising Committee* during which the Principles on Parental Responsibilities were prepared and drafted took place in:

LEUVEN	23-25 January 2004
FRANKFURT/ODER	19 March 2004
BARCELONA	6-8 May 2004
UTRECHT	9 December 2004
BRUSSELS	10-13 February 2005
LYON	7-10 April 2005
UTRECHT	15-18 September 2005
UPPSALA	8 December 2005
FRANKFURT/ODER	16-19 March 2006
BRUSSELS	23-26 November 2006

The meeting of the *Expert Group* during which the draft of the Principles on Parental Responsibilities was discussed took place in:

UPPSALA	8-10 December 2005

Conferences

The essence of the pioneering work carried out by CEFL is such that it needs constant backing in a broader academic forum. For this purpose, the CEFL organises family law conferences on a regular basis. Its inaugural conference was organised in Utrecht from the 11th–14th of December 2002. It was largely dedicated to the theoretical aspects of the unification and harmonisation of family law in Europe and aimed to discuss the theoretical and practical premises upon which the CEFL had developed its activities and the initial results achieved by CEFL at that stage (BOELE-WOELKI (ed), *Perspectives for the Unification and Harmonisation of Family Law in Europe*, European Family Law Series No. 4, 2003). In order to keep CEFL's work in regular contact and dialogue with the broader academic community the first results of its work were presented at the 2nd CEFL Conference which was again held in Utrecht from the 9th–11th December 2004. At that conference the CEFL presented the Principles of European Family Law for the first two chosen fields: divorce and maintenance between former spouses. In addition, the initial results in the second working field – parental responsibilities – were presented. The main scientific objective of the conference was to subject the choices and working method of the CEFL to a critical assessment by both academics and practitioners in order to obtain feedback concerning the work which had been accomplished up to that time. Building upon the experience of CEFL's inaugural conference the plenary sessions with presentations by prominent experts was combined with three workshops containing presentations by young researchers which were selected after a call for papers (BOELE-WOELKI (ed), *Common Core and Better Law in European Family Law*, European Family Law Series No. 10, 2005). CEFL's third conference on the European Challenges in Contemporary Family Law in Europe will take place in Oslo from the 7th–9th June 2007. It is organised in collaboration with the Department of Private Law of the University of Oslo in Norway. Various subjects are addressed, such as human rights and the harmonisation of family law in Europe, the attempts to reharmonise Nordic family law, the rights of children and the responsibilities owed to them, the new European instruments in the field of private international law in family matters, the migration in Europe and, finally, the position of cohabitants upon the termination of their relationship either by means of death or dissolution. Once again, this conference will provide selected young researchers with the opportunity to present their research.

European Family Law series

CEFL's Organising Committee established the *European Family Law* series which includes comparative legal studies and materials as well as studies on the effects of international and European law-making within the national legal systems in Europe. The books in this series are published by the Belgian publisher Intersentia (Antwerp-Oxford-New York) in cooperation with the Swiss publisher Stämpfli (Bern). Since March 2003 sixteen volumes have been published in the series. Further information is available at CEFL's website.

Financial support

The activities of the CEFL have been largely financed by the European Commission under the Framework Programme on Judicial Cooperation in Civil Matters 2004. In addition, financial support has been received from the Netherlands Organisation for Scientific Research (NWO), the Dutch Ministry of Justice, the Royal Dutch Academy of Science (KNAW), the Deutsche Forschungsgemeinschaft (DFG), the Bank of Sweden Tercentenary Foundation (RJ), the Wenner-Gren Foundation, the Ius Commune Research School, and the publishers Intersentia (Antwerp) and Stämpfli (Bern). The Universities of Barcelona, Cardiff, Frankfurt/Oder, Leuven, Lyon, Uppsala and Utrecht finally met a significant part of the expenses incurred by the CEFL meetings.

The CEFL is very grateful to all these sponsors for their substantial contributions.

Katharina Boele-Woelki

Utrecht, January 2007

TABLE OF CONTENTS

APPENDICES

GENERAL INTRODUCTION

Unification and harmonisation of (international) family law within the European Union

For the Member States of the European Union the general legal background in family law is not only endowed by human rights conventions but also provided by the *Treaty establishing the European Community* of 25th March 1975. Article 12 EC Treaty contains the prohibition of discrimination on grounds of nationality whereas Article 17 EC Treaty establishes the citizenship of the Union for nationals of the Members States. According to Article 18(1) EC Treaty all citizens have the right to move and to reside freely within the Member States. This right of free movement has gradually gained more significance in the discussion on the unification of private international law in family matters as well as the harmonisation of substantive family law. A closer look at the concept of the free movement of persons within the Member States reveals that interesting arguments have been proffered by the European Court of Justice in the *Garcia Avello v. Belgium* case[1] and by Advocate General Jacobs in his opinion in the *Standesamt Stadt Niebüll v. Grunkin Paul* case.[2] The emerging European citizenship not only requires measures to be taken in the field of private international law but also to a certain extent in the field of substantive family law. Regarding cross-border family relationships it is interesting to note that the European legislator has been extremely active since 1998.[3] Although Articles 61 under c and 65 of the EC Treaty require restraint, these measures are finally considered as being necessary for the proper functioning of the internal market. Apparently, with regard to all areas where legislative

---

1 Europan Court of Justice 2.10.2003, *Garcia Avello v. Belgium*, Case C-148/02. See PINTENS, "Family Law – A Challenge For Europe?", in Àrea de Dret Civil Universitat de Girona (ed), *Nous reptes del Dret de família*, 2005, pp. 21–37; LAGARDE, "L'oeuvre de la Commission Internationale de l'Etat Civil en matière de nom des personnes", in: MANSEL/PFEIFFER/KRONKE/KOHLER/HAUSMANN (eds), *Festschrift für Erik Jayme*, 2004, pp. 1291–1305.

2 The European Court of Justice delivered its judgment on 27th April 2006, Case C-96/04. It was held that the European Court of Justice had no jurisdiction to answer the question referred by the Niebüll Local Court because there was no dispute between the parties as both parents were seeking the same outcome, that is, that their son be allowed to use a double-barrelled name containing both their surnames. See MANSEL, "Anerkennung als Grundprinzip des Europäischen Rechtsraums", *RabelsZ* 2006, pp. 654–731 (687–711).

3 See MEEUSEN/PERTEGÁS/STRAETMANS/SWENNEN (eds.), *International Family Law for the European Union*, 2007.

measures have either already been taken (divorce,[4] parental responsibilities[5]) or will be realised[6] in the near future (maintenance obligations,[7] property law between married and unmarried couples[8] and the law of succession and wills[9]) the answers were positive. Private international law and substantive law are however interrelated. The European family law instruments will only be successful in the long run when the similarities between the substantive family law systems will increase. Thus, the harmonisation of substantive family law is the next natural step to be taken.

The first working fields: Divorce and Maintenance between Former Spouses

In 2004, the Commission on European Family Law (CEFL) published its first set of Principles of European Family Law in the field of Divorce and Maintenance Between Former Spouses.[10] On the basis of twenty-two national reports, the CEFL formulated ten Principles concerning Divorce (Part 1) and ten Principles concerning Maintenance between Former Spouses (Part 2).

The second working field: Parental Responsibilities

Shortly after its establishment in 2001, the CEFL selected the field of parental responsibilities as the second working field. This choice was based on different grounds. First, there are significant and natural links between, on the one hand, the question of divorce and its consequences and, on the other, between the question of parental responsibilities and the financial consequences of divorce. Secondly, the subject of parental responsibilities is linked to the recent unification of the rules concerning jurisdiction and the recognition and enforcement of judgments on parental responsibilities in the European Union. Thirdly, many European countries are bound by international child conventions, most of which, however, deal with cross-border

4 *Brussels II bis Regulation* and Proposal for the Regulation amending Regulation (EC) No. 2201/2003 as regards jurisdiction and introducing rules concerning applicable law in matrimonial matters, COM (2006) 399 final. See also the Green Paper on Applicable Law and Jurisdiction in Divorce Matters, COM (2005) 82 final.

5 *Brussels II bis Regulation.*

6 The EU Council and Commission adopted a Programme of Measures for Implementation of the Principle of Mutual Recognition of Decisions in Civil and Commercial Matters, OJ 15.1.2001, C12/1.

7 Proposal for a Council Regulation on Jurisdiction, Applicable Law, Recognition and the Enforcement of Decisions and Cooperation in Matters Relating to Maintenance Obligations (COM (2005) 649. See also the Green Paper on Maintenance Obligations, COM (2004) 254 final.

8 Green Paper on Conflicts of Laws in Matters Concerning Matrimonial Property Regimes, Including the Question of Jurisdiction and Mutual Recognition COM (2006) 400 final.

9 Green Paper Succession and Wills, COM (2005) 65 final.

10 See Boele-Woelki/Ferrand/González Beilfuss/Jänterä-Jareborg/Lowe/Martiny/Pintens, *Principles of European Family Law Regarding Divorce and Maintenance Between Former Spouses*, European Family Law Series No. 7, 2004.

relationships. For many decades, important international organisations, such as the United Nations, the Hague Conference on Private International Law, the Council of Europe and recently also the European Union have been specifically engaged in the field of parental responsibilities in order to improve the legal position of the child. The international unification of the law relates to the protection of children including all civil matters concerning the attribution, exercise, delegation, restriction and termination of parental responsibilities. The Principles presented in this volume are based on national reports which were finalised in December 2004. Several reforms in the national systems which have taken place since then, could not be taken into account.

The third working field: Matrimonial Property

In December 2006, CEFL's Organising Committee decided that the third set of Principles should address matrimonial property law. This field of law was already extensively discussed when the CEFL commenced its activities in 2001. At that time it was considered that it would prove to be too complicated an endeavour to draft the first Principles in the field of matrimonial property law given the great diversity of legal regimes within Europe and their different technical nature. In general, three basic concepts are to be distinguished: the separation of property with judicial adjudication, the limited community of property and the deferred community of property.[11]

Since 2001, however, important changes have taken place, in particular within the European Union. First and foremost, it is notable that the European Commission also considers the law of property relations between spouses and partners as an area where unified private international law rules will contribute to a better functioning of the internal market. In July 2006 the European Commission published the *Green Paper on Conflicts of Laws in Matters Concerning Matrimonial Property Regimes, Including the Question of Jurisdiction and Mutual Recognition.*[12] According to the Hague Programme of 10th May 2005,[13] the purpose of which is to strengthen freedom, security and justice in the EU, the legislative instrument, which most likely will be a Regulation, should be completed by 2011. In order to prepare this legislative measure the current legal situation in the Member States with regard to substantive and private interna-

[11] See ANTOKOLSKAIA, *Harmonisation of Family Law in Europe: A Historical Perspective*, European Family Law Series No. 13, 2006, pp. 455–484.

[12] COM (2006) 400 final.

[13] http://ec.europa.eu/justice_home/news/information_dossiers/the_hague_priorities/doc/09_area_of_justice_en.pdf.

tional law was investigated.[14] Moreover, several other studies and overviews of European systems are available.[15] In the Hague Programme for 2005 it was announced that the instrument should only cover matters of private international law and should not be based on harmonised concepts of 'family', 'marriage' or other concepts. Rules of uniform substantive law should only be introduced as an accompanying measure, wherever necessary, to effect the mutual recognition of decisions or to improve judicial co-operation in civil matters. This intention has been kept in mind. The *Green Paper* does not investigate the possibility as to whether one optional European matrimonial regime should be introduced even though the preparatory comparative study has strongly favoured this idea. In addition, this has been suggested earlier and supported by several distinguished experts in the field of matrimonial property law, private international law and comparative law.[16] The CEFL has always been of the opinion that family law problems in Europe cannot be solved only through unified private international law rules. In addition, substantive family law needs to be harmonised. In this respect it should be mentioned that the European Group for Private International Law[17] in its answers to the questions posed in the *Green Paper* also shows an interest in the establishment of a European matrimonial property regime, which, for instance, could consist of two models amongst which the parties could choose: a community of property or a separation of property regime. Finally, particular attention should be paid to the current situation in the common law countries where there has been a consistent refusal to impose any formal regime of property rights upon entering into a marriage. Three ground-breaking decisions by the English House of Lords in

---

14 This study was completed in 2002. It was carried out by researchers of the TMC Asser Institute in The Hague and researchers from the Belgian University Louvain la Neuve. The research contains 16 national reports and a comparative analysis. See *Étude sur les regimes matrimoniaux des couples mariés et sur le patrimoine des couples non mariés dans le droit international privé et le droit interne des états members de l'union européen,* JAI/A3/2001/03 (2002).

15 See VERBEKE, "Euroepan Marital Property Law. Survey 1988–1994", *European Review of Private Law* 1995, pp. 445–482; HENRICH/SCHWAB, *Eheliche Gemeinschaft, Partnerschaft und Vermögen im europäischen Vergleich, Beiträge zum europäischen Familienrecht,* 1999; VERWILGHEN, *Régimes matrimoniaux, successons et libéralités dans les relations internationals et internes,* Union Internationale du Notariat Latin, 2003; BRAAT, *Indépendance et interdépendance des époux dans le régime matrimonial légal des droits français, néerlandais et suisse,* European Family Law series No. 6, 2004; BONOMI/STEINER, *Les régimes matrimoniaux en droit comparé et en droit international privé,* 2006.

16 See AGELL, "Towards Uniforming Spouses' Property Rights Especially in International Marriages?", Council of Europe, Proceedings of the 3rd European Conference on Family Law, 1995, pp. 63–80; VERBEKE, "Perspectives for an International Marital Contract", *Maastricht Journal of European and Comparative Law* 2001, pp. 189–200; HENRICH, "Zur Zukunft des Güterrechts in Europa", *Zeitschrift für das gesamte Familienrecht* 2002, pp. 1521–1526; MARTINY, "Ein zusätzlicher Güterstand für Europa?", in: HOFER/KLIPPEL/WALTER (eds.), *Perspektiven des Familienrechts – Festschrift für Dieter Schwab,* 2005, pp. 1189–1207; STEENHOFF, "A Matrimonial Property System for the European Union?", *International Family Law* 2005, pp. 74–77.

17 Drafted at its meeting in Coimbra in 2006. See http://www.gedip-egpil.eu/documents/gedip-documents-26.html.

2001[18] and 2006[19] have given rise to claims that ENGLAND AND WALES has in practice adopted a system of a deferred community of property.[20] In IRELAND the feasibility of adopting a community of property regime has also been discussed.[21]

All these developments signify a growing need to draft Principles of European Family Law regarding Matrimonial Property.

Methodology

Also regarding CEFL's second working field the same working method as with regard to the first CEFL Principles has been followed.[22] On the basis of a detailed questionnaire containing 62 questions the expert members prepared twenty-two comprehensive national reports based on the law as it stood in 2004. These national reports, together with the relevant legal provisions, are available on CEFL's website www.law.uu.nl/priv/cefl under working field 2. In addition, an integrated version of all the reports has been published.[23] On the basis of a systematic analysis of this comparative material, to which the comparative overviews comprehensively refer,[24] and the relevant international and European instruments in this field the CEFL formulated 39 Principles concerning Parental Responsibilities. They were drafted by the Organising Committee and have been discussed with the drafters of the national reports at a meeting of the Expert Group in Uppsala from 8th–10th December 2005.

Frame of reference

Like the Principles Regarding Divorce and Maintenance Between Former Spouses the Principles Regarding Parental Responsibilities are primarily directed towards national, European and international legislators who are considering modernising the law in this field. They may serve as a frame of reference and inspiration.[25] In using the CEFL Principles it should be kept in mind that the drafters lack a political mandate and that

---

18 *White v. White* [2001] I Law Reports, Appeal Cases 596.

19 *Miller v. Miller: McFarlane v. McFarlane* [2006] United Kingdom House of Lords 24.

20 See COOKE/BARLOW/CALLUS, *Community of Property, A Regime for England and Wales?*, The Nuffield Foundation 2006.

21 See BUCKLEY, "Matrimonial Property and Irish Law: A Case for Community?", *Northern Ireland Legal Quarterly*, 2002, vol 53, no. 39.

22 See BOELE-WOELKI, "The Working Method of the Commission on European Family Law", in: BOELE-WOELKI (ed.), *Common Core and Better Law in European Family Law*, European Family Law Series No. 10, 2005, pp. 15–38.

23 See BOELE-WOELKI/BRAAT/CURRY-SUMNER (eds.), *European Family Law in Action, Volume III: Parental Responsibilities*, European Family Law Series No. 9, 2005.

24 Reference is made to the national reports by citing the author's name, the jurisdiction concerned and the number of the question where the specific answer is provided.

25 See in general on the nature of the CEFL Principles, *ibid.*, note 10, p. 3.

they do not represent their national system. Instead they have distanced themselves from their own legal background because the European perspective ultimately prevails. In respect of the adopted results it is considered to be absolutely vital to reveal the criteria upon which the choices were based. This aspect is one of the major objectives and, as a result, one of the concerns of the CEFL, because its Principles may only aspire to be used not *ratione imperii*, but *imperio rationis*. Therefore, the utmost care has been given to the explanation of both the commonly shared desires and the underlying considerations, which are either of a general or specific nature. The comments associated with each Principle contain this fundamental information.

Languages

CEFL's working language is English. However, the Principles are formulated in three languages: English, French and German. No version is a translation of one of the two other languages. All three versions have been drafted at the same time. They are equally authentic. The present publication has been completed with a translation of the Principles into Dutch, Spanish and Swedish.

PREAMBLE
PREAMBULE
PRÄAMBEL

PREAMBLE

Recognising that, notwithstanding the existing diversities of national family law systems, there is nevertheless a growing convergence of laws;

Recognising that the free movement of persons within Europe is hindered by the remaining differences;

Desiring to contribute to common European values regarding the child's rights and welfare;

Desiring to contribute to the harmonisation of family law in Europe and to further facilitate the free movement of persons within Europe;

The Commission on European Family Law recommends the following Principles:

PREAMBULE

Reconnaissant que, malgré les diversités existantes entre les systèmes nationaux de droit de la famille, la convergence entre les lois tend à s'accroître;

Reconnaissant que la libre circulation des personnes en Europe est entravée par les différences qui demeurent;

Souhaitant contribuer à des valeurs communes européennes concernant les droits et le bien être de l'enfant;

Souhaitant contribuer à l'harmonisation du droit de la famille en Europe et faciliter encore davantage la libre circulation des personnes en Europe;

La Commission pour le Droit Européen de la Famille recommande les Principes suivants:

PRÄAMBEL

In Anerkennung, dass es trotz der bestehenden Unterschiede in den nationalen Familienrechten gleichwohl eine zunehmende Übereinstimmung gibt;

In Anerkennung, dass die bestehenden Unterschiede die Freizügigkeit der Personen in Europa behindern;

In dem Wunsch zu den gemeinsamen europäischen Werten in Bezug auf die Rechte und das Wohlergehen des Kindes beizutragen.

In dem Wunsch zur Angleichung des Familienrechts in Europa beizutragen und die Freizügigkeit der Personen in Europa weiter zu erleichtern;

Empfiehlt die Kommission für Europäisches Familienrecht die folgenden Prinzipien:

COMMENT

1. Subsequent to the Preamble of CEFL's Principles of European Family Law Regarding Divorce and Maintenance Between Former Spouses[26] the Principles Regarding Parental Responsibilities are preceded by a Preamble. Both Preambles are similar. The second Preamble includes both generally acknowledged considerations and commonly felt desires with regard to the situation of family law in Europe as well as the notion of the child's rights and welfare which functioned as the main guideline in the drafting process.

2. The Preamble refers to the free movement of persons in Europe which is hindered by the existing diversities of family law systems. It is generally acknowledged that, to date, in cross-border situations people cannot rely on the continuity of their family relationships when changing residence. The unification of the private international law rules (jurisdiction, applicable law, recognition and enforcement) by the *Brussels II bis Regulation* and by the *Hague Child Protection Convention 1996* is unable to completely eliminate the obstacles experienced by European citizens moving across jurisdictions.

3. Likewise, the Preamble to CEFL's first set of Principles, the Preamble preceding the Principles Regarding Parental Responsibilities, also contains two specific reflections. First, reference is made to the common European values regarding the child's rights and welfare which encompasses not only the protection of the best interests of the child, but also the equal treatment of children born within and outside

[26] See BOELE-WOELKI/FERRAND/GONZÁLEZ BEILFUSS/JÄNTERÄ-JAREBORG/LOWE/MARTINY/PINTENS, *ibid.*, note 10, pp. 7–9.

marriage as well as the participation of the child in the decision making and the autonomy of the holders of parental responsibilities to agree on parental responsibility matters. Generally, however, this freedom is subject to scrutiny by the competent authority. Secondly, CEFL's main objective regarding its Principles is mentioned. The Principles Regarding Parental Responsibilities can also be used as a frame of reference in the harmonisation process of family law in Europe.

PART 3. PARENTAL RESPONSIBILITIES

INTRODUCTION

Historical developments

The legal relationship between parents and children has been profoundly affected by the transformation of the traditional family into its modern equivalent.[27] As a result, the law regarding the parent-child relationship has significantly changed within the last two hundred years. Essentially the same social, economic and political changes took place, which as a result led to a considerable convergence of the laws in respect of the relationship between the child and his or her parents. All these transformations, however, did not always take place within the same time periods. Some jurisdictions were about twenty to fifty years more advanced and liberal than others. In all European family law systems, however, the following similar developments can be discerned. In this process the most important progress was achieved through the social and legal emancipation of women, which led to the replacement of the more or less absolute power of the married father as the head of the family by the equal responsibility of both the mother and the father. The next momentous step was the abandoning of the morally indefensible attitude towards illegitimate children.[28] Gradually, they were equated with legitimate children in all respects. As a result, parental responsibilities may also jointly be obtained by unmarried couples. In particular, the possibility of the unmarried father to obtain parental responsibilities under certain conditions or at least to have contact with his child were made possible. Whereas in the case of a divorce or a separation up until about twenty years ago parental responsibilities were usually only granted to one of the parents, the conviction steadily gained ground that neither divorce nor a separation between the parents should affect the joint exercise of parental responsibilities. Hence joint parental responsibilities on the part of the spouses automatically continue after divorce or separation. Progressively, many international organisations, such as the United Nations, the Hague Conference on Private International Law, the Council of Europe and the European Union, recognised the rights of the child in their respective instruments. In 1989 these international acknowledgments culminated in the *Convention on the Rights of the Child*, which is the most central international legislation in the field of child law. It had a substantial impact on the national family law systems in Europe. Alongside these developments

---

[27] See STOLJAR, Volume IV *Persons and Family*, Chapter 7, *Children, Parents and Guardians*, International Encyclopedia of Comparative Law, 1973, nos. 1–89.

[28] See ANTOKOLSKAIA, *ibid.*, note 11, pp. 443–453.

the decisions of the European Court of Human Rights regarding Article 8 of the *European Convention on the Protection of Human Rights and Fundamental Freedoms* of 4th November 1950 influenced not only the law of parentage but also the law of parental responsibilities. Finally, also in the field of public law considerable changes took place. The responsibility of the State and other public authorities for the welfare of children enormously increased. At last all changes in the relationship between parents and children were simultaneously accompanied by a change of terminology, which indicates the shift from the traditional concept of parental power and parental authority to parental rights and duties as well as parental care and ultimately to parental responsibilities.

The concept of parental responsibilities

Parental responsibilities is a broad concept consisting of a collection of rights and duties that concerns the taking care of the child's person and properties. The CEFL opted for this concept which likewise is increasingly used in international and European and instruments. Concepts like guardianship and custody, that are still used in national systems, have been left behind. Many international and recent European instruments use the concept of parental responsibilities. An analysis of its use, however, has not yet been provided by those organizations which drafted and adopted the different instruments. Normally, parental responsibilities belong to parents. Once parental responsibilities belong to a person, he or she cannot divest him or herself of the whole package of rights and duties. The exercise of parental responsibilities can, however, under certain circumstances be restricted and delegated to a third person or institution.

Children and the holders of parental responsibilities

CEFL's concept of parental responsibilities only applies to children from the moment of their birth until they have reached majority. Generally, majority is attained at the age of 18 years. Automatically, parental responsibilities cease and full legal capacity begins. These Principles, however, do not deal with majority issues as such. A difference between younger and adolescent children has been recognized, although the indication of an age limit has intentionally not been provided. It not only depends on the child's age but also upon his/her maturity whether his or her opinion should be taken into account. This notion has been expressed in Principles 3:6, 3:20 (3)(a), 3:21 (3)(a), 3:37. Generally, however, it should be left to national law whether a child is meant to be a child of the family. On the other hand, these Principles refer to the holders of parental responsibilities (Principle 3:2). In almost all cases the child has two holders of parental responsibilities who are his/her parents at the same time. However, also a person other than a parent, who has no legal ties with the child, can also hold parental responsibilities. Hence preference is given to the rather long-winded term 'holder or holders of parental responsibilities'.

International and European instruments

The international and European instruments in the field of parental responsibilities[29] have played a significant role in the drafting of the Principles of European Family Law in this field. The most relevant international organisations and their respective instruments are listed here.

1. The United Nations

The *Convention on the Rights of the Child 1989* entered into force on 2nd September 1990. Currently, 191 countries are bound by this convention.[30] All twenty-two countries that are represented in the CEFL by a national report with regard to parental responsibilities have either ratified or acceded to this convention. As summarized in the Preamble to the Convention the need to extend particular care to the child was already stated in the *Declaration on the Rights of the Child 1924*, in the *Declaration on the Rights of the Child 1959* and recognized in the *Universal Declaration of Human Rights 1948*, in the *International Covenant on Civil and Political Rights 1966*, in the *International Covenant on Economic, Social and Cultural Rights 1966* and in the *Declaration on Social and Legal Principles relating to the Protection and Welfare of Children 1986*. Finally, the *Convention on the Elimination of Discrimination against Women 1979*[31] should be mentioned. Among the 185 contracting states are all the countries which are represented in the CEFL.

2. The Hague Conference on Private International Law

The *Hague Child Protection Convention 1996*[32] entered into force on 1st January 2002. BULGARIA, CZECH REPUBLIC, HUNGARY and LITHUANIA are among the thirteen contracting states. It is expected that in the near future all Member States of the European Union will have ratified this convention.[33] In the relations between the contracting states the 1996 Convention replaces the *Hague Child Protection Convention 1961*. This convention entered into force on 4th February 1969. Only ten European

29 See for an overview, pp 279–282.

30 untreaty.un.org.

31 www.un.org/womenwatch/daw/cedaw.

32 www.hcch.net.

33 In total 19 EU Member States which are represented in the CEFL will by then be bound by the convention. This does not apply to NORWAY, RUSSIA and SWITZERLAND.

countries which are represented in the CEFL are contracting states.[34] The *Hague Child Abduction Convention 1980*, on the other hand, which entered into force on 1st December 1983, has been ratified by all in the CEFL represented countries except by RUSSIA. To a lesser extent this also applies to the *Hague Adoption Convention 1993* which entered into force on 1st May 1995.[35]

3. The Council of Europe

The central human rights instrument in Europe is the *European Convention on Human Rights 1950*,[36] which was concluded under the auspices of the Council of Europe.[37] Regarding family relations, Article 8, which contains the right to respect for "private and family life", is considered to be the key provision in the Convention. The European Court of Human Rights and the European Commission on Human Rights[38] have found *inter alia* that "family life" includes the relationship between:

- married parents and their legitimate minor child
- cohabiting parents and their minor child
- the mother and her minor child within and outside marriage
- the man and the minor child which has been recognised
- the biological father and the minor child in specific circumstances
- close relatives, such as grandparents, and the minor child
- foster parents and the minor child
- the non-biological parent and the minor child.

In addition to the ECHR, five specific conventions relating to child matters have been concluded. The most recent *Convention on Contact Concerning Children 2003*[39] became effective as of 1st September 2005. The *Convention on the Exercise of Children's Rights 1996*[40] entered into force on 1st July 2000. Many countries that have ratified the *Hague Convention on Child Abduction 1980* are also a contracting state to the *Convention on Recognition and Enforcement of Decisions Concerning Custody 1980*.[41] Two older

---

34 These are: AUSTRIA, CZECH REPUBLIC, GERMANY, FRANCE, ITALY, THE NETHERLANDS, POLAND, PORTUGAL, SPAIN and SWITZERLAND.

35 Only GREECE, IRELAND and RUSSIA are non-contracting states.

36 CETS n° 5. All jurisdictions represented in the CEFL belong to the 46 contracting states.

37 conventions.coe.int.

38 Since 1st November 1998 the only treaty-monitoring body of the ECHR is the European Court of Human Rights pursuant to Protocol 11 of the Convention. This single-body system replaced the two tier system of the Court and a European Commission on Human Rights.

39 CETS n° 192. The CZECH REPUBLIC is one of the Member States.

40 CETS n° 160. The CZECH REPUBLIC, GERMANY, GREECE, ITALY and POLAND are among the 19 Member States.

41 CETS n°105. All jurisdictions save RUSSIA represented in the CEFL have ratified this convention.

conventions, the *Convention on the Legal Status of Children Born out of Wedlock 1975*[42] and the *Convention on the Adoption of Children 1967*[43] came into force on 11th August 1978 and 26th April 1968 respectively.

In addition, the Committee of Ministers (CM) and the Parliamentary Assembly (PA) of the Council of Europe agreed on a number of recommendations and resolutions which are relevant in the field of parental responsibilities. They are listed in chronological order:

1. (CM) Resolution (77)33 of 11th March 1977 on placement of children;
2. (PA) Recommendation 874(1979) on a European Charter on the Rights of the Child;
3. (CM) Recommendation (79)17 of 13th September 1979 concerning the protection of children against ill-treatment;
4. (CM) Recommendation (84)4 of 28th February 1984 on parental responsibilities;
5. (PA) Recommendation 1065 of 6th October 1987 on the traffic in children and other forms of child exploitation;
6. (PA) Recommendation 1071 of 23 March 1988 on child welfare – Providing institutional care for infants and children;
7. (PA) Recommendation 1121 of 1 February 1990 on the rights of children;
8. (CM) Recommendation (95)6 of 7th February 1995 on the application of the European Convention on recognition and enforcement of decisions concerning custody of children and on restoration of custody of children;
9. (PA) Recommendation 1286 of 24 January 1996 on a European strategy for children;
10. (CM) Recommendation No. R (98)1 of 21st January 1998 on family mediation;
11. (PA) Recommendation 1371 of 23 April 1998 on abuse and neglect of children;
12. (CM) Recommendation (98)8 of 18th September 1998 on children's participation in family and social life;
13. (CM) Recommendation (99) of 23rd February 1999 on the application of the European Convention on recognition and enforcement of decisions concerning custody of children and on restoration of custody of children.

Finally, the Council of Europe drafted a *White Paper on Principles Concerning the Establishment and Legal Consequences of Parentage 2002* which also contains principles regarding parental responsibilities. The drafters noted that "with the legal and social

[42] CETS n° 85. AUSTRIA, CZECH REPUBLIC, DENMARK, ENGLAND AND WALES, GREECE, IRELAND, LITHUANIA, NORWAY, POLAND, PROTUGAL, SWEDEN and SWITZERLAND are among the 21 Member States.

[43] CETS n° 58. AUSTRIA, CZECH REPUBLIC, DENMARK, ENGLAND AND WALES, GERMANY, GREECE, IRELAND, ITALY, NORWAY, POLAND, PORTUGAL and SWITZERLAND are among the 18 Member States.

changes which have occurred at the national and international level, in particular, as regards human rights and the protection of the rights of the child, as well as the newly available medical techniques, there is an increased need for the member States of the Council of Europe to update their laws in order to clarify and reinforce the legal status of the child."

4. The European Union

Based on Article 61 (c) and Article 67 (1) of the *EC Treaty 1975*, which has been amended by the *Treaty of Amsterdam 1997*, the Council of the European Union has subsequently adopted two communitarian instruments in the field of parental responsibilities. As from 1st March 2005 the *Brussels II bis Regulation*[44] repealed and replaced the *Brussels II* Regulation.[45] The new Regulation covers all decisions on parental responsibility, including measures for the protection of the child, independently of any link with a matrimonial proceeding.[46] As regards the property of the child the *Brussels II bis Regulation* only applies to measures for the protection of the child, i.e. (i) the designation and functions of a person or body having charge of the child's property, representing or assisting the child, and (ii) the administration, conservation or disposal of the child's property. In this context, the Regulation should, for instance, apply in cases where the parents are in dispute as regards the administration of the child's property. The *Proposal for the Regulation amending Brussels II bis as regards jurisdiction and introducing rules concerning the applicable law in matrimonial matters* was published in July 2006.[47] Its main objective is to introduce the prorogation of jurisdiction in divorce proceedings and to unify the conflict of law rules in matters of divorce and legal separation. The proposal does not contain any changes regarding the provisions relating to parental responsibilities. In consultation with the European Judicial Network in Civil and Commercial Matters the Commission Services have drawn up the *Practice Guide* for the application of the Brussels Regulation.[48] The *Practice Guide* only deals with the provisions concerning matters of parental responsibilities. It provides guidance for parties, judges, lawyers, notaries and central

---

44 Official Journal 2003 L 338/1. The following 19 countries which are represented in the CEFL are EU Member States: AUSTRIA, BELGIUM, BULGARIA, CZECH REPUBLIC, DENMARK, FINLAND, FRANCE, GERMANY, GREECE, HUNGARY, IRELAND, ITALY, LITHUANIA, THE NETHERLANDS, POLAND, PORTUGAL, SPAIN, ENGLAND AND WALES and SWEDEN. The *Brussels II bis Regulation* is not applicable in DENMARK.

45 Official Journal 2000 L 160/19. This Regulation was in force from 1st March 2001 until 28th February 2005.

46 See BOELE-WOELKI/GONZÀLEZ BEILFUSS, *Brussels II bis: Its Impact and Application in the Member States*, European Family Law series No. 14, 2007.

47 COM (2006) 399 final.

48 europa.eu.int/comm/justice_home/ejn/parental_resp/parental_resp_ec_vdm_en.pdf.

authorities as to how to apply the *Brussels II bis Regulation*[49] as well as advice to Member States as to how best to ensure its implementation.[50]

At the level of human rights, in its *Draft Treaty for a European Constitution 2003*, the European Union has proposed that the child's best interests should be considered a primary consideration in all actions relating to children, whether taken by public authorities or private institutions (Article II–84.2). A corresponding provision (Article 24.2) is found in the *European Charter of Fundamental Rights 2000.* Certain human rights, however, have an exclusive or particular application to children, for example the right to education and the right to maintain relations with both parents. In its Communication on *Strategic Objectives 2005–2009*,[51] the European Commission identified children's rights as one of its main priorities since they should be recognized as a self-standing set of concerns and not simply subsumed into wider efforts to mainstream human rights in general. In order to establish a comprehensive EU strategy on the rights of the child, future EU actions have been proposed in the European Commission's Communication *Towards an EU Strategy on the Rights of the Child.*[52] The Commission will develop a complete strategy to ensure that the European Union contributes to promoting and safeguarding children's rights in all its internal and external actions and will support the efforts of the Member States in this field. In addition, the Commission calls on the Member States, on the European institutions and on other stakeholders to take an active part in the development of this strategy since the idea of creating child-friendly societies within the EU cannot be separated from the need to further deepen and consolidate European integration.

Current national legislation

In all jurisdictions which are represented in the CEFL the current law of parental responsibilities is codified.[53] The most important sources of the law governing parental responsibilities are either part of the Civil Code (AUSTRIA, BELGIUM, FRANCE, GERMANY,

---

49 See COESTER-WALTJEN, "Die Berücksichtigung der Kindesinteressen in der neuen EU-Verordnung "Brüssel IIa", *Zeitschrift für das gesamte Familienrecht* 2005, pp. 241–248.

50 The Practice Guide is not legally binding, and does not prejudge any opinion delivered by the European Court of Justice, or any decision issued by national courts, concerning the interpretation of the *Brussels II bis Regulation.*

51 Europe 2010: A Partnership for European Renewal, Prosperity, Solidarity and Security, COM (2005) 12.

52 COM (2006) 367 final. See also the Commission Staff Working Document which contains a Preliminary Inventory of EU Actions Affecting Children's Rights, SEC (2006) 889.

53 See the answers in the national reports in BOELE-WOELKI/BRAAT/CURRY-SUMNER, *ibid.*, note 23, Q 4.

GREECE, ITALY, LITHUANIA, NETHERLANDS, PORTUGAL, SPAIN and SWITZERLAND),[54] of the Family Code (BULGARIA, CZECH REPUBLIC, HUNGARY and RUSSIA) or contained in specific Acts on Children, Parental Authority, Custody or Guardianship (DENMARK, IRELAND, ENGLAND AND WALES, FINLAND, NORWAY and SWEDEN).

Parental Responsibilities and other fields of law

For many issues, there are different rules in various contexts. As regards the scope of the Principles regarding Parental Responsibilities it should be emphasized that the CEFL generally only address private law issues. However, several fields of family law have been excluded from the scope of these Principles in spite of their private law nature and their interrelationship with parental responsibilities. Firstly, the establishment or contesting of a parent-child relationship (parentage) has not been dealt with.[55] The same applies to adoption,[56] child abduction[57] and the name and forename of the child.[58] In these fields of law specific international conventions are in effect. This is also the case with regard to child maintenance which is generally considered to be an independent legal consequence of parentage, but is directly linked to the possible duties of the parents concerning their child.[59] Several international conventions that specifically apply to or include child maintenance obligations have been concluded under the auspices of the United Nations[60] and the Hague Conference on Private

54 In some jurisdictions additional rules are provided by the national constitution, the codes for civil and non-contentious procedures as well as specific acts relating to children.

55 See for references under 2. Council of Europe. Under the auspices of the International Commission on Civil Status (ICCS) the following Conventions have been concluded: *Convention extending the competence of authorities empowered to receive declarations acknowledging natural children*, Rome 14th September 1961 (Member States that are represented in the CEFL are BELGIUM, FRANCE, GERMANY, GREECE, THE NETHERLANDS and SWITZERLAND); *Convention on the establishment of maternal descent of natural children*, Brussels 12th September 1962 (Member States that are represented in the CEFL are GERMANY, GREECE, THE NETHERLANDS and SWITZERLAND); *Convention on legitimating by marriage*, Rome 10th September 1970 (Member States that are represented in the CEFL are AUSTRIA, FRANCE, GREECE, ITALY and THE NETHERLANDS); *Convention on the voluntary acknowledgement of children born out of wedlock*, Munich 5th September 1980. This convention is not yet in force.

56 See for references under 2. Hague Conference on Private International Law and 3. Council of Europe.

57 *Ibid.*

58 The ICCS has concluded the following conventions: *Convention on changes of surnames and forenames*, Istanbul 4th September 1958 (Member States that are represented in the CEFL are AUSTRIA, FRANCE, GERMANY, ITALY, PORTUGAL, SPAIN, and THE NETHERLANDS); *Convention on the law applicable to surnames and forenames*, Munich 5th September 1980 (Member States that are represented in the CEFL are ITALY, PORTUGAL, SPAIN and THE NETHERLANDS). The *Convention on the recognition of surnames*, Strasbourg 17 March 2005, has not yet become effective.

59 In this sense Principle 18 No. 65 of the *White Paper 2002.*

60 *New York Convention of 20th June 1956 on the recovery abroad of maintenance.* This convention has been ratified by all countries represented in the CEFL except for BULGARIA, LITHUANIA and RUSSIA.

International Law.[61] In addition, *Regulation (EC) of 22nd December 2000 on Jurisdiction and Recognition and Enforcement of Judgements in Civil and Commercial Matters* (Brussels I)[62] is applicable to child maintenance claim procedures as well as *Regulation (EC) of 21st April 2004 Creating a European Enforcement Order for Uncontested Claims.*[63] Pursuant to the Green Paper on Maintenance Obligations[64] a *Proposal for a Council Regulation on Jurisdiction, Applicable Law, Recognition and the Enforcement of Decisions and Cooperation in Matters Relating to Maintenance Obligations* was published in December 2005.[65]

There are close links with more or less every other field of law, in particular with respect to the administration of the child's property. Aspects of contract law, property law, inheritance law and the law of civil procedure have not been included. With regard to the latter, however, a few exceptions have been made. Some specific procedural Principles have been drafted with regard to the competent authority to intervene and/or to decide in parental responsibility matters (Principle 3:35), the position of alternative dispute resolution mechanisms (Principle 3:36), the hearing of the child (Principle 3:37), the appointment of a legal representative for the child (Principle 3:38) and the enforcement of agreements and decisions (Principle 3:39). CEFL's general decision to restrict the Parental Responsibilities Principles to private law issues consequently excludes public welfare, intervention by the state, measures taken as a

61 *Convention of 1st June 1956 on the law applicable to maintenance obligations towards children* (Member States that are represented in the CEFL are: AUSTRIA, BELGIUM and THE NETHERLANDS); *Convention of 15th April 1958 concerning the recognition and enforcement of decisions relating to maintenance obligations towards children* (Member States that are represented in the CEFL are AUSTRIA, BELGIUM, HUNGARY and THE NETHERLANDS); *Convention of 2nd October 1973 on the Law Applicable to Maintenance Obligations* (Member States that are represented in the CEFL are FRANCE GERMANY, GREECE, ITALY, LITHUANIA, THE NETHERLANDS, POLAND, PORTUGAL, SPAIN and SWITZERLAND) and the *Convention of 2nd October 1973 on the recognition and enforcement of decisions relating to maintenance obligations* (Member States that are represented in the CEFL are the CZECH REPUBLIC, DENMARK, ENGLAND AND WALES, FINLAND, FRANCE, GERMANY, GREECE ITALY, LITHUANIA, THE NETHERLANDS, NORWAY, POLAND, PORTUGAL, SPAIN, SWEDEN and SWITZERLAND). Currently, a new Hague Maintenance Convention is being prepared.

62 No. 44/2001, Official Journal L 236/33. This Regulation replaces, as of 1st March 2002, the *Brussels Convention of 27th September 1968 on jurisdiction and the enforcement of judgments in civil and commercial matters*, as amended by Conventions on the Accession of the New Member States to that Convention in relations between the EU Member States. The following 19 countries which are represented in the CEFL are EU Member States: AUSTRIA, BELGIUM, BULGARIA, CZECH REPUBLIC, DENMARK, FINLAND, FRANCE, GERMANY, GREECE, HUNGARY, IRELAND, ITALY, LITHUANIA, THE NETHERLANDS, POLAND, PORTUGAL, SPAIN, ENGLAND AND WALES and SWEDEN. The *Brussels I Regulation* is not applicable in DENMARK. NORWAY and SWITZERLAND are bound by the *Lugano Convention of 16th September 1988 on jurisdiction and the enforcement of judgments in civil and commercial matters*, which is a parallel Convention to the 1968 Brussels Convention.

63 No. 805/2004, Official Journal L 143/15. Effective as of 21st October 2005.

64 COM (2004) 254 final.

65 COM (2005) 649.

result of criminal offences committed by children and, in particular, health law and the law regarding foster care. Only certain aspects of the last two areas have been addressed. In this context it should be underlined, however, that "the relations between parent and child are as profoundly 'private' as they are also eminently public ones. The interests of the child must be ultimately accessible to public scrutiny; its interests inviting outside intervention are thus as public as anything in the history of civilisation has been."[66]

Statistical information

Do parents always have joint parental responsibilities even if their relationship has come to an end? Is there a difference between married and divorced parents, on the one hand, and parents who are living in or have dissolved their non-marital relationship? How often – if indeed this is possible, has the exercise of parental responsibilities been attributed to one of the parents and to whom? No statistical information with regard to these kinds of questions is available in BELGIUM, CZECH REPUBLIC, ENGLAND AND WALES, HUNGARY, IRELAND, NORWAY, POLAND and SPAIN. In some jurisdictions this lack of information is based on the fact that the break up of the parents relationship has no affect upon the attribution of parental responsibilities. The statistical information provided from the other jurisdictions must be considered with great care. The most interesting figures refer to the situation after divorce. In BULGARIA,[67] GREECE,[68] ITALY,[69] PORTUGAL[70] and SWITZERLAND[71] where generally in the case of divorce one of the parents is awarded parental rights and duties, in the majority of cases (50–85%) it is consistently the mother who holds and/or exercises these rights and duties. In contrast, in the majority of jurisdictions (DENMARK,[72] FINLAND,[73] FRANCE,[74] GERMANY,[75] THE NETHERLANDS,[76] RUSSIA[77] AND SWEDEN[78]) where statistical information is available, joint parental responsibilities after the dissolution of the parents' relationship has become the norm. The figures vary between 75% in DENMARK and GERMANY up to 97%

66 See STOLJAR, *ibid.*, note 27, No. 2.
67 See TODOROVA, Bulgarian Report, Q 19.
68 See KOUTSOURADIS/ZERVOGIANNI, Greek Report, Q 19.
69 See PATTI/BELLISARIO/ROSSI CARLEO, Italian Report, Q 19.
70 See DE OLIVEIRA, Portuguese report, Q 19.
71 See HAUSHEER/ACHERMANN-WEBER/WOLF, Swiss Report, Q 19. Since 2000, however, the instances of jointly held parental responsibilities after divorce have increased considerably.
72 See LUND-ANDERSEN/JEPPESEN-DE BOER Danish Report, Q 19.
73 See KURKI-SUONIO, Finnish Report, Q 19.
74 See FERRAND, French Report, Q 19.
75 See DETHLOFF/MARTINY, German Report, Q 19.
76 See BOELE-WOELKI/SCHRAMA/VONK, Dutch Report, Q 19.
77 See ANTOKOLSKAIA, Russian Report, Q 19.
78 See JÄNTERÄ-JAREBORG/SINGER/SÖRGJERD, Swedish Report, Q 19.

in SWEDEN. In AUSTRIA[79] this percentage is about 45% and in PORTUGAL[80] no more than 13%. With regard to the situation in AUSTRIA, it has been specifically reported that, on average, three weeks' more visitation days are agreed upon with joint parental responsibilities than with sole parental responsibilities. In addition, fathers with joint parental responsibilities spend almost six weeks more time with their children than when the mothers have the so-called *Obsorge* for the child. In those countries where joint parental responsibilities after the dissolution of the parents' relationship is the general rule, the child predominately resides with the mother (80–90%), whereas in LITHUANIA[81] in 45% of cases the child's residence was established with the father and only in 34% of the cases with the mother. Finally, in SWEDEN[82] in 2002 it was estimated that approximately 17% of all children with divorced or separated parents lived alternately with both parents. How often children have their residence in two households in the other European jurisdictions has not been reported.

Structure and content of the Principles regarding Parental Responsibilities

Due to the fact that in the field of parental responsibilities many international and European instruments are to be taken into account, the structure and content of the Principles regarding Parental Responsibilities is to some extent different to the structure of CEFL's first Principles regarding Divorce and Maintenance between Former Spouses. Each section containing a Principle consists of four parts. The text of the Principle itself (1) is followed by an overview of the relevant international and European provisions regarding the issue addressed in the Principle (2) in order to recall the international commitments that have previously been achieved. The international obligations build the framework along which the Principles have been drafted. The comparative overviews (3) and the comments (4) do not only refer to the twenty-two national reports, but include, in addition, the related international and European instruments.

The Parental Responsibilities Principles constitute Part 3 of CEFL's Principles of European Family Law.[83] It contains a Preamble and 39 Principles classified into eight Chapters.

- The *first Chapter* contains two Definitions: the Concept of Parental Responsibilities (Principle 3:1) and the Holder of Parental Responsibilities (Principles 3:2).

[79] See ROTH, Austrian Report, Q 19.
[80] See DE OLIVEIRA, Portuguese Report, Q 19.
[81] See MIKELENAS, Lithuanian Report, Q 19.
[82] See JÄNTERÄ-JAREBORG/SINGER/SÖRGJERD, Swedish Report, Q 19.
[83] Part 1 is devoted to Divorce and Part 2 to Maintenance Between Former Spouses.

- *Chapter two* encapsulates the Rights of the Child: the Best Interests of the Child (Principle 3:3), the Autonomy of the Child (Principle 3:4), Non-discrimination of the Child (Principle 3:5), the Child's Right to be Heard (Principle 3:6) and Conflict of Interests (Principle 3:7).
- *Chapter three* deals with the Parental Responsibilities of Parents and Third Persons: Parents (Principle 3:8), Third Persons (Principle 3:9) and the Effect of Dissolution and Separation (Principle 3:10).
- *Chapter four* on the Exercise of Parental Responsibilities consists of two Sections. *Section A* is dedicated to the Exercise by Parents: Joint Exercise (Principle 3:11), Daily Matters, Important and Urgent Decisions (Principle 3:12), (Dis-)Agreement on Exercise (Principles 3:13 and 3:14) and Sole Exercise upon Agreement or Decision and Exercise by one Parent (Principles 3:15 and 3:16). *Section B* includes the Principles regarding the Exercise by Third Persons in Addition to or instead of the Parents (Principle 3:17) and Decisions in Daily Matters (Principle 3:18).
- *Chapter five* on the Contents of Parental Responsibilities also is divided into two Sections. *Section A* on the Child's Person and Property deals with Care, Protection and Education (Principle 3:19), Residence (Principle 3:20), Relocation (Principle 3:21), Administration of the Child's Property (Principle 3:22), Restrictions (Principle 3:23) and Legal Representation (Principle 3:24). *Section B* covers the Maintenance of Personal Relationships: Contact with Parents or Other Persons (Principle 3:25), Content of Contact (Principle 3:26), Agreement (Principle 3:27), Restrictions (Principle 3:28) and Information to Parents (Principle 3:29).
- *Chapter six* regulates the Termination of Parental Responsibilities: Termination (Principle 3:30) and the Death of the Parents (Principle 3:31).
- *Chapter seven* consists of the Principles regarding the Discharge and Restoration of Parental Responsibilities: Discharge of Parental Responsibilities (Principle 3:32), Request for Discharge of Parental Responsibilities (Principle 3:33) and Restoration of Parental Responsibilities (Principle 3:34).
- *Chapter eight* is devoted to Procedure: Competent Authority (Principle 3:35), Alternative Dispute Resolution (Principle 3:36), Hearing of the Child (Principle 3:37), Appointment of a Special Representative for the Child (Principle 3:38) and Enforcement (Principle 3:39).

CHAPTER I: DEFINITIONS
CHAPITRE I: DÉFINITIONS
KAPITEL I: BEGRIFFSBESTIMMUNGEN

Principle 3:1 Concept of parental responsibilities

Parental responsibilities are a collection of rights and duties aimed at promoting and safeguarding the welfare of the child. They encompass in particular:

(a) care, protection and education;
(b) maintenance of personal relationships;
(c) determination of residence;
(d) administration of property, and
(e) legal representation.

Principe 3:1 Notion de responsabilité parentale

La responsabilité parentale est un ensemble de droits et devoirs destinés à favoriser et à sauvegarder le bien-être de l'enfant. Elle comprend notamment

(a) soins, protection et éducation;
(b) maintien des relations personnelles;
(c) détermination de la résidence;
(d) administration des biens et
(e) représentation légale.

Prinzip 3:1 Begriff der elterlichen Verantwortung

Elterliche Verantwortung ist ein Bündel von Rechten und Pflichten, die auf die Förderung und Sicherung des Wohles des Kindes abzielen. Sie umfasst insbesondere:

(a) Sorge, Schutz und Erziehung;
(b) Unterhalten persönlicher Beziehungen;
(c) Bestimmung des Aufenthaltes;
(d) Verwaltung des Vermögens und
(e) gesetzliche Vertretug.

INTERNATIONAL INSTRUMENTS

The following definitions of parental responsibilities are used in international and European instruments:

1. Article 1 para. 2 of the *Hague Child Protection Convention 1996*:

For the purposes of this Convention, the term "parental responsibility" includes parental authority, or any analogous relationship of authority determining the rights, powers and responsibilities of parents, guardians or other legal representatives in relation to the person or the property of the child.

2. Article 2 para. 6 of *Brussels IIbis*:

The term "parental responsibility" shall mean all rights and duties relating to the person or the property of a child which are given to a natural or legal person by judgment by operation of law or by agreement having legal effect. The term shall include rights of custody and rights of access.

3. Principle 18 of the *White Paper 2002*:

Parental responsibilities are a collection of duties and powers, which aim at ensuring the moral and material welfare of children, in particular:

- Care and protection
- Maintenance of personal relationships
- Provision of education
- Legal representation
- Determination of residence and
- Administration of property.

COMPARATIVE OVERVIEW

Terminology

The term "parental responsibilities" or "parental responsibility" is not commonly used as a basic concept in all jurisdictions surveyed. Only in the NORWEGIAN Children Act

1981[84] and the ENGLISH Children Act 1989 is the term explicitly used.[85] In SWEDEN the introduction of the concept of parental responsibilities was rejected in 1990 after several discussions during the last thirty years.[86] However, due to the use of this term either in the singular or in the plural in the Brussels II and II*bis* Regulation and other international and European instruments, the term "parental responsibilities" is becoming increasingly established in Europe. In the existing laws the following concepts are used: parental rights and obligations (BULGARIA[87]), custody (FINLAND[88]), custody and guardianship (IRELAND,[89] SWEDEN[90]), parental care (GERMANY[91]), parental authority (DENMARK,[92] FRANCE,[93] ITALY,[94] LITHUANIA,[95] THE NETHERLANDS,[96] POLAND,[97] SPAIN[98] and SWITZERLAND[99]), parental care and guardianship (GREECE[100]), parental supervision (HUNGARY[101]), parental power (PORTUGAL[102]) and parental rights (RUSSIA[103]). In particular in the Nordic countries a clear distinction is made between, on the one hand, custody/parental responsibility or authority which refers to the legal responsibility of taking care of and protecting the child and deciding for the child in personal matters, and on the other hand, guardianship which refers to the legal representation and administration of the child's property. Normally, a child's parents are both the child's custodians and guardians. Seen together, both concepts correspond with the general concept of parental responsibilities. In this context, it is noteworthy, that (official) translations of national concepts into English[104] often differ and therefore the lack of an uniform terminology should not be considered as problematic.

---

84 See however SVERDRUP/LØDRUP, Norwegian Report, Q 5: The Children Act 1981 introduced the concept 'parental responsibility' instead of 'parental authority' – a change that reflects a shift in attitude, more than a shift in content.

85 In the report of the CZECH REPUBLIC reference is made to the term 'parental responsibilities', see HRUSAKOVÁ, Czech Report, Q 1.

86 See JÄNTERÄ-JAREBORG/SINGER/SÖRGJERD, Swedish Report, Q 1 note 39.

87 Art. 68 Bulgarian Family Code.

88 See KURKI-SUONIO, Finnish Report, Q 1.

89 See SHANNON, Irish Report, Q 7.

90 Ch. 6 and 9–15 Swedish Children and Parents Code.

91 § 1626 para. 1 German Civil Code.

92 See LUND-ANDERSEN/JEPPESEN-DE BOER, Danish Report, Q 1.

93 Art. 371 para. 1 French Civil Code.

94 Title IX, Book 1 Italian Civil Code.

95 Art. 3.155 Lithuanian Civil Code.

96 Art. 1:247 Dutch Civil Code.

97 Art. 92 Polish Family and Guardianship Code.

98 Art. 154 Spanish Civil Code.

99 Art. 301 para. 1 and 2 Swiss Civil Code.

100 Art. 1511 and 1648 Greek Civil Code.

101 See WEISS/SZEIBERT, Hungarian Report, Q 1.

102 Art. 122–124, 129 Portuguese Civil Code.

103 See ANTOKOLSKAIA, Russian Report, Q 1.

104 See ROTH, Austrian Report, Q 1 refers to the German term: "The Austrian term for parental responsibilities is *Obsorge*."

Conversely, the content of the concept of parental responsibilities is of significant importance.

Content of parental responsibilities

With regard to the concepts of parental responsibilities a common core exists. In all jurisdictions the concept of parental responsibilities encompasses the following aspects: care and protection, the provision of education, maintenance of the personal relationship, the determination of the child's residence, the administration of the child's property and legal representation. This collection of rights and duties, which aims to ensure the moral and material welfare of children, is entirely in accordance with Principle 18 of the *White Paper 2002.*

Care, protection and education

In some jurisdictions certain aspects of parental responsibilities such as care and protection, the maintenance of personal relationships or the provision of education are explicitly regulated in the national constitution (BULGARIA,[105] GERMANY,[106] ITALY,[107] RUSSIA[108] and SPAIN[109]). In all jurisdictions it is generally acknowledged that the concept of care is the most important part of parental responsibilities. It includes the protection of the child's mental and physical health, security and morality. The duty to take care of the child must be exercised on the basis of the child's interests and needs which includes the development of its personality. The law of all jurisdictions embraces this key feature as being the most characteristic element of the relationship between the child and it's holders of parental responsibilities.[110]

Maintenance of personal relationships

The maintenance of personal relationships expresses the fundamental bond between the holders of parental responsibilities and the child. Family life in the sense of Article 8 of the *European Convention on Human Rights 1950* is based on the existence of daily

105 See TODOROVA, Bulgarian Report, Q 2.
106 See DETHLOFF/MARTINY, German Report, Q 2.
107 See PATTI/BELLISARIO/ROSSI CARLEO, Italian Report, Q 2.
108 See ANTOKOLSKAIA, Russian Report, Q 2.
109 See GONZÁLEZ BEILFUSS, Spanish Report, Q 2.
110 See the answers in the national reports in BOELE-WOELKI/BRAAT/CURRY-SUMNER, *ibid.*, note 23, Q 7 and Q 8a. See also the Comparative Overview under Principle 3:16.

or at least regular contact between the family members. All jurisdictions surveyed encompass this principle.[111]

Determination of residence

The holders of parental responsibilities should have the right to determine the child's residence.[112] Normally they live together. After a breakdown of their personal relationship the child's residence may eventually change. In all cases the holders of parental responsibilities should agree upon the child's residence. In particular, in view of the principle of the free movement of persons within the EU the determination of the child's residence has gained increasing importance when one of the parents wants to relocate to another jurisdiction. This aspect has not yet received the attention it really deserves.

Administration of the child's property

The issue of parental administration arises when the child owns his or her own property. The majority of European jurisdictions treat the administration of the child's property as a part of parental responsibilities.[113] In most legal systems there is a parallel between the care for the person and the care for the property of the child (AUSTRIA,[114] BELGIUM,[115] BULGARIA,[116] CZECH REPUBLIC,[117] FRANCE,[118] GERMANY,[119] GREECE,[120] HUNGARY,[121] ITALY,[122] LITHUANIA,[123] THE NETHERLANDS,[124] POLAND,[125] PORTUGAL,[126]

---

111 See all the answers in the national reports in BOELE-WOELKI/BRAAT/CURRY-SUMNER, *ibid.*, note 23, Q 7 and Q 8a. See also the Comparative Overview under Principles 3:17, 3:28, 3:29 and 3:30.

112 See all the answers in the national reports in BOELE-WOELKI/BRAAT/CURRY-SUMNER, *ibid.*, note 23, Q 2e. See also the Comparative Overview under Principles 3:18 and 3:19.

113 See all the answers in the national reports in BOELE-WOELKI/BRAAT/CURRY-SUMNER, *ibid.*, note 23, Q 2f. See also the Comparative Overview under Principles 3:20 and 3:21.

114 § 144, § 149 and § 150 Austrian Civil Code. See ROTH, Austrian Report, Q 2f and Q 10.

115 Art. 376 ff. Belgian Civil Code and PINTENS/PIGNOLET, Belgian Report, Q 2 f and Q 10.

116 See TODOROVA, Bulgarian Report, Q 2 f and Q 10.

117 § 31 para. 1 Czech Family Code. See HRUSAKOVÁ, Czech Report, Q 2f and Q 10.

118 See FERRAND, French Report, Q 2 f and Q 10.

119 § 1626 para. 1 German Civil Code. See DETHLOFF/MARTINY, German Report, Q 2f and Q 10.

120 Art. 1510 Greek Civil Code. See KOUTSOURADIS/ZERVOGIANNI, Greek Report, Q 2f and Q 10.

121 See WEISS/SZEIBERT, Hungarian Report, Q 2 f and Q 10.

122 Art. 320 Italian Civil Code and PATTI/BELLISARIO/ROSSI CARLEO, Italian Report, Q 2f and Q 10.

123 Art. 3.185 ff. Lithuanian Civil Code. See MIKELENAS, Lithuanian Report, Q 2f and Q 10.

124 Art. 1:245 para. 4 Dutch Civil Code. See BOELE-WOELKI/SCHRAMA/VONK, Dutch Report, Q 2f and Q 10.

125 Art. 101 para. 1 Polish Family and Guardianship Code. See MĄCZYŃSKI/MĄCZYŃSKA, Polish Report, Q 2f and Q 10.

126 Art. 1878 No. 1 Portuguese Civil Code. See DE OLIVEIRA, Portuguese Report, Q 2f and Q 10.

RUSSIA,[127] SPAIN[128] and SWITZERLAND[129]). Consequently the holders of parental responsibilities have by law the right and the obligation to administer the child's property. In DENMARK,[130] FINLAND,[131] NORWAY[132] and SWEDEN[133] there is a distinction between the care for the person which is understood as a question of custody and the care for the property which belongs to the law of guardianship. Therefore the holders of parental responsibilities, the parents, are the legal guardians of the minor child and basically the same rules as for guardians apply. At Common Law, a parent has no inherent authority over the assets of the child.[134] Therefore the traditional legal approach was to solve the arising questions mainly by the law of guardianship and the law of trusts. A parent may be appointed as a guardian or a trustee. Nevertheless, under modern child legislation in ENGLAND AND WALES[135] the court can decide also property issues of parental responsibility and the position of the holder of parental responsibilities is similar to a guardian of the estate.

Legal representation

Another element repeatedly described as forming a constituent part of parental responsibilities is that of legal representation.[136] Broadly speaking, the child cannot perform legal acts until he or she has reached the age of majority. In almost all systems surveyed statute law expressly confers the right of the holders of parental responsibilities to act as the child's legal representative.[137]

COMMENT

1. The CEFL uses the term parental responsibilities. Several European and international organisations have used this term in their respective instruments either in the singular (Hague Conference on Private International Law, European Commission)

---

127 See ANTOKOLSKAIA, Russian Report, Q 2f and Q 10.

128 Art. 155 Spanish Civil Code. See GONZÁLEZ BEILFUSS, Spanish Report, Q 2f and Q 10.

129 Art. 318 para. 1 Swiss Civil Code. See HAUSHEER/ACHERMANN-WEBER/WOLF, Swiss Report, Q 2f and Q 10.

130 Ch. 5 Danish Act on Guardianship. See LUND-ANDERSEN/JEPPESEN-DE BOER, Danish Report, Q 2f and Q 10.

131 § 4 Finnish Guardianship Services Act. See KURKI-SUONIO, Finnish Report, Q 2f.

132 § 3 Norwegian Act on Guardianship. See SVERDRUP/LØDRUP, Norwegian Report, Q 2f and Q 10.

133 Ch. 9 – 15 Swedish Children and Parents Code and JÄNTERÄ-JAREBORG/SINGER/SÖRGJERD, Swedish Report, Q 2f and Q 10.

134 See LOWE, English Report, Q 10; STOLJAR, *ibid.*, note 27, no. 206.

135 S. 3 (1) (2) English Children Act 1989. See LOWE, English Report, Q 10.

136 See all national reports, Q 2d. See also the Comparative Overview under Principle 3:22.

137 Under ENGLISH law this notion is based on common law and practice, see LOWE, English report, Q 2d and Q 8f.

or in the plural (Council of Europe). The CEFL has given preference to the latter, although in the French and German languages the concept can only be expressed in the singular. The concept parental responsibilities is a broad concept. It encompasses not only one package of rights and duties but consists of many different rights and duties. In addition, parental responsibilities are not only held by a parent but may also be held by third persons in whole or in part. Moreover, the use of the plural permits a more flexible approach.

2. CEFL's Questionnaire on Parental Responsibilities has initially used the definition of the Council of Europe in its *White Paper 2002* as a working definition. The CEFL definition of parental responsibilities in Principle 3:1 slightly differs from the Council of Europe definition. Preference is given to the wording of "rights and duties" instead of "duties and powers". In addition, the order of the constituent elements of parental responsibilities has been adjusted to the structure of the CEFL Principles regarding Parental Responsibilities.

3. Parental responsibilities can be divided among different holders of parental responsibilities. A person other than a parent, for instance, may, by a decision of the competent authority, exercise some rights and duties in addition to the parent(s) (Principle 3:19) and parents may agree on the exercise of parental responsibilities (Principle 3:13). Consequently, a division of rights and duties between the parents is possible.

4. Principle 3:1 contains CEFL's general concept of parental responsibilities. The content of all aspects (rights and duties) are specifically elaborated in Chapter V. In this chapter a distinction is made between, on the one hand, the *child's person and property* (Section A: Principles 3:19 to 3:24) and, on the other, the *maintenance of personal relationships* (Section B: Principles 3:25 to 3:29). Principle 3:19 deals with the right and duty of the holders of parental responsibilities to take *care of, protect* and *educate* the child in more detail. In Principle 3:20 and Principle 3:21 various matters concerning the *child's residence* and *relocation* are dealt with. The *administration of the child's property* is considered to be another constituent element of parental responsibilities. This has resulted in two separate Principles (Principles 3:22 and 3:23). The *legal representation* of the child is dealt with in Principle 3:24 and Principle 3:38 (Appointment of a legal representative for the child). The *maintenance of personal relationships*, which is usually indicated by the term "contact", is of paramount importance within the concept of parental responsibilities. Four specific Principles address this issue (Principles 3:25 to 3:28) whereas Principle 3:29 contains the right of the parent to be informed about the personal situation of the child.

Principle 3:2 Holder of parental responsibilities

(1) A holder of parental responsibilities is any person having the rights and duties listed in Principle 3:1 either in whole or in part.

(2) Subject to the following Principles, holders of parental responsibilities are:

(a) the child's parents, as well as

(b) persons other than the child's parents having parental responsibilities in addition to or instead of the parents.

Principle 3:2 Titulaires de la responsabilité parentale

(1) Est titulaire de la responsabilité parentale toute personne ayant, en tout ou partie, les droits et devoirs mentionnés au Principe 3:1.

(2) Sous réserve des Principes suivants, les titulaires de la responsabilité parentale sont:

(a) les parents de l'enfant, ainsi que

(b) les personnes autres que les parents de l'enfant qui ont la responsabilité parentale en complément ou à la place des parents.

Prinzip 3:2 Inhaber der elterlichen Verantwortung

(1) Inhaber der elterlichen Verantwortung ist jede Person, der die in Prinzip 3:1 genannten Rechte und Pflichten ganz oder teilweise zustehen.

(2) Vorbehaltlich der folgenden Prinzipien, sind Inhaber der elterlichen Verantwortung

(a) die Eltern des Kindes, so wie

(b) andere Personen als die Eltern des Kindes, denen elterliche Verantwortung zusätzlich mit oder statt der Eltern zusteht.

INTERNATIONAL INSTRUMENTS

Only recent international instruments define the term "holder of parental responsibilites". According to Article 2 sub. b of the *Convention on the Exercise of Children's Rights 1996* this term means parents and other persons or bodies entitled to exercise some or all parental responsibilities. The Convention's commentary states that, where appropriate, foster parents or establishments in which children are placed could therefore be included in this definition. In Principle 19 of the *White Paper 2002* it is stated that parental responsibilities should in principle belong jointly to both parents and in Principle 20 (3) it is submitted that a person other than a parent may, upon a decision by a competent authority, exercise some or all parental responsibilities in addition to or instead of parents. The *Brussels II bis Regulation* refers in respect to the term "holder of parental responsibility" to any person having parental responsibility over a child (Art. 2 no. 8).

COMPARATIVE OVERVIEW

Parents

In all systems surveyed parents are the primary holders of parental responsibilities. This is not explicitly stated but automatically follows from the establishment of legal parentage. Legal parentage either follows *ex lege* or is established through acknowledgment or adoption. See the detailed COMPARATIVE OVERVIEW under Principle 3:8.

Persons other than parents

A definition of persons other than parents can be found in a few international instruments that were drafted in recent years. However, national systems allow persons other than parents to exercise parental responsibilities. These persons are a step-parent, the parent's partner, the child's grandparent, foster parents and other persons who have close family ties or other ties with the child. See the detailed COMPARATIVE OVERVIEW under Principle 3:9. In the exceptional case of discharge of parental responsibilities also public bodies exercise parental responsibilities in whole or in part.

COMMENT

1. The definition provided in Principle 3:2 is deemed to be necessary for two reasons. Firstly, the CEFL has adopted a broad concept of parental responsibilities. Secondly, the Principles make a distinction between parents and third persons. The rights and duties described in Principle 3:1 cannot only be exercised by parents who are normally the most important persons in a child's life. Primarily they are in charge of the exercise of parental responsibilities. However, physical persons other than the parents as well as public bodies can also have parental responsibilities.

2. Principle 3:2 is further elaborated in Principle 3:8 where a definition of a parent is provided and in Principles 3:9 and 3:17 where the person other than a parent (third person) is defined. For decisions to be taken in daily matters Principle 3:18 specifically refers to the parent's partner.

3. Principle 3:2 clarifies that according to the CEFL Principles it is possible that there might be even more than two holders of parental responsibilities.

CHAPTER II: RIGHTS OF THE CHILD
CHAPITRE II : DROITS DE L'ENFANT
KAPITEL II: RECHTE DES KINDES

Principle 3:3 Best interests of the child
In all matters concerning parental responsibilities the best interests of the child should be the primary consideration.

Principe 3:3 Meilleur intérêt de l'enfant
Dans toutes les questions relatives à la responsabilité parentale, doit être pris en considération, à titre prépondérant, le meilleur intérêt de l'enfant.

Prinzip 3:3 Kindeswohl
In allen Angelegenheiten, die die elterliche Verantwortung betreffen, ist das Kindeswohl als oberster Gesichtspunkt in Betracht zu ziehen.

INTERNATIONAL INSTRUMENTS

A general principle establishing that children's interests should be given priority is laid down in numerous more recent international instruments.[138] The most important of these instruments is the *Convention on the Rights of the Child 1989*. According to its Article 3, "in all actions concerning children, whether undertaken by public or private social welfare institutions, courts of law, administrative authorities or legislative bodies, the best interests of the child shall be a primary consideration". The Contracting States shall "ensure the child such protection and care as is necessary for his or her well-being, taking into account the rights and duties of his or her parents, legal guardians, or other individuals legally responsible for him or her". To achieve this, the States parties are obliged to take all appropriate legislative and administrative measures. The Contracting States shall, furthermore, "ensure that the institutions, services and facilities responsible for the care and protection of children shall conform with the standards established

[138] In earlier instruments concerns like this were not as explicit, although express welfare concerns were. According to the *UN Declaration on the Rights of the Child 1959* "mankind owes the child the best it has to give". The *Convention on the Rights of the Child 1989* is the first international instrument to establish the human rights of the child.

by competent authorities, particularly in areas of safety, health, in the number and suitability of their staff as well as competent supervision".

The best interests of the child is not only one of the general principles of the *Convention on the Rights of the Child 1989*, but also a criterion in assessing the rights of the child. Specific references to the best interests of the child are made within the context of, for example, the separation of the child from his or her family setting (Art. 9), parental responsibility for the upbringing and development of the child (Art. 18) and the system of adoption and comparable arrangements (Art. 20 and 21). It embraces the treatment of children in all areas covered by the Convention, summing up the other principles established by the Convention which aim to make a child a subject of his or her own rights, and not merely an object of various conflicting interests.[139] Already in the *Convention on the Elimination of Discrimination against Women 1979* the interests of children are considered to be of paramount importance. Article 16.1.d guarantees equality between men and women in all matters relating to marriage and family relations. They should have the same rights and responsibilities as parents, irrespective of their marital status, in matters relating to their children. According to the *European Charter of Fundamental Rights 2000* (Art. 24.2), as well as the *Draft Treaty for a European Constitution 2003* (Art. II–84.2), "in all actions relating to children, whether taken by public authorities or private institutions, the child's best interests must be a primary consideration".

Recent international instruments dealing with issues concerning parental responsibilities all confirm that the best interests of the child is to be a primary consideration, to be promoted by the instrument in question.[140] Neither these instruments nor the previously mentioned more general instruments provide any particular definition as to what constitutes the best interests of the child.

COMPARATIVE OVERVIEW

A well-established principle

The principle of the best interests of the child is well established in all the twenty-two jurisdictions surveyed. This is due not least to the fact that they are all parties to the *Convention on the Rights of the Child 1989*. In many of them, also many of the other

[139] See GRAS, *Monitoring the Convention on the Rights of the Child*, 2001, p. 19.

[140] See the Preamble to the *Hague Child Protection Convention 1996*, the Preamble to the *Convention on the Exercise of Children's Rights 1996*, the Preamble to the *Convention on Contact Concerning Children 2003* and the Preamble to the *Brussels II bis Regulation*.

international instruments referred to above are in force. In some of the surveyed jurisdictions the law merely refers to the "interests of the child" (BELGIUM,[141] BULGARIA,[142] HUNGARY,[143] LITHUANIA[144] and PORTUGAL[145]) instead of the "best interests of the child', but in essence this difference in expression would seem to be without relevance. The same applies to ENGLAND AND WALES[146] and IRELAND[147], where the law refers to "the welfare of the child". Similarly, the laws of AUSTRIA, GERMANY and SWITZERLAND, in a literal sense, refer to the child's well-being ("Kindeswohl").

No precise statutory definitions

None of the jurisdictions surveyed have a statutory provision explicitly defining what is meant by "the best interests of the child" or other corresponding expressions. An explanation is that it is not possible to establish these interests generally, irrespective of the individual child and the culture, values and morals prevailing in the society where the child lives. The best interests of the child is also a notion whose content cannot be permanently fixed, but must reflect the prevailing values in the society in question and the concrete situation of the child in question. Certain goals stipulated by the law may, however, be interpreted as a definition of what is meant, such as the child's right to care, protection, a good upbringing, and an autonomy which increases with the child's growing maturity. This is the approach taken in, e.g., AUSTRIA[148], FINLAND,[149] FRANCE,[150] PORTUGAL[151] and SWEDEN.[152]

The guiding principle or the primary consideration

In light of the national reports the best interests of the child appears to be a flexible concept enabling an individual assessment by the competent authority. The best interests of the child may be regarded as the "guiding principle" (FRANCE,[153]

141 See PINTENS/PIGNOLET, Belgian Report, Q 35.
142 See TODOROVA, Bulgarian Report, Q 5.
143 See WEISS/SZEIBERT, Hungarian Report, Q 35.
144 See MIKELENAS, Lithuanian Report, Q 35.
145 See DE OLIVEIRA, Portuguese Report, Q 35.
146 See LOWE, English Report, Q 35.
147 See SHANNON, Irish Report, Q 35.
148 See ROTH, Austrian Report, Q 35.
149 See KURKI-SUONIO, Finnish Report, Q 35.
150 See FERRAND, French Report, Q 35.
151 See DE OLIVEIRA, Portuguese Report, Q 9.
152 See JÄNTERÄ-JAREBORG/SINGER/SÖRGJERD, Swedish Report, Q 35.
153 See FERRAND, French Report, Q 35.

GERMANY,[154] HUNGARY,[155] SPAIN[156] and SWITZERLAND[157]) or the "primary" or "paramount consideration" (ENGLAND AND WALES,[158] FINLAND,[159] IRELAND,[160] NORWAY,[161] PORTUGAL[162] and SWEDEN[163]) in addressing issues of parental responsibilities. Some of the national reports (ITALY[164] and LITHUANIA[165]) emphasize that issues concerning parental responsibilities must de decided exclusively in the interests of the child whereas others, on the other hand, point out that, outside of litigation, the holders of parental responsibilities ultimately decide, and that also, generally speaking, there are limits to pursuing the child's interests at the expense of, for example, the interests of the parents (BULGARIA,[166] ENGLAND AND WALES,[167] POLAND[168] and RUSSIA[169]). Where these interests are in conflict with each other, ultimately the child's interests should be given priority.

COMMENT

1. Principle 3:3 places the best interests of the child as *the* primary consideration, i.e., the ultimate, decisive consideration. The wording used is stronger than that of the *Convention on the Rights of the Child 1989* according to which "the best interests of the child shall be *a* primary consideration". It is also stronger, or at least clearer, than the expression used in both the *European Charter of Fundamental Rights 2000* and the *Draft Treaty for a European Constitution 2003*, according to which "the child's best interests must be *a* primary consideration". It roughly equates to the expression of "the paramount consideration"[170] used in the law of ENGLAND AND WALES. The aim

154 See DETHLOFF/MARTINY, German Report, Q 35.
155 See WEISS/SZEIBERT, Hungarian Report, Q 35.
156 See GONZÁLEZ BEILFUSS, Spanish report, Q 35.
157 See HAUSHEER/ACHERMANN-WEBER/WOLF, Swiss Report, Q 35.
158 See LOWE, English Report, Q 35.
159 See KURKI-SUONIO, Finnish Report, Q 5.
160 See SHANNON, Irish Report, Q 35.
161 See SVERDRUP/LØDRUP, Norwegian Report, Q 35.
162 See DE OLIVEIRA, Portuguese Report, Q 5.
163 See JÄNTERÄ-JAREBORG/SINGER/SÖRGJERD, Swedish Report, Q 35.
164 See PATTI/BELLISARIO/ROSSI CARLEO, Italian Report, Q 35. The Report, however, also claims that this does not apply in practice, Q 5.
165 See MIKELENAS, Lithuanian Report, Q 35.
166 See TODOROVA, Bulgarian Report, Q 5.
167 See LOWE, English Report, Q 35.
168 See MĄCZYŃSKI/MĄCZYŃSKA, Polish Report, Q 35.
169 See ANTOKOLSKAIA, Russian Report, Q 35.
170 It has, however, been suggested that the wording of the *Convention on the Rights of the Child 1989* might be more realistic, "in the light of human rights obligations towards adult parties", than the "paramount consideration" expressed in English law. See BAINHAM, *Children – The Modern Law*, 2005, pp. 70–71. It should also be noted that the principle of paramountcy in ENGLISH law applies

is to mark the criterion's exceptional weight. It is not a primary consideration, to be taken into account among other important concerns, but *the decisive criterion*. The assessment of the child's best interests should always be made from the child's perspective, regard being had to his or her present and future interests and needs. Where there is a clash between the interests of the child and those of the holders of parental responsibilities or those of other persons, the interests of the child should prevail, see Principle 3:7.

2. Principle 3:3 leaves the content of the "best interests of the child" undefined as do the various international instruments and all of the national jurisdictions surveyed. The "best interests of the child" is a changing notion, dependent not only on the prevailing values in the society in question as regards children, but also on the individual child and his or her present situation (age, maturity, personality, needs, abilities, etc.). It is a general principle to be taken into account as *the* primary consideration in all matters concerning children. Indirectly, its content is developed in all the following Principles, as these are aimed to materialize what constitutes the child's best interests in different kinds of situations.

3. Whereas, for example, the *Convention on the Rights of the Child 1989* refers to all *actions* concerning children and undertaken by different types of public or private bodies, Principle 3:3 refers to "all matters concerning parental responsibilities". "Matters" is a broader concept aimed to cover not only measures taken by competent authorities but also agreements between the holders of parental responsibilities as well as daily decisions by the parents or other holders of parental responsibilities relating to the child's care.

---

in litigation, but it does not directly apply to parents or other holders of parental responsibilities in their exercise of parental responsibilities. See LOWE, English Report, Q 35.

Principle 3:4 Autonomy of the child
The child's autonomy should be respected in accordance with the developing ability and need of the child to act independently.

Principe 3:4 Autonomie de l'enfant
L'autonomie de l'enfant est respectée en tenant compte de la capacité et du besoin croissants de l'enfant d'agir de façon indépendante.

Prinzip 3:4 Autonomie des Kindes
Die Autonomie des Kindes wird respektiert, wobei den wachsenden Fähigkeiten und Bedürfnissen des Kindes selbständig zu handeln, Rechnung getragen wird.

INTERNATIONAL INSTRUMENTS

The *Convention on the Rights of the Child 1989* recognizes the child as an autonomous individual with the right to exercise influence over his or her own life. The Convention broke the trend from viewing children primarily or merely as vulnerable objects of their parents and in need of protection, to recognizing children as autonomous individuals with rights and integrity of their own and a human dignity of their own. Almost every right protected by the Convention includes elements of participation in decision-making processes.[171] Earlier instruments of the United Nations, such as the *Declaration on the Rights of the Child 1924* and the *Declaration of the Rights of the Child 1959*, reflected a more conservative and patronizing approach to children, focusing on the care and protection of children.[172] Nevertheless, the Convention also recognizes that children, due to their physical and mental immaturity, are vulnerable and in need of protection. It follows that the child's right to autonomy does not exclude the child's right to protection. On the contrary, both concerns are of the utmost importance under the Convention.

The view of children as autonomous individuals with rights of their own, confirmed by the *Convention on the Rights of the Child 1989*, is reflected in more recent international instruments, e.g., the *European Charter of Fundamental Rights 2000*, the *Convention on the Exercise of Children's Rights 1996*, the *Convention on Contact Concerning Children 2003* and the *White Paper 2002*. This approach is expressed in general principles emphasizing the child's best interests as a primary consideration

---

171 See STERN, *The Child's Right to Participation – Reality or Rhetoric?*, 2006, pp. 16–17.
172 See GRAS, *ibid.*, note 139, p. 3. In the words of the 1959 Declaration, "the child, by reason of his physical and mental immaturity, needs special safeguards and care, including appropriate legal protection".

that must be taken into account in all decisions concerning the child and, in particular, in principles concerning the child's right to participation, i.e, to be heard in all matters concerning him or her and to exercise his or her rights. These principles, as expressed in international instruments, are described and commented upon under Principle 3:3 and Principle 3:6. Similarly with the *Convention on the Rights of the Child 1989*, also these instruments strive to combine the recognition of the child's autonomy with the child's need for protection. Thus, according to the *European Charter of Fundamental Rights 2000*, children shall have the right to such protection and care as is necessary for their well-being (Art. 24.1). This provision is repeated in the *Draft Treaty for a European Constitution 2003* (Art. II–84.1).

COMPARATIVE OVERVIEW

Striking a balance between the child's autonomy and the need for protection

In all the jurisdictions surveyed the child is recognized not only as a vulnerable person in need of care and protection, but also – in theory at least – as an autonomous individual.[173] This development, which in many of the jurisdictions materialized only after the State's ratification of the *Convention on the Rights of the Child 1989* (e.g. HUNGARY[174]), has in some cases resulted in a change of terminology from concepts such as "parental power" (BELGIUM[175]), or "parental authority" (GERMANY[176] and NORWAY[177]) to more child-centred concepts such as "parental care" or "parental responsibility". A balance between the different concerns is found by emphasizing the child's age and maturity. A younger and less mature child needs more care and protection than an older and more mature child who may enjoy rights of participation in decisions concerning him or her and who may also, within certain limits, take decisions and act independently on his or her own. The parents or other holders of parental responsibilities with corresponding rights and duties are expected to assist the child in making

---

173 The Italian Report claims that in practice the child continues to be seen as an "incendental addressee of a series of decisions taken by others". See PATTI/BELLISARIO/ROSSI CARLEO, Italian Report, Q 5. International studies show that the child's right to participation, protected by the *Convention on the Rights of the Child 1989*, has turned out to be the most difficult right to implement in most of the States parties to the Convention. See STERN, *ibid.*, note 171.

174 See WEISS/SZEIBERT, Hungarian Report, Q 5.

175 See PINTENS/PIGNOLET, Belgian Report, Q 5.

176 See DETHLOFF/MARTINY, German Report, Q 5.

177 See SVERDRUP/LØDRUP, Norwegian Report, Q 5.

his or her own decisions, taking into account the child's age and maturity (see, e.g., CZECH REPUBLIC,[178] FRANCE,[179] PORTUGAL[180] and SWEDEN[181])

When may a child act on his or her own?

Normally parents with parental responsibilities or other corresponding holders of parental responsibilities act as the *legal representatives* of the child when taking actions, on behalf of the child, in matters concerning both the person of the child and the child's economic affairs. Normally this function of the parents or other holders of parental responsibilities lasts until the child reaches the age of majority, including both judicial and extra-judicial representation. In certain situations and under certain conditions, however, the minor child may validly act on his or her own.

In many of the countries surveyed the child is given a limited legal capacity at a certain age, which varies between fourteen to sixteen years, but may also depend on the nature of the issue at stake. From that age onwards the child may act more or less freely regarding certain types of legal actions. In some countries, the consent of the parents is required in addition. Alternatively, the child's consent is required before a decision concerning the child can be taken, e.g. regarding medical treatment, when the child has reached a certain age or maturity (AUSTRIA, BULGARIA, CZECH REPUBLIC, DENMARK, ENGLAND AND WALES, FINLAND, FRANCE, THE NETHERLANDS and PORTUGAL).[182] In BULGARIA, once the child attains the age of fourteen, he or she may act independently subject to the condition that the parents consent to this.[183] In HUNGARY[184] and LITHUANIA[185] and RUSSIA,[186] the child also acquires a limited legal capacity at the age of fourteen. In FINLAND,[187] a child who has reached the age of fifteen has the right of self-representation in cases relating to the child's person, whereas in SPAIN[188] it is sufficient that the child has reached the age of fourteen.

---

178 See HRUSKAKOVÁ, Czech Report, Q 8.
179 See FERRAND, French Report, Q 35.
180 See DE OLIVEIRA, Portuguese Report, Q 5 and Q 8.
181 See JÄNTERÄ-JAREBORG/SINGER/SÖRGJERD, Swedish Report, Q 35.
182 See all the answers in the national reports in BOELE-WOELKI/BRAAT/CURRY-SUMNER, *ibid.*, note 23, Q 8.
183 See TODOROVA, Bulgarian Report, Q 8 and Q 9.
184 See WEISS/SZEIBERT, Hungarian Report, Q 8.
185 See MIKELENAS, Lithuanian Report, Q 8.
186 See ANTOKOLSKAIA, Russian Report, Q 8.
187 See KURKI-SUONIO, Finnish Report, Q 8.
188 See GONZÁLES BEILFUSS, Spanish Report, Q 8.

In the other jurisdictions, the law fixes no generally applicable age requirement.[189] The child's right to act independently with legal validity depends on the nature of the issue at hand, and an assessment of whether the child has reached a sufficient age and maturity to understand the consequences of his or her actions. This is the position taken in, e.g., CZECH REPUBLIC,[190] ENGLAND AND WALES,[191] FRANCE,[192] THE NETHERLANDS,[193] and PORTUGAL.[194] Furthermore, in FINLAND[195] and SWEDEN,[196] the child may independently administer assets which he or she has acquired through his or her own labour. In ITALY,[197] a minor child may validly exercise rights and duties deriving from employment.

COMMENT

1. Principle 3:4 explicitly recognizes the child's autonomy. The child should be viewed as the subject of his or her own rights, which also means that the child should be able to participate in decisions concerning him or her and, within necessary limits, should also be permitted to act independently. Principle 3:4 is closely linked to Principle 3:3 and Principle 3:6. It is also of relevance for the application of Principle 3:7. It should, furthermore, be taken into account in the application of all the subsequent Principles. Principle 3:4 is addressed to both competent authorities and the holders of parental responsibilities.

2. Children are young by definition, inexperienced and vulnerable, which justifies limitations to their right to self-determination. International instruments and national laws refer to the child's age and maturity as relevant criteria. Some of the national laws have fixed age limits for certain types of decisions by the child. Principle 3:4 emphasizes the link between the child's developing ability and his or her increasing need to act independently, without explicitly referring to the child's age and maturity. The idea is that a person's age should not as such be decisive for his or her autonomy, but that autonomy requires a certain capacity. The more able the child, the greater is his or her need to act independently. Ability, in turn, is dependent on the child's maturity.

---

189 It must be pointed out, however, that not all of the national reports explicitly touch upon the relevance of the child's age but leave it open. See, e.g., KOUTSOURADIS/ZERVOGIANNI, Greek Report, Q 8.

190 See HRUSKAKOVÁ, Czech Report, Q 8.

191 See LOWE, English Report, Q 8 and Q 59.

192 See FERRAND, French Report, Q 8.

193 See BOELE-WOELKI/SCHRAMA/VONK, Dutch Report, Q 2d.

194 See DE OLIVEIRA, Portuguese Report, Q 8.

195 See KURKI-SUONIO, Finnish Report, Q 8.

196 See JÄNTERÄ-JAREBORG/SINGER/SÖRGJERD, Swedish Report, Q 8.

197 See PATTI/BELLISARIO/ROSSI CARLEO, Italian Report, Q 8.

3. The child's developing ability to feel and take responsibility should be reflected in increasing autonomy for the child. The child's need for protection is correspondingly reduced, but is still present. The holders of parental responsibilities, normally the child's parents, should assist the child in taking actions and making decisions on his or her own.

Principle 3:5 Non-discrimination of the child
Children should not be discriminated on grounds such as sex, race, colour, language, religion, political or other opinion, national, ethnic or social origin, sexual orientation, disability, property, birth or other status, irrespective of whether these grounds refer to the child or to the holders of parental responsibilities.

Principe 3:5 Non-discrimination de l'enfant
Les enfants ne font l'objet d'aucune discrimination fondée notamment sur le sexe, la race, la couleur, la langue, la religion, les opinions politiques ou autres, l'origine nationale, ethnique ou sociale, l'orientation sexuelle, le handicap, le patrimoine, la naissance ou tout autre état, que ces motifs se rapportent à l'enfant ou aux titulaires de la responsabilité parentale.

Prinzip 3:5 Nichtbenachteiligung des Kindes
Kinder dürfen nicht benachteiligt werden aus Gründen wie Geschlecht, Rasse, Hautfarbe, Sprache, Religion, politische oder andere Anschauungen, nationale, ethnische oder soziale Herkunft, sexueller Ausrichtung, Behinderung, Vermögen, Geburt oder anderem Status, unabhängig davon, ob diese Gründe sich auf das Kind oder die Inhaber der elterlichen Verantwortung beziehen.

INTERNATIONAL INSTRUMENTS

Article 2 of the *Convention on the Rights of the Child 1989* obliges the Contracting States to respect and ensure the rights set forth in the Convention to each child within their jurisdiction "without discrimination of any kind, irrespective of the child's or his or her parent's or legal guardian's race, colour, sex, language, religion, political or other opinion, national, ethnic or social origin, property, disability, birth or other status". The Contracting States "shall take all appropriate measures to ensure that the child is protected against all forms of discrimination or punishment on the basis of the status, activities, expressed opinion, or beliefs of the child's parents, legal guardians, or family members". The cited principle of non-discrimination of the child is one of the Convention's general provisions. The enlisted grounds of discrimination correspond to those of the *International Covenant on Civil and Political Rights 1966* (Art. 2.1).[198] The list should not be considered to be exhaustive but merely indicative.

[198] According to Article 2.1 of the *International Covenant on Civil and Political Rights 1966*, "each State Party to the present Covenant undertakes to respect and to ensure to all individuals within their territory and subject to its jurisdiction the rights recognized in the present Covenant, without distinction of any kind, such as race, colour, sex, language, religion, political or other opinion, national or social origin, property, birth or other status". The same listing is followed in the

The contracting states of the *Convention on the Elimination of Discrimination against Women 1979* have committed themselves to taking all appropriate measures to eliminate discrimination against women in all matters relating to marriage and family relations and in particular to ensure, on a basis of equality between men and women, that they have the same rights and responsibilities as parents, irrespective of their marital status, in matters relating to their children (Art. 16.1.d).

Another more general provision prohibiting discrimination is found in Article 14 of the *European Convention on Human Rights 1950.* "The enjoyment of the rights and freedoms set forth in this Convention shall be secured without discrimination on any ground such as sex, race, colour, language, religion, political or other opinion, national or social origin, association with a national minority, property, birth or other status." The *Treaty Establishing the European Community* of 25th March 1975 not only prohibits discrimination on grounds of nationality (Art. 12), but also authorizes the Council to take appropriate action to combat discrimination based on sex, racial or ethnic origin, religion or belief, disability, age or sexual orientation (Art. 14). According to the *European Charter of Fundamental Rights 2000* "any discrimination based on any ground such as sex, race, colour, ethnic or social origin, genetic features, language, religion or belief, political or any other opinion, membership of a national minority, property, birth, disability, age or sexual orientation" is prohibited (Art. 21) in addition to discrimination on grounds of nationality. This provision is reproduced in the *Draft Treaty for a European Constitution 2003* (Art. II–81).

In recent international instruments on parental responsibilities[199] no distinction is made between children on grounds such as the above-mentioned. The *Brussels II bis Regulation* covers all decisions on parental responsibility, including measures for the protection of the child, independently of any link with a matrimonial proceeding. The aim is to "ensure equality for all children".[200] When drafting the new Regulation the limitation of the repealed Regulation to decisions on parental responsibility for the children of both spouses, rendered on the occasion of matrimonial proceedings, was found to be untenable.

International Covenant on Economic, Social and Cultural Rights 1966. Both have been inspired by the *United Nations Universal Declaration on Human Rights 1948*, Article 2.1.

199 See above Principle 3:3.

200 See Preamble, paragraph 5 of the *Brussels II bis Regulation.*

COMPARATIVE OVERVIEW

There is a clear trend in the jurisdictions surveyed towards the equal treatment of children. The pace of the development varies, however. Unequal treatment of a child often also entails unequal treatment of a parent or another person close to the child. It is also evident that unequal treatment of children often has to do with a ground directly connected to another person close to the child, such as that person's homosexuality. The national reports focus on two grounds for unequal treatment, i.e., the effect of the child's birth within or out of wedlock on the attribution of parental responsibilities, and the effect of the homosexuality of the parent's partner on his or her prospects of acquiring parental responsibilities. It is not reported that the child's sex is a ground for discrimination in any of the countries concerned.[201]

Unequal treatment on the basis of the child's birth

As regards children born *within wedlock* a patriarchic order, according to which the father was the legal holder of parental responsibilities prevailed until after the Second World War in countries such as GERMANY[202] (until 1949), HUNGARY[203] (until 1945), ITALY[204] (until 1948), and THE NETHERLANDS[205] (until 1947). In the majority of the jurisdictions surveyed, however, both of the married parents were by this time the holders of parental responsibilities, although in some countries (BELGIUM[206] and PORTUGAL[207]), the father's rights were superior to those of the mother.[208] In FRANCE,[209] the married parents of a child were only placed on an equal footing in 1970 and in GREECE[210] as late as in 1983. If the child was born to an unmarried mother, i.e. *out of wedlock*, parental responsibilities belonged for a long time in all of the jurisdictions to the mother, to the exclusion of the father.

---

201 In RUSSIA, however, during a period following the 1917 Revolution, different age limits applied to the termination of parental responsibilities as regards girls (16 years) and boys (18 years). See ANTOKOLSKAIA, Russian Report, Q 5. The national reports do not touch upon the issue of whether different marriage ages are applied to boys and girls. Globally, discrimination against girls is a huge problem.

202 See DETHLOFF/MARTINY, German Report, Q 5. The German Basic Law of 1949 established equality between men and women. All statutes that were not in conformity with this principle were to cease to be valid as of 1953.

203 See WEISS/SZEIBERT, Hungarian Report, Q 5.

204 See PATTI/BELLISARIO/ROSSI CARLEO, Italian Report, Q 5.

205 See BOELE-WOELKI/SCHRAMA/VONK, Dutch Report, Q 5.

206 See PINTENS/PIGNOLET, Belgian Report, Q 5.

207 See DE OLIVEIRA, Portuguese Report, Q 5.

208 Until married women received full legal capacity, the husband's parental responsibilies continued to be more extensive than the wife's.

209 See FERRAND, French Report, Q 5.

210 See KOUTSOURADIS/ZERVOGIANNI, Greek Report, Q 5.

The distinction between children born within wedlock and children born out of wedlock has successively been abandoned in all the jurisdictions.[211] In spite of this, different rules continue to apply to the attribution of parental responsibilities following the birth of the child, depending on whether the parents are (or have been) married to each other or whether they have never been married to each other.[212] A certain development towards the equal treatment of the parents as the holders of parental responsibilities, irrespective of the child's birth within or out of wedlock (or other formalized relationship), is however conceivable.[213]

Unequal treatment on the basis of sexual orientation

In the majority of the jurisdictions homosexual couples do not enjoy the same rights regarding parental responsibilities as are enjoyed by (married) heterosexual couples. The common core found in most of the jurisdictions is that *adoption* is the only way for a parent's partner to acquire full parental responsibilities jointly with the child's parent. In many of the countries, however, same-sex partners are excluded from adoption (AUSTRIA,[214] CZECH REPUBLIC,[215] ITALY,[216] LITHUANIA[217] and PORTUGAL[218]). Those countries that, in principle, place homosexual couples on an equal footing with heterosexual couples as regards parental responsibilities are still a minority (BELGIUM,[219] THE NETHERLANDS[220] and SWEDEN[221]). On the other hand, certain countries in Europe have recently introduced legislation on registered partnerships (ENGLAND AND WALES[222] and SWITZERLAND[223]), or are considering such legislation. In the future, a person's sexual orientation is likely to be of less importance also as regards the acquisition and exercise of parental responsibilities.

The national reports contain no documentation on discrimination against children on the basis of the child's sexual orientation.

---

211 See all the national reports in BOELE-WOELKI/BRAAT/CURRY-SUMNER, *ibid.*, note 23, Q 5.
212 See all the national reports in BOELE-WOELKI/BRAAT/CURRY-SUMNER, *ibid.*, note 23, Q 5.
213 See all the national reports in BOELE-WOELKI/BRAAT/CURRY-SUMNER, *ibid.*, note 23, Q 5.
214 See ROTH, Austrian Report, Q 28.
215 See HRUSAKOVÁ, Czech Report, Q 28.
216 See PATTI/BELLISARIO/ROSSI CARLEO, Italian Report, Q 28.
217 See MIKELENAS, Lithuanian Report, Q 28.
218 See DE OLIVEIRA, Portuguese Report, Q 28.
219 See PINTENS/PIGNOLET, Belgian Report, Q 28.
220 See BOELE-WOELKI/SCHRAMA/VONK, Dutch Report, Q 28.
221 See JÄNTERÄ-JAREBORG/SINGER/SÖRGJERD, Swedish Report, Q 28.
222 The Civil Partnership Act 2004 became effective as of 5th December 2005.
223 The Registered Partnership Act entered into force on the 1st January 2007.

COMMENT

1. The grounds of prohibited discrimination enlisted in Principle 3:5 correspond to those found in leading international instruments. Compared with the *Convention on the Rights of the Child 1989* and the *European Convention on Human Rights 1950*, the list is more comprehensive in also including sexual orientation which, on the other hand, is explicitly mentioned in the *EC Treaty 1975*, the *European Charter of Fundamental Rights 2000* and the *Draft Treaty for a European Constitution 2003*. Similarly with these instruments, the list is not meant to be exhaustive, but only indicative. Also other grounds than the ones explicitly mentioned may constitute forbidden discrimination. Discrimination is understood to mean any distinction, exclusion, restriction or preference, based on grounds such as the above-mentioned, where the aim is to nullify or impair the recognition, enjoyment or exercise, on an equal footing, of rights and freedoms.[224]

2. The grounds prohibiting discrimination enlisted in Principle 3:5 refer not only to the child but also to the holders of parental responsibilities, who are normally the child's parents. Likewise, these grounds should also be interpreted to refer to all those other persons who, according to national law, are regarded, or may come into consideration, as the holders of parental responsibilities, instead of, or in addition to, the child's parents. Prohibited discrimination may also relate to a family member of the child, not holding parental responsibilities, as stated in Article 2.2 of the *Convention on the Rights of the Child 1989.* It is important to keep in mind that the list contained in Principle 3:5 is not exhaustive, but only indicative. In reality, the unequal treatment of a child is often based on a ground or grounds relating to a person other than the child.

3. Principle 3:5 goes further than the majority of the jurisdictions surveyed in prohibiting discrimination against children. At present, differences in treatment may apply in particular depending on whether the parents of the child are or have been married to each other. Furthermore, a person's homosexuality may as such in certain countries disqualify him or her as a (potential) holder of parental responsibilities. Principle 3:5 also prohibits the unequal treatment of children on grounds such as the status of the child's residence. Children who reside illegally in a country should enjoy the same rights, e.g., in respect of the right to medical care and education, as are enjoyed by the children legally resident in that country. Only then can the holders of parental responsibilities exercise their rights and duties on an equal footing with others.

---

[224] See DETRICK, *A Commentary on the United Nations Convention on the Rights of the Child*, 1999, p. 73.

Principle 3:6 Child's right to be heard
Having regard to the child's age and maturity, the child should have the right to be informed, consulted and to express his or her opinion in all matters concerning the child, with due weight given to the views expressed by him or her.

Principe 3:6 Droit de l'enfant d'être entendu
Eu égard à son âge et à sa maturité, l'enfant a le droit d'être informé, consulté et d'exprimer son opinion dans tous les domaines le concernant, l'opinion exprimée par l'enfant étant dûment prise en considération.

Prinzip 3:6 Recht des Kindes auf Gehör
Entsprechend seinem Alter und seiner Reife hat das Kind das Recht, informiert und konsultiert zu werden, und seine Meinung zu äußern in allen das Kind berührenden Angelegenheiten, wobei der vom Kind geäusserten Auffasung des Kindes angemessenes Gewicht zu geben ist.

INTERNATIONAL INSTRUMENTS

Article 12 of the *Convention on the Rights of the Child 1989* obliges the Contracting States to "assure to the child who is capable of forming his or her own views the right to express those views freely in all matters affecting the child, the views of the child being given due weight in accordance with the age and maturity of the child. For this purpose, the child shall in particular be provided with the opportunity to be heard in any judicial or administrative proceedings affecting the child, either directly, or through a representative or an appropriate body, in a manner consistent with the procedural rules of national law."

Once again, we are dealing with one of the guiding principles of the Convention. This principle is supplemented by Article 13 establishing the child's right to obtain and to make known certain information and to express his or her views, unless this would violate the rights of others. General instruments, recognizing the child's right to express his or her own opinion, include the *European Charter of Fundamental Rights 2000.* According to its Article 24.1 children "may express their views freely". "Such views shall be taken into consideration on matters which concern them in accordance with their age and maturity". The same provision is repeated in the *Draft Treaty for a European Constitution 2003* (Art. II–84.1).

The child's right to be heard, to express his or her opinion as well as to participate in decisions concerning him or her is also confirmed in other instruments of relevance for the assessment of parental responsibilities.[225] The *Convention on the Exercise of Children's Rights 1996* should be mentioned in particular, it being a specialist instrument aiming, in the best interests of children, to grant children procedural rights and to facilitate the exercise of these rights in family law proceedings, in particular those involving the exercise of parental responsibilities such as residence and access to children (Art. 1).[226] The Convention ensures any child considered by internal law as having sufficient understanding, in the case of proceedings before a judicial authority affecting him or her, the right (a) to receive all relevant information, (b) to be consulted and express his or her views, and (c) to be informed of the possible consequences of compliance with these views and the possible consequences of any decision (Art. 3). The *Convention on Contact Concerning Children 2003* also distinguishes between the child's right (a) to receive (all relevant) information, (b) to be consulted and (c) to express his or her views (Art. 6). According to the Convention, these rights apply to a child considered by internal law as having sufficient understanding, unless this would be manifestly contrary to the child's best interests. According to the *White Paper 2002,* "when exercising parental rights and responsibilities the child should have a right to express his or her views" and "due weight should be given to the views expressed by the child according to his age and maturity" (Principle 21).

COMPARATIVE OVERVIEW

Obligatory or voluntary hearing of the child

All of the jurisdictions surveyed recognize the child's right to be heard in proceedings concerning parental responsibilities. In the great majority of these jurisdictions, this right of the child entails a duty on the court to hear the child, either directly or by delegating the hearing of the child to a suitable person or body, such as a social worker or a representative of a social welfare committee (AUSTRIA, BULGARIA, CZECH REPUBLIC, DENMARK, ENGLAND AND WALES, FINLAND, GERMANY, GREECE, HUNGARY, LITHUANIA, THE NETHERLANDS, NORWAY, POLAND, PORTUGAL, RUSSIA, SPAIN, SWEDEN and SWITZERLAND).[227] In some of the other jurisdictions, the court is not obliged to hear the child,

---

225 In addition to the instruments referred to in the text above, also the *Hague Child Protection Convention 1996*, (Art. 23.2.b) and the *Brussels II bis Regulation* (Art. 23.b, see also para. 19 of the Preamble to the *Brussels II bis Regulation*) should be mentioned.

226 Among the jurisdictions surveyed, this Convention is in force in the CZECH REPUBLIC, GERMANY, GREECE, ITALY, and POLAND. Judging on the basis of which states have signed it, its ratification is expected by AUSTRIA, FINLAND, FRANCE, IRELAND, PORTUGAL, RUSSIA, SLOVAKIA, SPAIN and SWEDEN.

227 See all the answers in the national reports in BOELE-WOELKI/BRAAT/CURRY-SUMNER, *ibid.*, note 23, Q 59.

but may still do so (BELGIUM,[228] FRANCE[229] and IRELAND[230]). It is also reported that in countries where the court should, according to the law, hear the child, this is not always the case in practice (CZECH REPUBLIC,[231] GREECE,[232] THE NETHERLANDS,[233] SPAIN[234] and SWEDEN[235]).

The national reports clearly indicate that the child's right to be heard is not regarded as an absolute right, not even when the child has reached a certain age stipulated by law. Exceptions are made where hearing the child would be detrimental to his or her interests or would risk harming him or her.[236] Giving priority to the child's best interests has in some cases resulted in the court abstaining from hearing the child.[237] The child's age and maturity are likely to influence this assessment.[238]

The nature of the proceedings

The position taken regarding the court's duty to hear the child depends, in addition, on several other factors. The type of proceedings concerned may be of relevance as to whether the court should hear the child or whether the court enjoys discretion in this respect. This is the case at least in BELGIUM[239] where hearing the child is an obligation as regards proceedings at the Juvenile Court or before the Justice of the Peace, on condition that the child is of a certain age. In other proceedings, hearing the child is at the court's discretion. Nevertheless, the general rule followed in the twenty-two jurisdictions surveyed is that a child should be heard irrespective of the type of proceedings.

---

228 See PINTENS/PIGNOLET, Belgian Report, Q 59.
229 See FERRAND, French Report, Q 59 and Q 9.
230 See SHANNON, Irish Report, Q 59.
231 See HRUSAKOVÁ, Czech Report, Q 59.
232 See KOUTSOURADIS/ZERVOGIANNI, Greek Report, Q 59.
233 See BOELE-WOELKI/SCHRAMA/VONK, Dutch Report, Q 59.
234 In a judgment from 1994 (STS, 24 June 1994) the Spanish Supreme Court held that in proceedings concerning the discharge of parental responsibilities children need not necessarily be heard even if they are above the age of twelve. See GONZÁLEZ BEILFUSS, Spanish Report, Q 59.
235 See JÄNTERÄ-JAREBORG/SINGER/SÖRGJERD, Swedish Report, Q 59.
236 See all the answers in the national reports in BOELE-WOELKI/BRAAT/CURRY-SUMNER, *ibid.*, note 23, Q 59 and Q 62.
237 See the Norwegian Supreme Court judgment Rt. 2004 p. 811, reported by SVEDRUP/LØDRUP, Norwegian Report, Q 59.
238 See, e.g., TODOROVA, Bulgarian Report, Q 62 and DETHLOFF/MARTINY, German Report, Q 62.
239 See PINTENS/PIGNOLET, Belgian Report, Q 59.

The effect of an agreement

In some of the countries the child is in practice not heard if the parents are in agreement on the issue affecting the interests of the child (BULGARIA,[240] CZECH REPUBLIC,[241] DENMARK,[242] ENGLAND AND WALES[243] and FINLAND[244]). This may apply even when the parental agreement must be approved by the court or by some other competent authority. A likely explanation for this is that a parental agreement is considered to be in the interests of the child and that hearing the child would in such a case not make any difference. As is pointed out in the FINNISH Report,[245] parents are always supposed to take the views and wishes of their children into consideration. The majority position would nevertheless seem to be that the child has the right to be heard, before the competent authority decides upon the approval of an agreement between the parents or other holders of parental responsibilities.

The child's age and maturity

The child's age and maturity is in most of the jurisdictions decisive as to whether the child should be heard. In approximately half of the countries surveyed, the law fixes a certain age at which the child should generally be heard, but making it in many cases also possible to hear a younger child who has attained the necessary maturity. In NORWAY,[246]a child who has reached the age of seven years has the right to be heard before a decision is taken in matters concerning the person of the child. According to the generally applicable rule in BULGARIA,[247] a child who has reached the age of ten years should always be heard, but even a younger child may be heard depending on the child's maturity. In DENMARK[248] and in THE NETHERLANDS,[249] a child aged twelve years or older must be heard, but also a younger child should be heard if the child is sufficiently mature and the child's opinion is of relevance to the decision.[250] The same applies in FINLAND[251] and SWEDEN[252] as regards proceedings concerning the enforce-

---

240 See TODOROVA, Bulgarian Report, Q 59.

241 See HRUSAKOVÁ, Czech Report, Q 59. The answer indicates, however, that a social worker would still need to investigate the child's opinion.

242 See LUND-ANDERSEN/JEPPESEN-DE BOER, Danish Report, Q 59.

243 See LOWE, English Report, Q 59.

244 See KURKI-SUONIO, Finnish Report, Q 59.

245 See KURKI-SUONIO, Finnish Report, Q 59.

246 See SVERDRUP/LØDRUP, Norwegian Report, Q 59.

247 See TODOROVA, Bulgarian Report, Q 59.

248 See LUND-ANDERSEN/JEPPESEN-DE BOER, Danish Report, Q 59.

249 See BOELE-WOELKI/SCHRAMA/VONK, Dutch Report, Q 59.

250 See LUND-ANDERSEN/JEPPESEN-DE BOER, Danish Report, Q 59.

251 § 2 Finnish Act on the Enforcement of a Decision on Child Custody and Right of Access. See KURKI-SUONIO, Finnish Report, Q 59.

252 Ch. 21 § 5 Swedish Children and Parents Code.

ment of decisions on custody and contact. In FINLAND this also applies to public law care proceedings, whereas the legislation in all other cases leaves the child's age open. Also in BELGIUM,[253] in special proceedings concerning the child's person, a child of twelve years should be heard, but also younger children may be heard depending on their maturity. Where an issue on parental responsibilities arises in connection with matrimonial proceedings in SPAIN,[254]a child aged twelve or over should be heard. Catalan law goes further in requiring that children who are at least twelve years old must be heard in all cases. In GERMANY[255] and HUNGARY,[256] a child who has reached the age of fourteen must be heard, but also younger children may and occasionally must be heard.

In the remainder of the countries (CZECH REPUBLIC,[257] ENGLAND AND WALES,[258] FRANCE,[259] GREECE,[260] IRELAND,[261] ITALY,[262] POLAND,[263] PORTUGAL[264] and SWITZERLAND[265]) no specific age is determined by legislation. This also applies as the general rule in BELGIUM[266] and in SPAIN.[267] In these countries, hearing the child is decided on the basis of the child's maturity and the child's ability to assess the issue at hand. In LITHUANIA[268] and RUSSIA,[269] following the wording of Article 12 of the *Convention on the Rights of the Child 1989*, the child is to be heard as soon as he or she is able to form his or her own views, irrespective of the child's age or level of maturity.

The weight of the child's opinion

Generally speaking, as regards the question of what weight should be given to the views expressed by the child, the older and more mature the child, the more weight is to be given to his or her opinions. In NORWAY,[270] where according to the law a child of seven

253 See PINTENS/PIGNOLET, Belgian Report, Q 59.
254 See GONZÁLEZ BEILFUSS, Spanish Report, Q 59 and Q 9.
255 See DETHLOFF/MARTINY, German Report, Q 59.
256 See WEISS/SZEIBERT, Hungarian Report, Q 59 and Q 9.
257 See HRUSAKOVÁ, Czech Report, Q 59.
258 See LOWE, English Report, Q 59 and Q 62.
259 See FERRAND, French Report, Q 62.
260 See KOUTSOURADIS/ZERVOGIANNI, Greek Report, Q 59.
261 See SHANNON, Irish Report, Q 62.
262 See PATTI/BELLISARIO/ROSSI CARLEO, Italian Report, Q 59.
263 See MĄCZYŃSKI/MĄCZYŃSKA, Polish Report, Q 59 and Q 62.
264 See DE OLIVEIRA, Portuguese Report, Q 62.
265 See HAUSHEER/ACHERMANN-WEBER/WOLF, Swiss Report, Q 62.
266 See PINTENS/PIGNOLET, Belgian Report, Q 59 and Q 62.
267 See GONZÁLEZ BEILFUSS, Spanish Report, Q 59 and Q 9.
268 See MIKELENAS, Lithuanian Report, Q 9 and Q 62.
269 See ANTOKOLSKAIA, Russian Report, Q 59.
270 § 31 Norwegian Children Act. See also SVERDRUP/LØDRUP, Norwegian Report, Q 59.

years has the right to be heard, the law also stipulates that the wishes of a child who has reached the age of twelve years must be given great importance. In RUSSIA,[271] the law provides that the opinion of a ten-year-old child must be considered. In all of the jurisdictions, case law provides important guidance. It should also be pointed out that regarding special issues such as medical treatment, religious upbringing and education, many of the jurisdictions have fixed specific age limits as regards when the child's consent is required or they follow slightly different standards than in respect of parental responsibilities in general.

COMMENT

1. Principle 3:6 follows the model laid down by modern international instruments establishing the child's right to be heard and to have his or her own views taken into account in all matters concerning the child. Since the adoption and entry into force of the *Convention on the Rights of the Child 1989* this Principle has become well established in different parts of the world and in all of the jurisdictions surveyed. It recognizes the child as an autonomous individual, capable of forming and expressing his or her own views and capable of participating in decisions concerning his or her own life. The Principle is closely connected with Principle 3:4. It is intended to cover the child's right to be heard not only when a competent authority takes a decision, but also outside of proceedings in situations where the holders of parental responsibilities make agreements or take decisions concerning the child. It also applies where a special representative has been appointed for the child. Procedural aspects of hearing the child are dealt with in Principle 3:37.

2. The Principle distinguishes explicitly between the child's right to receive information, the child's right to be consulted and the child's right to express his or her opinion. The underlying idea is that a child can truly take part in decision-making only when he or she has the right to receive (and to request) all relevant information, to be consulted and to express his or her own views. The right to relevant information includes information as to the possible consequences of the child's views as well as of any decision that can be taken. In this respect, the Principle follows in particular the *Convention on the Exercise of Children's Rights 1996* although, unlike that Convention, it is not limited to proceedings in a competent authority. The opinion of the child is established on the basis of the "views expressed" by the child which in turn include "the ascertainable wishes and feelings of the child".[272] This Principle recognizes the

---

[271] See ANTOKOLSKAIA, Russian Report, Q 62.

[272] According to the *Convention on Contact Concerning Children 2003*, due weight shall be given to the views and "to the ascertainable wishes and feelings of the child" (Art. 6.2).

child's right to information on all matters of relevance to the child, i.e., also in cases where no measure can be taken or agreement made, such as when a parent or another person close to the child has died.

3. Giving the child the rights laid down in Principle 3:6 is not at the discretion of the competent authority or at the discretion of the parents or other holders of parental responsibilities taking decisions on behalf of the child, but an obligatory point of departure. The scope of the obligations set forth in this Principle depends, however, on the child's age and maturity. This criterion is well established in all relevant international instruments and in all the jurisdictions surveyed. It applies not only to the assessment regarding whether the child should be informed, consulted and given the opportunity to express his or her opinion, but also to what weight should be given to the views expressed by the child. In the latter respect the child's capability of forming his or her own views is, implicitly, of relevance.[273] The Principle does not fix any special age or degree of maturity but states generally that they are factors that should always be taken into account. The older and more mature the child, the greater is the weight to be attached to the views expressed by the child.

4. Principle 3:6 does not explicitly state that exceptions should be made if informing and hearing the child would be manifestly incompatible with the child's best interests. That this is the case follows from the interplay between Principles 3:3 and 3:6. Principle 3:6 is thus completely in line with the position taken in international instruments and in the jurisdictions surveyed. Principle 3:6 takes for granted that the child should have the right to express his or her own views freely. To keep the drafting as brief as possible, this is not stated explicitly.

---

[273] The *Convention on the Rights of the Child 1989*, on the other hand, explicitly refers to the child "capable of forming his or her own views" (Art. 12.1). The *Convention on the Exercise of Children's Rights 1996* refers to children considered as having "sufficient understanding" (Art. 3).

Principle 3:7 Conflict of interests
The interests of the child should be protected whenever they may be in conflict with the interests of the holders of parental responsibilities.

Principe 3:7 Conflit d'intérêts
Les intérêts de l'enfant doivent être protégés dans tous les cas où ils peuvent se trouver en opposition avec ceux des titulaires de la responsabilité parentale.

Prinzip 3:7 Interessenkonflikt
Die Belange des Kindes sind zu schützen, wann immer sie den Belangen des (der) Inhaber der elterlichen Verantwortung widersprechen können.

INTERNATIONAL INSTRUMENTS

The child's best interests are "a primary consideration" in all actions concerning children whether taken by public authorities or private institutions. This is explicitly stated as a general principle in such major instruments as the *Convention on the Rights of the Child 1989* (Art. 3), the *European Charter of Fundamental Rights 2000* (Art. 24.2) and in the *Draft Treaty for a European Constitution 2003* (Art. II–84 par. 2). It follows that the child's interests are a most important, although not the sole, factor to be fully taken into account in any conflict of interests.

The obligation to take full account of the child's best interests means that these interests must also be protected in cases of conflict. This may, for example, require the appointment of an independent representative for the child. According to the *Convention on the Exercise of Children's Rights 1996*, "the child shall have the right to apply, in person or through other persons or bodies, for a special representative in proceedings before a judicial authority affecting the child where internal law precludes the holders of parental responsibilities from representing the child as a result of a conflict of interest with the latter" (Art. 4.1).

COMPARATIVE OVERVIEW

In the majority of the jurisdictions surveyed a third person, such as a guardian, a curator, a specially appointed custodian or a property administrator, may be appointed to take care of the child's interests where they risk conflicting with the interests of the holders of parental responsibilities (BELGIUM,[274] CZECH REPUBLIC,[275] ENGLAND AND WALES,[276] FINLAND,[277] FRANCE,[278] GERMANY,[279] GREECE,[280] HUNGARY,[281] IRELAND,[282] LITHUANIA,[283] THE NETHERLANDS,[284] NORWAY,[285] POLAND,[286] RUSSIA,[287] SPAIN,[288] SWEDEN[289] and SWITZERLAND[290]). This person then becomes a holder of parental responsibilities within the scope of his or her mandate. In legal proceedings, on the other hand, where the child's interests risk coming into conflict with the interests of the holders of parental responsibilities, a special representative may in many jurisdictions be appointed for the child.

The appointment of a special representative for the child as regards proceedings on parental responsibilities is developed further in the COMPARATIVE OVERVIEW and COMMENTS to Principle 3:38.

COMMENT

1. The Principles recognize the child as the holder of his or her own rights. It follows that the child also has interests of his or her own that need to be protected. Normally the holders of parental responsibilities protect the child's interests. Principle 3:7 concerns situations where the child's interests may conflict with the interests of the holders of parental responsibilities.

2. Principle 3:7 is to be read against the background of the previous Principles, in particular Principle 3:3. This means, *inter alia*, that the child's interests prevail over those of any holder of parental responsibilities. Also Principles 3:4 and 3:6, recognizing the child's right to autonomy and the child's right to participation, are of relevance

---

274 Art. 378 Belgian Civil Code.
275 See HRUSKOVÁ, Czech Report, Q 8.
276 See LOWE, English Report, Q 59.
277 See KURKI-SUONIO, Finnish Report, Q 8 and Q 59.
278 See FERRAND, French Report, Q 59.
279 See DETHLOFF/MARTINY, German Report, Q 61.
280 See KOUTSOURADIS/ZERVOGIANNI, Greek Report, Q 61.
281 See WEISS/SZEIBERT, Hungarian Report, Q 61.
282 See SHANNON, Irish Report, Q 61.
283 See MIKELENAS, Lithuanian Report, Q 61.
284 See BOELE-WOELKI/SCHRAMA/VONK, Dutch Report, Q 2d.
285 See SVERDRUP/LØDRUP, Norwegian Report, Q 61.
286 See MĄCZYŃSKI/MĄCZYŃSKA, Polish Report, Q 2d, 8 and Q 61.
287 See ANTOKOLSKAIA, Russian Report, Q 8.
288 See GONZALÉZ BEILFUSS, Spanish Report, Q 8.
289 See JÄNTERÄ-JAREBORG/SINGER/SÖRGJERD, Swedish Report, Q 8.
290 See HAUSHEER/ACHERMANN-WEBER/WOLF, Swiss Report, Q 61.

when assessing the child's interests and any conflict between them and those of holders of parental responsibilities. In this assessment, also the subsequent Principles are of relevance.

3. Parental responsibilities may not be exercised in a manner which harms or risks harming the physical, psychological or moral health and development of the child or the child's property. A clash of interests between the child's interests and those of a holder of parental responsibilities may occur in many different types of situations and that is why Principle 3:7 only states that, in the case of conflict, which should also include any risk of conflict, the child's interests should be protected. The manner in which the protection should take place is left open, depending on the situation and the issue at hand. One means is by appointing a special representative for the child as provided for in Principle 3:38. Other solutions include the discharge of parental responsibilities, in full or in part (Principle 3:32), limitations to the right of contact with the child (Principle 3:28) or appointing an additional holder of parental responsibilities to exercise, for example, a certain function of parental responsibilities (Principle 3:17). A competent authority may, for example, appoint a person to supervise the manner in which the holders of parental responsibilities should administer the child's property.

CHAPTER III: PARENTAL RESPONSIBILITIES OF PARENTS AND THIRD PERSONS
CHAPITRE III: RESPONSABILITÉ PARENTALE DES PARENTS ET DE TIERS
KAPITEL III: ELTERLICHE VERANTWORTUNG DER ELTERN UND DRITTER

Principle 3:8 Parents
Persons, whose legal parentage has been established, should have parental responsibilities for the child.

Principe 3:8 Parents
Les personnes dont la parenté légale a été établie envers l'enfant ont la responsabilité parentale à l'égard de ce dernier.

Prinzip 3:8 Eltern
Personen, deren gesetzliche Abstammung feststeht, haben die elterliche Verantwortung für das Kind.

INTERNATIONAL INSTRUMENTS

Uniform law is rather poor on the attribution of parental responsibilities. Article 18 of the *Convention on the Rights of the Child 1989* states in very general terms, without distinguishing between children born within or outside wedlock, that the States Parties shall use their best efforts to ensure the recognition of the principle that both parents have common responsibilities for the upbringing and development of the child. The principle of common responsibilities implies that both parents are holders of parental responsibilities.

In its *Recommendation on Parental Responsibilities 1984* the Committee of Ministers of the Council of Europe suggests several principles on the attribution of parental responsibilities. Principle 2 underlines the equality of the partners. This rule finds expression in Principle 5 on parental responsibilities for a child born within wedlock. In this case parental responsibilities should belong jointly to both parents. Principle 7 states that when the child is born out of wedlock and a legal filiation link is established with regard to one parent only, the parental responsibilities should belong to that parent (para. 1). Concerning children born out of wedlock where a legal filiation link is established with regard to both parents, the Principle does not mention the attribution but only the exercise of parental responsibilities. However, one can presume that the Committee of Ministers had a similar system in mind for the attribution and exercise of such responsibilities. Here the Principle does not propose a unique system, but leaves a choice to national law that covers all existing systems at the time (Principle 7 para. 2).

Twenty years later the Council of Europe stated in its *White Paper 2002* that parental responsibilities should in principle belong jointly to both parents (Principle 19 para. 1). The underlying idea is that joint parental responsibilities are in the best interest of the child. Therefore, the Principle makes no distinction between married and unmarried parents. If legal parentage has been established, it is irrelevant whether the parents are married or not, and the joint attribution is seen as the ideal situation for the child (Expl. No. 66). In cases where only one parent has parental responsibilities by the operation of law, the other parent should have an opportunity to acquire parental responsibilities, unless this is against the best interests of the child. A lack of consent or opposition by the parent having parental responsibilities should not as such be an obstacle for such an acquisition (Principle 19 para. 2).

COMPARATIVE OVERVIEW

Maternity and paternity established

Since parental responsibilities are not a consequence of marriage but of filiation, the attribution of those responsibilities in principle only depends in the majority of the legal systems on the establishment of maternity and paternity. They do not make a distinction between children born within or outside wedlock. The parents' relationship has no influence on their ability to be the holders of parental responsibilities, and only their legal relationship with the child is relevant.[291] If the relationship is established

[291] See also BOELE-WOELKI, "Parental responsibilities – CEFL's Initial Results", in: BOELE-WOELKI (ed.), *Common Core and Better Law in European Family Law*, p. 152 f.

(for the mother by the operation of law after the birth and for the father concerning children born within wedlock through the presumption *pater is est quem nuptiae demonstrant* and for children born out of wedlock through recognition or determination by the court), the parents have joint parental responsibilities (BELGIUM,[292] BULGARIA,[293] CZECH REPUBLIC,[294] FRANCE,[295] ENGLAND AND WALES,[296] GREECE,[297] HUNGARY,[298] ITALY,[299] LITHUANIA,[300] POLAND,[301] RUSSIA[302] and SPAIN[303]). Some of those systems do have certain peculiarities. Under FRENCH[304] and ITALIAN[305] law the unmarried mother has to recognise her child or the court must determine her maternity. As a consequence, joint parental responsibilities start with the recognition of the child by both parents or with the court determination. In HUNGARIAN[306] and ITALIAN[307] law the rule of joint parental responsibilities only applies if the unmarried parents live together. If they do not, then under HUNGARIAN law only the mother is the holder of parental responsibilities; under ITALIAN law the parent who first recognised the child is the holder of parental responsibilities, but a judge can take another decision in the interest of the child.

Other systems differentiate between children born within wedlock, where the parents have joint parental responsibilities, and children born out of wedlock where in principle only the mother has parental responsibilities and where joint parental responsibilities can only be acquired upon the basis of the registration of an agreement or a court order (AUSTRIA,[308] DENMARK,[309] ENGLAND AND WALES,[310] GERMANY,[311]

292 Art. 373 Belgian Civil Code. See PINTENS/PIGNOLET, Belgian Report, Q 15 and Q 20.
293 See TODOROVA, Bulgarian Report, Q 15 and Q 20.
294 See HRUSAKOVÁ, Czech Report, Q 15 and Q 20.
295 Art. 372 French Civil Code. See FERRAND, French Report, Q 15 and Q 20.
296 See LOWE, English Report, Q 15 and Q 20.
297 Art. 1510 and Art. 1515 Greek Civil Code. See KOUTSOURADIS/ZERVOGIANNI, Greek Report, Q 15 and Q 20.
298 See WEISS/SZEIBERT, Hungarian Report, Q 15 and Q 20.
299 Art. 280 and Art. 316 para. 2 Italian Civil Code. See PATTI/BELLISARIO/ROSSI CARLEO, Italian Report, Q 15 and Q 20.
300 Art. 3.137 Lithuanian Civil Code. See MIKELENAS, Lithuanian Report, Q 15 and Q 20.
301 Art. 93 para. 1 Polish Family and Guardianship Code. See MĄCZYŃSKI/MĄCZYŃSKA, Polish Report, Q 15 and Q 20. An exception is made for paternity established by the Court.
302 Art. 48 para. 1 Russian Family Code. See ANTOKOLSKAIA, Russian Report, Q 15 and Q 20.
303 See GONZÁLEZ BEILFUSS, Spanish Report, Q 15 and Q 20.
304 Art. 372 French Civil Code. See FERRAND, French Report, Q 20.
305 Art. 317*bis* Italian Civil Code. See PATTI/BELLISARIO/ROSSI CARLEO, Italian Report, Q 20.
306 See WEISS/SZEIBERT, Hungarian Report, Q 20.
307 Art. 317*bis* Italian Civil Code. See PATTI/BELLISARIO/ROSSI CARLEO, Italian Report, Q 20.
308 § 166 and § 167 Austrian Civil Code. See ROTH, Austrian Report, Q 20.
309 § 5 para. 1 Danish Act on Parental Authority and Contact. See LUND-ANDERSEN/JEPPESEN-DE BOER, Danish Report, Q 20.
310 See LOWE, English Report, Q 15, 20 and Q 22.
311 § 1626 a para. 1 No. 1 German Civil Code. See DETHLOFF/MARTINY, German Report, Q 20.

IRELAND,[312] THE NETHERLANDS,[313] PORTUGAL,[314] SWEDEN[315] and SWITZERLAND[316]). In these latter legal systems one can recognise four types: (1) In AUSTRIA, DENMARK, ENGLAND AND WALES and GERMANY the unmarried father who does not have joint parental responsibilities can obtain such responsibilities by means of an agreement with the holder (the mother) of parental responsibilities; (2) In THE NETHERLANDS, the unmarried parents who wish to exercise joint parental responsibilities have to register their joint request with the Registrar of the Custody Register; in PORTUGAL, the parents have to make a declaration before the official of the Registry Office,[317] (3) In SWITZERLAND, the guardianship authority may, upon a joint petition, confer joint parental responsibilities on unmarried parents subject to the approval of a parental agreement; (4) In IRELAND and SWEDEN, unmarried parents can obtain joint parental responsibilities through a court order or through registration with the tax authority whereas in ENGLAND AND WALES the unmarried father can obtain parental responsibilities upon being registered as the father on the child's birth certificate.

The influence of a later marriage

When the filiation between the child and the father is not established at the time of birth, in most legal systems a later marriage between the parents has no influence on the attribution of parental responsibilities. Only the establishment of the filiation is decisive (BELGIUM,[318] BULGARIA,[319] CZECH REPUBLIC,[320] FINLAND,[321] FRANCE,[322] GREECE,[323] HUNGARY,[324] ITALY,[325] LITHUANIA,[326] THE NETHERLANDS,[327] PORTUGAL,[328] RUSSIA,[329]

---

312 See SHANNON, Irish Report, Q 15, 20 and Q 22.

313 Art. 1:252 Dutch Civil Code. See BOELE-WOELKI/SCHRAMA/VONK, Dutch Report, Q 20 and Q 22.

314 Art. 1911 No. 3 Portuguese Civil Code. See DE OLIVEIRA, Portuguese Report, Q 20 : There is no such an agreement for the joint exercise of parental care in case of children born out of wedlock. There is only a declaration of both parents in the sense of the joint exercise of parental care.

315 Ch. 6 § 4 para. 2 Swedish Children and Parents Code. See JÄNTERÄ-JAREBORG/SINGER/SÖRGJERD, Swedish Report, Q 20.

316 Art. 298a para. 1 Swiss Civil Code. See HAUSHEER/ACHERMANN-WEBER/WOLF, Swiss Report, Q 20.

317 Art. 1911 No. 3 Portuguese Civil Code.

318 See PINTENS/PIGNOLET, Belgian Report Q 15.

319 See TODOROVA, Bulgarian Report, Q 15.

320 See HRUSAKOVÁ, Czech Report, Q 15.

321 See KURKI-SUONIO, Finnish Report, Q 15.

322 See FERRAND, French Report, Q 15.

323 See KOUTSOURADIS/ZERVOGIANNI, Greek Report, Q 15.

324 See WEISS/SZEIBERT, Hungarian Report, Q 15.

325 Art. 280 Italian Civil Code. See PATTI/BELLISARIO/ROSSI CARLEO, Italian Report, Q 15.

326 See MIKELENAS, Lithuanian Report, Q 15.

327 See BOELE-WOELKI/SCHRAMA/VONK, Dutch Report, Q 15.

328 Art. 1901 No. 1 and Art. 1911 No. 1 Portuguese Civil Code. See DE OLIVEIRA, Portuguese Report, Q 15: the parental care belongs to both parents during their marriage even if they were not married when the child was born.

329 See ANTOKOLSKAIA, Russian Report, Q 15.

SPAIN[330] and SWITZERLAND.[331] In AUSTRIA the child is legitimated by the marriage, with the consequence that in any case the father has parental responsibilities from the marriage onwards.[332] In POLAND the unmarried father does not obtain parental responsibilities when paternity has been established by a court decision. The later marriage can be a ground for the court to grant parental responsibilities.[333] In DENMARK,[334] ENGLAND AND WALES,[335] GERMANY,[336] IRELAND[337] and SWEDEN[338] the parents acquire joint parental responsibilities.

The influence of a formalized relationship

In most legal systems a formalized relationship (registered partnership, civil union, etc.) has no influence on the attribution of parental responsibilities. Only the establishment of the filiation is relevant (BELGIUM,[339] CZECH REPUBLIC,[340] FRANCE,[341] LITHUANIA,[342] PORTUGAL,[343] RUSSIA[344] and SPAIN[345]). In THE NETHERLANDS there has been a certain development. When the registered partnership was introduced in 1998 it had no legal consequences for the children of the partners. However, since 2001, Article 1:253aa Dutch Civil Code gives parents joint parental responsibilities over children born during their registered partnership. If the biological father has not recognized his child, he will also be attributed with joint parental responsibilities together with the mother concerning a child born during their registered partnership, unless legal family ties exist between the child and another parent.[346]

---

330 See GONZÁLEZ BEILFUSS, Spanish Report, Q 15.

331 Art. 259 para. 1 and Art. 297 para. 1 Swiss Civil Code. See HAUSHEER/ACHERMANN-WEBER/WOLF, Swiss Report, Q 15.

332 § 161 Austrian Civil Code. See ROTH, Austrian Report, Q 15.

333 Art. 93 para. 2 Polish Family and Guardianship Code. See MĄCZYŃSKI/MĄCZYŃSKA, Polish Report, Q 15.

334 § 4 Danish Act on Parental Authority and Contact. See LUND-ANDERSEN/JEPPESEN-DE BOER, Danish Report, Q 15.

335 S. 2(1) and (3) English Children Act and S. 1(3)(b) English Family Reform Act. See LOWE, English Report, Q 15.

336 § 1626 a para. 1 German Civil Code. See DETHLOFF/MARTINY, German Report, Q 15.

337 See SHANNON, Irish Report, Q 15.

338 Unless the Court has awarded custody to one or two specially appointed custodians; Ch. 6 § 3 para. 1 Swedish Children and Parents Code. See JÄNTERÄ-JAREBORG/SINGER/SÖRGJERD, Swedish Report, Q 15.

339 Art. 373 Belgian Civil Code. See PINTENS/PIGNOLET, Belgian Report, Q 21.

340 See HRUSAKOVÁ, Czech Report, Q 21.

341 See FERRAND, French Report, Q 21.

342 See MIKELENAS, Lithuanian Report, Q 21.

343 See DE OLIVEIRA, Portuguese Report, Q 20.

344 See ANTOKOLSKAIA, Russian Report, Q 21.

345 See GONZÁLEZ BEILFUSS, Spanish Report, Q 21.

346 Art. 1:253sa Dutch Civil Code. See BOELE-WOELKI/SCHRAMA/VONK, Dutch Report, Q 21.

Also in legal systems where a registered partnership only concerns partners of the same sex, every influence on the attribution of parental responsibilities is excluded. The adoption of a stepchild is the only possibility for same-sex partners to become the parent of the child (DENMARK,[347] FINLAND,[348] GERMANY,[349] NORWAY[350] and SWEDEN[351]).

Only maternity established

If no legal relationship is established before or after the birth of the child with respect to the (biological) father, the mother has sole parental responsibilities. In all systems the mother is attributed those responsibilities *ex lege* upon the birth of the child, except for FRANCE and ITALY, where the maternity is established through recognition or a court decision (cf. supra) and therefore parental responsibilities are attributed at that moment. Some legal systems have specific provisions providing solutions by way of guardianship in the case of the legal incapacity of the mother e.g. when the mother is a minor (HUNGARY[352] and THE NETHERLANDS[353]).

COMMENT

1. The Principle states that persons whose legal parentage has been established should have parental responsibilities. It applies both in cases where the legal parentage of two persons has been established as well as in cases where the legal parentale of only one person has been established. In these cases each parent should be the holder of parental responsibilities by operation of law.

2. The Principle does not deal with the establishment of parentage and leaves this matter to national law.

3. That the sole parent should be attributed with full parental responsibilities is accepted by all the legal systems surveyed. The Principle includes the position that after the death of a parent the surviving parent will be the sole holder of parental responsibilities (see Principle 3:21 para. 1).

347 § 4 para. 1 Danish Registered Partnership Act and § 4 Danish Act on Parental Authority and Contact. See LUND-ANDERSEN/JEPPESEN-DE BOER, Danish Report, Q 21.

348 § 9 Finnish Act Concerning Registered Partnership. See KURKI-SUONIO, Finnish Report, Q 21.

349 § 9 para. 7 Registered Partnership Act. See DETHLOFF/MARTINY, German Report, Q 21.

350 See SVERDRUP/LØDRUP, Norwegian Report, Q 21.

351 See JÄNTERÄ-JAREBORG/SINGER/SÖRGJERD, Swedish Report, Q 21.

352 See WEISS/SZEIBERT, Hungarian Report, Q 22.

353 Art. 1:246 Dutch Civil Code. See BOELE-WOELKI/SCHRAMA/VONK, Dutch Report, Q 22.

4. The majority of the legal systems fully accept that parental responsibilities are a consequence of filiation. Therefore those systems attribute parental responsibilities by operation of law not only to the one parent who has an established legal relationship with the child, but also to both parents when they have such an established legal relationship with the child irrespective of the relationship between the parents themselves. Here the Principle is in accordance with the common core and excludes any influence of a later marriage or other formalised relationships. Only the establishment of a legal relationship between the child and the parent is relevant. Moreover, this rule is based on the idea that joint attribution is in the best interests of the child and that both parents have equal rights and obligations. If parental responsibilities for one of the parents are not in the interest of the child, protection can be found by way of revising the exercise of such responsibilities or even completely discharging a parent from parental responsibilities (see Principles 3:15 para. 2 and 3:32). For all those reasons the Principle relies on the *White Paper 2002.*

Principle 3:9 Third persons
Parental responsibilities may in whole or in part also be attributed to a person other than a parent.

Principe 3:9 Tiers
La responsabilité parentale peut également être attribuée en tout ou partie à une personne autre que les père ou mère.

Prinzip 3:9 Dritte
Elterliche Verantwortung kann auch einer anderen Person als einem Elternteil ganz oder teilweise zuerkannt werden.

INTERNATIONAL INSTRUMENTS

Explicit or implied distinction between attribution and exercise

Several international instruments on parental responsibilities or including parental responsibilities make a distinction between the attribution of parental responsibilities and the exercise of such responsibilities. Such a distinction is made explicitly in the *Brussels II bis Regulation* and in the *Hague Child Protection Convention 1996*. Also the *White Paper 2002* distinguishes between to whom parental responsibilities should "belong" and who should exercise them. In other international instruments this distinction is implied or is even not made at all. In those instruments where this distinction is of relevance, it is not limited to the parental responsibilities of the child's parents, but may also concern parental responsibilities of third persons, i.e., persons other than the child's parents.

None of the international instruments define what is meant by the attribution of parental responsibilities, on the one hand, and the exercise of parental responsibilities, on the other. The more recent instruments, such as the *Brussels II bis Regulation* and the *Hague Child Protection Convention 1996*, are furthermore based on a very comprehensive concept of parental responsibilities, which clearly deviates from national law in most countries. Due to the fact that it is not always clear how the line should be drawn between attribution and exercise, the description given here of the international instruments is of relevance also as regards Principle 3:17 concerning the exercise of parental responsibilities by third persons.

Parental responsibilities of third persons are recognised

As regards parental responsibilities the emphasis in the *Convention on the Rights of the Child 1989* lies on the protection of the parent-child relationship, although it also recognizes the parental responsibilities of third persons. The Convention obliges the States Parties "to ensure the child such protection and care as is necessary for his or her well-being, taking into account the rights and duties of his or her parents, *legal guardians, or other individuals legally responsible for him or her*" (Art. 3.2). Furthermore, the States are obliged to "respect the responsibilities, rights and duties of the parents or, where applicable, the *members of the extended family or community* as provided by local custom, *legal guardians or other persons legally responsible for the child*" (Art. 5). Parents or, as the case may be, *legal guardians*, have the primary responsibility for the upbringing and development of the child, the best interests of the child being their basic concern (Art. 18). Alternative care, such as foster placement, kafalah under Islamic Law, adoption or necessary placement in suitable child care institutions, shall be ensured for a child who is deprived of his or her family environment, due regard being paid to the desirability of continuity in the child's upbringing and to the child's ethnic, religious, cultural and linguistic background (Art. 20).[354] Alternative care, in the sense of the Convention, can be understood to entail that parental responsibilities are transferred, in whole or in part, to the persons caring for the child, instead of, or in addition to the parents. The content of the alternative care arrangements depends on the national law of the country in question. Often they entail both the attribution and exercise of parental responsibilities.

The *European Convention on Human Rights 1950* establishes in its Article 8 that "everyone has the right to respect for his or her family life". According to the case law of the European Court of Human Rights this provision may provide a legal ground for certain kinds of parental responsibilities, such as the right of grandparents to contact with the child.[355] Grandparents are then "attributed" a right of contact to be "exercised" by them. Also according to the *European Charter of Fundamental Rights 2000* (Art. 7) and the *Draft Treaty for a European Constitution 2003* (Art. II–67) "everyone has the right to respect for his or her private and family life".

The *Hague Child Protection Convention 1996* defines "parental responsibility" as including "parental authority, or any analogous relationship of authority determining the rights, powers and responsibilities of parents, *guardians or other legal representatives* in relation to the person or property of the child" (Art. 1.2). Third persons are thus

354 See also *Declaration on Social and Legal Principles relating to the Protection and Welfare of Children 1986.*

355 European Court of Human Rights, 13.7.2000, *Scozzari and Giunta v. Italy.*

included among the holders of parental responsibilities. Parental responsibilities may, according to the Convention, be attributed by operation of law without the intervention of a judicial or administrative authority, or by an agreement or a unilateral act without the intervention of a judicial or administrative authority (Art. 16), in addition to measures of attribution (Art. 3.1) taken by a competent authority. The Convention contains separate choice of law rules as regards the attribution of parental responsibilities (Art. 16), on the one hand, and the exercise of such responsibilities (Art. 17), on the other.

The *Hague Child Abduction Convention 1980* defines the removal or the retention of a child as being wrongful where "it is in breach of rights of custody *attributed to a person, an institution or any other body*, either jointly or alone" under the law of the State where the child was habitually resident. These rights may arise in particular by operation of law or by reason of a judicial or administrative decision, or by reason of an agreement having legal effect under the law of that State (Art. 3). The *Convention on Recognition and Enforcement of Decisions concerning Custody 1980* refers to "any person" as regards the right to apply for the recognition or enforcement of decisions on custody, etc. (Art. 4.1). It follows that parental responsibilities, also under this Convention, may belong to persons other than the child's parents.

According to the *Convention on Contact Concerning Children 2003* contact may be established between the child and *persons other than his or her parents having family ties with the child* (Art. 5.1). States are, furthermore, free to establish contact between the child and *other persons than those with family ties with the child* (Art. 5.2). As pointed out before, contact rights may entail both the attribution and exercise of the right to contact.

The *Brussels II bis Regulation* applies, *inter alia*, in civil matters relating to the attribution, exercise, delegation, restriction or termination of parental responsibility (Art. 1.1.b). Parental responsibility is defined as "all rights and duties to the person or the property of the child which are given to a natural or legal person by judgment, by operation of law or by agreement having legal effect" (Art. 2.7). The "holder of parental responsibility" is defined as *any person* having parental responsibility over a child (Art. 2.8). It follows that parental responsibilities of third persons are covered by the Regulation. For the purposes of the *Convention on the Exercise of Children's Rights 1996*, the term "holders of parental responsibilities" is defined to mean parents and *other persons or bodies* entitled to exercise some or all parental responsibilities (Art. 2.b).

According to the *White Paper 2002* parental responsibilities belong primarily to the child's parents who should exercise them jointly (Principles 19 and 20.1). However, in certain situations the *White Paper 2002* acknowledges that parental responsibilities, in full or in part, need to be exercised by third persons. Thus, according to Principle 20.3, in cases determined by law, *a person other than a parent* may, upon a decision by a competent authority, exercise some or all parental responsibilities in addition to, or instead of parents. Upon the death of a parent, the parental responsibilities may, subject to certain conditions, be transferred to a third person (Principles 23.2–23.4). The last mentioned situation would seem to fall under "the attribution of parental responsibilities" to a person other than the child's parent.

COMPARATIVE OVERVIEW

It is not always clear where the borderline lies between the attribution and exercise of parental responsibilities and what their interrelationship is. Unless otherwise stated, the point of departure in the text below is that the reported solutions involve the attribution of parental responsibilities. In many cases, however, both attribution and exercise are covered.

Attribution of parental responsibilities to the parent's partner

In the majority of the jurisdictions the parent's spouse, registered partner or informal partner cannot obtain, i.e. be attributed, parental responsibilities with *equal* rights and duties to those of the parent.[356] Adoption is the only general exception to this point of departure. But even regarding adoption, the majority position is that it is only available if the parent and his or her partner are *married* to each other. A further condition is that the child's parent is the holder of sole parental responsibilities. In certain countries also the parent's *registered partner* may adopt his or her partner's child, again on condition that the parent is the holder of sole parental responsibilities (BELGIUM,[357] DENMARK,[358] GERMANY,[359] THE NETHERLANDS[360] and SWEDEN[361]). Only in PORTUGAL,[362] RUSSIA,[363] and SPAIN[364] is a formal relationship not a condition, with the result that also the parent's cohabitant may adopt, as is also exceptionally the case in LITHUANIA.[365]

---

356 See the national reports, BOELE-WOELKI/BRAAT/CURRY-SUMNER, *ibid.*, note 23, Q 27.
357 Art. 343 para 1 a) – b) Belgian Civil Code which has taken effect as of 1st September 2005.
358 See LUND-ANDERSEN/JEPPESEN-DE BOER, Danish Report, Q 21.
359 § 9 para. 7 German Registered Partnership Act (in force since 1 January 2005).
360 Art. 1:228 para. 1 (g) Dutch Civil Code.
361 See JÄNTERÄ-JAREBORG/SINGER/SÖRGJERD, Swedish Report, Q 27.
362 Art. 7 Portuguese Law No. 7/2001 of 11 May 2001. DE OLIVEIRA, Portuguese Report, Q 27.
363 See ANTOKOLSKAIA, Russian Report, Q 27.
364 See GONZÁLEZ BEILFUSS, Spanish Report, Q 27. This is only the case under Catalan law.
365 See MIKELENAS, Lithuanian Report, Q 27.

In BULGARIA,[366] in addition to adoption, the parent's partner may obtain joint parental responsibilities together with the parent by recognizing the child, on condition that a second person's parentage of the child has not been established. The same applies in LITHUANIA,[367] on condition that the parent recognizing the child is the child's biological parent. In DENMARK,[368] the *spouse* of a parent with sole parental authority can obtain parental authority by agreement with the parent, but this agreement must also be approved by the competent authority in order to become valid. In ENGLAND AND WALES,[369] a step-parent can obtain parental responsibility through a residence order in his or her favour (determining with whom the child is to live), irrespective of whether he or she lives in a formalised or non-formalised relationship with the child's parent. The step-parent's parental responsibility will end upon the termination of the residence order.[370] After the full entry into force of the ENGLISH Adoption and Children Act of 2002, a step-parent who has married or registered a partnership with the child's parent may obtain parental responsibility either by a formal agreement with the parent or by a court order. In FINLAND,[371] a married or registered partner of the child's parent, as well as a person living in a non-formalised relationship with the parent, may obtain custody of the child, but only by a court order. In THE NETHERLANDS,[372] joint parental responsibilities belong *ex lege* to a parent and his or her spouse who is not the child's parent, if the child was born during the marriage and does not have legal ties with the other parent. Basically, this also applies as regards a child born during a registered partnership.[373]

In AUSTRIA,[374] a step-parent (whether married to or living with the child's parent in a non-formalised relationship) is placed on the same footing as a foster parent and may apply to the court for the transfer of parental responsibilities. If the application is granted, however, it takes place at the expense of the rights belonging to a previous holder of parental responsibilities.[375] To the extent that parental responsibilities are granted to the step-parent, the parent then loses them.[376] In FRANCE,[377] the court may grant a step-parent some personal rights regarding the child, such as a right of contact, but full parental responsibilities have until recently been excluded. Recent case law

366 See TODOROVA, Bulgarian Report, Q 27.
367 See MIKELENAS, Lithuanian Report, Q 27.
368 See LUND-ANDERSEN/JEPPESEN-DE BOER, Danish report, Q 27.
369 See LOWE, English Report, Q 27.
370 S. 12(2) English Children Act 1989.
371 See KURKI-SUONIO, Finnish Report, Q 27.
372 Art. 1:253sa Dutch Civil Code. See BOELE-WOELKI/SCHRAMA/VONK, Dutch Report, Q 27.
373 Art. 1:253sa Dutch Civil Code. See BOELE-WOELKI/SCHRAMA/VONK, Dutch Report, Q 27.
374 § 186a Austrian Civil Code.
375 See ROTH, Austrian Report, Q 27.
376 See ROTH, Austrian Report, Q 27
377 See FERRAND, French Report, Q 27.

implies that a change may be under way, irrespective of whether or not the relationship between the parent and his or her partner is formalised. In THE NETHERLANDS,[378] the court may, under special conditions, grant the parent and his or her non-formalised partner joint parental responsibilities.

In some countries (GERMANY[379] and SWITZERLAND[380]) the law recognizes "limited parental responsibilities" regarding daily matters for the parent's partner. This kind of right is, essentially, a right to *exercise* parental responsibilities, and it will be separately commented upon under Principle 3:18.

In the majority of the jurisdictions the sex of the parent's partner basically has no significance in respect of the attribution (or exercise) of parental responsibilities (BELGIUM,[381] ENGLAND AND WALES,[382] FINLAND,[383] FRANCE,[384] GERMANY,[385] THE NETHERLANDS,[386] NORWAY,[387] SPAIN[388] and SWEDEN[389]). Nevertheless, as has been pointed out above,[390] the prospects for joint parental responsibilities are best in a marriage. A marriage, in turn, is at present only available to opposite sex couples, save in BELGIUM, THE NETHERLANDS, and SPAIN. In some of the countries, there is no clear position on this issue (BULGARIA,[391] GREECE,[392] HUNGARY,[393] POLAND[394] and RUSSIA[395]) due to the absence of legislation and case law. A minority of the countries (AUSTRIA,[396] CZECH

378 Art. 1:253t Dutch Civil Code. See BOELE-WOELKI/SCHRAMA/VONK, Dutch Report, Q 27.
379 § 1687 b paras 1–3 German Civil Code and § 9 German Registered Partnership Act.
380 Art. 299, 90 para. 2, 260 para. 2, 265a para. 1 Swiss Civil Code. See HAUSHEER/ACHERMANN-WEBER/WOLF, Swiss Report, Q 27.
381 See PINTENS/PIGNOLET, Belgian Report, Q 28.
382 See LOWE, English Report, Q 28.
383 See KURKI-SUONIO, Finnish Report, Q 28.
384 See FERRAND, French Report, Q 28.
385 See DETHLOFF/MARTINY, German Report, Q 28.
386 See BOELE-WOELKI/SCHRAMA/VONK, Dutch Report, Q 28.
387 See SVERDRUP/LØDRUP, Norwegian Report, Q 28.
388 See GONZÁLEZ BEILFUSS, Spanish Report Q 28.
389 See JÄNTERÄ-JAREBORG/SINGER/SÖRGJERD, Swedish Report, Q 28.
390 See also the Comparative Overview regarding Principle 3:5.
391 See TODOROVA, Bulgarian Report, Q 28.
392 See KOUTSOURADIS/ZERVOGIANNI, Greek Report, Q 28.
393 See WEISS/SZEIBERT, Hungarian Report, Q 28, describing the questions as "meaningless" with regard to the content of Hungarian law.
394 See MĄCZYŃSKI/MĄCZYŃSKA, Polish Report Q 27 and Q 28.
395 See ANTOKOLSKAIA, Russian Report, Q 28.
396 See the decision by the Austrian Supreme Court (*Oberster Gerichtshof*) 25.09.2002 and ROTH, Austrian Report, Q 28.

REPUBLIC,[397] ITALY,[398] LITHUANIA[399] and PORTUGAL[400]) refuse to grant same sex couples joint parental responsibilities and exclude a same sex partner from, e.g., stepchild adoption.

Attribution of parental responsibilities to a person other than the parent's partner

As regards the prospects for "other persons" than a parent's partner to be attributed (or given the right to exercise) parental responsibilities, three groups of persons enjoy priority, subject to the best interests of the child. These persons consist of (1) the child's grandparents, (2) foster parents, and (3) other persons who have close family ties or other ties with the child. Former step-parents may also belong to the last-mentioned category. In many countries the foster parents of a child are given preference over step-parents, relatives of the child and other persons with close ties to the child.

The approaches vary between the jurisdictions surveyed as to whether placing the child in the care of a third person carries with it the transfer of parental responsibilities (in full or in part), in which case it has an affect on the attribution of parental responsibilities, or whether it only entails entrusting the third person with the right to exercise certain parental responsibilities, besides the parents retaining their parental responsibilities. Since not all of the national reports explicitly address the difference between the attribution and exercise of parental responsibilities, doubt remains in many cases as to the approach chosen in a given State. In some countries (e.g. FRANCE,[401] GREECE,[402] SPAIN[403] and SWEDEN[404]) both models may be available, depending on the circumstances of the case, such as the reason for the placement and its factual duration.

In AUSTRIA[405] the court can entrust one or both grandparents or foster parents with parental responsibilities. Those to be considered as foster parents include step-parents, relatives and other persons who have close ties with the child and who are prepared to care for the child on a permanent basis. If no such persons can be found, parental responsibilities can be attributed to any suitable private individuals or, as a last resort, the youth welfare agency. If parental responsibilities are judicially transferred from the parent or parents to foster parents, the parent loses them to the extent that they

397 See HRUSAKOVÁ, Czech Report, Q 28.
398 See PATTI/BELLISARIO/ROSSI CARLEO, Italian Report, Q 28.
399 See MIKELENAS, Lithuanian Report, Q 28.
400 See DE OLIVEIRA, Portuguese Report, Q 28.
401 See FERRAND, French Report, Q 28.
402 See KOUTSOURADIS/ZERVOGIANNI, Greek Report, Q 28.
403 See GONZÁLEZ BEILFUSS, Spanish Report Q 28.
404 See JÄNTERÄ-JAREBORG/SINGER/SÖRGJERD, Swedish Report, Q 28
405 See ROTH, Austrian Report, Q 31.

pass to the foster parent.[406] In FRANCE,[407] when a child needs to be entrusted to the care of a third person, for example because the parents are deprived of parental responsibilities, the child is placed with his or her grandparents as a matter of priority. Parental responsibilities may also be entrusted, by order of the court on the application of a parent, to a member of the family or a reliable close person.[408] Entrusting the child to the care of a third person does not entail any automatic changes in the exercise of parental responsibilities other than ordinary acts relating to the child's supervision and upbringing.[409] The last option under FRENCH law is to place the child under *tutelle* (guardianship), giving the guardian full parental responsibilities, but subject to the supervision of a special board.[410] A corresponding system ("tutela") applies in SPAIN.[411]

In BELGIUM[412] and BULGARIA,[413] third persons may, by a court order, be granted the right to exercise parental responsibilities in respect of children placed with them, but without parental responsibilities being attributed to them. In the CZECH REPUBLIC[414] and GERMANY,[415] placing the child in the care of foster parents does not affect the parental responsibilities of the (biological or adoptive) parents, except as regards deciding on matters relating to the everyday life of the child in a long-time placement. The same approach is followed in SWEDEN[416] even if, exceptionally, the foster parents may, by a court order, be appointed as special custodians of the child, in which case full parental responsibilities are transferred to them and the parents are deprived of these corresponding rights and duties. In GREECE,[417] the parents' parental responsibilities may be transferred to a guardian. When the parents are not able to effectively exercise their parental responsibilities the child may also be placed in the care of foster parents, but without this affecting the attribution of parental responsibilities. Only when the child's placement in the foster family has become of long duration and the ties with the child's parents or guardian have weakened, may the foster parents be attributed parental responsibilities in whole or in part.[418] In HUNGARY,[419] when the parents are unsuitable to exercise or are prevented from exercising parental responsibilities, the child is placed in the care of a third person who will exercise parental

406 See ROTH, Austrian Report, Q 27.
407 Art. 371-4 French Civil Code. See also FERRAND, French Report, Q 27.
408 Art. 377 French Civil Code. See FERRAND, French Report, Q 32.
409 Art. 374–4 French Civil Code. See also FERRAND, French Report, Q 27.
410 See FERRAND, French Report, Q 31.
411 See GONZÁLEZ BEILFUSS, Spanish Report, Q 31.
412 See PINTENS/PIGNOLET, Belgian Report, Q 14.
413 See TODOROVA, Bulgarian Report, Q 31.
414 See HRUSAKOVÁ, Czech Report, Q 31.
415 § 1688 German Civil Code. See also DETHLOFF/MARTINY, German Report, Q 31.
416 See JÄNTERÄ-JAREBORG/SINGER/SÖRGJERD, Swedish Report, Q 31.
417 See KOUTSOURADIS/ZERVOGIANNI, Greek Report, Q 31.
418 Art. 1660 and 1661 Greek Civil Code.
419 See WEISS/SZEIBERT, Hungarian Report, Q 31.

responsibilities as the child's guardian. The person with whom the child is placed is normally chosen from among the child's relatives. If there is no such person, the child is taken into state care to live with foster parents or in a children's home. The person acting as the child's guardian is entrusted with full parental responsibilities, although the parents may retain certain rights such as the right of contact. In IRELAND,[420] the parental responsibilities of the child's parent may only be substituted by invoking the wardship jurisdiction of a court. In ITALY,[421] a guardian is appointed to exercise parental responsibilities in the absence, impossibility or incapacity of the parents. The guardian is primarily chosen from among the child's relatives and next of kin. In LITHUANIA,[422] in cases where the child is separated from the parents or the parents' parental responsibilities are restricted by a court order, the parental responsibilities are transferred to a specially appointed guardian. In POLAND,[423] a guardian may be appointed, substituting the parents as the holders of parental responsibilities. The guardian is normally chosen from among the child's relatives or persons close to the child or the child's parents.[424] If the child is placed in a foster family, the foster parents may be appointed as guardians. In PORTUGAL,[425] a child may only exceptionally, due to abuse of the child by the parents or other grave misconduct on the part of the parents, be entrusted to the care of a child-care establishment or a third person who then exercises the necessary parental responsibilities.[426]

Both in ENGLAND AND WALES and in FINLAND, a third person's acquisition of parental responsibilities is in principle *an addition* to and not a substitution of the existing parental responsibilities and has a wide scope. In ENGLAND AND WALES,[427] a residence order always confers parental responsibility. Such acquisition does not affect the legal position of parents who will continue to have parental responsibility. In FINLAND, a child may have more than two custodians, meaning that there may be several persons to whom parental responsibilities have been attributed.[428] The court may, upon an application by a parent, the child's custodian or the local social authority,[429] order that one or more persons who have consented thereto shall have the custody of a child

---

420 See SHANNON, Irish Report, Q 31. By issuing a wardship order the court will assume responsibility for exercising parental rights and duties concerning the child. The court will then appoint a guardian for the child.

421 See PATTI/BELLISARIO/ROSSI CARLEO, Italian Report, Q 31.

422 Art. 3.160, Part 2, Lithuanian Civil Code. See MIKELENAS, Lithuanian Report, Q 31.

423 See MĄCZYŃSKI/MĄCZYŃSKA, Polish Report, Q 31.

424 Art. 149 § 2 Polish Family and Guardianship Code.

425 Art. 1905 No. 2 and 1915 Portuguese Civil Code; Art. 194 Portuguese Child Protection Law.

426 Art. 1907 No. 2 Portuguese Civil Code.

427 See LOWE, English Report, Q 14 and Q 31.

428 See KURKI-SUONIO, Finnish Report, Q 14.

429 § 14 para. 1 Finnish Child Custody and Access Rights Act.

instead of, or together with, the parent(s).[430] Custody of the child may be transferred from a parent only on condition that it is manifestly in the best interests of the child.[431] Exceptionally, also in LITHUANIA[432] other persons may be entrusted with some aspects of parental authority without infringing upon the parents' parental authority and without the child being separated from the parents. These persons consist of a specially appointed guardian or close relatives of the child, such as grandparents or adult siblings.

It is reported that in NORWAY,[433] third persons can obtain parental responsibilities only in the case of the death of the parents. In RUSSIA,[434] and in SWITZERLAND,[435] parental responsibilities cannot be transferred, save by adoption.

Attribution of parental responsibilities by agreement

The clear majority position is that the *attribution* of parental responsibilities to a person other than a parent falls outside the scope of party autonomy (AUSTRIA,[436] BULGARIA,[437] ENGLAND AND WALES,[438] FINLAND,[439] FRANCE,[440] GERMANY,[441] GREECE,[442] HUNGARY,[443] IRELAND,[444] ITALY,[445] LITHUANIA,[446] NORWAY,[447] POLAND,[448] PORTUGAL,[449] RUSSIA,[450] SPAIN,[451] SWEDEN[452] and SWITZERLAND[453]). Only in a minority of the countries surveyed

---

430 § 9 para. 1 point 4 Finnish Child Custody and Access Rights Act.
431 § 9 para. 2 Finnish Child Custody and Access Rights Act. See also KURKI-SUONIO, Finnish Report, Q 27.
432 See MIKELENAS, Lithuanian Report, Q 31.
433 See SVERDRUP/LØDRUP, Norwegian Report, Q 31.
434 See ANTOKOLSKAIA, Russian Report, Q 31.
435 See HAUSHEER/ACHERMANN-WEBER/WOLF, Swiss Report, Q 31.
436 See ROTH, Austrian Report, Q 30.
437 See TODOROVA, Bulgarian Report, Q 30.
438 See LOWE, English Report, Q 30. A change is under way, however, as the English Adoption and Children Act fully enters into force.
439 See KURKI-SUONIO, Finnish Report, Q 30.
440 See FERRAND, French Report, Q 30.
441 See DETHLOFF/MARTINY, German Report, Q 30.
442 See KOUTSOURADIS/ZERVOGIANNI, Greek Report, Q 30.
443 See WEISS/SZEIBERT, Hungarian Report, Q 30.
444 See SHANNON, Irish Report, Q 30.
445 See PATTI/BELLISARIO/ROSSI CARLEO, Italian Report, Q 30.
446 See MIKELENAS, Lithuanian Report, Q 30.
447 See SVERDRUP/LØDRUP, Norwegian Report, Q 30.
448 See MĄCZYŃSKI/MĄCZYŃSKA, Polish Report, Q 30.
449 See DE OLIVEIRA, Portuguese Report, Q 30.
450 See ANTOKOLSKAIA, Russian Report, Q 30.
451 See GONZÁLEZ BEILFUSS, Spanish Report, Q 30.
452 See JÄNTERÄ-JAREBORG/SINGER/SÖRGJERD, Swedish Report, Q 30.
453 See HAUSHEER/ACHERMANN-WEBER/WOLF, Swiss Report, Q 30.

does the law recognize a limited autonomy to the parties, modifying the above-mentioned point of departure. Thus, in BELGIUM,[454] most parental responsibilities may, by agreement and subject to certain conditions, such as the consent of the child if he or she has reached the age of 15 years, be transferred to a third person who then acquires them instead of the parent. In DENMARK,[455] parental responsibilities may be transferred by agreement with their holders, subject to approval by the competent authority. In THE NETHERLANDS,[456] a parent may apply for joint parental responsibilities together with any person who has a close personal relationship with the child. In still other countries (HUNGARY[457] and POLAND[458]), when appointing a guardian, the parents' wishes may be taken into account. This kind of influence by the parents falls short of party autonomy, however. The autonomy of the parents or other holders of parental responsibilities to authorize a third person to *exercise* parental responsibilities is commented upon under Principle 3:17. The appointment of holders of parental responsibilities in the case of the death of the parents is dealt with under Principle 3:31.

COMMENT

1. All of the above-mentioned international instruments on parental responsibilities recognize that persons other than the child's parents may be holders of parental responsibilities. As third persons who may be attributed with and/or exercise parental responsibilities the instruments may explicitly refer to "legal guardians" or "other individuals legally responsible for the child" as well as to "members of the extended family or community".[459] They may also leave the issue more open by simply referring to "any person".[460] Also "institutions" or "other bodies"[461] as well as "legal persons"[462] may be included. The international instruments leave it open as to who these third persons are to whom parental responsibilities may be attributed or who may exercise parental responsibilities. The instruments do not make any clear distinction between the attribution and exercise of parental responsibilities[463] and also do not define what

454 Art. 475 ter Belgian Civil Code. See PINTENS/PIGNOLET, Belgian Report, Q 31.

455 § 11 Danish Act on Parental Authority and Contact. See also LUND-ANDERSEN/JEPPESEN-DE BOER, Danish Report, Q 31.

456 Art. 1:253t Dutch Civil Code.

457 See WEISS/SZEIBERT, Hungarian Report, Q 31.

458 Art. 149 § 1 Polish Family and Guardianship Code.

459 See the *Convention on the Rights of the Child 1989*, Art. 3 para. 2 and 5. See also the *Hague Child Protection Convention 1996*, Art. 1 para. 2.

460 See the *Hague Child Abduction Convention 1980*, Art. 3 and 8. See also Art. 4 of the *Convention on Recognition and Enforcement of Decisions of Custody 1980.*

461 See the *Hague Child Abduction Convention* 1980, Art. 3 and 8.

462 See *Brussels II bis* Regulation, Art. 2 para. 7.

463 An exception is the separate choice of law rules in the *Hague Child Protection Convention 1996.*

is meant by the one or the other. A comprehensive concept of parental responsibilities is followed in the more recent instruments, such as the *Hague Child Protection Convention 1996*, the *Brussels II bis Regulation* and the *White Paper 2002*, making it possible for different persons to be in charge not only of the whole bulk of parental responsibilities but also in different degrees and of different aspects of parental responsibilities. It is important to notice that this terminology clearly differs from that followed in the national law of the majority of the jurisdictions.

2. This terminology and approach is also followed in the Principles, which make a distinction between the attribution of parental responsibilities to a third person (Principle 3:9) and a third person's exercise of parental responsibilities (Principle 3:17). Attribution and exercise are namely not synonymous expressions and the Principles aim to cover all situations where a person other than a parent holds parental responsibilities. The term "attribution" in Principle 3:9 corresponds, more or less, to expressions such as "the acquisition of parental responsibilities". Once attributed, they "belong" to that person who "has" corresponding parental responsibilities.

3. Principle 3:9 is a natural "follow-up" to Principle 3:8. Contrary to the situation of the child's parents, parental responsibilities of third persons remain an exception. Third persons may, nevertheless, under certain conditions be attributed with parental responsibilities which either correspond to those normally enjoyed by a parent, i.e. *parental responsibilities enjoyed as a whole*, e.g., by a guardian or a specially appointed custodian, or which are limited to a certain issue, such as the grandparent's right (duty) of contact with the child, i.e. *parental responsibilities in part.*

4. Principle 3:9 only states that parental responsibilities may be attributed to a third person, leaving it open as to *how* and *on what conditions* this attribution takes place and *to whom* parental responsibilities may be attributed. In the jurisdictions surveyed, the attribution may take place by operation of law (*ex lege*), through a decision by a competent authority or through an agreement having legal effect.[464] The common core is through the parent's partner adopting the parent's child. Another common solution is by placing the child under the care of a third person, but this solution does not in all of the countries involve an attribution of parental responsibilities to the third person; in many cases it is only a right of exercise and the parents retain their parental responsibilities. Adoption, *ex lege* acquisition of parental responsibilities by a third person (at present THE NETHERLANDS) and the attribution of parental responsibilities to a third person by a decision of a competent authority are, nevertheless, intended

464 The *Hague Child Abduction Convention 1980*, for example, refers to rights of custody arising by operation of law or by reason of a judicial or administrative decision or by reason of an agreement having legal effect under the law of the child's habitual residence, Art. 3 para. 2.

to be included within the scope of Principle 3:9, whereas the effect of agreements regarding the attribution of parental responsibilities is left to national law. "A person other than a parent" may be the parent's partner (step-parent), but it may also be any suitable third person, as defined by national law, except a legal person or a public body. The last mentioned falls outside the scope of the principles which do not deal with public law aspects, such as State intervention in the care and upbringing of a child.

Principle 3:10 Effect of dissolution and separation
Parental responsibilities should neither be affected by the dissolution or annulment of the marriage or other formal relationship nor by the legal or factual separation between the parents.

Principe 3:10 Incidence de la dissolution et de la séparation
La responsabilité parentale n'est affectée ni par la dissolution, l'annulation du mariage ou de toute autre union formalisée, ni par la séparation légale ou la séparation de fait des parents.

Prinzip 3:10 Wirkungen der Auflösung und der Trennung
Die elterliche Verantwortung wird weder von der Auflösung oder Nichtigerklärung der Ehe oder einer anderen formalisierten Lebensgemeinschaft noch von der gesetzlichen oder tatsächlichen Trennung der Eltern berührt.

INTERNATIONAL INSTRUMENTS

There is no uniform law on the influence of the dissolution or weakening of a marriage and of cohabitation on the attribution of parental responsibilities. The *Convention on the Rights of the Child 1989* does not mention this issue. The *Recommendation on Parental Responsibilities 1984* by the Council of Europe only considers the effect of a dissolution of a marriage or the separation of the parents on the exercise of parental responsibilities, but not on their attribution. The principles contained in the Council of Europe's *White Paper 2002* also only contain a rule concerning the influence of a dissolution or separation on the exercise and not on the attribution of parental responsibilities (Principle 22). However, the explanations speak in general terms about the automatic continuation of joint parental responsibilities (Expl. No. 66).

COMPARATIVE OVERVIEW

Marriage

In the great majority of the legal systems a divorce, a legal separation,[465] a marriage annulment[466] or a factual separation do not affect the attribution of parental

[465] Legal separation is not known in AUSTRIA, BULGARIA, CZECH REPUBLIC, FINLAND, GERMANY, GREECE, HUNGARY, RUSSIA and SWEDEN. See all the answers in the national reports in BOELE-WOELKI/BRAAT/CURRY-SUMNER, *ibid.*, note 23, Q 16.

[466] A marriage annulment is not known in FINLAND and SWEDEN. See KURKI-SUONIO, Finnish Report, Q 16 and JÄNTERÄ-JÄREBORG/SINGER/SÖRGJERD, Swedish Report, Q 16.

responsibilities. The position of the holders of parental responsibilities is not changed since parental responsibilities are a consequence of parenthood and not of marital status (BELGIUM,[467] BULGARIA,[468] CZECH REPUBLIC,[469] DENMARK,[470] ENGLAND AND WALES,[471] FINLAND,[472] FRANCE,[473] GERMANY,[474] GREECE,[475] IRELAND,[476] ITALY,[477] THE NETHERLANDS,[478] NORWAY,[479] POLAND,[480] PORTUGAL,[481] RUSSIA,[482] SPAIN[483] and SWEDEN[484]). In LITHUANIA a divorce, legal separation and factual separation have no effect on the attribution of parental responsibilities, with the exception of the right to administer the child's property. This right belongs to the parent with whom the child lives.[485] In HUNGARY the attribution of parental responsibilities does not *ex lege* continue: a court has to decide.[486] The same solution is adopted in AUSTRIA[487] and SWITZERLAND,[488] where sole parental responsibilities are attributed by a court order to the parent with whom the child is residing unless the parents request that their joint parental responsibilities should continue. In all legal systems, maintaining the joint attribution of parental responsibilities does not exclude that court orders or parental agreements on the exercise of those responsibilities can turn the joint attribution into something of an empty shell.

---

467 Art. 373 Belgian Civil Code. See PINTENS/PIGNOLET, Belgian Report, Q 16.

468 Art. 71 para. 2, Art. 98, Art. 99, Art. 106 Bulgarian Family Code. See TODOROVA, Bulgarian Report, Q 16.

469 § 17 para. 2, § 26 and § 50 Czech Family Code. See HRUSAKOVÁ, Czech Report, Q 16.

470 § 8 Danish Act on Parental Authority and Contact. See LUND-ANDERSEN/JEPPESEN-DE BOER, Danish Report, Q 16.

471 See LOWE, English Report, Q 16.

472 § S.31–32 Finnish Marriage Act. See KURKI-SUONIO, Finnish Report, Q 16.

473 Art. 373–2 French Civil Code. See FERRAND, French Report, Q 16.

474 § 1671 German Civil Code. See DETHLOFF/MARTINY, German Report, Q 16.

475 Art. 1510 para. 1, Art. 1513 and Art. 1514 Greek Civil Code. See KOUTSOURADIS/ZERVOGIANNI, Greek Report, Q 16.

476 S. 10(2) and S. 41 Irish Family Law (Divorce) Act, S. 2 Irish Guardianship of Infants Act as amended by the Irish Children Act. See SHANNON, Irish Report, Q 16.

477 Art. 317 para. 2 Italian Civil Code. See PATTI/BELLISARIO/ROSSI CARLEO, Italian Report, Q 16.

478 See BOELE-WOELKI/SCHRAMA/VONK, Dutch Report, Q 16.

479 § 34 para. 2 Norwegian Children Act. See SVERDRUP/LØDRUP, Norwegian Report, Q 16.

480 Art. 107 para. 1 Polish Family and Guardianship Code. See MĄCZYŃSKI/MĄCZYŃSKA, Polish Report, Q 16.

481 Art. 1905 and Art. 1909 Portuguese Civil Code. See DE OLIVEIRA, Portuguese Report, Q 16.

482 Art. 30 para. 3 and Art. 61 para. 1 Russian Family Code. See ANTOKOLSKAIA, Russian Report, Q 16.

483 See GONZÁLEZ BEILFUSS, Spanish Report, Q 16.

484 Ch. 6 § 3 para. 2 Swedish Children and Parents Code. See JÄNTERÄ-JAREBORG/SINGER/SÖRGJERD, Swedish Report, Q 16.

485 Art. 3.190 Lithuanian Civil Code. See MIKELENAS, Lithuanian Report, Q 16.

486 See WEISS/SZEIBERT, Hungarian Report, Q 16.

487 § 177 Austrian Civil Code. See ROTH, Austrian Report, Q 16.

488 Art. 133 para. 3 Swiss Civil Code. See HAUSHEER/ACHERMANN-WEBER/WOLF, Swiss Report, Q 16.

Cohabitation

In most systems the ending of the unmarried parents' relationship has no effect on the attribution of parental responsibilities (AUSTRIA,[489] BELGIUM,[490] CZECH REPUBLIC,[491] DENMARK,[492] ENGLAND AND WALES,[493] FINLAND,[494] FRANCE,[495] GERMANY,[496] GREECE,[497] HUNGARY,[498] IRELAND,[499] ITALY,[500] LITHUANIA,[501] THE NETHERLANDS,[502] NORWAY,[503] POLAND,[504] PORTUGAL,[505] RUSSIA,[506] SPAIN[507] and SWEDEN[508]). In SWITZERLAND a court can reorganise the attribution of parental responsibilities at the request of one parent.[509]

COMMENT

The Principle states that the dissolution or the weakening of a marriage or other formal relationships has, as such, no influence on the attribution of parental responsibilities. The Principle is in accordance with the common core of the legal systems as well as with the *White Paper 2002* of the Council of Europe (Principle 22). Similar to married or unmarried partners who live together (see Principle 3:6, COMMENT under 3), the interests of the child can be protected by restricting the exercise of such responsibilities or even by completely discharging a parent from parental responsibilities (see Principles 3:15 para. 1 and 3:32).

---

489 § 167 Austrian Civil Code. See ROTH, Austrian Report, Q 23.

490 Art. 373 Belgian Civil Code. See PINTENS/PIGNOLET, Belgian Report, Q 23.

491 But the court can decide otherwise: § 50 Czech Family Code. See HRUSAKOVÁ, Czech Report, Q 23.

492 The parents can apply for sole parental authority (§8 and §12 Danish Act on Parental Authority and Contact. See LUND-ANDERSEN/JEPPESEN-DE BOER, Danish Report, Q 23).

493 See LOWE, English Report, Q 23.

494 See KURKI-SUONIO, Finnish Report, Q 23.

495 Art. 373–2 French Civil Code. See FERRAND, French Report, Q 23.

496 § 1626 a German Civil Code. See DETHLOFF/MARTINY, German Report, Q 23.

497 See KOUTSOURADIS/ZERVOGIANNI, Greek Report, Q 23.

498 See WEISS/SZEIBERT, Hungarian Report, Q 23.

499 See SHANNON, Irish Report, Q 23.

500 See PATTI/BELLISARIO/ROSSI CARLEO, Italian Report, Q 23.

501 See MIKELENAS, Lithuanian Report, Q 23.

502 See BOELE-WOELKI/SCHRAMA/VONK, Dutch Report, Q 23.

503 See SVERDRUP/LØDRUP, Norwegian Report, Q 23.

504 See MĄCZYŃSKI/MĄCZYŃSKA, Polish Report, Q 23.

505 Art. 1904–1907 and Art. 1912 Portuguese Civil Code. See DE OLIVEIRA, Portuguese Report, Q 23.

506 See ANTOKOLSKAIA, Russian Report, Q 23.

507 See GONZÁLEZ BEILFUSS, Spanish Report, Q 23.

508 See JÄNTERÄ-JAREBORG/SINGER/SÖRGJERD, Swedish Report, Q 23.

509 Art. 298a para. 2 Swiss Civil Code. See HAUSHEER/ACHERMANN-WEBER/WOLF, Swiss Report, Q 23.

CHAPTER IV: EXERCISE OF PARENTAL RESPONSIBILITIES
CHAPITRE IV: EXERCICE DE LA RESPONSABILITÉ PARENTALE
KAPITEL IV: AUSÜBUNG DER ELTERLICHEN VERANTWORTUNG

SECTION A: PARENTS
SECTION A: LES PARENTS
ABSCHNITT A: ELTERN

Principle 3:11 Joint exercise
Parents having parental responsibilities should have an equal right and duty to exercise such responsibilities and whenever possible they should exercise them jointly.

Principe 3:11 Exercice en commun
Les parents détenant la responsabilité parentale ont dans l'exercice de celle-ci les mêmes droits et devoirs. Dans la mesure du possible, ils l'exercent en commun.

Prinzip 3:11 Gemeinsame Ausübung
Eltern, denen die elterliche Verantwortung zusteht, haben bei der Ausübung dieser Verantwortung die gleichen Rechte und Pflichten. Soweit möglich üben sie sie gemeinsam aus.

INTERNATIONAL INSTRUMENTS

Principle 20 para. 1 of the *White Paper 2002* concerning the establishment and legal consequences of parentage establishes that parents having parental responsibilities should have an equal right to exercise such responsibilities. It further states that parents should exercise parental responsibilities together unless the best interests of the child determine otherwise. However, the *White Paper 2002* does not establish a corresponding duty for parents to exercise parental responsibilities

COMPARATIVE OVERVIEW

Equal exercise

When parental responsibilities are held jointly by both parents, they are held equally in virtually all systems (AUSTRIA,[510] BELGIUM,[511] BULGARIA,[512] CZECH REPUBLIC,[513] DENMARK,[514] ENGLAND AND WALES,[515] FRANCE,[516] GERMANY,[517] GREECE,[518] ITALY,[519] LITHUANIA,[520] THE NETHERLANDS,[521] NORWAY,[522] PORTUGAL,[523] RUSSIA,[524] SPAIN,[525] SWEDEN[526] and SWITZERLAND[527]). In most of the systems it makes no difference whether or not the parents are married (BELGIUM,[528] BULGARIA,[529] CZECH REPUBLIC,[530]

---

[510] § 137 para. 3 Austrian Civil Code. See ROTH, Austrian Report, Q 36.
[511] Art. 373 para. 1 Belgian Civil Code. See PINTENS/PIGNOLET, Belgian Report, Q 36.
[512] Art. 72 Bulgarian Family Code. See TODOROVA, Bulgarian Report, Q 36.
[513] § 44 Czech Family Code. See HRUSAKOVÁ, Czech Report, Q 36.
[514] See LUND-ANDERSEN/JEPPESEN-DE BOER, Danish Report, Q 36.
[515] See LOWE, English Report, Q 36.
[516] See FERRAND, French Report, Q 36.
[517] See DETHLOFF/MARTINY, German Report, Q 36.
[518] See KOUTSOURADIS/ZERVOGIANNI, Greek Report, Q 36.
[519] Art. 316 para. 2 Italian Civil Code. See PATTI/BELLISARIO/ROSSI CARLEO, Italian Report, Q 36.
[520] Art. 38 Lithuanian Constitution and Art. 3156 Lithuanian Civil Code. See MIKELENAS, Lithuanian Report, Q 36.
[521] See BOELE-WOELKI/SCHRAMA/VONK, Dutch Report, Q 36.
[522] See SVERDRUP/LØDRUP, Norwegian Report, Q 36.
[523] Art. 36. 3 Portuguese Constitution and Nos1 and 2 Portuguese Civil Code 1901. See DE OLIVEIRA, Portuguese Report, Q 36.
[524] Art. 38 para,Russian Constitution and Art. 61 para. 1 Russian Family Code. See ANTOKOLSKAIA, Russian Report, Q 36.
[525] See GONZÁLEZ BEILFUSS, Spanish Report, Q 36.
[526] See JÄNTERÄ-JAREBORG/SINGER/SÖRGJERD, Swedish Report, Q 36.
[527] Art. 297 § 1 Swiss Civil Code. See HAUSHEER/ACHERMANN-WEBER/WOLF, Swiss Report, Q 36.
[528] See PINTENS/PIGNOLET, Belgian Report, Q 14.
[529] See TODOROVA, Bulgarian Report, Q 14.
[530] See HRUSAKOVÁ, Czech Report, Q 14.

DENMARK,[531] FRANCE,[532] GREECE,[533] HUNGARY,[534] ITALY,[535] LITHUANIA,[536] THE NETHERLANDS,[537] NORWAY,[538] PORTUGAL,[539] RUSSIA,[540] SPAIN,[541] SWEDEN[542] and SWITZERLAND[543]).

In some systems, however, civil status still makes a difference. Under ENGLISH law an unmarried father who has been registered as the father on the child's birth certificate will only gain parental responsibility with the mother's agreement or by having a parental responsibility or residence order made in his favour.[544] The situation is very similar in IRELAND.[545] In AUSTRIA[546] and GERMANY[547] an unmarried father will only have joint custody if there is a common declaration to that effect by the parents.

Exceptions to equal exercise

There are exceptions to the equal exercise of parental responsibilities. Under GERMAN law one parent will exercise sole parental responsibilities despite the parents having joint parental responsibility rights where the other parent is factually prevented from exercising such rights or his or her rights have been temporarily suspended.[548] The same holds true under AUSTRIAN law if one parent is partially not able to exercise parental responsibilities.[549] In RUSSIA a minor unmarried parent is only partially legally capable of exercising these rights; thus if the other parent is not also a minor, he or she will be able to exercise parental responsibilities to a greater extent.[550] When parental responsibilities are attributed jointly to a parent and to a person or persons who are not the parent(s), certain rights are only attributed to the actual parent (ENGLAND AND WALES[551]). Similarly under PORTUGUESE law third persons or childcare establishments

---

531 See LUND-ANDERSEN/JEPPESEN-DE BOER, Danish Report, Q 14.
532 See FERRAND, French Report, Q 14.
533 See KOUTSOURADIS/ZERVOGIANNI, Greek Report, Q 14.
534 See WEISS/SZEIBERT, Hungarian Report, Q 14.
535 See PATTI/BELLISARIO/ROSSI CARLEO, Italian Report, Q 14.
536 See MIKELENAS, Lithuanian Report, Q 14.
537 See BOELE-WOELKI/SCHRAMA/VONK, Dutch Report, Q 14.
538 See SVERDRUP/LØDRUP, Norwegian Report, Q 14.
539 See DE OLIVEIRA, Portuguese Report, Q 14.
540 See ANTOKOLSKAIA, Russian Report, Q 14.
541 See GONZÁLEZ BEILFUSS, Spanish Report, Q 14.
542 See JÄNTERÄ-JAREBORG/SINGER/SÖRGJERD, Swedish Report, Q 14.
543 See HAUSHEER/ACHERMANN-WEBER/WOLF, Swiss Report, Q 14.
544 See LOWE, English Report, Q 14 and Q 22.
545 See SHANNON, Irish Report, Q 14.
546 § 166 and § 167 Austrian Civil Code. See ROTH, Austrian Report, Q 14, 22a and Q 22b.
547 § 1626a para. 1 No. 2 German Civil Code. See DETHLOFF/MARTINY, German Report, Q 14.
548 § 1678 para. 1 clause 1 German Civil Code. See DETHLOFF/MARTINY, German Report, Q 36.
549 See ROTH, Austrian Report, Q 36.
550 See ANTOKOLSKAIA, Russian Report, Q 36.
551 See LOWE, English Report, Q 36

may acquire parental responsibilities and exercise them simultaneously with the parent(s). In these cases the third party or institution will only acquire limited parental responsibilities.[552]

COMMENT

1. Principle 3:11 reflects the common core of European jurisdictions and also Principle 20 (1) of the Council of Europe's *White Paper 2002*. It establishes that parental responsibilities are held equally whenever they are held jointly. It moreover stresses that there is not only an equal right to exercise parental responsibilities, but also an equal duty to do so.

2. Exceptions to the joint and equal exercising of parental responsibilities are however recognised because it is realised that parental responsibilities should be exercised by the parents together "whenever possible". According to Principle 3:15 parental responsibilities may be exercised by one of the holders of parental responsibilities when this is jointly agreed by the holders of parental responsibilities according to Principle 3:13, or upon a decision to that effect by the competent authority.

3. The fact that parental responsibilities should be exercised jointly does not mean that parents have to act together in all circumstances. This issue is further developed under Principle 3:12 which grants the authority to act alone in daily matters.

4. According to Principle 3:10 the exercise of parental responsibilities as such is not affected by the fact that the marriage or other formal relationship of the holders of parental responsibilities has been dissolved or annulled or that they have legally or factually separated.

---

552 Art. 1907 Portuguese Civil Code. See De Oliveira, Portuguese Report, Q 36.

Principle 3:12 Daily matters, important and urgent decisions
(1) Parents having joint parental responsibilities should have the right to act alone with respect to daily matters.
(2) Important decisions concerning matters such as education, medical treatment, the child's residence, or the administration of his or her property should be taken jointly. In urgent cases a parent should have the right to act alone. The other parent should be informed without undue delay.

Principe 3:12 Actes de la vie courante, décisions importantes et urgentes
(1) Les parents titulaires en commun de la responsabilité parentale ont le droit d'accomplir seuls les actes de la vie courante.
(2) Les décisions importantes concernant des domaines tels que l'éducation de l'enfant, son traitement médical, sa résidence ou l'administration de ses biens, sont prises conjointement. En cas d'urgence, un parent a le droit d'agir seul. L'autre parent doit être informé sans retard.

Prinzip 3:12 Tägliche Angelegenheiten, wichtige und dringende Entscheidungen
(1) Eltern, denen die elterliche Verantwortung gemeinsam zusteht, haben das Recht, in täglichen Angelegenheiten alleine zu handeln.
(2) Wichtige Entscheidungen bezüglich Angelegenheiten wie Erziehung, medizinische Behandlung, Aufenthalt des Kindes oder Sorge für sein Vermögen sind gemeinsam zu treffen. In dringenden Fällen hat ein Elternteil, das Recht alleine zu handeln. Der andere Elternteil ist unverzüglich zu unterrichten.

INTERNATIONAL INSTRUMENTS

Principle 20 para. 1 of the *White Paper 2002* establishes that parents should exercise parental responsibilities together whenever possible. In Principle 20 (2) it is further specified that, subject to the best interests of the child, parental responsibilities may be exercised by one parent alone. There are no further details, however, as to when and under which conditions this is admissible. Principle 10 of the Council of Europe's *Recommendation on Parental Responsibilities 1984* subjects decisions affecting the interests of the child to the agreement of both parents holding parental responsibilities. Although neither the *Hague Child Protection Convention 1996* nor the *Brussels II bis Regulation* deal with substantive law, both instruments imply that an international relocation is a matter upon which both parents should agree. If the removal of a child from one jurisdiction to another is in breach of custody rights it will be considered wrongful and both instruments will intervene in order to obtain the prompt return of the child. This is further developed under Article 3. 11 b) of the *Brussels II bis*

Regulation which establishes that custody shall be considered to be exercised jointly when, pursuant to a judgment or by operation of the law, one holder of parental responsibilities cannot decide on the child's place of residence without the consent of the other holder of such responsibilities.

COMPARATIVE OVERVIEW

Power to act alone

The fact that parental responsibilities are held jointly does not mean that parents must always act together. In many systems there exists a legal presumption that each parent acts with the agreement of the other parent (BELGIUM,[553] CZECH REPUBLIC,[554] FRANCE,[555] HUNGARY,[556] PORTUGAL,[557] RUSSIA[558] and SPAIN[559]). This presumption may apply to all acts (BELGIUM[560]), only to routine decisions (FRANCE,[561] SPAIN[562]) or to decisions which are not considered to be of major importance (RUSSIA[563]). In some systems the presumption only applies to decisions concerning the child's property (HUNGARY[564]). In BELGIAN and FRENCH law the presumption is rebuttable in relation to *bona fide* third parties.[565] In SPAIN the presumption is a *iuris et de iure* presumption.[566]

In other systems each holder of parental responsibilities is authorized to act alone, except concerning decisions of major importance (DENMARK,[567] ENGLAND AND WALES,[568]

553 Art. 373 para. 2 Belgian Civil Code for acts concerning the person of the child and Art. 376 para. 2 Civil Code for other acts. See PINTENS/PIGNOLET, Belgian Report, Q 36 and Q 39.
554 See HRUSAKOVÁ, Czech Report, Q 36 and Q 39.
555 Art. 372–2 French Civil Code. See FERRAND, French Report, Q 36.
556 See WEISS/SZEIBERT, Hungarian Report, Q 39.
557 See DE OLIVEIRA, Portuguese Report, Q 37.
558 Art. 79 Russian Familiy Code. See ANTOKOLSKAIA, Russian Report, Q 39.
559 See GONZÁLEZ BEILFUSS, Spanish Report, Q 37 and Q 39.
560 In BELGIAN law there is only one exception: the removal of an organ of the child which requires the express consent of both holders of parental responsibilities. See PINTENS/PIGNOLET, Belgian Report, Q 36.
561 See FERRAND, French Report, Q 36.
562 See GONZÁLEZ BEILFUSS, Spanish Report, Q 37.
563 See ANTOKOLSKAIA, Russian Report, Q 39.
564 See WEISS/SZEIBERT, Hungarian Report, Q 39.
565 See PINTENS/PIGNOLET, Belgian Report, Q 36; FERRAND, French Report, Q 36.
566 See GONZÁLEZ BEILFUSS, Spanish Report, Q 37.
567 See LUND-ANDERSEN/JEPPESEN-DE BOER, Danish Report, Q 39.
568 S. 2(7) English Children Act 1989. See LOWE, English Report, Q 39.

POLAND,[569] GREECE,[570] IRELAND,[571] ITALY[572] and LITHUANIA[573]). In some systems this power to act alone is confined to certain matters (THE NETHERLANDS[574] and NORWAY[575]). Under SWISS law it is sufficient for the other parent to give his or her prior or subsequent, explicit or implicit consent.[576]

Urgent matters

In an emergency either parent can act alone (FINLAND,[577] GERMANY,[578] GREECE,[579] ITALY,[580] SPAIN[581] and SWITZERLAND[582]). GERMAN law specifies that the other parent must be informed immediately.[583] A power to act alone is also granted in the case of the illness or absence of one of the holders of parental responsibilities (SPAIN[584] and SWEDEN[585]).

Important decisions

In some systems the law provides that important decisions concerning, for example, the choice of education or a change of residence have to be taken together (CZECH REPUBLIC,[586] HUNGARY,[587] ITALY[588] and SPAIN[589]). CATALAN law provides that, in situations where communication between the holders of parental responsibilities is difficult, once a parent is informed that the other parent intends to make a decision,

---

569 Art. 97 para.1 and 2 Polish Family And Guardianship Code. See MĄCZYŃSKI/MĄCZYŃSKA, Polish Report, Q 36.

570 See KOUTSOURADIS/ZERVOGIANNI, Greek Report, Q 39.

571 See SHANNON, Irish Report, Q 39.

572 See PATTI/BELLISARIO/ROSSI CARLEO, Italian Report, Q 39.

573 See MIKELENAS, Lithuanian Report, Q 39.

574 Art. 1:253i para. 1 Dutch Civil Code; BOELE-WOELKI/SCHRAMA/VONK, Dutch Report, Q 39.

575 Financial Matters – Art. 3 Norwegian Act on Guardianship 1927. See SVERDRUP/LØDRUP, Norwegian Report, Q 39.

576 Art. 304 para. 2 Swiss Civil Code. See HAUSHEER/ACHERMANN-WEBER/WOLF, Swiss Report, Q 36.

577 See KURKI-SUONIO, Finnish Report, Q 39.

578 § 1629 para. 2 clause 2 German Civil Code. See DETHLOFF/MARTINY, German Report, Q 39.

579 See KOUTSOURADIS/ZERVOGIANNI, Greek Report, Q 39.

580 See PATTI/BELLISARIO/ROSSI CARLEO, Italian Report, Q 39.

581 See GONZÁLEZ BEILFUSS, Spanish Report, Q 37.

582 See HAUSHEER/ACHERMANN-WEBER/WOLF, Swiss Report, Q 39.

583 See DETHLOFF/MARTINY, German Report, Q 39.

584 Art. 156 Spanish Civil Code and Art. 137.3 Catalan Family Code. See GONZÁLEZ BEILFUSS, Spanish Report, Q 39.

585 See JÄNTERÄ-JAREBORG/SINGER/SÖRGJERD, Swedish Report, Q 39.

586 See HRUSAKOVÁ, Czech Report, Q 39.

587 § 72/B para. 1 and 2 Hungarian Family Act.

588 See PATTI/BELLISARIO/ROSSI CARLEO, Italian Report, Q 14.

589 See GONZÁLEZ BEILFUSS, Spanish Report, Q 36.

he or she has a right of veto. If this right is not exercised within thirty days of having been informed, the other parent will be allowed to proceed alone.[590]

COMMENT

1. Principle 3:12 (1) establishes that each parent having joint parental responsibilities is allowed to act alone in daily matters. It further develops Principle 3:11 which stipulates that parents having joint parental responsibilities should exercise such responsibilities jointly. "Joint exercise" does not mean that parents have to act together at all times as this would be impracticable.

2. There are generally three reasons for authorizing each holder of parental responsibilities to act alone in daily matters instead of establishing a presumption that each parent acts with the consent of the other. A presumption is more difficult from a technical point of view and results in uncertainty if it is rebuttable. If the presumption is not rebuttable it can be equated with a power to act alone and it seems to be more straightforward to grant this authority directly. Since CEFL's Principles do not distinguish between whether the parents are a couple or have separated (Principle 3:10), it seems clearer and more close to reality to establish an individual right to act alone in daily matters.

3. Principle 3:12 (2) requires that parents take decisions on important matters together.

4. Important matters requiring joint action are not defined by the Principles. Principle 3:12 (2) contains a non-exhaustive list which serves as an illustration. It refers to issues such as the determination of the child's residence, his or her education, medical treatment and the administration of property. Not all matters in these areas require a joint decision; this is only so if the matter is important. The Principles do not provide a criterion in order to evaluate whether or not an issue is important. Decisions with a long-lasting effect for the child should, however, be considered important. For example, whereas authorizing a child to attend a language course will not be deemed to be an important decision on education requiring the consent of both parents, a change of school would probably be regarded as such. Much will however depend on the circumstances of the case.

5. Principle 3:12 (2) allows each parent to act alone in urgent situations even when important matters are at stake. Urgent situations are those requiring immediate action,

[590] Art. 139 Catalan Family Code, GONZÁLEZ BEILFUSS, Spanish Report, Q 36.

where a decision cannot be postponed until the other holder of parental responsibilities agrees. An example could be authorizing surgery after an accident. The other parent should however be informed without undue delay.

Principle 3:13 Agreement on exercise
(1) Subject to the best interests of the child, parents having joint parental responsibilities may agree on the exercise of parental responsibilities.
(2) The competent authority may scrutinize the agreement.

Principe 3:13 Accord sur l'exercice
(1) Eu égard au meilleur intérêt de l'enfant, les parents détenant en commun la responsabilité parentale peuvent s'entendre sur l'exercice de celle-ci.
(2) L'autorité compétente peut contrôler l'accord.

Prinzip 3:13 Vereinbarung über die Ausübung
(1) In Übereinstimmung mit dem Kindeswohl können Eltern, denen die elterliche Verantwortung gemeinsam zusteht, eine Vereinbarung über die Ausübung der elterlichen Verantwortung treffen.
(2) Die zuständige Behörde kann die Vereinbarung überprüfen.

INTERNATIONAL INSTRUMENTS

International instruments generally only guarantee joint parental responsibilities as such. However, Principle 20 para. 1 of the Council of Europe's *White Paper 2002* states that parents having parental responsibilities should have an equal right to exercise such responsibilities and, whenever possible, should exercise such responsibilities together unless the best interests of the child require otherwise. According to Principle 20 para. 2, subject to the best interests of the child, parental responsibilities may be exercised by one parent alone or the exercise may be divided between the two parents according to the decision of the competent authority or on the basis of an agreement between them. Agreements are also mentioned in the *Brussels II bis Regulation* (Art. 2 No. 7, 11 (a), 46). According to the Principle 10 of the *Recommendation on Parental Responsibilities 1984*, where parental responsibilities are exercised jointly by both parents, any decision affecting the interests of the child should be taken by the agreement of both.

COMPARATIVE OVERVIEW

Joint exercise of parental responsibilities

When both of the parents are the holders of parental responsibilities the joint exercise thereof is the rule; both have an equal right to exercise parental responsibilities (e.g.

AUSTRIA,[591] BELGIUM,[592] CZECH REPUBLIC,[593] DENMARK,[594] FRANCE,[595] GERMANY,[596] ITALY,[597] LITHUANIA,[598] THE NETHERLANDS,[599] PORTUGAL,[600] SPAIN,[601] SWEDEN[602] and SWITZERLAND[603]). The question whether the holders of parental responsibilities have to agree on all issues is dealt with in the comparative overview under Principle 3:12 on daily matters, important and urgent decisions. In many jurisdictions the fact that the holders of parental responsibilities live separately has no influence on the distribution of legal responsibilities. The holders of parental responsibilities have to reach an agreement also under these circumstances (BELGIUM[604], FRANCE,[605] LITHUANIA[606] and RUSSIA[607]). However, in some jurisdictions the parents' independence to decide is stressed (ENGLAND and WALES[608]). Moreover, also applicable here is the rule that decisions of minor importance can be taken by one parent alone, which means that the parent with whom the child lives can so decide (LITHUANIA[609] and POLAND[610]); see the COMPARATIVE OVERVIEW under Principle 3:12.

Agreements

Agreements between the holders of parental responsibilities are in general respected in all the jurisdictions surveyed. Such agreements play an increasingly important role in the field of parental responsibilities. However, in the jurisdictions surveyed several types of agreements are distinguished which are dealt with in the context of the subject-matter, see for agreements on the joint exercise of parental responsibilities the comparative overview under Principle 3:11 (1), for agreements on important matters see the comparative overview under Principle 3:12 (2), on contact see the comparative overview under Principle 3:27, and on the residence of the child see the comparative

591 § 144 Austrian Civil Code and ROTH, Austrian Report, Q 37.
592 See PINTENS/PIGNOLET, Belgian Report, Q 37.
593 See HRUSAKOVÁ, Czech Report, Q 37.
594 See LUND-ANDERSEN/JEPPESEN-DE BOER, Danish Report, Q 37.
595 See FERRAND, French Report, Q 37.
596 § 1627 German Civil Code and see DETHLOFF/MARTINY, German Report, Q 37.
597 See PATTI/BELLISARIO/ROSSI CARLEO, Italian Report, Q 37.
598 See MIKELENAS, Lithuanian Report, Q 37.
599 See BOELE-WOELKI/SCHRAMA/VONK, Dutch Report, Q 37.
600 See DE OLIVEIRA, Portuguese Report, Q 37.
601 See GONZÁLEZ BEILFUSS, Spanish Report, Q 37.
602 See JÄNTERÄ-JAREBORG/SINGER/SÖRGJERD, Swedish Report, Q 37.
603 See HAUSHEER/ACHERMANN-WEBER/WOLF, Swiss Report, Q 37.
604 Art. 374 Belgian Civil Code. See PINTENS/PIGNOLET, Belgian Report, Q 37.
605 See FERRAND, French Report, Q 37.
606 See MIKELENAS, Lithuanian Report, Q 37.
607 See ANTOKOLSKAIA, Russian Report, Q 37.
608 See LOWE, English Report, Q 37.
609 See MIKELENAS, Lithuanian Report, Q 37.
610 See MĄCZYŃSKI/MĄCZYŃSKA, Polish Report, Q 37.

overview under Principle 3:20 (1), (2). For an agreement between the holders of parental responsibilities which leads to the sole exercise of parental responsibilities by one of the parents alone, see under Principle 3:15 (2). Generally, parental responsibilities also include the legal representation of the child (see the COMPARATIVE OVERVIEW under Principle 3:24). The holder of parental responsibilities may enter into an agreement on behalf of the underage child. Nearly all jurisdictions follow the rule that one parent can give the other parent an authorization to exercise this legal representation (e.g. FRANCE,[611] GERMANY,[612] HUNGARY,[613] NORWAY,[614] RUSSIA,[615] and SPAIN[616]). Therefore one parent can act alone.

COMMENT

1. Principle 3:13 (1) lays down the general principle that there may be agreements concerning the exercise of parental responsibilities. This means that the holders of parental responsibilities may agree on several matters or on a specific issue. Para. 1 follows Principle 20 subs. 1 of the *White Paper 2002* on Parentage. The holders of parental responsibilities should have an equal right to exercise such responsibilities and whenever possible should exercise them together unless the best interests of the child require otherwise (see Principle 3:11 (1)). This is in accordance with the common core of the legal systems.

2. There can be several kinds of agreements between the holders of parental responsibilities. Principle 3:13 only deals with agreements on the exercise of parental responsibilities in the case of joint exercise. The attribution of parental responsibilities is dealt with in Principles 3:8 and 3:9. Contact issues are dealt with in Principle 3:27.

3. The holders of parental responsibilities should generally exercise their parental responsibilities together. They have to come to an agreement concerning issues affecting the child. Important decisions have to be jointly taken by the holders of parental responsibilities (see Principle 3:12 (2)). Principle 3:13 (2) states that, in accordance with Principle 3:7, agreements are only binding if they respect the child's best interests. The freedom of the holders of parental responsibilities to enter into an agreement and to determine its content is thereby restricted. Principle 3:7 already states that the interests of the child should be protected whenever they may be in conflict

[611] See FERRAND, French Report, Q 37.
[612] See DETHLOFF/MARTINY, German Report, Q 37.
[613] See WEISS/SZEIBERT, Hungarian Report, Q 37.
[614] § 4 para. 1 Norwegian Act on Guardianship.
[615] See ANTOKOLSKAIA, Russian Report, Q 37.
[616] See GONZÁLEZ BEILFUSS, Spanish Report, Q 37.

with the interests of the holders of parental responsibilities. However, the importance of the child's best interests is stressed here once again as a reminder that they have to be respected also in the case of agreements.

4. Principle 3:13 (3) states that agreements may be subject to the scrutiny of the competent authority. However, in general no such scrutiny is required. In particular for the exercise of parental responsibilities, the parents have to find their own solutions without any formalities. The agreement can be made orally or in writing. Only in the case of a divorce by mutual consent should an agreement be in writing (Principle 1:6 (2) of the CEFL Divorce Principles). Agreements are modifiable. If there is a disagreement between the holders of parental responsibilities and disputes arise then Principle 3:14 applies. In the case of a divorce by mutual consent the spouses should have reached an agreement on their parental responsibilities, where necessary including a contact agreement according to Principle 1:6 (1)(a) of the CEFL Divorce Principles. The competent authority should determine the consequences for the children, but takes into account an admissible agreement between the spouses (Principle 1:7 (1) Divorce Principles).

5. The scope of an agreement can cover all aspects of parental responsibilities listed in Principle 3:1, in particular care, protection and education. However, some aspects are dealt with separately in the Principles. Agreements on the joint exercise of parental responsibilities are recognised in Principle 3:11 (1). Agreements on important matters are mentioned in Principle 3:12 (2).

6. An agreement between the holders of parental responsibilities may also lead to the sole exercise of parental responsibilities by one of the parents; see Principle 3:15 (a).

7. With regard to specific issues there should be, as far as possible, an agreement between the holders of parental responsibilities. The maintenance of personal relationships is dealt with in Principle 3:27, the residence of the child in Principle 3:20 (1), (2).

Principle 3:14 Disagreement on exercise
(1) Where parents having joint parental responsibilities cannot agree on an important matter they may apply to the competent authority.
(2) The competent authority should promote agreement between the parents.
(3) Where agreement cannot be reached the competent authority should divide the exercise of parental responsibilities between the parents or decide the dispute.

Principe 3:14 Désaccord en matière d'exercice
(1) Si les parents détenant en commun la responsabilité parentale ne parviennent pas à s'entendre sur une question importante, ils peuvent saisir l'autorité compétente.
(2) L'autorité compétente s'efforce de favoriser un accord entre les parents.
(3) Si aucun accord ne peut être conclu, l'autorité compétente divise l'exercice de la responsabilité parentale entre les parents ou tranche le désaccord.

Prinzip 3:14 Meinungsverschiedenheit über die Ausübung
(1) Können Eltern, denen die elterliche Verantwortung gemeinsam zusteht, sich über wichtige Angelegenheiten nicht einigen, können sie die zuständige Behörde anrufen.
(2) Die zuständige Behörde versucht eine Einigung zwischen den Eltern zu fördern.
(3) Kann keine Einigung erzielt werden, teilt die zuständige Behörde die Ausübung der elterlichen Verantwortung unter den Eltern auf oder entscheidet die Meinungsverschiedenheit.

INTERNATIONAL INSTRUMENTS

International instruments deal with agreements between the holders of parental responsibilities,[617] but in general not expressly with disagreements. However, Principle 10 para. 2 of the *Recommendation on Parental Responsibilities 1984* deals with disagreements. Where there is a disagreement and the matter is referred to the competent authority, it should, insofar as the interests of the child so require, try to reconcile the parents, and, if this fails, take the appropriate decision.

---

617 See under Principle 3:11.

COMPARATIVE OVERVIEW

Disagreement between the holders of parental responsibilities

The issue of a disagreement arises when both parents are the holders of joint parental responsibilities. This problem has several dimensions which cannot easily be distinguished. One is the lack of consent between the holders themselves in respect of care and/or the administration of property, the other issue is the ability to make a valid decision and to represent the child in dealings with third persons.[618] Therefore any disagreement as such between the holders of parental responsibilities has to be distinguished from the issue of legal representation in dealings with third parties. Since the extent of the authority of one parent to act alone and without the consent of the other parent is different in the jurisdictions surveyed, the problems have different dimensions.

When the holders of parental responsibilities have joint parental responsibilities, their joint exercise is the general rule. If the holders of parental responsibilities do not agree on an issue neither parent has a superior right to make a decision; they have to try to find a common solution. In some cases, apart from the general rules, there is special legislation concerning some issues which are deemed to be important and where the consent of the parents is required. Such provisions exist, for example, on the name of the child (FINLAND[619]), the issuing of a passport for the child (BULGARIA[620]) or taking the child outside the jurisdiction without the other parent's consent (ENGLAND AND WALES[621] and NORWAY[622]).

If the holders of parental responsibilities are unable to agree on specific issues relating to parental responsibilities, the question arises whether they can apply to a competent authority to have their dispute resolved. Only in the DANISH[623] and NORWEGIAN[624] legal systems is the intervention of the competent authority limited to disputes relating to contact. If the parents holding joint parental responsibilities do not agree on an issue in NORWAY, there is no public authority to which they can apply to have the dispute resolved as long as they remain living together. In contrast, according to the laws of nearly all jurisdictions the intervention of a competent authority is provided for all kinds of disagreements, although, in general, unimportant disputes regarding daily

618 See the Comparative Overview under Principle 3:24.
619 See KURKI-SUONIO, Finnish Report, Q 37.
620 See TODOROVA, Bulgarian Report, Q 37.
621 See LOWE, English Report, Q 37.
622 § 40 para. 2 Norwegian Children Act. See SVERDRUP/LØDRUP Norwegian Report, Q 37.
623 See LUND-ANDERSEN/JEPPESEN-DE BOER, Danish Report, Q 38.
624 See SVERDRUP/LØDRUP, Norwegian Report, Q 38.

issues fall outside the scope of legal regulation and should be resolved by the parents themselves (FRANCE,[625] GERMANY,[626] ITALY,[627] PORTUGAL,[628] RUSSIA[629] and SWITZERLAND[630]). It should be avoided that parents are able to offload their responsibilities on to a competent authority.

Dispute resolution

Different mechanisms for resolving disputes can be distinguished: The competent authority can try to conciliate the parents (FRANCE[631] and SWEDEN[632]). However, the intensity of any intervention varies. In some systems the competent authority can itself resolve the problem in the interest of the child and leave the joint exercise of parental responsibilities to both parents (AUSTRIA,[633] BELGIUM,[634] BULGARIA,[635] CZECH REPUBLIC,[636] DENMARK,[637] ENGLAND AND WALES,[638] FRANCE,[639] GREECE,[640] HUNGARY,[641] IRELAND,[642] LITHUANIA,[643] THE NETHERLANDS,[644] POLAND[645] and PORTUGAL[646]). In other systems it can authorise one of the parents to act alone with regard to one or more specific decisions (BELGIUM,[647] FINLAND,[648] GERMANY,[649] ITALY[650] and SPAIN[651]), it can charge one of the parents with the exclusive exercise of parental authority (BELGIUM[652]), it can

625 See FERRAND, French Report, Q 38.
626 See DETHLOFF/MARTINY, German Report, Q 38.
627 See PATTI/BELLISARIO/ROSSI CARLEO, Italian Report, Q 38.
628 See DE OLIVEIRA, Portuguese Report, Q 38.
629 See ANTOKOLSKAIA, Russian Report, Q 38.
630 See HAUSHEER/ACHERMANN/WOLF, Swiss Report, Q 38.
631 See FERRAND, French Report, Q 38.
632 See JÄNTERÄ-JAREBORG/SINGER/SÖRGJERD, Swedish Report, Q 38.
633 § 176 Austrian Civil Code. See Roth, Austrian Report, Q 38.
634 See PINTENS/PIGNOLET, Belgian Report, Q 38.
635 Art. 72 Bulgarian Family Code and TODOROVA, Bulgarian Report, Q 37.
636 See HRUSAKOVÁ, Czech Report, Q 38.
637 See LUND-ANDERSEN/JEPPESEN-DE BOER, Danish Report, Q 38.
638 See LOWE, English Report, Q 38.
639 Art. 373–2–11 French Civil Code with a list of the relevant criteria. See FERRAND, French Report, Q 37 and Q 38.
640 See KOUTSOURADIS/ZERVOGIANNI, Greek Report, Q 38.
641 See WEISS/SZEIBERT, Hungarian Report, Q 37 and Q 38.
642 S. 11 Irish Guardianship of Infants Act. See SHANNON, Irish Report, Q 37.
643 Art. 3.165 Lithuanian Civil Code. See MIKELENAS, Lithuanian Report, Q 38
644 See BOELE-WOELKI/SCHRAMA/VONK, Dutch Report, Q 38.
645 See MĄCZYŃSKI/MĄCZYŃSKA, Polish Report, Q 38.
646 Art. 1901 No. 2 Portuguese Civil Code. See DE OLIVEIRA, Portuguese Report, Q 38.
647 See PINTENS/PIGNOLET, Belgian Report, Q 38.
648 See KURKI-SUONIO, Finnish Report, Q 37 and Q 38.
649 § 1628 German Civil Code. See DETHLOFF/MARTINY, German Report, Q 38.
650 See PATTI/BELLISARIO/ROSSI CARLEO, Italian Report, Q 37 and Q 38.
651 Art. 156 Spanish Civil Code. See GONZÁLEZ BEILFUSS, Spanish Report, Q 38.
652 See PINTENS/PIGNOLET, Belgian Report, Q 38.

determine with whom the child lives (ENGLAND AND WALES[653]), it can determine what visiting or other contact arrangements there should be (ENGLAND AND WALES[654] and SWITZERLAND[655]), or it can give instructions as to how the dispute should be resolved (RUSSIA[656]).

Protective measures

In some cases the law itself resolves the problem by providing a certain solution where the holders of parental responsibilities cannot agree. Generally, if the child's welfare is endangered by the parents' disagreement then the protection of the interests of the child can be ensured by measures for the protection of the child in accordance with the general provisions on parental responsibilities.

Attribution of sole parental responsibilities

In nearly all the legal systems a possible solution is also that the competent authority can attribute sole parental responsibilities to one of the parents. However, this is generally only a measure of last resort (GERMANY[657] and SWEDEN[658]), whereas in some legal systems where there is no specific mechanism for deciding on disputes, this is a general solution (DENMARK[659]).

COMMENT

1. The holders of parental responsibilities generally have to come to an agreement on issues affecting the child; see Principle 3:13. However, if no agreement can be reached, according to Principle 3:14 (1) the competent authority should be able to resolve the dispute. Both parents or only one of them may submit such an application. Principle 3:14 (1) deals only with important matters (see Principle 3:12 (2)), such as education and health. The holders of parental responsibilities have to determine their own solutions for issues of a daily nature. Nevertheless, the competent authority's competence should not be limited to certain issues. A disagreement on specific issues is dealt with separately in the context of residence (Principle 3:20 (2)) and relocation (Principle 3:21 (2)).

---

653 See LOWE, English Report, Q 38.
654 See LOWE, English Report, Q 38.
655 See HAUSHEER/ACHERMANN-WEBER/WOLF, Swiss Report, Q 38.
656 Art. 65 para. 2 Russian Family Code. See ANTOKOLSKAIA, Russian Report, Q 38.
657 See DETHLOFF/MARTINY, German Report, Q 38.
658 See JÄNTERÄ-JAREBORG/SINGER/SÖRGJERD, Swedish Report, Q 37 and Q 38.
659 See LUND-ANDERSEN/JEPPESEN-DE BOER, Danish Report, Q 37.

2. According to Principle 3:14 (2) the competent authority should attempt to reach an agreement between the parties in the proceedings because it is generally in the interests of the child that the holders of parental responsibilities should exercise such responsibilities together whenever possible. This is in line with Principle 3:36 according to which methods of alternative dispute resolution should also be used.

3. There is no common core as to whether the competent authority can decide for itself or is restricted to authorising one of the parents to act alone with regard to one or more issues. The second alternative avoids any unnecessary intervention in family life. However, the practical result will often be the same, because deciding on the most competent parent will be difficult without taking into account the disputed issue itself. Therefore Principle 3:14 (3) leaves it open whether parental responsibilities may be exercised by one holder of parental responsibilities alone or the dispute itself may be decided by the competent authority. Authorising one of the parents to act alone will be preferable where it can be established that a specific, separable issue has to be resolved and one of the holders of parental responsibilities has a sufficient degree of competence or knowledge to pursue the best interests of the child concerning this question. In any case the competent authority has to observe the principle of the best interests of the child and also has to take into account the former practice of the parents.

4. The dispute between the holders of parental responsibilities may also lead to protective measures being taken by the competent authority in order to protect the child. See also Principle 3:32.

Principle 3:15 Sole exercise upon agreement or decision
Subject to the best interests of the child a parent may exercise parental responsibilities alone
(a) upon agreement between the parents according to Principle 3:13, or
(b) upon a decision of the competent authority.

Principe 3:15 Exercice unilatéral en vertu d'un accord ou d'une décision
Eu égard au meilleur intérêt de l'enfant, la responsabilité parentale peut être exercée par un seul parent
(a) en vertu d'unaccord entre les parents, conformément au Principe 3:13 ; ou
(b) en vertu d'une décision de l'autorité compétente.

Prinzip 3:15 Alleinige Ausübung aufgrund Vereinbarung oder Entscheidung
Vorbehaltlich des Kindeswohls kann ein Elternteil die elterliche Verantwortung alleine ausüben
(a) aufgrund einer Vereinbarung der Eltern gemäß Prinzip 3:13 oder
(b) aufgrund einer Entscheidung der zuständigen Behörde.

INTERNATIONAL INSTRUMENTS

Only a few international instruments deal more or less directly with the issue of the sole exercise of parental responsibilities. The *Convention on the Rights of the Child 1989* contains only a provision stating very generally that the State Parties shall make their best efforts to recognise the principle that both parents have a common responsibility for the upbringing and the development of the child; the best interests of the child must be their basic concern.[660] But this does not contain any direct and concrete assertion on the question whether or not the sole exercise of parental responsibilities should be possible.

The *White Paper 2002* lays down the principle that parental responsibilities should in principle belong jointly to both parents (Principle 19 para. 1).[661] Nevertheless, Principle 20 allows some exceptions: subject to the best interests of the child (which are, in this context, also the paramount consideration), parental responsibilities may be exercised

---

660 Art. 9 states the general principle that the child should not be separated from his or her own parents against their will, except when the competent authorities, subject to judicial review, determine that such separation is necessary in the best interests of the child.

661 Principle 19 para. 2 even promotes, in cases where only one parent has parental responsibilities by the operation of law, the opportunity for the other parent to acquire parental responsibilities, unless it is against the best interests of the child.

by one parent alone, or the exercise may be divided between the two parents. According to Principle 20, such a sole or divided exercise of parental responsibilities can be founded either on the decision of the competent authority or on an agreement between the two parents. The *White Paper 2002* does not therefore exclude the possibility of the sole exercise of parental responsibilities, but it is subject to the condition that such a solution shall be in the best interests of the child.

COMPARATIVE OVERVIEW

In case both parents have parental responsibilities, a comparative study of the jurisdictions surveyed shows that it may be possible in some countries for one of the parents to exercise those responsibilities alone, either on the ground of an agreement between both parents, or on the basis of a decision made by the competent authority.

Agreement on the sole exercise of parental responsibilities by one parent

The national reports do not generally deal with the possibility for the parents to enter into an agreement on the sole exercise of parental responsibilities by one of them. While agreements on the joint exercise of parental responsibilities between unmarried parents are generally favoured (see e.g. AUSTRIA,[662] DENMARK,[663] FRANCE,[664] GERMANY,[665] SWEDEN[666] and SWITZERLAND[667]),[668] it remains uncertain whether the parents are allowed to agree on the sole exercise of parental responsibilities by one of them. Only one question in the Questionnaire[669] covers this subject, but only with regard to the *attribution* (and not the exercise) of parental responsibilities and to unmarried parents. However, this distinction between the attribution and the exercise of parental responsibilities is not always relevant in the national laws. According to the answers to Question 25, in several of the jurisdictions surveyed, unmarried parents are free to agree upon parental responsibilities after the ending of their relationship (AUSTRIA[670] where the parents can also agree that one of them will have sole parental responsibili-

662 See ROTH, Austrian Report, Q 20.

663 See LUND-ANDERSEN/JEPPESEN-DE BOER, Danish Report, Q 20.

664 See FERRAND, French Report, Q 20 and Art. 372 para. 3 French Civil Code.

665 See DETHLOFF/MARTINY, German Report, Q 20.

666 See JÄNTERÄ-JAREBORG/SINGER/SÖRGJERD, Swedish Report, Q 20.

667 See HAUSHEER/ACHERMANN-WEBER/WOLF, Swiss Report, Q 20.

668 In some countries, they are not even necessary because parental responsibilities, as a rule, are exercised jointly subject to the condition that parenthood has been established in relation to both parents.

669 See Q 25: "To what extent, if at all, are unmarried parents free to agree upon the attribution of parental responsibilities after the ending of their relationship?"

670 § 177 para. 1 and 3, § 177b Austrian Civil Code. See ROTH, Austrian Report, Q 16a, c, d.

ties, BULGARIA,[671] CZECH REPUBLIC,[672] DENMARK,[673] FINLAND[674] and FRANCE[675] on the exercise of parental responsibilities, GERMANY for joint parental responsibilities,[676] GREECE,[677] HUNGARY[678] and IRELAND[679] for conferring on the father the status of a guardian, ITALY,[680] LITHUANIA,[681] NORWAY,[682] PORTUGAL[683] and SPAIN[684] and on the exercise of parental responsibilities, SWEDEN[685]). In contrast, agreements on parental responsibilities between unmarried parents which confer sole parental responsibilities on one parent are not allowed in THE NETHERLANDS,[686] POLAND[687] and SWITZERLAND.[688] Those countries that do allow agreements between the parents on the exercise of parental responsibilities sometimes require that the agreement shall be scrutinised and approved by the competent authority[689] which will consider the child's best interests.

Decision of the competent authority on the sole exercise of parental responsibilities

The competent authority may have to decide on the sole exercise of parental responsibilities especially after a separation between the parents, or if one of the parents has disappeared or is more generally unfit to exercise such responsibilities. In most

[671] See TODOROVA, Bulgarian Report, Q 25: the agreement is a private matter, neither scrutiny nor registration is required.
[672] See HRUSAKOVÁ, Czech Report, Q 25: the court may approve the parents' agreement.
[673] See LUND-ANDERSEN/JEPPESEN-DE BOER, Danish Report, Q 25: agreements on joint or sole parental responsibilities. Such agreements between unmarried parents are not subject to judicial scrutiny.
[674] See KURKI-SUONIO, Finnish Report, Q 25.
[675] See FERRAND, French Report, Q 25: the family judge shall approve the agreement unless it does not protect the child's interests.
[676] See DETHLOFF/MARTINY, German Report, Q 25.
[677] See KOUTSOURADIS/ZERVOGIANNI, Greek Report, Q 25.
[678] See WEISS/SZEIBERT, Hungarian Report, Q 25: unmarried couples are not obliged to obtain approval from the court or any other competent authority.
[679] See SHANNON, Irish Report, Q 25.
[680] See PATTI/BELLISARIO/ROSSI CARLEO, Italian Report, Q 25.
[681] See MIKELENAS, Lithuanian Report, Q 25.
[682] See SVERDRUP/LØDRUP, Norwegian Report, Q 25: there is no public scrutiny of the agreement. To be valid, the agreement must be reported to the National Population registry, § 39 Norwegian Children Act 1981.
[683] See DE OLIVEIRA, Portuguese Report, Q 25.
[684] See GONZÁLEZ-BEILFUSS, Spanish Report, Q 25.
[685] See JÄNTERÄ-JAREBORG/SINGER/SÖRGJERD, Swedish Report, Q 25: the agreement must be in writing and approved by the social welfare committee.
[686] See BOELE-WOELKI/SCHRAMA/VONK, Dutch Report, Q 25: unmarried parents who want to terminate existing joint parental responsibilities must apply to the court for this purpose.
[687] See MĄCZYŃSKI/MĄCZYŃSKA, Polish Report, Q 25.
[688] See HAUSHEER/ACHERMANN-WEBER/WOLF, Swiss Report, Q 25.
[689] See e.g. AUSTRIA, BULGARIA, CZECH REPUBLIC, FINLAND, FRANCE, GREECE, HUNGARY, IRELAND, ITALY, LITHUANIA, PORTUGAL, RUSSIA, SPAIN and SWEDEN. Some countries do not require such approval, see e.g. LUND-ANDERSEN/JEPPESEN-DE BOER, Danish Report, Q 25 and SVERDRUP/LØDRUP, Norwegian Report, Q 25.

of the jurisdictions surveyed, a separation or divorce does not generally mean that the joint exercise of parental responsibilities should cease (see e.g. BELGIUM,[690] BULGARIA,[691] CZECH REPUBLIC,[692] DENMARK,[693] FRANCE[694] in principle, GERMANY,[695] IRELAND,[696] ITALY,[697] LITHUANIA,[698] THE NETHERLANDS,[699] NORWAY,[700] RUSSIA,[701] SPAIN with some nuances[702] and SWEDEN[703]).

In contrast, in a few of the jurisdictions surveyed, in such cases the competent authority shall entrust one parent with sole parental responsibilities (or the sole exercise thereof), especially when the parents are not able to reach an agreement on joint parental responsibilities after the separation or divorce (see e.g. AUSTRIA[704] and HUNGARY[705]). In SWITZERLAND,[706] the court may decide to attribute parental responsibilities to one parent or, upon a petition, to leave parental responsibilities with both parents if this corresponds with the child's welfare. In several countries, the competent authority may decide that one parent be entrusted with the sole exercise of parental responsibilities if the child's interests so require (see e.g. CZECH REPUBLIC if the unmarried parents of a minor child do not cohabit and do not reach an agreement on the upbringing and the maintenance of the child,[707] DENMARK,[708] FRANCE[709] and GREECE[710] if the parents do not want to continue to exercise joint parental responsibilities and if one of them submits a petition to the court to regulate parental care, HUNGARY,[711] IRELAND,[712]

690 See PINTENS/PIGNOLET, Belgian Report, Q 16.
691 See TODOROVA, Bulgarian Report, Q 16.
692 See HRUSAKOVÁ, Czech Report, Q 16 on divorce and separation between married parents.
693 See LUND-ANDERSEN/JEPPESEN-DE BOER, Danish Report, Q 16 on divorce and separation between married parents.
694 See FERRAND, French Report, Q 16.
695 See DETHLOFF/MARTINY, German Report, Q 16.
696 See SHANNON, Irish Report, Q 16.
697 See PATTI/BELLISARIO/CARLEO ROSSI, Italian Report, Q 16.
698 See MIKELENAS, Lithuanian Report, Q 16.
699 See BOELE-WOELKI/SCHRAMA/VONK, Dutch Report, Q 16.
700 See SVERDRUP/LØDRUP, Norwegian Report, Q 16.
701 See ANTOKOLSKAIA, Russian Report, Q 16.
702 See GONZÁLEZ BEILFUSS, Spanish Report, Q 16 and Q 18.
703 See JÄNTERÄ-JAREBORG/SINGER/SÖRGJERD, Swedish Report, Q 16.
704 See ROTH, Austrian Report, Q 16 and Q 23.
705 See WEISS/SZEIBERT, Hungarian Report, Q 16: maintaining joint parental responsibilities after divorce is rather exceptional in Hungary.
706 See HAUSHEER/ACHERMANN-WEBER/WOLF, Swiss Report, Q 16.
707 See HRUSAKOVÁ, Czech Report, Q 23 for unmarried parents and § 50 Czech Family Code.
708 See LUND-ANDERSEN/JEPPESEN-DE BOER, Danish Report, Q 23 on unmarried parents: the parents may apply to be given sole parental responsibilities on the basis of the termination of the relationship.
709 See FERRAND, French Report, Q 16 and Art. 373–2–1 French Civil Code.
710 See KOUTSOURADIS/ZERVOGIANNI, Greek Report, Q 16.
711 See WEISS/SZEIBERT, Hungarian Report, Q 23 on unmarried parents.
712 See SHANNON, Irish Report, Q 16.

ITALY,[713] THE NETHERLANDS,[714] NORWAY,[715] SPAIN,[716] SWEDEN[717] and SWITZERLAND[718]). When the competent authority delivers its decision, it has to take into consideration the child's best interests, which are the central criterion.

COMMENT

1. Even if the general principle should be the joint exercise of parental responsibilities by both parents (see Principle 3:11), and subject to Principle 3:25 which lays down the right of the child and of the holders of parental responsibilities to obtain and maintain regular contact with each other, Principle 3:15 determines two cases in which only one parent will exercise parental responsibilities although parenthood is established with regard to both parents and although both parents have parental responsibilities. Both retain those responsibilities, but only one of them exercises them.

2. This can apply in two cases: when both holders agree upon the sole exercise of parental responsibilities by one of them or when the competent authority so decides. In the first case, the conditions laid down in Principle 3:13 (especially the requirement that this agreement should be in the child's best interests) must be fulfilled. This means that, subject to national law, the agreement may be scrutinised by the competent authority that will have to check whether the agreement reached by the holders of parental responsibilities really corresponds with the best interests of the child and it may refuse to approve this agreement if this is not the case. Like Principle 3:13, Principle 3:15 refers to the best interests of the child as a primary consideration.

3. If the holders of parental responsibilities cannot reach an agreement on the issue of the sole exercise of those responsibilities (either because they do not share the same views on this issue or e.g. because one of them is absent, mentally ill etc.), the competent authority (in practice a court or an administrative authority) may be called upon to decide the issue. It shall decide – always taking the child's best interests into account – whether the sole exercise of parental responsibilities should be granted to one parent. This may apply e.g. in cases where one holder is not at all interested in

---

713 See PATTI/BELLISARIO/CARLEO ROSSI, Italian Report, Q 23.

714 See BOELE-WOELKI/SCHRAMA/VONK, Dutch Report, Q 23.

715 § 56 Norwegian Children Act 1981. See SVERDRUP/LØDRUP, Norwegian Report, Q 23.

716 See GONZÁLEZ-BEILFUSS, Spanish Report, Q 18 and Q 23.

717 See JÄNTERÄ-JAREBORG/SINGER/SÖRGJERD, Swedish Report, Q 23.

718 Art. 298a para. 2 Swiss Civil Code: "upon the request of one parent, the child or the guardianship authority…, the attribution of parental responsibilities is to be reorganized by the guardianship authority, if this is necessary for the child's welfare due to significant changes in circumstances". See HAUSHEER/ACHERMANN-WEBER/WOLF, Swiss Report, Q 23.

taking care of the child (or is unable to do so) after a divorce or a separation, or in cases where one holder of parental responsibilities is not present (this can be a legal or actual impediment, for instance if a holder is mentally ill, abroad, or has disappeared).

Principle 3:16 Exercise by one parent
If only one parent has parental responsibilities he or she should exercise them alone.

Principe 3:16 Exercice par un seul parent
Si un seul parent détient la responsabilité parentale, il l'exerce seul.

Prinzip 3:16 Ausübung durch einen Elternteil
Hat nur ein Elternteil die elterliche Veranwortung, übt er sie alleine aus.

INTERNATIONAL INSTRUMENTS

The same international instruments apply as under Principle 3:15.

COMPARATIVE OVERVIEW

It generally appears that in two kinds of situations, one parent can exercise parental responsibilities alone *ex lege*: when parenthood has been established only in relation to this parent, but also in some cases where parenthood has been established as regards both parents.

Parenthood established only in relation to one parent

Where parenthood is established only in relation to one of the child's parents, only this parent can exercise parental responsibilities. Even if the national reports do not always deal directly with this issue, such a common core solution may be indirectly deduced from the answer to several questions in the Questionnaire[719] (see AUSTRIA,[720] BELGIUM,[721] BULGARIA,[722] CZECH REPUBLIC,[723] DENMARK,[724] FINLAND,[725] ENGLAND AND

719 See BOELE-WOELKI/BRAAT/CURRY-SUMNER, *ibid.*, note 23, especially Q 15, 16, 20 and Q 22.
720 See ROTH, Austrian Report, Q 22.
721 See PINTENS/PIGNOLET, Belgian Report, Q 15 and Q 22.
722 See TODOROVA, Bulgarian Report, Q 15.
723 See HRUSAKOVÁ, Czech Report, Q 15.
724 See LUND-ANDERSEN/JEPPESEN-DE BOER, Danish Report, Q 20.
725 See KURKI-SUONIO, Finnish Report, Q 15.

WALES,[726] FRANCE,[727] GERMANY,[728] GREECE,[729] HUNGARY,[730] IRELAND,[731] ITALY,[732] LITHUANIA,[733] THE NETHERLANDS,[734] NORWAY,[735] POLAND,[736] PORTUGAL,[737] RUSSIA,[738] SPAIN,[739] SWEDEN[740] and SWITZERLAND[741]).

Parenthood established in relation to both parents

In several European countries, the mere fact that the mother is not married leads to the exercise of parental responsibilities by her alone, even if the father has acknowledged the child or even if the fatherhood has been determined by a court or by any other competent authority. This is e.g. the case in AUSTRIA,[742] FINLAND,[743] GERMANY,[744] GREECE,[745] IRELAND,[746] NORWAY,[747] SWEDEN[748] and SWITZERLAND[749]). In ITALY,[750] the unmarried father can obtain parental responsibilities if he lives with the child or if he was the first to recognise the child, unless the court decides that the child's interests

726 See LOWE, English Report, Q 20.
727 See FERRAND, French Report, Q 15 and Art. 372 para. 2 French Civil Code.
728 See DETHLOFF/MARTINY, German Report, Q 15 and 22.
729 See KOUTSOURADIS/ZERVOGIANNI, Greek Report, Q 15, 20 and Q 22.
730 See WEISS/SZEIBERT, Hungarian Report, Q 20.
731 See SHANNON, Irish Report, Q 15.
732 See PATTI/BELLISARIO/ROSSI CARLEO, Italian Report, Q 22.
733 See MIKELENAS, Lithuanian Report, Q 20.
734 See BOELE-WOELKI/SCHRAMA/VONK, Dutch Report, Q 20.
735 See SVERDRUP/LØDRUP, Norwegian Report, Q 20.
736 See MĄCZYŃSKI/MĄCZYŃSKA, Polish Report, Q 20.
737 See DE OLIVEIRA, Portuguese Report, Q 20 and Art. 1910 Portuguese Civil Code.
738 See ANTOKOLSKAIA, Russian Report, Q 20: parental responsibility is coupled with legal filiation between a child and a parent rather than with marriage between the parents.
739 See GONZÁLEZ-BEILFUSS, Spanish Report, Q 20.
740 See JÄNTERÄ-JAREBORG/SINGER/SÖRGJERD, Swedish Report, Q 20.
741 See HAUSHEER/ACHERMANN-WEBER/WOLF, Swiss Report, Q 20.
742 See ROTH, Austrian Report, Q 22: the unmarried mother is entitled to be given sole parental responsibilities, § 166 Austrian Civil Code.
743 See KURKI-SUONIO, Finnish Report, Q 20.
744 See DETHLOFF/MARTINY, German Report, Q 15 and § 1626a para. 1 sent. 2 German Civil Code.
745 See KOUTSOURADIS/ZERVOGIANNI, Greek Report, Q 20: the exercise of parental responsibilities belongs to the mother if the parents are not married to each other. If the father has voluntarily recognized the child or has not appeared as a defendant in a case concerning judicial recognition, he will also take part in the parental care. But he will only exercise this duty if the mother's parental care has ceased, or if she is unable to do so. In some cases, the court may attribute the exercise of parental care to the father alone.
746 See SHANNON, Irish Report, Q 20.
747 See SVERDRUP/LØDRUP, Norwegian Report, Q 20 and § 35 para. 1 Norwegian Children Act 1981.
748 See JÄNTERÄ-JAREBORG/SINGER/SÖRGJERD, Swedish Report, Q 20: but the parents who are in agreement can obtain joint custody by means of registration with the tax authority after a joint notification to the social welfare committee. The father must have acknowledged his paternity.
749 Art. 298 para. 1 Swiss Civil Code. See HAUSHEER/ACHERMANN-WEBER/WOLF, Swiss Report, Q 20.
750 See PATTI/BELLISARIO/ROSSI CARLEO, Italian Report, Q 22.

require otherwise.[751] In PORTUGAL,[752] if the parents are not married to each other, the exercise of parental responsibilities falls to the parent who has custody of the child, and the law presumes that the mother has custody.[753] Nevertheless, this favouring of the mother in some countries does not seem to be the absolute prevailing tendency. In a more or less equivalent number of jurisdictions surveyed, where parenthood has been established in relation to both parents, the parents normally share the exercise of parental responsibilities (see e.g. BELGIUM,[754] CZECH REPUBLIC,[755] FRANCE,[756] HUNGARY,[757] ITALY under some circumstances,[758] LITHUANIA,[759] POLAND,[760] RUSSIA[761] and SPAIN[762]). For a nuanced solution, see DENMARK,[763] where the parents who are not married to each other have joint parental responsibilities if they have made a statement to the effect that they will care for the child together.[764] If no such statement has been made and if no agreement on joint parental responsibilities has been reached between the parents, the mother has sole parental responsibilities.

Some jurisdictions surveyed make a distinction between the legal act which determines parenthood: voluntary recognition or a court order. In the CZECH REPUBLIC,[765] parental responsibilities also arise by operation of law for the father whose paternity has been determined by a court, while in some other countries, the fact that the paternity has been established by a court judgement leads to sole parental responsibilities in favour of the mother (see e.g. FRANCE[766] and HUNGARY[767]). In RUSSIA,[768] parental responsibilities only belong to the father whose paternity has been established by a court order

---

751 Art. 317 bis Italian Civil Code.
752 See DE OLIVEIRA, Portuguese Report, Q 20.
753 Art. 1911 n°2 Portuguese Civil Code.
754 See PINTENS/PIGNOLET, Belgian Report, Q 20.
755 See HRUSAKOVÁ, Czech Report, Q 20.
756 See FERRAND, French Report, Q 20.
757 See WEISS/SZEIBERT, Hungarian Report, Q 20.
758 See PATTI/BELLISARIO/ROSSI CARLEO, Italian Report, Q 20.
759 See MIKELENAS, Lithuanian Report, Q 20.
760 See MĄCZYŃSKI/MĄCZYŃSKA, Polish Report, Q 20.
761 See ANTOKOLSKAIA, Russian Report, Q 20.
762 See GONZÁLEZ BEILFUSS, Spanish Report, Q 20.
763 See LUND-ANDERSEN/JEPPESEN-DE BOER, Danish Report, Q 20.
764 § 5 para. 1 Danish Act on Parental Authority and Contact.
765 See HRUSAKOVÁ, Czech Report, Q 15.
766 Art. 372 para. 2 French Civil Code. If the father acknowledges the child later than one year after the child's birth or if the paternity is not established by voluntary recognition but by a judicial decision, only the parent that has acknowledged the child (or acknowledged the child earlier than the other parent) has parental responsibilities. See FERRAND, French Report, Q 15.
767 See WEISS/SZEIBERT, Hungarian Report, Q 22: a father whose legal affiliation has been established by a judicial decision generally does not want to take part in the exercise of parental responsibilities.
768 See ANTOKOLSKAIA, Russian Report, Q 20.

against his will if the child's mother is unknown, has died or has been declared by a court to have disappeared.

COMMENT

1. Contrary to Principle 3:15 which deals with the situation in which both parents have parental responsibilities, but only one of them exercises them on the ground of an agreement between the parents or on the ground of a decision made by the competent authority, Principle 3:16 deals with the situation where there is only one parent.

2. Principle 3:16 determines an exception which is required in specific circumstances. Logically, the sole exercise of parental responsibilities should be allowed where parenthood is only established in relation to one parent. This is the clear common core in the national laws of the 22 jurisdictions surveyed. Where only one person is recognised by the law as a parent, only this person may be entitled to exercise parental responsibilities.

SECTION B: THIRD PERSONS
SECTION B: LES TIERS
ABSCHNITT B: DRITTE

Principle 3:17 Exercise in addition to or instead of the parents
A person other than a parent may exercise some or all parental responsibilities in addition to or instead of the parents.

Principe 3:17 Exercice en complément ou en lieu et place des parents
Une personne autre qu'un parent peut exercer tout ou partie de la responsabilité parentale en complément ou en lieu et place des parents.

Prinzip 3:17 Zusätzliche oder an die Stelle der Eltern tretende Ausübung
Eine andere Person als ein Elternteil kann zusätzlich oder an Stelle der Eltern die elterliche Verantwortung ganz oder teilweise ausüben.

INTERNATIONAL INSTRUMENTS

Numerous international instruments recognize the parental responsibilities of third persons but without making a clear distinction between, on the one hand, the *attribution* and, on the other, the *exercise* of parental responsibilities. The identification and description of the relevant international instruments above under Principle 3:9 in respect of the attribution of parental responsibilities to third persons are relevant also as regards the exercise of parental responsibilities under Principle 3:17.

COMPARATIVE OVERVIEW

Exercise by the parent's partner

Normally, the attribution of parental responsibilities also entails the exercise of corresponding parental responsibilities. Where the parent's partner has been attributed with parental responsibilities, he or she can also be expected to take part in the exercise of those parental responsibilities. Therefore, the COMPARATIVE OVERVIEW under Principle 3:9 concerning the prospects for the parent's partner to acquire parental responsibilities is an adequate description also as regards the exercise of parental responsibilities by a parent's partner.

Placing the child in the care of a third person

A common solution in the countries surveyed is to place the child under the care of a third person. This placement may involve the attribution of parental responsibilities to the third person, but in many cases it is merely a right to exercise such responsibilities and the parents retain their parental responsibilities. Since not all of the national reports explicitly address the difference between the attribution and the exercise of parental responsibilities, doubts may remain regarding the approach chosen in a given State. In some of the countries both models are available, depending on the circumstances of the case, such as the reason for the placement and its factual duration. The national models are described in more detail in the COMPARATIVE OVERVIEW under Principle 3:9.

In addition to or substituting the parents?

Appointing a third person to exercise parental responsibilities is often a measure of protection, used in situations where the parents are not able to fulfil their parental responsibilities at all or only partly. This solution is described in detail in the COMPARATIVE OVERVIEW under Principle 3:9. But it may also serve other kinds of purposes, such as when the competent authority establishes a contact right between the child and a third person, such as the child's grandparent, or when a third person is appointed to control the parents' administration of the child's property. These kinds of limited parental responsibilities held by a third person supplement the parental responsibilities of the parents.

An interesting minority position is found in ENGLAND AND WALES[769] and FINLAND[770] where a third person's acquisition of parental responsibilities may be far-reaching, but is still in principle *an addition* and not a substitution of the existing parental responsibilities. In ENGLAND AND WALES,[771] a residence order always confers parental responsibility. Such acquisition does not affect the legal position of parents who will continue to have parental responsibility. In FINLAND,[772] a child may have more than two custodians, meaning that there may be several persons to whom parental responsibilities have been attributed. The court may order, upon an application by

769 See LOWE, English Report, Q 14.
770 See KURKI-SUONIO, Finnish Report, Q 14.
771 See LOWE, English Report, Q 31.
772 See KURKI-SUONIO, Finnish Report, Q 27.

a parent, the child's custodian or the local social authority,[773] that one or more persons who have consented thereto shall have the custody of a child instead of, or together with, the parent or the parents.[774] Custody of the child may only be transferred from a parent subject to the condition that it is manifestly in the best interests of the child.[775] Exceptionally, in LITHUANIA,[776] other persons may be entrusted with some aspects of parental authority without infringing upon the parents' parental authority and without the child being separated from the parents. These persons consist of a specially appointed guardian or close relatives of the child, such as grandparents or adult siblings.

Agreements granting the exercise of parental responsibilities to third persons

The jurisdictions surveyed leave a certain scope for agreements granting the right to exercise parental responsibilities to third persons.[777] In BELGIUM[778] it is permitted to transfer most parental responsibilities to a third person by agreement, subject to certain conditions such as the consent of the child if he or she has reached the age of 15 years or otherwise of the parent. In DENMARK,[779] a parent holding parental responsibilities may validly, but subject to approval by the competent authority, agree with his or her spouse (who is not the child's parent) on joint parental responsibilities. In ENGLAND AND WALES,[780] the parent and his or her partner may agree upon the exercise of parental responsibilities but not on the formal allocation thereof. In GERMANY,[781] the parents holding parental responsibilities may, on a revocable basis, engage third persons to exercise parental responsibilities, the parental responsibility as such remaining with the parents.

The exercise of parental responsibilities by a public body

Although not all of the national reports expressly address this issue, it is evident that in all of the jurisdictions a public body may, where necessary, intervene in the exercise of parental responsibilities and take measures to protect the child. In several of the countries, a public body may under special conditions also exercise parental

773 § 14 para. 1 Finnish Child Custody and Access Rights Act.

774 § 9 para. 1 point 4 Finnish Child Custody and Access Rights Act.

775 § 9 para. 2 Finnish Child Custody and Access Rights Act and KURKI-SUONIO, Finnish Report, Q 27.

776 See MIKELENAS, Lithuanian Report, Q 31.

777 Also as regards agreements, it is not always clear how the borderline is drawn between attribution and exercise of parental responsibilities.

778 See PINTENS/PIGNOLET, Belgian Report, Q 31.

779 § 11 Danish Act on Parental Authority and Contact. See also LUND-ANDERSEN/JEPPESEN-DE BOER, Danish Report, Q 31.

780 See LOWE, English Report, Q 30.

781 See DETHLOFF/MARTINY, German Report, Q 31.

responsibilities (AUSTRIA,[782] BELGIUM,[783] GERMANY,[784] GREECE,[785] IRELAND (care order),[786] ITALY,[787] LITHUANIA,[788] THE NETHERLANDS,[789] PORTUGAL,[790] SPAIN[791] and SWITZERLAND[792]). This solution is normally only available as a "last resort" when the parents, for one reason or another, are not able or suitable to exercise parental responsibilities and there is no other suitable person to whom the exercise of parental responsibilities could be entrusted. It may, however, also apply as a complementary solution, supplementing another person's, normally the child's parents', restricted or partial exercise of parental responsibilities. In these cases the public body in question exercises parental responsibilities in addition to other persons. This may be the case in BELGIUM,[793] ENGLAND AND WALES[794] (care orders and emergency protection orders), FINLAND,[795] FRANCE,[796] and LITHUANIA.[797] In HUNGARY,[798] a civil servant may act in his or her professional status as a child's guardian, often in a limited manner complementing the exercise of parental responsibilities by, for example, foster parents.

In other systems, it is not possible to entrust public bodies with the exercise of parental responsibilities. This is at least the starting point of countries such as BULGARIA,[799] CZECH REPUBLIC,[800] DENMARK,[801] NORWAY,[802] POLAND,[803] RUSSIA,[804] and SWEDEN.[805] On the other hand, also in these countries the public bodies may still be involved in the exercise of parental responsibilities, e.g., in RUSSIA[806] where a public body may fulfil

782 See ROTH, Austrian report, Q 31.
783 See PINTENS/PIGNOLET, Belgian Report, Q 31.
784 § 1791 b para. 1 German Civil Code. See DETHLOFF/MARTINY, German Report, Q 32.
785 See KOUTSOURADIS/ZERVOGIANNI, Greek Report, Q 32.
786 See SHANNON, Irish Report, Q 32.
787 See PATTI/BELLISARIO/ROSSI CARLEO, Italian Report, Q 32.
788 See MIKELENAS, Lithuanian Report, Q 32.
789 See BOELE-WOELKI/SCHRAMA/VONK, Dutch Report, Q 32.
790 See DE OLIVEIRA, Portuguese Report, Q 32.
791 See GONZÁLEZ BEILFUSS, Spanish Report, Q 32.
792 See HAUSHEER/ACHERMANN-WEBER/WOLF, Swiss Report, Q 32.
793 See PINTENS/PIGNOLET, Belgian Report, Q 32.
794 See LOWE, English Report, Q 32.
795 See KURKI-SUONIO, Finnish Report, Q 32.
796 See FERRAND, French Report, Q 32.
797 See MIKELENAS, Lithuanian Report, Q 32.
798 See WEISS/SZEIBERT, Hungarian Report, Q 32. According to the Report, a professional guardian is not a public body in a strict sense. Such a guardian may be responsible for up to 40 children, e.g., administering their property.
799 See TODOROVA, Bulgarian Report, Q 32.
800 See HRUSAKOVÁ, Czech Report, Q 32.
801 See LUND-ANDERSEN/JEPPESEN-DE BOER, Danish Report, Q 32.
802 See SVERDRUP/LØDRUP, Norwegian Report, Q 32.
803 See MĄCZYŃSKI/MĄCZYŃSKA, Polish Report, Q 32.
804 See ANTOKOLSKAIA, Russian Report, Q 32.
805 See JÄNTERÄ-JAREBORG/SINGER/SÖRGJERD, Swedish Report, Q 32.
806 See ANTOKOLSKAIA, Russian Report, Q 32.

the functions of a child's guardian or in SWEDEN[807] where public bodies are under the duty to supervise the care of children who have been removed from the parents' care but without appointing foster parents as special custodians of the child. In the light of the answers given in the national reports, it is not always possible to draw a clear borderline between the different systems.

COMMENT

1. International instruments recognize the exercise of parental responsibilities by persons other than the child's parents, but without always making a clear distinction between the attribution and the exercise of parental responsibilities, see COMMENT above under Principle 3:9. A comprehensive concept of parental responsibilities is followed in the more recent instruments, such as the Hague Child Protection Convention, the *Brussels II bis Regulation* and the *White Paper 2002*, making it possible for different persons to be in charge not only of the whole bulk of parental responsibilities but also in different degrees and of different aspects of parental responsibilities. The modern concept of parental responsibilities normally involves both attribution and exercise but may also be limited to only one of the two. It is important to notice that this terminology clearly differs from that followed in the national law of the majority of the jurisdictions.

2. Also Principle 3:17 recognises that parental responsibilities may be exercised by third persons. The wording of the Principle is inspired in particular by the *White Paper 2002* (Principle 20 para. 3) according to which "a person other than a parent may … exercise some or all parental responsibilities in addition to or instead of parents". Other important sources of inspiration are the laws of ENGLAND AND WALES and FINLAND, where a third person's acquisition and exercise of parental responsibilities is normally an addition and not a limitation to the parents' parental responsibilities. Principle 3:17 also covers, however, situations where a third person exercises parental responsibilities instead of the parents. The Principle is based on a "better law" approach.

3. Principle 3:17 leaves it to national law to decide how and subject to what conditions the third persons exercising some or all parental responsibilities end up in this position, e.g., by a decision of a competent authority, by agreement, *ex lege*, etc. This differs, e.g., from the position of the *White Paper 2002*, according to which a third person can be appointed to exercise parental responsibilities only by a decision of a competent authority. Principle 3:17 also leaves it to national law to decide which persons are eligible to exercise parental responsibilities besides or instead of the parents, how many

807 See JÄNTERÄ-JAREBORG/SINGER/SÖRGJERD, Swedish Report, Q 32.

persons may be in charge of parental responsibilities concerning a child, and which kinds of parental responsibilities may be concerned.

4. Principle 3:17 does not include the exercise of parental responsibilities by public bodies. The position taken by the jurisdictions surveyed varies in this respect, but they all agree that parents or other (physical) persons should primarily be in charge of exercising parental responsibilities. Where provided by national law, a public body may exercise such parental responsibilities that cannot suitably be undertaken by a parent or other holders of parental responsibilities.

Principle 3:18 Decisions in daily matters
The parent's partner living with the child may take part in decisions with respect to daily matters unless the other parent having parental responsibilities objects.

Principe 3:18 Décisions de la vie courante
Le partenaire d'un parent qui vit avec l'enfant peut prendre part aux décisions de la vie courante, sauf objection de l'autre parent détenant la responsabilité parentale.

Prinzip 3:18 Entscheidungen in täglichen Angelegenheiten
Der Partner des Elternteils, der mit dem Kind zusammenlebt, kann in täglichen Angelegenheiten mitentscheiden, soweit der andere Elternteil dem nicht widerspricht.

INTERNATIONAL INSTRUMENTS

The situation covered by this Principle may well be included within the general scope of various international instruments, e.g., the *Hague Child Protection Convention 1996*, but without being expressly addressed by any of them.

COMPARATIVE OVERVIEW

Parent's partner enjoys wide parental responsibilities

The right of the parent's partner to be attributed with and/or to exercise parental responsibilities is described above under the COMPARATIVE OVERVIEWS under Principles 3:9 and 3:17. In these situations, the scope of the parental responsibilities is wide and may, more or less, correspond to those enjoyed by the child's parent.

Parent's partner may participate in decisions regarding daily matters

There exists yet another kind of system with much more limited implications. In GERMANY,[808] the parent's spouse or registered partner is, directly by force of law, entitled to participate in decision-making on matters relating to the child's everyday life, the so-called "kleines Sorgerecht". This right to exercise limited parental responsibilities exists on condition that the parent in question enjoys sole parental responsibilities and it ends upon the termination of the marriage or the registered partnership. In situations where the parent lives in a non-formalised relationship, the

808 § 1687 b paras. 1–3 German Civil Code and § 9 German Registered Partnership Act.

parent may authorize his or her partner to exercise certain parental responsibilities. This authorization ends upon the termination of the relationship. In the CZECH REPUBLIC[809] and SWITZERLAND,[810] a person married to the child's parent is entrusted with the exercise of certain limited parental responsibilities. The step-parent automatically loses his or her rights to exercise parental responsibilities upon the ending of the relationship. The German "kleines Sorgerecht" and the step-parent's duty under CZECH and SWISS laws to assist the parent in his or her exercise of parental responsibilities are limited in scope and dependent on an existing relationship between the parent and his or her partner. The national reports (e.g. HUNGARY[811]) indicate that *in practice* in most of the countries step-parents living with the child and his or her parent participate in decision-making on daily matters concerning the child with the consent of the parent.

COMMENT

1. Principle 3:18 concerns situations falling outside the scope of Principle 3:9 and Principle 3:17. It is limited to the right of the "parent's partner" to take part in decisions regarding ordinary issues in the child's everyday life, such as deciding on the child's bedtime or how much time the child may spend watching television or playing computer games. A similar right is recognized by law in GERMANY and SWITZERLAND, and in practice it seems to apply in the majority of the countries surveyed. Principle 3:18 thus reflects a common core.

2. The mandate of the parent's partner is dependent on the "other parent's" express or tacit consent, but Principle 3:18 also requires that the other parent has not been discharged of his or her parental responsibilities. If the other parent holds parental responsibilities and objects, Principle 3:18 does not apply. This corresponds with the prevailing national law or practice in the countries surveyed. The "other parent" refers to the parent with whom the partner does not have a formal or informal relationship. Although it is not expressly stated, also the parent with whom the partner lives in a formal or informal relationship must consent.

3. By the "parent's partner" is meant his or her spouse, registered partner or partner in an informal relationship. Normally such a person is called the child's step-parent For Principle 3:18 to apply, the parent's partner must live together with the child,

---

809 § 33 Czech Family Code. See HRUSAKOVÁ, Czech Report, Q 27.

810 Art. 299, 90 § 2, 260 § 2, 265a § 1 Swiss Civil Code. See HAUSHEER/ACHERMANN-WEBER/WOLF, Swiss Report, Q 27.

811 See WEISS/SZEIBERT, Hungarian Report, Q 27.

permanently or on an alternate basis. When the parent and the parent's partner separate permanently, the Principle ceases to apply.

CHAPTER V: CONTENT OF PARENTAL RESPONSIBILITIES
CHAPITRE V: CONTENU DE LA RESPONSABILITÉ PARENTALE
KAPITEL V: INHALT DER ELTERLICHEN VERANTWORTUNG

SECTION A: THE CHILD'S PERSON AND PROPERTY
SECTION A: PERSONNE ET BIENS DE L'ENFANT
ABSCHNITT A: PERSON UND VERMÖGEN DES KINDES

Principle 3:19 Care, protection and education

(1) The holders of parental responsibilities should provide the child with care, protection and education in accordance with the child's distinctive character and developmental needs.

(2) The child should not be subjected to corporal punishment or any other humiliating treatment.

Principe 3:19 Soins, protection et éducation

(1) Les titulaires de la responsabilité parentale assurent à l'enfant soins, protection et éducation conformément à la personnalité de l'enfant et aux besoins de son développement.

(2) L'enfant ne doit pas subir de châtiments corporels ou tout autre traitement humiliant.

Prinzip 3:19 Sorge, Schutz und Erziehung

(1) Die Inhaber der elterlichen Verantwortung haben für die Sorge, den Schutz und die Erziehung des Kindes gemäß seiner Persönlichkeit und den Bedürfnissen seiner Entwicklung zu sorgen.

(2) Das Kind darf keiner körperlichen Bestrafung oder anderer entwürdigenden Behandlung ausgesetzt werden.

INTERNATIONAL INSTRUMENTS

Care and protection

In Article 18 para. 1 of the *Convention on the Rights of the Child 1989* it is submitted that both parents have common responsibilities for the upbringing and development of the child. Parents or, as the case may be, legal guardians, have primary responsibility for the upbringing and development of the child, whereby the best interests of the child should be their basic concern. In addition, the Council of Europe's *Recommendation on Abuse and Neglect 1998* considers that children must be afforded legal and social protection against paedophilia, exploitation for pornography, prostitution, incest, inappropriate criminal proceedings, repetition of offences of sexual violence against minors, abusive sterilisation, violations and mutilations of girls, abuse, including abuse within the family, refusal of necessary care and fraudulent actions with a view to adoption.

Education

In Article 28 of the *Convention on the Rights of the Child 1989* it is agreed to that the States Parties recognize the right of the child to receive education. According to Article 29 this education shall be directed towards, *inter alia*, the development of the child's personality, talents and mental and physical abilities to their fullest potential. The right to determine the child's religious education is guaranteed by Article 14 paras. 1 and 2 of the same Convention which provides that the States Parties shall respect the right of the child to freedom of thought, conscience and religion and that they shall respect the rights and duties of the parents or legal guardians to provide direction to the child in the exercise of his or her right in a manner which is consistent with the evolving capacities of the child.

Corporal punishment

Article 19 para. 1 of the *Convention on the Rights of the Child 1989* provides that the States Parties shall take all appropriate legislative, administrative, social and educational measures to protect the child from all forms of physical or mental violence, injury or abuse, neglect or negligent treatment, maltreatment or exploitation, including sexual abuse, while in the care of parent(s), legal guardian(s) or any other person who has the care of the child. The Council of Europe has addressed the protection of children against ill-treatment and violence in its *Recommendation Concerning the Protection of Children Against Ill-Treatment 1979*. States are recommended to take all necessary measures to ensure the safety of abused children by: promoting a better awareness of the problem, improving the organisation of the child welfare and protection systems, taking into account certain principles and suggestions (relating to prevention, detention, management, training of personnel), facilitating a multidisciplinary approach and by promoting research and reviewing child protection legislation.

COMPARATIVE OVERVIEW

Care and protection

In all jurisdictions it is generally acknowledged that the concept of care is the most important part of parental responsibilities. It includes the protection of the child's mental and physical health, security and morality. The duty to take care of the child must be exercised on the basis of the child's interests and needs which includes the development of its personality.[812] In some jurisdictions certain aspects of parental responsibilities such as care and protection, the maintenance of personal relationships or the provision of education are explicitly regulated in the national constitution (BULGARIA,[813] GERMANY,[814] ITALY,[815] RUSSIA,[816] SPAIN[817] and PORTUGAL[818]).

Education

With regard to education, a distinction is to be made between rules concerning the child's compulsory education and its right to be educated. Only in ITALY,[819]IRELAND[820], GERMANY,[821] RUSSIA[822] and SPAIN[823] the national Constitutions impose the parental obligation to educate the children. In many jurisdictions education is part and parcel of the right and duty to care for the child and is therefore not explicitly defined by the

812 See all the national reports, BOELE-WOELKI/BRAAT/CURRY-SUMNER, *ibid.*, note 23, Q 7 and Q 8a.
813 See TODOROVA, Bulgarian Report, Q 2.
814 See DETHLOFF/MARTINY, German Report, Q 2.
815 See PATTI/BELLISARIO/ROSSI CARLEO, Italian Report, Q 2.
816 See ANTOKOLSKAIA, Russian Report, Q 2.
817 SEE GONZÁLEZ BEILFUSS, SPANISH REPORT, Q 2.
818 Art. 67 No. 2 Portuguese Constitution.
819 Art. 30 para.1 Italian Constitution and Art. 147 Italian Civil Code.
820 Art. 42 Irish Constitution.
821 Art. 6 para. 2 German Constitution.
822 Art. 28 para. 2 Russian Constitution.
823 Art. 27 Spanish Constitution.

legislator (CZECH REPUBLIC,[824] FINLAND,[825] GERMANY,[826] GREECE,[827] HUNGARY[828] and THE NETHERLANDS[829]), whereas a comprehensive legal definition of the duty to educate children is provided in the AUSTRIAN Civil Code. Article 146 para. 2 states that "education includes the development of the child's physical, mental, psychological and moral strengths, the fostering of its aptitudes, abilities, inclinations and developmental capabilities and its education in school and in an occupation." Similar, but less detailed definitions are used by the legislators, courts and legal literature in the other jurisdictions. Education not only depends on the child's particular capacities, talents and natural inclinations (explicitly mentioned in the reports of GREECE,[830] ITALY,[831] POLAND,[832] PORTUGAL,[833] NORWAY,[834] SWEDEN[835] and SWITZERLAND[836]), but its extent is also based on the parents' living conditions and means (AUSTRIA,[837] IRELAND,[838] and PORTUGAL[839]). In all jurisdictions the holders of parental responsibilities have the right to choose a state or private school. In BELGIUM,[840] BULGARIA,[841] FRANCE,[842] GERMANY,[843] IRELAND,[844] ITALY,[845] LITHUANIA,[846] THE NETHERLANDS,[847] and SPAIN[848] children must attend school, while in DENMARK[849] and ENGLAND AND WALES[850] under certain circumstances children can also be educated at home. In the NORWEGIAN Children Act it is expressly stated that a child of 15 years or older may take all decisions concerning his or her education without the consent of his or her parents.[851] The

[824] See HRUSAKOVÁ, Czech Report, Q 8b.
[825] See KURKI-SUONIO, Finnish Report, Q 8b.
[826] § 1631 para. 1 German Civil Code.
[827] Art. 1510 para. 1 and 1603 Greek Civil Code.
[828] See WEISS/SZEIBERT, Hungarian Report, Q 2c.
[829] Art. 1:247 para. 2 Dutch Civil Code.
[830] Art. 1518 para. 2 Greek Civil Code.
[831] See PATTI/BELLISARIO/ROSSI CARLEO, Italian Report, Q 8b.
[832] Art. 96.2 Polish Family and Guardianship Code.
[833] Art. 1885 No. 2 Portuguese Civil Code.
[834] § 30 PARA. 2 NORWEGIAN CHILDREN ACT 1981.
[835] Ch. 6 § 2 para. 2 Swedish Childrens and Parents Code.
[836] Art. 302 para. 3 Swiss Civil Code.
[837] See ROTH, Austrian Report, Q 8b.
[838] See SHANNON, Irish Report, Q 8b.
[839] Art. 1885 No. 1 Portuguese Civil Code.
[840] See PINTENS/PIGNOLET, Belgian Report, Q 8b.
[841] See TODOROVA, Bulgarian Report, Q 8b.
[842] See FERRAND, French Report, Q 8b.
[843] See DETHLOFF/MARTINY, German Report, Q 8b.
[844] See SHANNON, Irish Report, Q 8b.
[845] See PATTI/BELLISARIO/ROSSI CARLEO, Italian Report, Q 8b.
[846] See MIKELENAS, Lithuanian Report, Q 8b.
[847] See BOELE-WOELKI/SCHRAMA/VONK, Dutch Report, Q 8b.
[848] See GONZÁLEZ BEILFUSS, Spanish Report, Q 8b.
[849] See LUND-ANDERSEN/JEPPESEN-DE BOER, Danish Report, Q 8b.
[850] See LOWE, English Report, Q 8b.
[851] § 32 Norwegian Children Act 1981.

obligation to take the opinion of the child into account is already required from the age of 12 years in HUNGARY[852] and 14 years in BULGARIA,[853] whereas this depends on the child's maturity in GREECE,[854] ITALY[855] and RUSSIA.[856] In BULGARIA,[857] DENMARK,[858] LITHUANIA[859] and THE NETHERLANDS[860] the right and duty to educate lasts until the child has reached the age of 16 years, in BELGIUM[861] and FRANCE[862] the child must have reached majority. Appropriate schooling is a matter of agreement between the parents. In the case of disputes, however, an order by the competent authority can be requested in BELGIUM[863] and ENGLAND AND WALES.[864]

Religious upbringing

The comparative overview shows that in all jurisdictions surveyed the religious upbringing of the child is considered to be a right of the holders of parental responsibilities. According to the national constitutions of three jurisdictions (LITHUANIA,[865] NORWAY[866] and POLAND[867]) the holders of parental responsibilities shall without restrictions ensure the religious education of their children in conformity with their own convictions. In five countries (AUSTRIA,[868] BULGARIA,[869] CZECH REPUBLIC,[870] FINLAND[871] and RUSSIA[872]) this freedom is regulated in separate legislation concerning the general position of religion and convictions. The decision whether to give the child a religious education is considered to be part of the rights and duties of the parents

852 See WEISS/SZEIBERT, Hungarian Report, Q 8b.
853 See TODOROVA, Bulgarian Report, Q 8b.
854 See KOUTSOURADIS/ZERVOGIANNI, Greek Report, Q 8b.
855 See PATTI/BELLISARIO/ROSSI CARLEO, Italian Report, Q 8b.
856 See ANTOKOLSKAIA, Russian Report, Q 8b.
857 See TODOROVA, Bulgarian Report, Q 8b.
858 See LUND-ANDERSEN/JEPPESEN-DE BOER, Danish Report, Q 8b.
859 See MIKELENAS, Lithuanian Report, Q 8b.
860 See BOELE-WOELKI/SCHRAMA/VONK, Dutch Report, Q 8b.
861 See PINTENS/PIGNOLET, Belgian Report, Q 8b.
862 See FERRAND, French Report, Q 8b.
863 See PINTENS/PIGNOLET, Belgian Report, Q 8b.
864 See LOWE, English Report, Q 8b.
865 Part 5 of Art. 26 of the Lithuanian Constitution.
866 The duty is however restricted to the inhabitants professing to the State Religion. Art. 2 para. 2 Norwegian Constitution states: The Evangelical-Lutheran religion shall remain the official religion of the State. The inhabitants professing it are bound to bring up their children in the same.
867 Art. 53 para. 3 Polish Constitution.
868 Federal Act on the Religious Education of Children of 1985.
869 Art. 6 para. 2 Bulgarian Law of Religious Beliefs 2002.
870 Act No. 3/2002 Coll. on Freedom of Religious Belief and Legal Status of Churches and Religious Communities.
871 Finnish Religious Freedom Act 2003.
872 Art. 5 para. 5 Federal Law on the Freedom of Conscience and Religious Organisations.

in general (DENMARK,[873] ENGLAND AND WALES,[874] FRANCE,[875] THE NETHERLANDS,[876] and SWEDEN[877]), their right to care for the child (BELGIUM,[878] GERMANY[879] and GREECE[880]) and/or their right to educate the child (AUSTRIA,[881] ITALY,[882] PORTUGAL,[883] RUSSIA[884] and SPAIN[885]). It is generally agreed that the child may not be torn between its parents' convictions if a different religion is imposed by one parent after the parents separate. In the case of disagreement between the parents the competent authority has to decide (AUSTRIA,[886] BELGIUM,[887] BULGARIA,[888] CZECH REPUBLIC,[889] FRANCE,[890] GERMANY,[891] IRELAND[892] and RUSSIA[893]). In contrast, parents cannot apply for a decision from the competent authority in HUNGARY[894] because the HUNGARIAN constitution does not allow state intervention in the exercise of religious upbringing. It has been reported by IRELAND[895] that the courts have often refused to award custody to a parent who was in a relationship with a person who had a different religious persuasion to that of the child. This court practice illustrates the tension between the constitutional preference for promoting the concept of being able to freely practise one's religion and the constitutional rule against discrimination on the basis of religious profession, status and belief. In eleven jurisdictions it is regulated by statute or has been decided by the courts that parents are to consider the child's wishes depending either on its age (10 years in RUSSIA,[896] 12 years in SWEDEN[897] and FINLAND,[898] 14 years in BULGARIA,[899] 15 years

873 See LUND-ANDERSEN/JEPPESEN-DE BOER, Danish Report, Q 8c.
874 See LOWE, English Report, Q 8c.
875 See FERRAND, French Report, Q 8c.
876 See BOELE-WOELKI/SCHRAMA/VONK, Dutch Report, Q 8c.
877 See JÄNTERÄ-JAREBORG/SINGER/SÖRGJERD, Swedish Report, Q 8c.
878 Art. 203 Belgian Civil Code.
879 See DETHLOFF/MARTINY, German Report, Q 8c.
880 See KOUTSOURADIS/ZERVOGIANNI, Greek Report, Q 8c.
881 See ROTH, Austrian Report, Q 8c.
882 See PATTI/BELLISARIO/ROSSI CARLEO, Italian Report, Q 8b and c.
883 See DE OLIVEIRA, Portuguese Report, Q 8b and c.
884 See ANTOKOLSKAIA, Russian Report, Q 8c.
885 See GONZÁLEZ BEILFUSS, Spanish Report, Q 8c.
886 See ROTH, Austrian Report, Q 8c.
887 See PINTENS/PIGNOLET, Belgian Report, Q 8c.
888 Art. 14 para. 2 Bulgarian Child Protection Act 2000.
889 See HRUSAKOVÁ, Czech Report, Q 8c.
890 See FERRAND, French Report, Q 8c.
891 See DETHLOFF/MARTINY, German Report, Q 8c.
892 See SHANNON, Irish Report, Q 8c.
893 Art. 65 para. 2 Russian Family Code.
894 See WEISS/SZEIBERT, Hungarian Report, Q 8c.
895 See SHANNON, Irish Report, Q 8c.
896 Art. 57 Russian Family Code.
897 Swedish Act (1998:1593) on Religious Communities.
898 § 3 Finnish Religious Freedom Act.
899 Art. 14 Bulgarian Law of Religious Beliefs.

in the CZECH REPUBLIC,[900] DENMARK[901] and NORWAY,[902] 16 years in PORTUGAL[903] and SWITZERLAND[904]) or its level of maturity (BELGIUM,[905] GREECE,[906] ITALY[907] and SPAIN[908]). Regardless of the different age limits, it is generally acknowledged that the child at a certain point acquires the freedom to take decisions of its own volition as regards religion.

Medical treatment

Decisions concerning the medical treatment of a child belong to the overall duty to take care for the child. The comparative overview shows, however, that the consent of the holders of parental responsibilities is not always decisive. This depends on the age or maturity of the child. In addition to the parents' consent the minor's consent is required if it has reached the age of 12 years (THE NETHERLANDS[909] and SPAIN[910]), 14 years (AUSTRIA[911]) or if it has reached "medical majority" (BELGIUM,[912] CZECH REPUBLIC,[913] FINLAND,[914] and GREECE[915]). Eleven jurisdictions have attributed exclusive rights to adolescents regarding their medical treatment. In these systems consent by the parents is no longer required if the child has reached the age of 15 years (DENMARK[916] and RUSSIA[917]), the age of 16 years (ENGLAND AND WALES,[918] IRELAND,[919] LITHUANIA,[920] NORWAY[921] and SPAIN[922]) or if he or she is sufficiently capable of

900 Czech Act No. 3/2002 Coll. on Freedom of Religious Belief and Legal Status of Churches and Religious Communities.
901 Art. 8 of Act No. 57 24.01.1992.
902 Art. 3 Norwegian Act on the Church of Norway 1996.
903 Art. 1886 Portuguese Civil Code.
904 Art. 303 para. 1 and 3 Swiss Civil Code.
905 See PINTENS/PIGNOLET, Belgian Report, Q 8c.
906 See KOUTSOURADIS/ZERVOGIANNI, Greek Report, Q 8c, note 80.
907 See PATTI/BELLISARIO/ROSSI CARLEO, Italian Report, Q 8c.
908 See GONZÁLEZ BEILFUSS, Spanish Report, Q 8c.
909 Art. 7:450 Dutch Civil Code.
910 See GONZÁLEZ BEILFUSS, Spanish Report, Q 8e.
911 § 146c para. 1 and 2 Austrian Civil Code.
912 Belgian Law of 22 August 20002 concerning the Rights of Patients.
913 See HRUSAKOVÁ, Czech Report, Q 8e.
914 § 7 Finnish Patient Act 785/1992.
915 See KOUTSOURADIS/ZERVOGIANNI, Greek Report, Q 8e.
916 § 8 para. 1 Danish Act on the Legal Position of Patients. A child under 18 needs the consent of the holders of parental responsibilities to obtain an abortion.
917 Art. 24 para. 5 Russian Federal Law on Health Protection.
918 See LOWE, English Report, Q 8e.
919 Sec. 23 Irish Non-Fatal Offences Against the Person Act 1997.
920 Art. 6.726 Lithuanian Civil Code.
921 Art. 4 sec. 3 Norwegian Act on Patient Rights 1999.
922 See GONZÁLEZ BEILFUSS, Spanish Report, Q 8e.

understanding the nature and the consequences of the treatment (ITALY,[923] SWEDEN[924] and SWITZERLAND[925]). The right to consent to medical treatment is not unlimited, however. Neither the child nor the child's parents can consent to a procedure that would render the child permanently incapable of reproduction (AUSTRIA,[926] ENGLAND AND WALES,[927] FRANCE,[928] and GERMANY[929]) and in BELGIUM[930] minor patients are excluded from the right to request euthanasia. Only in THE NETHERLANDS[931] may a patient who is between 16 and 18 years of age and who is capable of a reasonable evaluation of his/her interest, request euthanasia or suicide assistance. If the life of the child is in danger and medical treatment must be provided immediately, neither the consent of the parent(s) nor of the child is necessary (AUSTRIA,[932] BULGARIA,[933] CZECH REPUBLIC,[934] ENGLAND AND WALES,[935] FINLAND,[936] FRANCE[937] and SPAIN[938]).

Finally, if the parents refuse to give consent,[939] the case may be brought before the competent authorities in BULGARIA,[940] ENGLAND AND WALES,[941] FINLAND,[942] GERMANY,[943]

---

923 Art. 12 Law of 22 May 1978, No. 194, (abortion, use of contraceptives), Art. 120 of the Consolidated Text on the Drugs Law and Art. 5 para. 4 of Law 135/1990 (the outcome of a HIV test may be exclusively communicated to the minor if she or he has requested such a test).

924 See JÄNTERÄ-JAREBORG/SINGER/SÖRGJERD, Swedish Report, Q 8e.

925 Art. 19 para. 2 Swiss Civil Code.

926 § 146d Austrian Civil Code.

927 See LOWE, English Report, Q 8e, only with leave of a High Court judge.

928 Art. L. 2123–1 and L. 2123–2 French Code of Public Health. See FERRAND, French Report, Q 8e with regard to the removal of a minor child's organs and biomedical research.

929 § 1631c German Civil Code.

930 Art. 3 para. 1 Belgian Law of 28 May 2002 Concerning Euthanasia.

931 Dutch Act Concerning Assessment of Termination of Life upon Request and Suicide Assistance 2001.

932 § 146c para. 3 Austrian Civil Code.

933 Art. 89 Bulgarian Law on Health.

934 § 23 para. 3 Czech Act No. 20/1966 Coll. on Care of People's Health.

935 See LOWE, English Report, Q 8e.

936 § 9 Finnish Patient Act 785/1992.

937 See FERRAND, French Report, Q 8e.

938 See GONZÁLEZ BEILFUSS, Spanish Report, Q 8e.

939 E.g. Jehova's Witnesses refuse a necessary blood transfusion.

940 See TODOROVA, Bulgarian Report, Q 8e.

941 See LOWE, English Report, Q 8e.

942 See KURKI-SUONIO, Finnish Report, Q 8e.

943 § 1666 German Civil Code.

GREECE,[944] IRELAND,[945] ITALY,[946] THE NETHERLANDS,[947] RUSSIA,[948] SPAIN[949] and SWITZERLAND.[950]

Disciplinary measures and corporal punishment

Caring for a child and ensuring its education implies that the child must follow its parents' directions. It is generally accepted that in enforcing such directions, parents must initially seek to influence the child's will through positive means. If this has failed, are disciplinary measures or even corporal punishment allowed in order to overcome the child's disobeyance? The answers to this question differ to a considerable extent.[951] It has been explicitly reported that disciplinary measures are allowed in CZECH REPUBLIC,[952] LITHUANIA,[953] PORTUGAL,[954] RUSSIA[955] and SWITZERLAND.[956] If, however, such disciplinary measures, are harmful and undermine the child's dignity they are prohibited in BULGARIA[957] and HUNGARY.[958] In two jurisdictions parental chastisement is still allowed and can be used as a defence to both criminal prosecution and a civil claim (IRELAND[959] and SPAIN[960]). In contrast, in twelve countries the use of corporal punishment, mental injury and other degrading measures is prohibited (AUSTRIA,[961] DENMARK,[962] FINLAND,[963] GERMANY,[964] GREECE,[965] NORWAY,[966] ITALY,[967] LITHUANIA,[968]

944 Art. 1534 Greek Civil Code.
945 See SHANNON, Irish Report, Q 8e.
946 See PATTI/BELLISARIO/ROSSI CARLEO, Italian Report, Q 8e.
947 Art. 1:264 Dutch Civil Code.
948 Art. 33 Russian Law on Health Protection.
949 See GONZÁLEZ BEILFUSS, Spanish Report, Q 8e.
950 Art. 307 ff. Swiss Civil Code.
951 See for a country-by-country overview of the legality of corporal punishment worldwide: www.endcorporalpunishment.org.
952 § 31 para. 2 Czech Family Code.
953 See MIKELENAS, Lithuanian Report, Q 8d.
954 See DE OLIVEIRA, Portuguese Report, Q 8d.
955 See ANTOKOLSKAIA, Russian Report, Q 8d.
956 See HAUSHEER/ACHERMANN-WEBER/WOLF, Swiss Report, Q 8d.
957 Art. 11 para. 2 Bulgarian Child Protection Act.
958 Hungarian Child Welfare Act.
959 Irish Non-Fatal Offences Against the Person Act 1997.
960 Art. 617.2 and 620 Spanish Criminal Code.
961 § 146a Austrian Civil Code.
962 § 2 para. 2 Danish Act on Parental Authority and Contact.
963 § 1 para. 3 Finnish Child Custody Act.
964 § 1631 German Civil Code.
965 Art. 1518 para. 2 and 1606 Greek Civil Code.
966 § 30 para. 3 Norwegian Children Act 1981.
967 See PATTI/BELLISARIO/ROSSI CARLEO, Italian Report, Q 8d.
968 Art. 49 of the Law on the Protection of the Rights of the Child of 14 March 1996.

PORTUGAL,[969] RUSSIA,[970] SWEDEN[971] and SWITZERLAND[972]). A third approach is applied in BELGIUM,[973] ENGLAND AND WALES[974] and FRANCE[975] where persons with parental responsibilities may lawfully chastise and inflict *reasonable* corporal punishment upon the child. What is reasonable is a question of fact and will depend upon the age and strength of the child and the nature and degree of punishment. Finally, it should be mentioned that legislation to ban physical and psychological violence towards children is envisaged in BELGIUM[976] and THE NETHERLANDS.[977] In the case of physical or mental mistreatment of the child by its parent(s) the competent authority will discharge the holders of his, her or their parental responsibilities. This consequence has been reported in the CZECH REPUBLIC,[978] RUSSIA[979] and SWEDEN.[980]

COMMENT

1. In all matters concerning the child's person his or her right to self-determination is applicable. Pursuant to Principle 3:4 the holders of parental responsibilities should promote the child's autonomy and respect the child's decision in personal matters.

2. According to Article 28 *Convention on the Rights of the Child 1989* the child has a right to education. This right can be invoked against both the State and the holders of parental responsibilities. The provision of education is considered to be an essential part of their rights and duties. The holders of parental responsibilities have common responsibilities concerning the upbringing and development of the child. This is expressed in Article 18 para. 1 of the *Convention on the Rights of the Child 1989.*

3. The religious upbringing of the child is considered to be a right of the holders of parental responsibilities. This right is either an element of "care and protection" or the "provision of education". For that reason it has not specifically been mentioned in Principle 3:19 (1). The right of the holders of parental responsibilities to determine the child's religious education is guaranteed by Article 14 paras. 1 and 2 of the

---

969 Art. 152 Portuguese Criminal Code.
970 Art. 65 para. 1 Russian Family Code.
971 Ch. 6 § 1 Swedish Children and Parents Code.
972 Art. 9 para. 1 and Art. 10 paras. 2 and 3 Federal Constitution.
973 See PINTENS/PIGNOLET, Belgian Report, Q 8d.
974 See LOWE, English Report, Q 8d.
975 See FERRAND, French Report, Q 8d.
976 See PINTENS/PIGNOLET, Belgian Report, Q 8d.
977 See BOELE-WOELKI/SCHRAMA/VONK, Dutch Report, Q 8d.
978 § 44 para. 4 Czech Family Code.
979 Art. 69 and 73 Russian Family Code.
980 Ch. 6 § 7 Swedish Children and Parents Code.

Convention on the Rights of the Child 1989. In all circumstances the holders of parental responsibilities are to consider the child's wishes depending on its age or discernment. The holders of parental responsibilities should jointly take decisions regarding the child's religious upbringing, see Principle 3:12 (daily matters, important and urgent decisions). Having regard to the child's age and maturity it acquires the freedom to take decisions of its own volition as regards religion.

4. Medical treatment for the child is part and parcel of the right and duty to care for the child. There is a degree of tension between, on the one hand, the right and duty of the holders of parental responsibilities to take all necessary steps concerning medical treatment in order to safeguard the physical and mental well-being of the child and, on the other, his or her right to self-determination. This tension requires a careful approach. The rights of the child as expressed in Chapter II must be taken into account prior to the child's medical treatment. If, in particular, the adolescent is sufficiently mature his or her consent should be required. However, whether or not, in addition to the minor's consent, the holders of parental responsibilities should consent or whether the minor can decide alone, should be left to national law. This also applies to abortion, sterilisation and euthanasia.

5. The corporal punishment of children by the holders of parental responsibilities should be prohibited. Included under this prohibition (Principles 3:19 (2)) is any treatment that is unreasonable and detrimental to the welfare of the child. It excludes not only inflicting physical pain but also any treatment that violates human dignity. Such a prohibition is consistent with Article 19 para. 1 of the *Convention on the Rights of the Child 1989*.

Principle 3:20 Residence

(1) If parental responsibilities are exercised jointly the holders of parental responsibilities who are living apart should agree upon with whom the child resides.

(2) The child may reside on an alternate basis with the holders of parental responsibilities upon either an agreement approved by a competent authority or a decision by a competent authority. The competent authority should take into consideration factors such as:

(a) the age and opinion of the child;

(b) the ability and willingness of the holders of parental responsibilities to cooperate with each other in matters concerning the child; as well as their personal situation;

(c) the distance between the residences of the holders of the parental responsibilities and to the child's school.

Principe 3:20 Résidence

(1) Si la responsabilité parentale est exercée en commun, ses titulaires, s'ils vivent séparés, doivent s'entendre pour déterminer avec lequel d'entre eux l'enfant résidera.

(2) L'enfant peut résider alternativement chez les titulaires de la responsabilité parentale en vertu ou bien d'un accord entre les titulaires approuvé par l'autorité compétente, ou bien d'une décision de l'autorité compétente. L'autorité compétente prend notamment en considération:

(a) l'âge et l'avis de l'enfant;

(b) la capacité et la volonté des titulaires de la responsabilité parentale de coopérer sur toutes questions concernant l'enfant ainsi que leur situation personnelle;

(c) la distance entre les résidences des titulaires de la responsabilité parentale ainsi que la distance avec l'école fréquentée par l'enfant.

Prinzip 3:20 Aufenthalt des Kindes

(1) Wird die elterliche Verantwortung von Personen gemeinsam ausgeübt, die getrennt leben, so haben sie sich zu einigen, bei wem das Kind seinen Aufenthalt hat.

(2) Das Kind kann sich abwechselnd bei den Inhabern der elterlichen Verantwortung aufhalten aufgrund einer von der zuständigen Behörde genehmigten Vereinbarung oder aufgrund einer Entscheidung der zuständigen Behörde. Die zuständige Behörde berücksichtigt Umstände wie:

(a) das Alter und die Auffassung des Kindes;

(b) die Fähigkeit und Bereitschaft der Inhaber der elterlichen Verantwortung, in den das Kind betreffenden Angelegenheiten zu kooperieren, sowie ihre persönliche Situation;

(c) die Entfernung zwischen den Aufenthaltsorten der Inhaber der elterlichen

INTERNATIONAL INSTRUMENTS

The habitual residence of the child is the most important connecting factor in private international law instruments concerning children's law. The concept of habitual residence is the key to the operation of all aspects of these Conventions and European regulations and yet it is not a term that is defined in these instruments themselves. The variety of different circumstances which can combine in a particular case makes it impossible to arrive at a more precise definition in legal terms. Therefore the habitual residence of a child has to be determined by the courts in each case on the basis of factual elements. Article 5 of the *Hague Child Abduction Convention 1980* determines that, for the purpose of the convention, "rights of custody" shall include rights relating to the physical care of the child and, in particular, the right to determine the child's place of residence. Regarding the latter, Article 3(b) of the *Hague Child Protection Convention 1996* reproduces the same formulation. Both conventions and the *Brussels II bis Regulation* establish that the most appropriate forum for matters of parental responsibilities is the court of the Member State of the child's habitual residence.

COMPARATIVE OVERVIEW

Determination of residence

If parental responsibilities are held by parents jointly and those parents live together, the child's legal residence is in virtually all systems the parents' domicile (BELGIUM,[981] BULGARIA,[982] FRANCE,[983] ITALY,[984] LITHUANIA,[985] POLAND,[986] SPAIN[987] and SWITZERLAND[988]). This does not exclude the fact that children can live elsewhere when there are justified reasons (BELGIUM,[989] BULGARIA[990] and SPAIN[991]). When the parents do not live together they have to decide jointly on the domicile of the child (BELGIUM,[992] BULGARIA,[993]

981 Art. 108 Belgian Civil Code. See PINTENS/PIGNOLET, Belgian Report, Q 2e.
982 Art. 71 Bulgarian Family Code. See TODOROVA, Bulgarian Report, Q 2e.
983 Art. 108–2 French Civil Code. See FERRAND, French Report, Q 2e.
984 See PATTI/BELLISARIO/ROSSI CARLEO, Italian Report, Q 2e.
985 Art. 3168 Lituanian Civil Code. See MIKELENAS, Lithuanian Report, Q 2e.
986 Art. 26 § 1 Polish Civil Code. See MĄCZYŃSKI/MĄCZYŃSKA, Polish Report, Q 2e.
987 Art. 154 Spanish Civil Code and 143 Catalan Family Code. See GONZÁLEZ BEILFUSS, Spanish Report, Q 2e.
988 See JÄNTERÄ-JAREBORG/SINGER/SÖRGJERD, Swedish Report, Q 2e.
989 See PINTENS/PIGNOLET, Belgian Report, Q 2e.
990 See TODOROVA, Bulgarian Report, Q 2e.
991 See GONZÁLEZ BEILFUSS, Spanish Report, Q 2e.
992 See PINTENS/PIGNOLET, Belgian Report, Q 2e.
993 See TODOROVA, Bulgarian Report, Q 2e.

FINLAND,[994] LITHUANIA,[995] THE NETHERLANDS,[996] RUSSIA[997] and SWEDEN[998]). Any disputes are resolved by the competent authorities (BELGIUM,[999] BULGARIA,[1000] LITHUANIA,[1001] THE NETHERLANDS[1002] and SWEDEN[1003]).

Alternating residence

An alternating residence is not possible in some systems (BULGARIA,[1004] DENMARK,[1005] HUNGARY[1006]). In other systems this is theoretically possible, but rarely occurs in practice (GERMANY,[1007] ITALY,[1008] THE NETHERLANDS,[1009] PORTUGAL,[1010] RUSSIA,[1011] SPAIN[1012] and SWITZERLAND[1013]). In some jurisdictions, however, it has been introduced or reinforced in recent legislation (CZECH REPUBLIC,[1014] FRANCE[1015] and SWEDEN[1016]) or in the case law (ENGLAND AND WALES[1017]).

Alternating residence subject to an agreement

Parents can agree that children should, on an alternating basis, reside with both holders of parental responsibilities according to all systems which allow an alternate or shared

994 See KURKI-SUONIO, Finnish Report, Q 2e.
995 Art. 3169 Lithuanian Civil Code. See MIKELENAS, Lithuanian Report, Q 2e.
996 See BOELE-WOELKI/SCHRAMA/VONK, Dutch Report, Q 2e.
997 Art. 65 para. 3 Russian Family Code. See ANTOKOLSKAIA, Russian Report, Q 2e.
998 See JÄNTERÄ-JAREBORG/SINGER/SÖRGJERD, Swedish Report, Q 2e.
999 See PINTENS/PIGNOLET, Belgian Report, Q 2e.
1000 See TODOROVA, Bulgarian Report, Q 2e.
1001 See MIKELENAS, Lithuanian Report, Q 2e.
1002 Art. 1:253 A Dutch Civil Code. See BOELE-WOELKI/SCHRAMA/VONK, Dutch Report, Q 2e.
1003 See JÄNTERÄ-JAREBORG/SINGER/SÖRGJERD, Swedish Report, Q 2e.
1004 See TODOROVA, Bulgarian Report, Q 41.
1005 See LUND-ANDERSEN/JEPPESEN-DE BOER, Danish Report, Q 41.
1006 See WEISS/SZEIBERT, Hungarian Report, Q 41.
1007 Amtsgericht Hannover 13.10. 2000, *FamRZ* 2001, 846. See DETHLOFF/MARTINY, German Report, Q 41.
1008 See PATTI/BELLISARIO/ROSSI CARLEO, Italian Report, Q 41.
1009 See BOELE-WOELKI/SCHRAMA/VONK, Dutch Report, Q 41.
1010 See DE OLIVEIRA, Portuguese Report, Q 41.
1011 See ANTOKOLSKAIA, Russian Report, Q 41.
1012 See GONZÁLEZ BEILFUSS, Spanish Report, Q 41.
1013 See HAUSHEER/ACHERMANN-WEBER/WOLF, Swiss Report, Q 41.
1014 Czech Law Reform 1998. See HRUSAKOVÁ, Czech Report, Q 41.
1015 Art. 373–2–9 French Civil Code (New Text of 4 March 2002). See FERRAND, French Report, Q 41.
1016 See JÄNTERÄ-JAREBORG/SINGER/SÖRGJERD, Swedish Report, Q 41.
1017 *D v D* (Shared Residence Order) [2001] 1 *Law Reports Family Division High Court* 495, Ca. See LOWE, English Report, Q 41.

residence (BELGIUM,[1018] CZECH REPUBLIC,[1019] FRANCE,[1020] GERMANY,[1021] GREECE,[1022] NORWAY,[1023] PORTUGAL,[1024] SPAIN,[1025] SWEDEN[1026] and SWITZERLAND[1027]). This agreement will be allowed by the competent authority unless it is against the best interests of the child. There are differences, however, as regards the law in action. In some systems alternating residence is the rule, which means that the competent authority will grant it unless it is obviously against the interests of the child (BELGIUM,[1028] FRANCE[1029] and SWEDEN[1030]), whereas in other jurisdictions it is only granted exceptionally, which means that the parents will have to show that their agreement is in the best interests of the child (CZECH REPUBLIC[1031] and SPAIN[1032]).

Alternating residence without an agreement to this effect

In some of the systems which allow for an alternating residence, this is not possible without the parents' agreement (GERMANY,[1033] THE NETHERLANDS[1034] and NORWAY[1035]). The competent authority can order an alternating residence for the child even without the parents' agreement if this is in the best interests of the child in BELGIUM,[1036] ENGLAND AND WALES,[1037] FRANCE,[1038] GREECE,[1039] IRELAND[1040] and SWEDEN.[1041]

1018 See PINTENS/PIGNOLET, Belgian Report, Q 41.
1019 See HRUSAKOVÁ, Czech Report, Q 41.
1020 Art. 373–2–7 French Civil Code. See FERRAND, French Report, Q 41.
1021 See DETHLOFF/MARTINY, German Report, Q 41.
1022 See KOUTSOURADIS/ZERVOGIANNI, Greek Report, Q 41.
1023 See SVERDRUP/LØDRUP Norwegian Report, Q 41.
1024 See DE OLIVEIRA, Portuguese Report, Q 41.
1025 See GONZÁLEZ BEILFUSS, Spanish Report, Q 41.
1026 See JÄNTERÄ-JAREBORG/SINGER/SÖRGJERD, Swedish Report, Q 41.
1027 See HAUSHEER/ACHERMANN-WEBER/WOLF, Swiss Report, Q 41.
1028 See PINTENS/PIGNOLET, Belgian Report, Q 41.
1029 See FERRAND, French Report, Q 41.
1030 See JÄNTERÄ-JAREBORG/SINGER/SÖRGJERD, Swedish Report, Q 41.
1031 Czech Law Reform 1998. See HRUSAKOVÁ, Czech Report, Q 41.
1032 See GONZÁLEZ BEILFUSS, Spanish Report, Q 41.
1033 See DETHLOFF/MARTINY, German Report, Q 41.
1034 See BOELE-WOELKI/SCHRAMA/VONK, Dutch Report, Q 41.
1035 See SVERDRUP/LØDRUP, Norwegian Report, Q 41.
1036 See PINTENS/PIGNOLET, Belgian Report, Q 41.
1037 See LOWE, English Report, Q 41.
1038 Art. 373–2–9 French Civil Code. See FERRAND, French Report, Q 41
1039 See KOUTSOURADIS/ZERVOGIANNI, Greek Report, Q 41.
1040 See SHANNON, Irish Report, Q 41.
1041 See JÄNTERÄ-JAREBORG/SINGER/SÖRGJERD, Swedish Report, Q

Factors to evaluate whether an alternating residence is in the child's best interests

Among the relevant factors to evaluate whether an alternating residence is in the best interests of the child are the distance between the parents' houses, the age of the child, the aptitude of the parents to communicate and cooperate with each other in matters concerning the child, the personal situation of both parents and the distance of their homes from the child's school.[1042]

COMMENT

1. In many national systems the determination of the child's residence is not a separate issue. In the context of the Principles of European Family law it seems to be necessary, however, to deal with the determination of the child's residence more in detail in order to adequately respond to higher divorce and separation rates in all European countries. It is increasingly common that the holders of parental responsibilities do not live together. Even if, in legal terms, parental responsibilities are not affected by the separation of holders of parental responsibilities and each holder continues to have parental responsibilities, in practice certain decisions will have to be taken. The most important of these is the determination of the child's residence.

2. Principle 3:12 allows each of the parents who hold joint parental responsibilities to act alone in daily matters and requires an agreement as regards important decisions. Paragraph 2 of Principle 3: 12 mentions the determination of residence among these important issues.

3. Paragraph 1 of Principle 3:20 recalls that any determination of the child's residence requires the holders of parental responsibilities to reach an agreement to this effect if the parents cease to live together. This is consistent with Principle 3:10 which establishes that parental responsibilities are as such unaffected by the fact that the holders of parental responsibilities divorce or separate. Principle 3:20 is moreover also applicable when parental responsibilities are held by persons other than parents. It applies whenever parental responsibilities are held by more than one person and the holders of parental responsibilities do not live together.

4. If the holders of parental responsibilities fail to agree about the child's residence, the matter will be deferred to the competent authority which will proceed according to Principle 3:14.

1042 See PINTENS/PIGNOLET, Belgian Report, Q 41; HRUSAKOVÁ, Czech Report, Q 41 and JÄNTERÄ-JAREBORG/SINGER/SÖRGJERD, Swedish Report, Q 41.

5. Principle 3:20 (2) deals with alternating residence. Alternating residence is a modern trend in recent legislation in, for example, FRANCE, BELGIUM and SWEDEN. It has also been one of the most controversial issues in the context of the recent SPANISH divorce legislation.[1043] It therefore seemed adequate to deal with the matter in the Principles.

6. Whether an alternating residence should be the rule or an exception is not decided by Principle 3:20 (2).It merely establishes that an alternating residence should be possible if this is agreed upon by the holders of parental responsibilities and the competent authority approves of such an agreement. The criteria which should be considered by the competent authority are listed under Principle 3:20 (2).

7. Principle 3:20 (2) also contemplates the possibility that an alternating residence will be decided upon by the competent authority failing an agreement by the holders of parental responsibilities, if this is considered to be in the child's best interests taking into account the factors mentioned under Principle 3:20 (2). Since the ability and willingness of the holders of parental responsibilities is one of the criteria mentioned, an alternating residence should be ordered only by the competent authority failing an agreement in exceptional cases.

8. Principle 3:20 (2) does not specify whether an alternating residence has to be requested by at least one of the holders of parental responsibilities or whether the competent authority can order this of its own motion. This matter is left to national law.

9. An alternating residence is only possible if it is in the best interests of the child. In order to help the competent authority to decide whether this is so, Principle 3:20 (2) contains a non-exhaustive list of factors which should be considered. This list of factors provides guidelines for scrutinising any agreement on an alternating residence for the child between the holders of parental responsibilities. It is also useful when there is no such agreement, but the competent authority is considering whether to decide on an alternating residence.

10. The factors listed reflect the CEFL's concern that notwithstanding the fact that an alternating residence may promote personal relationships with both holders of parental responsibilities, it may also deprive the child of a stable environment and thus be harmful for the child. The competent authority should therefore consider, among other relevant elements, the age and opinion of the child (thus recalling Principle 3:6), the

[1043] New Art. 92 Spanish Civil Code according to Law 15/2005 of 8 July.

ability and willingness of the holders of parental responsibilities to cooperate with each other in matters concerning the child as well as their personal situation and the distance between the residences of the holders of parental responsibilities and the child's school.

Principle 3:21 Relocation

(1) If parental responsibilities are exercised jointly and one of the holders of parental responsibilities wishes to change the child's residence within or outside the jurisdiction, he or she should inform the other holder of parental responsibilities.

(2) If the other holder of parental responsibilities objects to the change of the child's residence, each of them may apply to the competent authority for a decision.

(3) The competent authority should take into consideration factors such as:

- (a) the age and opinion of the child;
- (b) the right of the child to maintain personal relationships with the other holders of parental responsibilities;
- (c) the ability and willingness of the holders of parental responsibilities to cooperate with each other;
- (d) the personal situation of the holders of personal responsibilities;
- (e) the geographical distance and accessibility;
- (f) the free movement of persons.

Principe 3:21 Changement de résidence

(1) Si la responsabilité parentale est exercée en commun et un des titulaires désire modifier la résidence de l'enfant à l'intérieur ou en dehors du territoire national, il doit en informer préalablement l'autre titulaire de la responsabilité parentale.

(2) Si l'autre titulaire de la responsabilité parentale s'oppose au changement de résidence de l'enfant, chacun des titulaires peut saisir l'autorité compétente afin qu'elle statue.

(3) L'autorité compétente prend notamment en considération:

- (a) l'âge et l'avis de l'enfant;
- (b) le droit de l'enfant d'entretenir des relations personnelles avec les autres titulaires de la responsabilité parentale;
- (c) la capacité et la volonté des titulaires de la responsabilité parentale de coopérer;
- (d) la situation personnelle des titulaires de la responsabilité parentale;
- (e) la distance géographique et les facilités d'accès;
- (f) la libre circulation des personnes.

Prinzip 3:21 Änderung des Aufenthalts
(1) Wird die elterliche Verantwortung gemeinsam ausgeübt und wünscht ein Inhaber der elterlichen Verantwortung den Aufenthalt des Kindes innerhalb oder ausserhalb des Staates zu ändern, hat er den anderen Inhaber der elterlichen Verantwortung vorher zu informieren.
(2) Sind die Inhaber der elterlichen Verantwortung nicht über die Änderung der Aufenhaltes des Kindes einig, so kann jeder Inhaber der elterlichen Verantwortung eine Entscheidung bei der zuständigen Behörde beantragen.
(3) Die zuständige Behörde berücksichtigt Umstände wie:
- (a) das Alter und die Auffassung des Kindes;
- (b) das Recht des Kindes, persönliche Beziehungen mit den Inhabern der elterlichen Verantwortung zu unterhalten;
- (c) die Fähigkeit und die Bereitschaft der Inhaber der elterlichen Verantwortung miteinander zu kooperieren;
- (d) die persönliche Situation der Inhaber der elterlichen Verantwortung;
- (e) die geographischen Entfernungen und die Erreichbarkeit;
- (f) die Freizügigkeit der Personen.

INTERNATIONAL INSTRUMENTS

There are no international instruments directly dealing with relocation. The issue is however relevant in the context of child abduction which is usually defined as the wrongful removal or retention of the child outside his or her State of residence. A relocation is wrongful and has to be considered as an abduction when it is in breach of the rights of custody of another person or institution. These rights of custody are generally defined in international instruments as rights related to the care of the person of the child and, in particular, the right to determine the child's place of residence. The instruments dealing with international child abduction are basically two Conventions drawn up by the Hague Conference on Private International Law, namely the *Hague Child Abduction Convention* of 1980 and the *Hague Child Protection Convention 1996*. International child abduction is also dealt with in the Council of Europe's *Convention on Recognition and Enforcement of Decisions Concerning Custody 1980*. In addition, child abduction is also regulated among EU Member States in the *Brussels II bis Regulation* (Art. 10, 11, 40, 42 and 55).

COMPARATIVE OVERVIEW

The power of unilateral relocation by the residential parent

In some systems the residential parent is free to relocate with the child even without the other parent's consent (CZECH REPUBLIC,[1044] IRELAND,[1045] NORWAY,[1046] RUSSIA[1047] and SPAIN[1048]). This power of unilateral relocation is sometimes restricted to relocation within the jurisdiction (CZECH REPUBLIC,[1049] ENGLAND AND WALES,[1050] NORWAY[1051] and RUSSIA[1052]). In some of these systems the holders of parental responsibilities can agree to subject relocation to mutual consent (RUSSIA[1053] and SPAIN[1054]). In others the courts can decide to limit this power of unilateral relocation (ENGLAND AND WALES[1055] and SPAIN[1056]). There are often more restrictions to so-called external relocation, that is relocation implying leaving the jurisdiction, than there are to internal relocation (ENGLAND AND WALES[1057]).

The power of relocation subject to the consent of both holders of parental responsibilities or the authorization of the competent authority

In other systems a change to the child's residence always requires the consent of both parents (CZECH REPUBLIC,[1058] DENMARK,[1059] BELGIUM,[1060] BULGARIA,[1061] FRANCE,[1062]

1044 See HRUSAKOVÁ, Czech Report, Q 40
1045 See SHANNON, Irish Report, Q 40.
1046 See SVERDRUP/LØDRUP, Norwegian Report, Q 40.
1047 See ANTOKOLSKAIA, Russian Report, Q 40.
1048 See GONZÁLEZ BEILFUSS, Spanish Report, Q 40.
1049 See HRUSAKOVÁ, Czech Report, Q 40
1050 See LOWE, English Report, Q 40.
1051 See SVERDRUP/LØDRUP, Norwegian Report, Q 40.
1052 See ANTOKOLSKAIA, Russian Report, Q 40.
1053 See ANTOKOLSKAIA, Russian Report, Q 40.
1054 See GONZÁLEZ BEILFUSS, Spanish Report, Q 40.
1055 See LOWE, English Report, Q 40.
1056 See GONZÁLEZ BEILFUSS, Spanish Report, Q 40.
1057 See LOWE, English Report, Q 40.
1058 See HRUSAKOVÁ, Czech Report, Q 40.
1059 § 8 Danish Act on Parental Authority and Contact. See LUND-ANDERSEN/JEPPESEN-DE BOER, Danish Report, Q 40.
1060 See PINTENS/PIGNOLET, Belgian Report, Q 40.
1061 Art. 71 para. 2 and 72 Bulgarian Family Code. See TODOROVA, Bulgarian Report, Q 40.
1062 Art. 373–2 para. 2 Civil Code. See FERRAND, French Report, Q

GERMANY,[1063] GREECE,[1064] HUNGARY,[1065] ITALY,[1066] LITHUANIA,[1067] THE NETHERLANDS[1068] and RUSSIA for external relocation,[1069] SPAIN[1070] and SWEDEN[1071]). If one of the holders of parental responsibilities does not consent, the competent authority will decide on any possible relocation (BELGIUM,[1072] BULGARIA,[1073] FRANCE,[1074] GREECE,[1075] HUNGARY,[1076] ITALY,[1077] THE NETHERLANDS[1078] and SPAIN[1079]). The guideline is the interests of the child (BELGIUM,[1080] GREECE,[1081] THE NETHERLANDS[1082] and RUSSIA[1083] for external relocation). In other systems the court does not decide directly on relocation. The parent opposing the move of the child can only request that the child be placed in his or her care (CZECH REPUBLIC,[1084] DENMARK,[1085] ENGLAND AND WALES,[1086] FINLAND,[1087] GERMANY[1088] and NORWAY for external relocation,[1089] RUSSIA[1090] for internal relocation and SWEDEN[1091]).

COMMENT

1. Principle 3:21 (2) establishes that the determination of the child's residence is an important matter which has to be decided by the parents having joint parental

1063 § 1631 para. 1 German Civil Code. See DETHLOFF/MARTINY, German Report, Q 40.
1064 See KOUTSOURADIS/ZERVOGIANNI, Greek Report, Q 40.
1065 See WEISS/SZEIBERT, Hungarian Report, Q 40.
1066 See PATTI/BELLISARIO/ROSSI CARLEO, Italian Report, Q 40.
1067 See MIKELENAS, Lithuanian Report, Q 40.
1068 See BOELE-WOELKI/SCHRAMA/VONK, Dutch Report, Q 40
1069 See ANTOKOLSKAIA, Russian Report, Q 40.
1070 See GONZÁLEZ BEILFUSS, Spanish Report, Q 40.
1071 See JÄNTERÄ-JAREBORG/SINGER/SÖRGJERD, Swedish Report, Q 40.
1072 See PINTENS/PIGNOLET, Belgian Report, Q 40.
1073 Art. 72 Bulgarian Family Code. See TODOROVA, Bulgarian Report, Q 40.
1074 Art. 373–2 para. 2 Civil Code. See FERRAND, French Report, Q
1075 Art. 1512 Greek Civil Code. See KOUTSOURADIS/ZERVOGIANNI, Greek Report, Q 40.
1076 See WEISS/SZEIBERT, Hungarian Report, Q 40.
1077 See PATTI/BELLISARIO/ROSSI CARLEO, Italian Report, Q 40
1078 See BOELE-WOELKI/SCHRAMA/VONK, Dutch Report, Q 40.
1079 See GONZÁLEZ BEILFUSS, Spanish Report, Q 40.
1080 See PINTENS/PIGNOLET, Belgian Report, Q 40.
1081 See KOUTSOURADIS/ZERVOGIANNI, Greek Report, Q 40.
1082 See BOELE-WOELKI/SCHRAMA/VONK, Dutch Report, Q 40.
1083 See ANTOKOLSKAIA, Russian Report, Q 40.
1084 See HRUSAKOVÁ, Czech Report, Q 40.
1085 § 8 Danish Act on Parental Authority and Contact. See LUND-ANDERSEN/JEPPESEN-DE BOER, Danish Report, Q 40.
1086 See LOWE, English Report, Q 40.
1087 See KURKI-SUONIO, Finnish Report, Q 40.
1088 See DETHLOFF/MARTINY, German Report, Q 40.
1089 See SVERDRUP/LØDRUP, Norwegian Report, Q 40.
1090 See ANTOKOLSKAIA, Russian Report, Q 40.
1091 See JÄNTERÄ-JAREBORG/SINGER/SÖRGJERD, Swedish Report, Q 40.

responsibilities together. If they cannot reach an agreement the matter is referred to the competent authority which proceeds according to Principle 3:14.

2. The CEFL decided to introduce a Principle specifically dealing with relocation in order to respond to an ever increasing mobility in European society which is closely linked to EU citizenship. Relocation is emerging as an important issue in the context of European integration and the free movement of persons and is likely to lead to many disputes, as it has already done in the United States where it has become "the most contentious and fastest growing custody litigation".[1092] The relocation of a parent is dealt with in § 2.17 of the American Law Institute's Principles of the Law of Family Dissolution.

3. Changing the child's residence within or outside the jurisdiction is such an important matter that it requires informing the other holders of parental responsibilities in advance. This applies in particular to such a holder of parental responsibilities who has the right to decide upon the child's residence. In most cases this will be the parent of the child having joint parental responsibilities.

4. Principle 3:21 establishes that the holder of parental responsibilities who lives with the child and wishes to relocate and change the child's residence has to inform the other holders of parental responsibilities in advance. This applies regardless of whether the change is within or outside the jurisdiction. Since the determination of the child's residence is considered to be an important matter requiring that parents should act in agreement, the duty to inform is in fact implicit when parental responsibilities are held jointly by the parents.

5. The Principles do not specify how the other holders of parental responsibilities have to be informed. The national legislator may further specify a time-limit or specific conditions which have to be fulfilled.

6. Principle 3:21 (2) partially recalls Principle 3:14. When there is no agreement on relocation, the matter has to be deferred to the competent authority. There is however no need for the competent authority to try to reconcile the parties as provided in Principle 3:14 (2).

7. Principle 3:21 (3) contains a non-exhaustive list of factors which have to be taken into consideration by the competent authority in order to take a decision on relocation. This decision requires that the competent authority tries to find a balance between

[1092] See GLENNON, "Mobility and the post-divorce family: resolution of relocation disputes in the U.S." in BOELE-WOELKI, *ibid.*, note 22, pp. 193–215.

the right of the child to maintain personal relationships with the non-residential parent and close relatives and persons with whom the child has a close relationship (Principle 3:25) and the right of the residential parent to move in pursuit of a valid purpose, in order to, for example, improve his or her professional situation or to accompany a new partner (free movement rights). Geographical distance and accessibility as well as the personal, particularly the financial, situation of the holders of parental responsibilities are crucial factors. As always, due weight should be given to the child's opinion, having regard to his or her age and maturity (Principle 3:6)

Principle 3:22 Administration of the child's property

(1) The holders of parental responsibilities should administer the child's property with due care and diligence in order to preserve and where possible increase the value of the property.

(2) In administering the child's property the holders of parental responsibilities should not make gifts unless the gifts are deemed to be made under a moral obligation.

(3) The income derived from the child's property which is not needed for the proper management of the property or for the maintenance and education of the child may, where necessary, be used for the needs of the family.

Principe 3:22 Administration des biens de l'enfant

(1) Les titulaires de la responsabilité parentale administrent les biens de l'enfant avec soin et diligence afin de préserver et, dans la mesure du possible, d'accroître la valeur des biens.

(2) Dans le cadre de l'administration des biens de l'enfant, les titulaires de la responsabilité parentale ne peuvent faire de donations, sauf si celles-ci sont fondées sur une obligation morale.

(3) Les revenus produits par les biens de l'enfant qui ne sont pas nécessaires à une administration adéquate des biens, ni à l'entretien ou à l'éducation de l'enfant, peuvent en cas de nécessité être employés pour les besoins de la famille.

Prinzip 3:22 Vermögensverwaltung

(1) Die Inhaber der elterlichen Verantwortung verwalten das Vermögen des Kindes mit der gebotenen Sorgfalt, um das Vermögen zu erhalten und soweit wie möglich den Wert des Vermögens zu vermehren.

(2) Bei der Verwaltung des Vermögens des Kindes dürfen die Inhaber der elterlichen Verantwortung keine Geschenke machen, es sei denn, diese Geschenke entsprechen einer moralischen Verpflichtung.

(3) Aus dem Vermögen des Kindes erzieltes Einkommen, das nicht für die ordnungsgemäße Verwaltung des Vermögens sowie den Unterhalt und die Erziehung des Kindes benötigt wird, kann, soweit notwendig, für die Bedürfnisse der Familie verwendet werden.

INTERNATIONAL INSTRUMENTS

In European and international instruments the administration, conservation and disposal of the child's property is expressly included as a part of parental responsibilities in the *Hague Child Protection Convention 1996* (Art. 1 para. 2, 3 (d), (g)), the *Brussels II bis Regulation* (Art. 1 para. 2 (e), 2 No. 7), in Principle 1 (a) *Recommendation*

R (84) 4 on parental responsibilities and in Principle 18 of the Council of Europe's *White Paper 2002*. However, these instruments do not go into detail.

COMPARATIVE OVERVIEW

Parental administration of property and parental responsibilities

The issue of parental administration arises when the child owns property. The majority of the surveyed jurisdictions treat the administration of the child's property as a part of parental responsibilities (see Principle 3:1). In most legal systems there is a parallel between caring for the child and caring for the property of that child (AUSTRIA,[1093] BELGIUM,[1094] BULGARIA,[1095] CZECH REPUBLIC,[1096] FRANCE,[1097] GERMANY,[1098] GREECE,[1099] HUNGARY,[1100] ITALY,[1101] LITHUANIA,[1102] THE NETHERLANDS,[1103] POLAND,[1104] PORTUGAL,[1105] RUSSIA,[1106] SPAIN[1107] and SWITZERLAND[1108]). Consequently, the holders of parental responsibilities have, by law, the right and the obligation to administer the child's property. In DENMARK,[1109] FINLAND,[1110] NORWAY[1111] and SWEDEN[1112] there is a distinction between caring for the person, which is understood as a question of custody, and caring for that person's property, which belongs to the law of guardianship. However, the holders of parental responsibilities, the parents, are the legal guardians of the minor

1093 § 144, § 149 and 150 Austrian Civil Code. See ROTH, Austrian Report, Q 2f and Q 10.
1094 Art. 376 ff. Belgian Civil Code. See PINTENS/PIGNOLET, Belgian Report, Q 2f and Q 10.
1095 See TODOROVA, Bulgarian Report, Q 2f and Q 10.
1096 § 31 para. 1 Czech Family Code. See HRUSAKOVÁ, Czech Report, Q 2f and Q 10.
1097 Art. 382 ff. French Civil Code. See FERRAND, French Report, Q 2f and Q 10.
1098 § 1626 para. 1 German Civil Code. See DETHLOFF/MARTINY, German Report, Q 2f and Q 10.
1099 Art. 1510 Greek Civil Code. See KOUTSOURADIS/ZERVOGIANNI, Greek Report, Q 2f and Q 10.
1100 See WEISS/SZEIBERT, Hungarian Report, Q 2f and 10.
1101 Art. 320 Italian Civil Code and PATTI/BELLISARIO/ROSSI CARLEO, Italian Report, Q 2f and Q 10.
1102 Art. 3.185 ff. Lithuanian Civil Code. See MIKELENAS, Lithuanian Report, Q 2f and Q 10.
1103 Art. 1:245 para. 4 Dutch Civil Code. See BOELE-WOELKI/SCHRAMA/VONK, Dutch Report, Q 2f and Q 10.
1104 Art. 95 para. 1, 101 para. 1 Polish Family and Guardianship Code. See MĄCZYŃSKI/MĄCZYŃSKA, Polish Report, Q 2f and Q 10.
1105 Art. 1878 No. 1 Portuguese Civil Code. See DE OLIVEIRA, Portuguese Report, Q 2f and Q 10.
1106 See ANTOKOLSKAIA, Russian Report, Q 2f and Q 10.
1107 Art. 155 Spanish Civil Code. See GONZÁLEZ BEILFUSS, Spanish Report, Q 2f and Q 10.
1108 Art. 318 para. 1 Swiss Civil Code. See HAUSHEER/ACHERMANN-WEBER/WOLF, Swiss Report, Q 2f and Q 10.
1109 § 1and § 2 Danish Act on Guardianship. See LUND-ANDERSEN/JEPPESEN-DE BOER, Danish Report, Q 2f and Q 10.
1110 § 4 Finnish Guardianship Services Act. See KURKI-SUONIO, Finnish Report, Q 2f and Q 10
1111 § 3 Norwegian Act on Guardianship. See SVERDRUP/LØDRUP, Norwegian Report, Q 2f and Q 10.
1112 Ch. 9 – 15 Swedish Children and Parents Code. See JÄNTERÄ-JAREBORG/SINGER/SÖRGJERD, Swedish Report, Q 1, 2f and Q 10.

child and basically the same rules as for guardians will apply. Under Common Law, a parent has no inherent authority over the assets of the child.[1113] Therefore the traditional legal approach was to solve any questions which may arise mainly by the law of guardianship and the law of trusts. However, today in ENGLAND AND WALES[1114] the court can also decide on the property issues of parental responsibility and the position of the holder of parental responsibilities is similar to that of a guardian of an estate.

Only one holder of parental responsibilities

Under FRENCH law[1115] if only one parent is the holder of parental responsibilities the administration of property is restricted and the holder of parental responsibilities is subject to judicial control. He or she may undertake acts of administration alone, but for acts of disposition he or she needs authorisation subject to the same conditions as a guardian. In BELGIUM[1116] the other parent only has the right to supervise the administration, to be kept informed and to apply to the competent authority. However, in most jurisdictions such a distinction between simple and supervised parental responsibilities is not made. There are, however, protective measures such as the drawing up of an inventory of the child's property under the administration of only one holder of parental responsibilities in the case of a remarriage (GERMANY[1117]).

Best interests of the child

Generally, the best interests of the child are the paramount consideration also for the administration of property (e.g. LITHUANIA[1118]). The content of the right to administer the child's property is generally to maintain and, if possible, to increase the property by acts of management. Due to the diversity of situations it is, however, not easy to circumscribe exactly the content and the limits of the power of administration. Legal representation of the child is closely related to the administration of property. Generally, parental responsibilities include the internal aspect of the power of managing property and the external aspect of legal representation of the child. In GERMANY,[1119] RUSSIA[1120] and ITALY[1121] it is expressly stated that the administration of

---

1113 See LOWE, English Report, Q 10; STOLJAR, *ibid.*, note 27, no. 206.
1114 S. 3 (1)(2) English Children Act 1989. See LOWE, English Report, Q 2f and Q 10.
1115 Art. 389–2, 389–6 French Civil Code. See FERRAND, French Report, Q 11.
1116 Art. 376 Belgian Civil Code. See PINTENS/PIGNOLET, Belgian Report, Q 10.
1117 § 1683 German Civil Code.
1118 Art. 3.186 Lithuanian Civil Code. See MIKELENAS, Lithuanian Report, Q 11.
1119 § 1629 German Civil Code. See DETHLOFF/MARTINY, German Report, Q 2d and Q 11.
1120 Art. 60 para. 3 Russian Family Code. See ANTOKOLSKAIA, Russian Report, Q 2f.
1121 Art. 320 Italian Civil Code. See PATTI/BELLISARIO/ROSSI CARLEO, Italian Report, Q 2f, 8f and Q 10.

property also encompasses legal representation in this respect. However, in other jurisdictions there is also such a link between the administration of property and legal representation (AUSTRIA,[1122] BELGIUM,[1123] BULGARIA,[1124] CZECH REPUBLIC,[1125] FRANCE,[1126] GREECE,[1127] HUNGARY,[1128] LITHUANIA,[1129] THE NETHERLANDS,[1130] POLAND,[1131] PORTUGAL,[1132] SPAIN[1133] and SWITZERLAND[1134]). In DENMARK,[1135] FINLAND,[1136] NORWAY[1137] and SWEDEN[1138] the guardian has the respective power, see Principle 3:24.

Costs of administration

In some jurisdictions it is expressly stated that the administration of property is, as such, free of charge; only the costs of administration are to be paid from the property (AUSTRIA[1139] and SPAIN[1140]). However, when the child has an income the issue arises whether this income can also be used by the holders of parental responsibilities for themselves, the family and/or the child. In some jurisdictions the traditional usufruct of Roman law origin still exists. There is an express right of parental use and enjoyment of the property of the child (BELGIUM,[1141] FRANCE,[1142] ITALY,[1143] LITHUANIA[1144] and THE NETHERLANDS[1145]). The extent of the right of usufruct differs. In principle, the parents are entitled to the use and the fruits of the goods of the child, but have to use these amounts first and foremost to maintain the child. In other jurisdictions the parental usufruct has been abolished, although analogous rights exist instead. The child's

1122 § 144 and § 154 Austrian Civil Code. See ROTH, Austrian Report, Q 2f and Q 8f.
1123 Art. 376 ff. Belgian Civil Code. See PINTENS/PIGNOLET, Belgian Report, Q 2f and Q 8f.
1124 See TODOROVA, Bulgarian Report, Q 2f.
1125 See HRUSAKOVÁ, Czech Report, Q 2f.
1126 Art. 389–3 para. 1 French Civil Code. See FERRAND, French Report, Q 2f and Q 8f.
1127 See KOUTSOURADIS/ZERVOGIANNI, Greek Report, Q 2f and Q 8f.
1128 See WEISS/SZEIBERT, Hungarian Report, Q 2f and Q 8f.
1129 See MIKELENAS, Lithuanian Report, Q 2f.
1130 See BOELE-WOELKI/SCHRAMA/VONK, Dutch Report, Q 2d, f.
1131 See MĄCZYŃSKI/MĄCZYŃSKA, Polish Report, Q 2f and Q 8f.
1132 See DE OLIVEIRA, Portuguese Report, Q 2f and Q 8f.
1133 See GONZÁLEZ BEILFUSS, Spanish Report, Q 2f.
1134 Art. 304, 318 Swiss Civil Code. See HAUSHEER/ACHERMANN-WEBER/WOLF, Swiss Report, Q 2f and Q 8f.
1135 See LUND-ANDERSEN/JEPPESEN-DE BOER, Danish Report, Q 2f.
1136 See KURKI-SUONIO, Finnish Report, Q 2f.
1137 See SVERDRUP/LØDRUP, Norwegian Report, Q 8f.
1138 See JÄNTERÄ-JAREBORG/SINGER/SÖRGJERD, Swedish Report, Q 2d, f.
1139 § 149 para. 2 Austrian Civil Code. See ROTH, Austrian Report, Q 11.
1140 See GONZÁLEZ BEILFUSS, Spanish Report, Q 11.
1141 Art. 387 Belgian Civil Code. See PINTENS/PIGNOLET, Belgian Report, Q 11.
1142 Art. 382, 384 ff. French Civil Code. See FERRAND, French Report, Q 11.
1143 Art. 324 Italian Civil Code. See PATTI/BELLISARIO/ROSSI CARLEO, Italian Report, Q 11.
1144 Art. 3.185 Lithuanian Civil Code. See MIKELENAS, Lithuanian Report, Q 2 f, 11.
1145 Art. 1:253l Dutch Civil Code. See BOELE-WOELKI/SCHRAMA/VONK, Dutch Report, Q 11.

income and earnings can, as far as these are not required for the child's own needs, be employed for the purposes of the family, also for the maintenance of siblings (GERMANY[1146] and POLAND[1147]). It is widely accepted that, to a certain extent, the holder of parental responsibilities has the right to use income from the child's property to meet the needs of the family (CZECH REPUBLIC[1148] and SWITZERLAND[1149]).

Conflicts of interest between the child and the holders of parental responsibilities

In administering the property conflicts of interest may arise between the child and the holders of parental responsibilities. This can occur when there is a contract between a spouse or a relative of the holder of parental responsibilities and the child. And it is particularly the case when parents in a transaction both give and accept on behalf of the child, i.e. the holders of parental responsibilities are themselves parties to the contract. In these situations the legal representation of the child is excluded (FRANCE[1150] and GERMANY[1151]); generally a guardian or custodian must be appointed (BELGIUM,[1152] FRANCE,[1153] GREECE,[1154] ITALY[1155] and LITHUANIA[1156]). Where there is a conflict of interests only with respect to one of the child's parents, the child shall be represented by the other parent whose interests do not conflict with those of the child.

Maintaining the value of the property

In all jurisdictions where the holders of parental responsibilities have extensive powers it is expected that they maintain and, if possible, increase the property unless the child's interests require otherwise (e.g. AUSTRIA[1157] and GREECE[1158]). As a consequence of this guideline precautions must be taken against any mismanagement of the property. The holders of parental responsibilities have to act with "due care" (CZECH REPUBLIC,[1159]

1146 § 1649 German Civil Code. See DETHLOFF/MARTINY, German Report, Q 11 and Q 12a.
1147 Art. 103 Polish Family and Guardianship Code. See MĄCZYŃSKI/MĄCZYŃSKA, Polish Report, Q 11.
1148 See HRUSAKOVÁ, Czech Report, Q 2f.
1149 Art. 319 para. 1 Swiss Civil Code. See HAUSHEER/ACHERMANN-WEBER/WOLF, Swiss Report, Q 11.
1150 Art. 389–3 para. 2 French Civil Code. See FERRAND, French Report, Q 12a.
1151 § 181 German Civil Code. See DETHLOFF/MARTINY, German Report, Q 12c.
1152 Art. 378 Belgian Civil Code. See PINTENS/PIGNOLET, Belgian Report, Q 12c.
1153 See FERRAND, French Report, Q 11.
1154 See KOUTSOURADIS/ZERVOGIANNI, Greek Report, Q 13.
1155 Art. 320 para. 6 Italian Civil Code. See PATTI/BELLISARIO/ROSSI CARLEO, Italian Report, Q 10 and Q 12c.
1156 Art. 3.188 Lithuanian Civil Code. See MIKELENAS, Lithuanian Report, Q 11.
1157 § 149 Austrian Civil Code. See ROTH, Austrian Report, Q 2f and Q 11.
1158 See KOUTSOURADIS/ZERVOGIANNI, Greek Report, Q 11.
1159 § 37a Czech Family Code. See HRUSAKOVÁ, Czech Report, Q 2f and Q 10.

POLAND[1160] and SWEDEN[1161]), the "care of proper parents" (AUSTRIA[1162]) or the same diligence they employ when administering their own property (GERMANY,[1163] HUNGARY,[1164] PORTUGAL[1165] and SPAIN,[1166]). Often very detailed rules on specific transactions cover the investment of money. Sometimes there are special rules for secure investment (e.g. AUSTRIA[1167]). Not only is the preservation of assets expected, there must also be "profitable property management" (GERMANY[1168] and GREECE[1169]).

Specific measures of protection

Where parental responsibilities encompass the administration of the child's property it is also necessary to limit the freedom of the holders of parental responsibilities. Specific measures are prescribed by law or can be ordered by the competent authority. One of these measures is the establishment of an inventory that lists at least all the most valuable items of the child's property (e.g. GREECE[1170]). Other protective measures are statements of accounts and reports. E.g. the parents are obligated to give an account of their administration of the property (CZECH REPUBLIC[1171]) or to provide a financial report (POLAND[1172]) if the child so requires after the termination of their administration. The ordering of deposits and the furnishing of securities are other protective measures (SWITZERLAND[1173]).

Prohibition on making gifts in the name of the child

Despite the wide power of administration belonging to the holders of parental responsibilities there are some transactions which are totally prohibited. In some jurisdictions it is expressly stated that the holder may not make gifts in the name of

1160 See MĄCZYŃSKI/MĄCZYŃSKA, Polish Report, Q 11.
1161 Ch. 12 § 3 Swedish Children and Parents Code. See JÄNTERÄ-JAREBORG/SINGER/SÖRGJERD, Swedish Report, Q 11.
1162 See ROTH, Austrian Report, Q 2f and Q 11.
1163 § 1664 German Civil Code. See DETHLOFF/MARTINY, German Report, Q 11.
1164 § 82 para. 1 Hungarian Family Act.
1165 See DE OLIVEIRA, Portuguese Report, Q 11.
1166 Art. 164 Spanish Civil Code. See GONZÁLEZ BEILFUSS, Spanish Report, Q 11 concerning the stricter Art. 145 Catalan Family Code.
1167 See ROTH, Austrian Report, Q 12c.
1168 § 1642 German Civil Code. See DETHLOFF/MARTINY, German Report, Q 11.
1169 See KOUTSOURADIS/ZERVOGIANNI, Greek Report, Q 13.
1170 Art. 1523, 1611 Greek Civil Code. See KOUTSOURADIS/ZERVOGIANNI, Greek Report, Q 13.
1171 § 37a para. 3 Czech Family Code. See HRUSAKOVÁ, Czech Report, Q 2f and Q 10.
1172 See MĄCZYŃSKI/MĄCZYŃSKA, Polish Report, Q 11.
1173 Art. 324 para. 2 Swiss Civil Code. See HAUSHEER/ACHERMANN-WEBER/WOLF, Swiss Report, Q 13.

the child (BULGARIA,[1174] GERMANY,[1175] GREECE,[1176] THE NETHERLANDS[1177] and SWITZERLAND[1178]). Only small gifts subject to some moral or social duty may be made (GERMANY,[1179] GREECE[1180] and THE NETHERLANDS[1181]). It is however the exception that in BULGARIA some economic transactions, especially in the field of securities and credit transactions, are deemed to be so risky that they are completely prohibited.[1182]

Protective measures

If there is no proper management of the property by the holders of parental responsibilities, the competent authority may take appropriate measures to protect the child's property (AUSTRIA,[1183] GERMANY,[1184] SWEDEN[1185] and SWITZERLAND[1186]). This is done, for example, by a request to provide security (GERMANY[1187] and HUNGARY[1188]), appointing an administrator or custodian (BELGIUM,[1189] CZECH REPUBLIC,[1190] LITHUANIA[1191] and SPAIN[1192]), a guardian (FINLAND[1193]) or an official adviser (SWITZERLAND[1194]), placing the estate or a part thereof under administration (THE NETHERLANDS[1195]) and by the removal of the parents from the management of the child's property (e.g. LITHUANIA[1196]). The standard of supervision is not the same in the surveyed jurisdictions and the intensity of the supervision often varies according to the amount of the assets (AUSTRIA,[1197] FINLAND,[1198] NORWAY[1199] and SWEDEN[1200]).

1174 Art. 73 para. 3 Bulgarian Family Code. See TODOROVA, Bulgarian Report, Q 2f.
1175 § 1641 German Civil Code. See DETHLOFF/MARTINY, German Report, Q 12c.
1176 Art. 1524, 1617 Greek Civil Code. See KOUTSOURADIS/ZERVOGIANNI, Greek Report, Q 12c and Q 13.
1177 Art. 1:345 Dutch Civil Code. See BOELE-WOELKI/SCHRAMA/VONK, Dutch Report, Q 12c.
1178 See HAUSHEER/ACHERMANN-WEBER/WOLF, Swiss Report, Q 12c.
1179 § 1641 German Civil Code. See DETHLOFF/MARTINY, German Report, Q 12c.
1180 See KOUTSOURADIS/ZERVOGIANNI, Greek Report, Q 12c.
1181 See BOELE-WOELKI/SCHRAMA/VONK, Dutch Report, Q 12c.
1182 Art. 73 para. 3 Bulgarian Family Code. See TODOROVA, Bulgarian Report, Q 2f.
1183 See ROTH, Austrian Report, Q 12a.
1184 § 1667 German Civil Code.
1185 See JÄNTERÄ-JAREBORG/SINGER/SÖRGJERD, Swedish Report, Q 11 and Q 12a.
1186 Art. 324, 325 Swiss Civil Code and HAUSHEER/ACHERMANN-WEBER/WOLF, Swiss Report, Q 13.
1187 § 1667 para. 3 German Civil Code.
1188 See WEISS/SZEIBERT, Hungarian Report, Q 13.
1189 Art. 378 Belgian Civil Code. See PINTENS/PIGNOLET, Belgian Report, Q 13.
1190 See HRUSAKOVÁ, Czech Report, Q 13.
1191 See MIKELENAS, Lithuanian Report, Q 11.
1192 Art. 167 Spanish Civil Code. See GONZÁLEZ BEILFUSS, Spanish Report, Q 13.
1193 See KURKI-SUONIO, Finnish Report, Q 13.
1194 Art. 325 Swiss Civil Code. See HAUSHEER/ACHERMANN-WEBER/WOLF, Swiss Report, Q 13.
1195 Art. 1:370 Dutch Civil Code. See BOELE-WOELKI/SCHRAMA/VONK, Dutch Report, Q 13.
1196 See MIKELENAS, Lithuanian Report, Q 11.
1197 See ROTH, Austrian Report, Q 12a.
1198 See KURKI-SUONIO, Finnish Report, Q 11.
1199 See SVERDRUP/LØDRUP, Norwegian Report, Q 11 and Q 12a.
1200 See JÄNTERÄ-JAREBORG/SINGER/SÖRGJERD, Swedish Report, Q 12a.

COMMENT

1. The holders of parental responsibilities should have the right and the obligation to administer the child's property. This is a necessary consequence and is in accordance with Principle 3:1. The fact that in the Nordic legal systems two different legal terms – custody of the person of the child and guardianship of the child's property – are used does not prevent the use of the broader concept of parental responsibilities. In the Common Law jurisdictions there is also a tendency to include property issues under child legislation.

2. Principle 3:22 (1) states that the holders of parental responsibilities should administer the child's property in the best interests of the child. This is in accordance with the common core of the legal systems. Detailed rules in the Principles would be difficult to establish due to the different contractual and procedural national rules.

3. Administration with "due care and diligence" means that the holders of parental responsibilities should increase the value of the property and invest the child's money in accordance with the protective provisions of the law of parental responsibilities. This is also in accordance with the common core of the legal systems, but the details vary greatly.

4. The power of administration has inherent limits. Therefore a prohibition for the holder of parental responsibilities to make gifts in representing the child has been inserted in Principle 3:22 (2). This is in accordance with the common core of the legal systems. Exceptions should be gifts which are deemed to be made under a moral obligation or out of common decency. This restriction seems necessary for practical reasons.

5. Another inherent limitation concerns conflicts of interests. It is the common core of the legal systems that where there is a conflict of interests between the child and the holder of parental responsibilities the legal representation of the child should be excluded. The details as to which third person has to be the representative are closely connected with procedural and administrative rules and belong to Principle 3:24 on legal representation.

6. The institution of a parental usufruct (a concept which is of Roman law origin) is only known in some legal systems. However, the idea that income derived from the child's property, which is not needed for the proper management of the property and for the maintenance of the child, may be used for the needs of the family is in accordance with the common core of the legal systems. Therefore Principle 3:22 (3) recognizes this power belonging to the holders of parental responsibilities. The details,

however, are closely related to maintenance law and other questions so that only a general rule seems to be appropriate. Who may be included within the "family" is also left to national law. Included are, however, members of the nuclear family, in particular the parents and siblings.

7. If the property of the child is in jeopardy the competent authority should take appropriate measures to protect that child's property. This is also in accordance with the common core of the legal systems. However, not only do the administrative and judicial structures differ, but the procedural rules are also not unified. Therefore this Principle does not go into detail. To a certain extent the issue is covered by Principles 3:35 ff. on procedure.

Principle 3:23 Restrictions

(1) The holders of parental responsibilities should not administer property acquired by a child through a testamentary disposition or a gift, if the testator or the donor so instructed.

(2) Similarly the earnings by the child should not be administered by the holders of parental responsibilities unless the child is not of sufficient age and maturity to decide himself or herself.

(3) Where transactions can have significant financial consequences for the child the authorisation of the competent authority should be necessary.

Principe 3:23 Limitations

(1) Les titulaires de la responsabilité parentale n'administrent pas les biens acquis par l'enfant en vertu de dispositions testamentaires ou d'une donation si le testateur ou le donateur en a disposé ainsi.

(2) De même, les gains et salaires de l'enfant ne sont pas administrés par les titulaires de la responsabilité parentale, sauf dans l'hypothèse où l'enfant n'a ni l'âge ni la maturité suffisants pour prendre lui-même les décisions.

(3) Lorsque des transactions peuvent entraîner pour l'enfant des conséquences financières importantes, l'autorisation de l'autorité compétente est requise.

Prinzip 3:23 Beschränkungen

(1) Die Inhaber der elterlichen Verantwortung verwalten nicht das Vermögen, das das Kind durch testamentarische Verfügung oder Schenkung erworben hat, sofern der von Todes wegen Verfügende oder Schenker dies so angeordnet hat.

(2) Der Verdienst des Kindes wird gleichfalls nicht von den Inhabern der elterlichen Verantwortung verwaltet, es sei denn, das Kind hat noch nicht das nötige Alter und die Reife, um selbst zu entscheiden.

(3) Soweit Geschäfte bedeutende wirtschaftliche Folgen für das Kind haben können, ist die Zustimmung der zuständigen Behörde notwendig.

INTERNATIONAL INSTRUMENTS

In international instruments the administration, conservation or disposal of the child's property is expressly included as a part of parental responsibilities in the *Hague Child Protection Convention 1996* (Art. 1 para. 2, 3 (d), (g)) and in Principle 18 of the Council of Europe's *White Paper 2002*. However, these instruments do not go into detail and do not deal with restrictions.

COMPARATIVE OVERVIEW

Restrictions with respect to certain goods and values

In the civil law jurisdictions the administration of property covers, in principle, the child's property in its entirety. There are, however, restrictions with respect to certain goods and values. In most jurisdictions the right of the holders of parental responsibility to administer the child's assets may be restricted through stipulations by a third party. This is especially the case when the child receives property as a gift or by a testamentary disposition subject to the condition that this property shall be administered by a person other than the holder of parental responsibilities (AUSTRIA,[1201] FRANCE,[1202] GERMANY,[1203] GREECE,[1204] HUNGARY,[1205] LITHUANIA,[1206] THE NETHERLANDS,[1207] NORWAY,[1208] POLAND,[1209] PORTUGAL,[1210] SPAIN,[1211] SWEDEN[1212] and SWITZERLAND[1213]). For the disposal of property generally, proceedings before the competent authority are necessary (GERMANY,[1214] SWEDEN[1215] and SWITZERLAND[1216]). These goods are exempted from the parental usufruct (ITALY[1217] and LITHUANIA[1218]) and often a third person appointed by the donor or testator or the court shall administer such property. In the Common law jurisdictions a donor or testator who desires to leave personal or real property to minor children may make use of a trust rather than a direct gift to accomplish this purpose. Therefore trustees, governed by special statutes and the general law of trusts, can control the property.

1201 § 145 c Austrian Civil Code. See ROTH, Austrian Report, Q 12c.
1202 Art. 389–3 para. 3 French Civil Code. See FERRAND, French Report, Q 12a.
1203 § 1638 para. 1 German Civil Code. See DETHLOFF/MARTINY, German Report, Q 12a.
1204 Art. 1521 Greek Civil Code. See KOUTSOURADIS/ZERVOGIANNI, Greek Report, Q 12a.
1205 See WEISS/SZEIBERT, Hungarian Report, Q 12a.
1206 Art. 3.187 Lithuanian Civil Code. See MIKELENAS, Lithuanian Report, Q 12a.
1207 Art. 1:253m Dutch Civil Code. See BOELE-WOELKI/SCHRAMA/VONK, Dutch Report, Q 12a.
1208 § 33 Norwegian Act on Guardianship. See SVERDRUP/LØDRUP, Norwegian Report, Q 12a.
1209 Art. 102 Polish Family and Guardianship Code. See MĄCZYŃSKI/MĄCZYŃSKA, Polish Report, Q 12a.
1210 See DE OLIVEIRA, Portuguese Report, Q 12a.
1211 See GONZÁLEZ BEILFUSS, Spanish Report, Q 12a.
1212 Ch. 12 § 1 in conjunction with Ch. 9 § 3, 4 Swedish Children and Parents Code. See JÄNTERÄ-JAREBORG/SINGER/SÖRGJERD, Swedish Report, Q 12a.
1213 Art. 321, 322 Swiss Civil Code. See HAUSHEER/ACHERMANN-WEBER/WOLF, Swiss Report, Q 12a.
1214 § 1643 in conjunction with § 1821, 1822 German Civil Code. See DETHLOFF/MARTINY, German Report, Q 12c.
1215 See JÄNTERÄ-JAREBORG/SINGER/SÖRGJERD, Swedish Report, Q 12a.
1216 See HAUSHEER/ACHERMANN-WEBER/WOLF, Swiss Report, Q 12a.
1217 Art. 324 para. 3 No. 3, 4 Italian Civil Code.
1218 Art. 3.187 Lithuanian Civil Code. See MIKELENAS, Lithuanian Report, Q 12a.

In other jurisdictions there are restrictions in respect of the administration of inherited property. The renunciation or acceptance of an inheritance or a legacy needs authorisation (AUSTRIA,[1219] BELGIUM,[1220] GERMANY,[1221] ITALY[1222] and SPAIN[1223]).

Restrictions with respect to the earnings of the child

In many jurisdictions there are restrictions on the holders of parental responsibilities with respect to the salary of the child. The salary is earned by the child's own efforts and his/her increasing independence has to be protected. In some jurisdictions the minor is generally free to dispose of his or her own earnings (BULGARIA,[1224] CZECH REPUBLIC,[1225] FINLAND,[1226] POLAND[1227] and SWITZERLAND[1228]). In most jurisdictions an age limit exists; a child of 14 years (AUSTRIA,[1229] GREECE,[1230] HUNGARY[1231] and RUSSIA[1232]) or of 15 years (DENMARK[1233] and NORWAY[1234]) or 16 years (PORTUGAL,[1235] SPAIN[1236] and SWEDEN[1237]) is free to spend the salary which he or she has earned; the child's salary is excluded from management by the holder of parental responsibilities. However, in these jurisdictions it is also recognized that the minor child may not be able to make proper decisions. Therefore the possibility of intervention exists where the child endangers his or her support or property (e.g. AUSTRIA[1238]). In a minority of jurisdic-

---

1219 See ROTH, Austrian Report, Q 12c.

1220 See PINTENS/PIGNOLET, Belgian Report, Q 10a.

1221 § 1643 para. 2 German Civil Code. See DETHLOFF/MARTINY, German Report, Q 12c.

1222 Art. 320 para. 3 Italian Civil Code. See PATTI/BELLISARIO/ROSSI CARLEO, Italian Report, Q 11.

1223 See GONZÁLEZ BEILFUSS, Spanish Report, Q 12c.

1224 Art. 4 para. 2 Bulgarian Act on the Persons and the Family. See TODOROVA, Bulgarian Report, Q 12b.

1225 § 9 Czech Family Code. See HRUSAKOVÁ, Czech Report, Q 12b.

1226 See KURKI-SUONIO, Finnish Report, Q 12b.

1227 Art. 101 § 2 Polish Family and Guardianship Code. See MĄCZYŃSKI/MĄCZYŃSKA, Polish Report, Q 2f and Q 12b.

1228 Art. 323 para. 1 Swiss Civil Code. See HAUSHEER/ACHERMANN-WEBER/WOLF, Swiss Report, Q 12b.

1229 § 151 para. 2 Austrian Civil Code. See ROTH, Austrian Report, Q 12b.

1230 Art. 135 Greek Civil Code. See KOUTSOURADIS/ZERVOGIANNI, Greek Report, Q 12b.

1231 See WEISS/SZEIBERT, Hungarian Report, Q 12b.

1232 Art. 26 para. 2 Russian Civil Code with the possibility of court intervention. See ANTOKOLSKAIA, Russian Report, Q 12b.

1233 § 42 para. 1 Danish Act on Guardianship. See LUND-ANDERSEN/JEPPESEN-DE BOER, Danish Report, Q 12b.

1234 § 33 Norwegian Act on Guardianship. See SVERDRUP/LØDRUP, Norwegian Report, Q 12b.

1235 Art. 1888 No. 1 (d), Art. 127 No. 1 (a) Portuguese Civil Code. See DE OLIVEIRA, Portuguese Report, Q 12b.

1236 As to the restrictions see GONZÁLEZ BEILFUSS, Spanish Report, Q 12b.

1237 Ch. 9 § 3 para. 1 Swedish Children and Parents Code. See JÄNTERÄ-JAREBORG/SINGER/SÖRGJERD, Swedish Report, Q 12b.

1238 § 151 para. 2 Austrian Civil Code. See ROTH, Austrian Report, Q 12b.

tions the child generally cannot dispose of its salary if there is no parental consent (BELGIUM[1239] and GERMANY[1240]).

The child's salary is excluded from the parents' right to use and enjoy the property of the child (BELGIUM,[1241] FRANCE,[1242] ITALY,[1243] LITHUANIA[1244] and THE NETHERLANDS[1245]). On the other hand, in some jurisdictions there is a provision that the child has to contribute to cover common family expenses (CZECH REPUBLIC,[1246] GREECE,[1247] THE NETHERLANDS[1248] and SWITZERLAND[1249]). In ENGLAND AND WALES the holder of parental responsibility has no claim to the child's salary.[1250]

Restrictions with respect to certain transactions

The general principle in the Civil Law jurisdictions seems to be that the holders are free to perform all the "ordinary" acts or "normal administrative transactions" in preserving or maintaining the property under their administration (ITALY[1251] and THE NETHERLANDS[1252]). However, some transactions, even when they are beneficial to the child, are considered "not to be ordinary" due to their nature, the risk for the property and the resulting obligations of the child. In some jurisdictions "in essential matters" (CZECH REPUBLIC[1253]) or for "non-ordinary acts of administration or management" (BULGARIA[1254]) the authorisation of the court is necessary (POLAND[1255]). In other jurisdictions in such situations basically the same or similar rules apply as for guardians (BELGIUM,[1256] THE NETHERLANDS,[1257] POLAND[1258] and RUSSIA[1259]). In RUSSIAN law there

1239 See PINTENS/PIGNOLET, Belgian Report, Q 12b.
1240 See DETHLOFF/MARTINY, German Report, Q 12b.
1241 See PINTENS/PIGNOLET, Belgian Report, Q 12b.
1242 Art. 387 French Civil Code. See FERRAND, French Report, Q 12b.
1243 Art. 324 para. 3 No. 1 Italian Civil Code.
1244 Art. 2.7, 3.187 Lithuanian Civil Code. See MIKELENAS, Lithuanian Report, Q 12a.
1245 Art. 1:253l § 1 Dutch Civil Code. See BOELE-WOELKI/SCHRAMA/VONK, Dutch Report, Q 12b.
1246 § 31 para. 4 Czech Family Code. See HRUSAKOVÁ, Czech Report, Q 12b.
1247 Art. 1529 Greek Civil Code. See KOUTSOURADIS/ZERVOGIANNI, Greek Report, Q 12c.
1248 Art. 1:253l § 1 Dutch Civil Code. See BOELE-WOELKI/SCHRAMA/VONK, Dutch Report, Q 12b.
1249 Art. 323 para. 2 Swiss Civil Code.
1250 See LOWE, English Report, Q 12b.
1251 Art. 320 Italian Civil Code. See PATTI/BELLISARIO/ROSSI CARLEO, Italian Report, Q 2f.
1252 Art. 1:345 Dutch Civil Code. See BOELE-WOELKI/SCHRAMA/VONK, Dutch Report, Q 12c.
1253 § 28 Czech Civil Code. See HRUSAKOVÁ, Czech Report, Q 10.
1254 See TODOROVA, Bulgarian Report, Q 2f and Q 11.
1255 Art. 101 para. 3 Polish Family and Guardianship Code. See MĄCZYŃSKI/MĄCZYŃSKA, Polish Report, Q 12a.
1256 Art. 378, 410 Belgian Civil Code. See PINTENS/PIGNOLET, Belgian Report, Q 1 a.
1257 See BOELE-WOELKI/SCHRAMA/VONK, Dutch Report, Q 11.
1258 See MĄCZYŃSKI/MĄCZYŃSKA, Polish Report, Q 11.
1259 See ANTOKOLSKAIA, Russian Report, Q 11.

is the restriction that generally for transactions on behalf of a child under the age of fourteen an authorisation from the Guardianship and curatorship department is needed.[1260]

There often exists a more or less extensive list of transactions where an authorisation by the competent authority is necessary (AUSTRIA,[1261] BELGIUM,[1262] DENMARK,[1263] FINLAND,[1264] FRANCE,[1265] GERMANY,[1266] ITALY,[1267] THE NETHERLANDS,[1268] PORTUGAL,[1269] RUSSIA,[1270] SPAIN[1271] and SWEDEN[1272]). Generally, authorisation is required for unusual and/or risky transactions. These transactions include especially the sale and encumbrance of real estate (AUSTRIA,[1273] BELGIUM,[1274] BULGARIA,[1275] FRANCE,[1276] GREECE,[1277] HUNGARY,[1278] ITALY,[1279] LITHUANIA,[1280] THE NETHERLANDS,[1281] PORTUGAL[1282] and SWEDEN[1283]). The waiver of the right of inheritance is also such a transaction (AUSTRIA,[1284] LITHUANIA[1285] and PORTUGAL[1286]). Financial transactions such as the granting of a loan or entering into a loan agreement are also restricted (AUSTRIA,[1287]

1260 See ANTOKOLSKAIA, Russian Report, Q 12a, c.
1261 See ROTH, Austrian Report, Q 12c and Q 37.
1262 Art. 410 Belgian Civil Code. See PINTENS/PIGNOLET, Belgian Report, Q 11 and Q 12a.
1263 See LUND-ANDERSEN/JEPPESEN-DE BOER, Danish Report, Q 11.
1264 See KURKI-SUONIO, Finnish Report, Q 12a, c.
1265 Art. 389–5 para. 3 French Civil Code. See FERRAND, French Report, Q 11.
1266 § 1643, § 1821 and § 1822 German Civil Code. See DETHLOFF/MARTINY, German Report, Q 12c.
1267 Art. 320 para. 3 Italian Civil Code. See PATTI/BELLISARIO/ROSSI CARLEO, Italian Report, Q 11.
1268 Art. 1:345 Dutch Civil Code. See BOELE-WOELKI/SCHRAMA/VONK, Dutch Report, Q 12c.
1269 Art. 1889 Portuguese Civil Code. See DE OLIVEIRA, Portuguese Report, Q 12c.
1270 See ANTOKOLSKAIA, Russian Report, Q 12c.
1271 See GONZÁLEZ BEILFUSS, Spanish Report, Q 12c.
1272 See JÄNTERÄ-JAREBORG/SINGER/SÖRGJERD, Swedish Report, Q 12c.
1273 § 154 para. 3 Austrian Civil Code. See ROTH, Austrian Report, Q 12c.
1274 See PINTENS/PIGNOLET, Belgian Report, Q 12a.
1275 See TODOROVA, Bulgarian Report, Q 11.
1276 See FERRAND, French Report, Q 11.
1277 See KOUTSOURADIS/ZERVOGIANNI, Greek Report, Q 12c.
1278 See WEISS/SZEIBERT, Hungarian Report, Q 12c.
1279 Art. 320 para. 3 Italian Civil Code. See PATTI/BELLISARIO/ROSSI CARLEO, Italian Report, Q 11.
1280 See MIKELENAS, Lithuanian Report, Q 12c.
1281 Art. 1:345 Dutch Civil Code. See BOELE-WOELKI/SCHRAMA/VONK, Dutch Report, Q 12c.
1282 Art. 1889 Portuguese Civil Code. See DE OLIVEIRA, Portuguese Report, Q 12c.
1283 See JÄNTERÄ-JAREBORG/SINGER/SÖRGJERD, Swedish Report, Q 12c.
1284 § 154 para. 3 Austrian Civil Code. See ROTH, Austrian Report, Q 12c.
1285 See MIKELENAS, Lithuanian Report, Q 12c.
1286 Art. 1889 Portuguese Civil Code. See DE OLIVEIRA, Portuguese Report, Q 12c.
1287 § 154 para. 3 Austrian Civil Code. See ROTH, Austrian Report, Q 12c.

BELGIUM,[1288] FINLAND,[1289] FRANCE,[1290] GERMANY,[1291] GREECE,[1292] ITALY,[1293] THE NETHERLANDS,[1294] PORTUGAL[1295] and SWEDEN[1296]). The holder of parental responsibilities may only deal with the estate of the represented person with the authorization of the court (CZECH REPUBLIC,[1297] GERMANY[1298] and HUNGARY[1299]).

In some jurisdictions there are far-reaching restrictions (RUSSIA[1300]), especially for financial transactions where authorisation is required (BULGARIA[1301] and HUNGARY[1302]). In other jurisdictions financial assets over a certain amount are under the special control of the competent authority (NORWAY[1303]). The approach to control is different in ENGLAND AND WALES, where the rights and powers of the holder of parental responsibilities are limited from the very beginning and are similar to those of a guardian of an estate.[1304]

Indebtedness of the child

In all jurisdictions the management of the child's property should not result in the indebtedness of the child, thus damaging the property and endangering the future of the child. However, only in some jurisdictions are there special provisions protecting children from indebtedness caused by the holders of parental responsibilities. These rules encompass the necessity of authorisation by the competent authority in order to incur a debt on the child's behalf (e.g. NORWAY[1305] and PORTUGAL[1306]), restrictions as to the amount of loan agreements entered into on behalf of underage children (LITHUANIA[1307]), special rules limiting the liability of the child up to the value of the child's property at the moment the child reaches the age of majority (GERMANY[1308])

1288 Art. 410, 407 Belgian Civil Code. See PINTENS/PIGNOLET, Belgian Report, Q 11 and Q 12a.

1289 See KURKI-SUONIO, Finnish Report, Q 12c.

1290 See FERRAND, French Report, Q 11.

1291 § 1643 and § 1822 No. 8 ff. German Civil Code. See DETHLOFF/MARTINY, German Report, Q 12c.

1292 See KOUTSOURADIS/ZERVOGIANNI, Greek Report, Q 12c.

1293 Art. 320 para. 3 Italian Civil Code. See PATTI/BELLISARIO/ROSSI CARLEO, Italian Report, Q 11.

1294 Art. 1:345 Dutch Civil Code. See BOELE-WOELKI/SCHRAMA/VONK, Dutch Report, Q 12c.

1295 Art. 1889 Portuguese Civil Code. See DE OLIVEIRA, Portuguese Report, Q 12c.

1296 See JÄNTERÄ-JAREBORG/SINGER/SÖRGJERD, Swedish Report, Q 13.

1297 See HRUSAKOVÁ, Czech Report, Q 12c.

1298 See DETHLOFF/MARTINY, German Report, Q 12c.

1299 See WEISS/SZEIBERT, Hungarian Report, Q 12c.

1300 See ANTOKOLSKAIA, Russian Report, Q 11.

1301 See TODOROVA, Bulgarian Report, Q 11.

1302 See WEISS/SZEIBERT, Hungarian Report, Q 12a, c.

1303 § 62 and § 63 Norwegian Act on Guardianship. See SVERDRUP/LØDRUP, Norwegian Report, Q 11, 12 a.

1304 See LOWE, English Report, Q 11.

1305 § 55 Norwegian Act on Guardianship 1927. See SVERDRUP/LØDRUP, Norwegian Report, Q 11.

1306 See DE OLIVEIRA, Portuguese Report, Q 13.

1307 See MIKELENAS, Lithuanian Report, Q 12c.

1308 See DETHLOFF/MARTINY, German Report, Q 13.

or giving the competent authority special powers (SWEDEN[1309]). In many jurisdictions only the general rules apply (e.g. BULGARIA,[1310] ENGLAND AND WALES,[1311] HUNGARY,[1312] IRELAND,[1313] ITALY,[1314] POLAND,[1315] and RUSSIA[1316]). A violation of these rules can lead to the liability of the holder of parental responsibilities (e.g. FRANCE[1317]) or the deprivation of parental responsibilities.

COMMENT

1. In accordance with the common core of the jurisdictions surveyed the administration of the child's property should not be unrestricted. Some objects must be excluded from administration by the holder of parental responsibilities. Principle 3:23 (1) follows this concept. The common core of the legal systems is that the administration of property should not include property acquired by a child *mortis causa* or received by him or her as a gift and there is a disposition by the testator or donor to this effect. Principle 3:23 (1) is in accordance with this meaning that the will of the testator or donor should be given preference.

2. The income earned by the child from work or from the carrying out of an independent gainful occupation shall not be administrated according to the general rules of parental responsibility. This is laid down in Principle 3:23 (2) and is in accordance with the common core of the majority of legal systems. However, the details, especially the age limits, do vary. Therefore Principle 3:23 (2) only mentions a sufficient age and maturity.

3. Principle 3:23 (3) contains another restriction. The holders of parental responsibilities should require authorisation from the competent authority for transactions carried out on behalf of the child in any case where such authorisation is required. The purpose of this rule – the conservation and the protection of the child's property – is in accordance with the common core of the legal systems. However, the details vary and there are more or less different catalogues of transactions. Due to the close relationship with other fields of law the principle only states that a list of transactions should be established where the protection of the child's interests is necessary.

1309 See JÄNTERÄ-JAREBORG/SINGER/SÖRGJERD, Swedish Report, Q 13.
1310 See TODOROVA, Bulgarian Report, Q 13.
1311 See LOWE, English Report, Q 13.
1312 See WEISS/SZEIBERT, Hungarian Report, Q 13.
1313 See SHANNON, Irish Report, Q 13.
1314 See PATTI/BELLISARIO/ROSSI CARLEO, Italian Report, Q 13.
1315 See MĄCZYŃSKI/MĄCZYŃSKA, Polish Report, Q 13.
1316 See ANTOKOLSKAIA, Russian Report, Q 13.
1317 Art. 389–5 para. 4 French Civil Code. See FERRAND, French Report, Q 13.

Principle 3:24 Legal representation
(1) The holders of parental responsibilities should legally represent the child in matters concerning the child's person or property.
(2) Legal representation should not take place where there is a conflict of interest between the child and the holders of parental responsibilities.
(3) Having regard to the child's age and maturity, the child should have the right to self-representation in legal proceedings concerning himself or herself.

Principe 3:24 Représentation légale
(1) Les titulaires de la responsabilité parentale représentent légalement l'enfant dans les affaires relatives à la personne ou aux biens de l'enfant.
(2) La représentation légale est exclue dans le cas d'un conflit d'intérêts entre l'enfant et les titulaires de la responsabilité parentale.
(3) Eu égard à son âge et à sa maturité, l'enfant a le droit de se représenter lui-même dans les procédures le concernant.

Prinzip 3:24 Gesetzliche Vertretung
(1) Die Inhaber der elterlichen Verantwortung vertreten kraft Gesetz das Kind in allen Angelegenheiten, die seine Person und sein Vermögen betreffen.
(2) Keine gesetzliche Vertretung findet statt, wenn ein Interessenkonflikt zwischen dem Kind und den Inhabern der elterlichen Verantwortung besteht.
(3) Entsprechend seinem Alter und seiner Reife hat das Kind das Recht, sich in Verfahren, die es betrifft, selbst zu vertreten.

INTERNATIONAL INSTRUMENTS

The legal representation of the child by the holders of parental responsibilities has not yet been addressed in general in European or international instruments. However, it has been mentioned as one of the elements that belong to the concept of parental responsibilities in Article 3(d) of the *Hague Child Protection Convention 1996* and in Principle 18 of the Council of Europe's *White Paper 2002*. The legal representation of children has been excluded from the scope of application of the *Hague Convention on the Law Applicable to Agency 1978* (Art. 2 under c).

COMPARATIVE OVERVIEW

Representation in legal proceedings and actions

The right of the holders of parental responsibilities to administer is joined by a legal right of representation. By operation of law the minor thus gets (a) representative(s) who is (are) not only entitled but indeed required to act for him.[1318] The meaning of the right and duty to legally represent the child refers not only to the position of the holders of parental responsibilities in legal proceedings but generally includes representation with regard to legal actions in both personal and economic matters. Legal representation constitutes the external relationship between the holders of parental responsibilities and third parties. In all European jurisdictions surveyed the right and duty to legally represent the child is an aspect of parental responsibilities. In the majority of jurisdictions this aspect has been regulated by statute (AUSTRIA,[1319] BELGIUM,[1320] BULGARIA,[1321] CZECH REPUBLIC,[1322] DENMARK,[1323] ENGLAND AND WALES,[1324] FINLAND,[1325] FRANCE,[1326] GERMANY,[1327] GREECE,[1328] HUNGARY,[1329] ITALY,[1330] LITHUANIA,[1331] THE NETHERLANDS,[1332] NORWAY,[1333] POLAND,[1334] PORTUGAL,[1335] RUSSIA,[1336] SPAIN,[1337] SWEDEN[1338] and SWITZERLAND[1339]). The legal representation of the child in cases where there are disputes between the child and the holders of parental responsibilities raises a different issue. In these cases a special representative for the child other than the holders of parental responsibilities is usually appointed by the competent authority.

1318 See STOLJAR, *ibid.*, note 27, no. 211.
1319 § 144 Austrian Civil Code.
1320 Art. 373–379 Belgian Civil Code.
1321 Art. 73 Bulgarian Family Code.
1322 § 39 and § 56 Czech Family Code.
1323 § 2 Danish Act on Parental Authority and Contact.
1324 Based on common law and practice rather than statute. See LOWE, English Report, Q 2d and Q 8f.
1325 § 4 Finnish Child Custody and the Right of Access Act.
1326 Art. 389 French Civil Code.
1327 § 1629 German Civil Code.
1328 Art. 1510 para. 1 and 1603 Greek Civil Code.
1329 § 86 Hungarian Family Act.
1330 Art. 320 and Art. 2 para 2 Italian Civil Code.
1331 Part. 2 of Art. 3.157 Lithuanian Civil Code.
1332 Art. 1:254 para. 4 Dutch Civil Code.
1333 Art. 3 Norwegian Act on Guardianship 1927.
1334 Art. 98 para. 1 Polish Family and Guardianship Code.
1335 Art. 1878 No. 1 Portuguese Civil Code.
1336 Art. 64 para. 1 Russian Family Code.
1337 Art. 162 Spanish Civil Code.
1338 Ch. 6 §11 and § 12 Swedish Children and Parents Code.
1339 Art. 304 para. 1 Swiss Civil Code.

Generally, each parent is individually entitled and obliged to represent the child. The parent's legal action is valid according to the law in AUSTRIA,[1340] BELGIUM,[1341] FRANCE,[1342] GERMANY,[1343] THE NETHERLANDS[1344] and POLAND[1345] even if the other parent has not given his/her consent. Normally, the legal representation of the child by the holders of parental responsibilities lasts until the age of majority. In addition to the consent of the parents to a legal action, however, the minor needs to consent if he or she is older than 14 years of age in BULGARIA,[1346] HUNGARY,[1347] LITHUANIA[1348] and RUSSIA,[1349] whereas in the CZECH REPUBLIC[1350] and PORTUGAL[1351] a minor possesses legal capacity only if the nature of such acts corresponds to the mental and moral maturity of the child in question.

Conflict of interest

In administrating the property of the child conflicts of interests may arise between the child and the holders of parental responsibilities. This can happen when there is a contract between a spouse or a relative of the holder of parental responsibilities. In particular, a conflict of interests may arise when parents in a transaction both give and accept for the child, i.e. the holders of the parental responsibilities are themselves parties to the contract. In these situations legal representation of the child is excluded (FRANCE[1352] and GERMANY[1353]); generally a guardian or custodian must be appointed (BELGIUM,[1354] FRANCE,[1355] GREECE,[1356] ITALY[1357] and LITHUANIA[1358]).

1340 § 154 para. 1 Austrian Civil Code.
1341 See PINTENS/PIGNOLET, Belgian Report, Q 8f.
1342 Art. 389–4 French Civil Code.
1343 1629 para. 1 German Civil Code (in some instances).
1344 Art. 1:253i para. 1 Dutch Civil Code.
1345 Art. 98 par. 1 Polish Family and Guardianship Code.
1346 SeeTODOROVA, Bulgarian Report, Q 8e.
1347 See WEISS/SZEIBERT, Hungarian Report, Q 8e.
1348 See MIKELENAS, Lithuanian Report, Q 8e.
1349 Art. 26 para. 1 Russian Civil Code (specific transactions).
1350 § 9 Czech Civil Code.
1351 Art. 1881 No. 1 Portuguese Civil Code.
1352 Art. 389–3 para. 2 French Civil Code. See FERRAND, French Report, Q 12a.
1353 § 181 German Civil Code. See DETHLOFF/MARTINY, German Report, Q 12c.
1354 Art. 378 Belgian Civil Code. See PINTENS/PIGNOLET, Belgian Report, Q 12c.
1355 See FERRAND, French Report, Q 11.
1356 See KOUTSOURADIS/ZERVOGIANNI, Greek Report, Q 13.
1357 Art. 320 para. 6 Italian Civil Code. See PATTI/BELLISARIO/ROSSI CARLEO, Italian Report, Q 10 and Q 12c.
1358 Art. 3.188 Lithuanian Civil Code. See MIKELENAS, Lithuanian Report, Q 11.

Personal and economic matters

As to the rights of the holders of parental responsibilities to legally represent the child, a distinction must be made between, on the one hand, actions of a personal nature (personal matters) and, on the other, actions that substantially affect the child's property (economic matters). Regarding personal matters both parents need to consent in the case of important actions, e.g. changing the child's name, the acquisition of citizenship or the minor's acknowledgment of paternity in AUSTRIA,[1359] FRANCE,[1360] and LITHUANIA.[1361] In BELGIUM[1362] and the CZECH REPUBLIC[1363] representation by the parents is however prohibited with regard to acts of a special personal character, such as making a will, consent to adoption or the declaration of paternity. Self-representation in cases relating to personal matters is possible in SPAIN[1364] and FINLAND[1365] if the child has reached the age of 14 or 15 years, respectively, or if he or she is of sufficient maturity and understanding in ENGLAND AND WALES[1366] and ITALY.[1367] In SPAIN[1368] and HUNGARY[1369] minors older than 14 years of age can even dispose of their property *mortis causa* in a will without the consent of the parents. Actions that affect the child's economic situation and that extend beyond the ordinary administration of the child's property, such as, for example, taking out a loan or renouncing an inheritance or donation, usually require judicial authorisation in most of the jurisdictions surveyed.

COMMENT

1. A child who has not attained majority does not have full legal capacity. It is a general accepted principle that by virtue of law the parents are the general representatives of the minor child. If parental responsibilities are attributed to a person other than a parent (Principle 3:9) this holder of parental responsibilities has the right and duty to represent the child There are two kinds of representation, namely representing the child in economic and personal matters and representing in litigation. As for transactions these comprise, e.g. all legal contracts or dispositions connected with the

1359 Art. 154 para. 2 Austrian Civil Code.

1360 Art. 389–5 French Civil Code.

1361 Part 3 Art. 3.142 and Lithuanian Civil Code.

1362 Art. 410 Belgium Civil Code.

1363 See HRUSAKOVÁ, Czech Report, Q 8e.

1364 Art. 162 Spanish Civil Code and Art. 155 Catalan Family Code.

1365 Ch. 12 § 1, 2 Finnish Code of Judicial Procedure, § 14 para. 2 Finnish Administrative Procedure Act.

1366 S. 8 order under the English Children Act 1989, England and Wales, Rule 9.2A Family Proceedings Rules 1991, added by Rule 6, Family Proceedings (Amendment) Rules 1992.

1367 See PATTI/BELLISARIO/ROSSI CARLEO, Italian Report, Q 8e.

1368 Art. 663.1 Spanish Civil Code.

1369 See WEISS/SZEIBERT, Hungarian Report, Q 8e, if the will is made by a public instrument.

management of the child's property. The transactional side of representation has been specifically addressed in Principles 3:22 and 3:23.

2. The holders of parental responsibilities are the legal representatives. Principle 3:24 (2) prohibits legal representation if there is a conflict of interests between the child and the holders of parental responsibilities. Where there is a conflict of interests only with one of the child's parents the child should be represented by the other parent whose interests do not conflict with those of the child.

3. Often the child's litigation will arise out of the administration of its property. The holders of parental responsibilities have a right to sue and to be sued on the child's behalf. Other proceedings are likely: the child may have suffered injury or have caused one; he or she may be entitled to social benefits which need to be claimed.

4. In representing the child in personal and economic matters the best interests of the child (Principle 3:3), the non-discrimination of the child (Principle 3:5) and the child's right to be heard (Principle 3:6) should always be taken into account.

5. Principle 3:24 (1), however, does not extend to all acts. In some spheres a child cannot be represented by another person but must act alone. This right of self-representation -to which in particular adolescents should be entitled is expressed in Principle 3:24 (3) and it often exists in matters of a special personal character. Whether in these matters the consent of the holders of parental responsibilities additionally should be required, is to be answered by national law.

SECTION B: MAINTENANCE OF PERSONAL RELATIONSHIPS
SECTION B: MAINTIEN DES RELATIONS PERSONNELLES
ABSCHNITT B: UNTERHALTEN PERSÖNLICHER BEZIEHUNGEN

Principle 3:25 Contact with parents and other persons

(1) The child and the parents should have the right to obtain and maintain regular contact with each other.

(2) Contact should be established between the child and his or her close relatives.

(3) Contact may be established between the child and persons with whom the child has close personal relations.

Principe 3:25 Relations personnelles avec ses père et mère et d'autres personnes

(1) L'enfant et ses père et mère ont le droit d'avoir et d'entretenir entre eux des relations personnelles régulières.

(2) Des relations personnelles sont établies entre l'enfant et ses parents proches.

(3) Des relations personnelles peuvent être établies entre l'enfant et les personnes avec lesquelles l'enfant entretient des relations personnelles étroites.

Prinzip 3:25 Umgang mit Eltern und anderen Personen

(1) Das Kind und die Eltern haben das Recht, regelmäßigen Umgang miteinander zu erhalten und zu unterhalten.

(2) Umgang erfolgt auch zwischen dem Kind und seinen nahen Verwandten.

(3) Umgang kann auch zwischen dem Kind und Personen erfolgen, mit denen das Kind eine enge persönliche Beziehung hat.

INTERNATIONAL INSTRUMENTS

The principle of "maintenance of personal relations" and of "direct contact" between parents and children is recognized by Article 9 para. 3 United Nations *Convention on the Rights of the Child 1989*. Under Article 8 of the *European Convention on Human Rights 1950* the right of contact of a non-custodial parent after divorce has also been recognized, but is subject to the child's interests.[1370] The European Court of Human Rights also recognises that the best interests of the child are of crucial importance.[1371] According to the *Draft Treaty for a European Constitution 2003* every child shall have the right to maintain on a regular basis a personal relationship and direct contact with both his or her parents, unless that is contrary to his or her interests (Art. II–84 para. 3). The most recent *Convention on Contact Concerning Children 2003* deals with general principles to be applied to contact orders and with measures to promote and improve transfrontier contact. Article 4 guarantees contact between a child and his or her parents. The Explanatory Report states that according to Article 4 para. 2 contact between the child and his or her parents may only be restricted or excluded where this is necessary in the best interests of the child. Moreover, Article 5 para. 1 *Convention on Contact Concerning Children 2003* recognises that it may be in the best interests of the child to have contact with persons other than his or her parents. These are only persons who have "family ties" with the child, however. According to the Explanatory Report this expression was borrowed from the case law of the European Court of Human Rights, in particular on Article 8 of the *European Convention on Human Rights 1950*.[1372] It is defined in Article 2 (d) of the *Convention on Contact Concerning Children 2003* as meaning a close relationship such as that between a child and his or her grandparents or siblings or a de facto relationship. The Explanatory Report specifies that this category comprises foster parents, a spouse or former spouse of the parent or a former cohabitee of the parent. States parties to the Convention are free to extend Article 5 to other persons (Art. 5 para. 2). The protection granted to the contact rights of these persons is rather weak. It is only stated that contact "may be established" between the child and these persons. Principle 18 of the Council of Europe's *White Paper 2002* mentions the maintenance of personal relationships as a part of parental responsibilities, but does not go into detail. According to *Recommendation on Parental Responsibilities 1984* by the Committee of Ministers of the Council of Europe the parent with whom the child does not live should have at least the possibility of maintaining personal relationships with the child unless such relationships would be seriously harmful to the interests of the child (Principle 8). "Rights of access" are also a part of parental responsibility in Article 1 para. 2 (a) and Article 2 No. 7 of the *Brussels II bis Regulation*. The right of the child to maintain contact with both parents is reinforced by ensuring that decisions on access rights are automatically recognised and enforceable in another Member State if certain

---

1370 European Court of Human Rights, 23.9.1994 *Hokkanen v. Finland;* 19.9.2000 *Glaser v. UK;* 21.10.2004 *L and U v. Sweden*; 23.6.2005 *Zawadka v. Poland*; 13.7.2006 *Lafargue v. Romania*; 21.9.2006 *Moser v. Austria*.

1371 European Court of Human Rights, 7.8.1996 *Johansen v. Norway*.

1372 European Court of Human Rights, 13.7.2000 *Scozzari v. Italy*.

procedural conditions are met (see Art. 40 ff. *Brussels II bis Regulation*). This right is also covered by the *Hague Child Protection Convention 1996* (Art. 3 lit. b).

COMPARATIVE OVERVIEW

Contact between a child and his or her parents

In all legal systems surveyed the child has a right of contact with its parents. Especially a parent holding parental responsibilities, but not living with the child, has a right of contact with the child (AUSTRIA,[1373] BELGIUM,[1374] BULGARIA,[1375] CZECH REPUBLIC,[1376] DENMARK,[1377] FINLAND,[1378] FRANCE,[1379] GERMANY,[1380] GREECE,[1381] HUNGARY,[1382] IRELAND,[1383] ITALY,[1384] LITHUANIA,[1385] THE NETHERLANDS,[1386] NORWAY,[1387] POLAND,[1388] PORTUGAL,[1389] RUSSIA,[1390] SPAIN,[1391] SWEDEN[1392] and SWITZERLAND[1393]). A child has the same right to personal contact with a non-custodial parent not holding parental responsibilities (in the sense of custody or parental authority) and not living in the same household with the child (AUSTRIA,[1394] BELGIUM,[1395] BULGARIA,[1396] CZECH

1373 § 148 Austrian Civil Code.
1374 See PINTENS/PIGNOLET, Belgian Report, Q 44a.
1375 See TODOROVA, Bulgarian Report, Q 44a.
1376 See HRUSAKOVÁ, Czech Report, Q 44a.
1377 § 16 Danish Act on Parental Authority and Contact.
1378 See KURKI-SUONIO, Finnish Report, Q 44a.
1379 Art. 373–2 para. 2 French Civil Code. See FERRAND, French Report, Q 44a.
1380 § 1626 para. 3 German Civil Code.
1381 Art. 1520 Greek Civil Code.
1382 See WEISS/SZEIBERT, Hungarian Report, Q 44a.
1383 See SHANNON, Irish Report, Q 44a.
1384 See PATTI/BELLISARIO/ROSSI CARLEO, Italian Report, Q 44a.
1385 See MIKELENAS, Lithuanian Report, Q 44a.
1386 See BOELE-WOELKI/SCHRAMA/VONK, Dutch Report, Q 44a.
1387 See SVERDRUP/LØDRUP, Norwegian Report, Q 44a.
1388 See MĄCZYŇSKI/MĄCZYŇSKA, Polish Report, Q 44a.
1389 See DE OLIVEIRA, Portuguese Report, Q 44a.
1390 Art. 55 para. 1 Russian Family Code.
1391 Art. 160 Spanish Civil Code; Art. 135.1 Catalan Family Code.
1392 Ch. 6 § 15 para. 1 Swedish Children and Parents Code.
1393 Art. 273 para. 1 Swiss Civil Code.
1394 § 148 para. 1 Austrian Civil Code.
1395 Art. 375bis Belgian Civil Code. See PINTENS/PIGNOLET, Belgian Report, Q 44b.
1396 See TODOROVA, Bulgarian Report, Q 44b.

REPUBLIC,[1397] DENMARK,[1398] FINLAND,[1399] GERMANY,[1400] GREECE,[1401] HUNGARY,[1402] IRELAND,[1403] ITALY,[1404] LITHUANIA,[1405] THE NETHERLANDS,[1406] NORWAY,[1407] POLAND,[1408] PORTUGAL,[1409] RUSSIA,[1410] SPAIN,[1411] SWEDEN[1412]and SWITZERLAND[1413]). This is the consequence of the prevailing approach that the maintenance of personal relationships is seen as an effect of parenthood. In some jurisdictions the right of contact depends mainly on whether there was a total loss of parental responsibilities which deprived the parent of all contact rights (FRANCE[1414] and ITALY[1415]). Although in ENGLISH law any talk of a "right" of contact with the parents is generally avoided, an enduring relationship with both parents is seen as desirable. A contact order will only be denied if there are cogent reasons.[1416]

Contact with other relatives

In the vast majority of jurisdictions the importance of contact between the child and persons other than his or her parents is recognised and the child has a right of contact with his or her grandparents. In most jurisdictions the grandparents' right of contact is based on the existing kinship relationship (BULGARIA,[1417] CZECH REPUBLIC,[1418]

1397 See HRUSAKOVÁ, Czech Report, Q 44a, b.
1398 § 16 Danish Act on Parental Authority and Contact.
1399 See KURKI-SUONIO, Finnish Report, Q 44b.
1400 § 1684 para. 1 German Civil Code.
1401 See KOUTSOURADIS/ZERVOGIANNI, Greek Report, Q 44b.
1402 See WEISS/SZEIBERT, Hungarian Report, Q 44b.
1403 See SHANNON, Irish Report, Q 44 a.
1404 See PATTI/BELLISARIO/ROSSI CARLEO, Italian Report, Q 44b.
1405 See MIKELENAS, Lithuanian Report, Q 44b
1406 Art. 1:377a para. 1 Dutch Civil Code. See BOELE-WOELKI/SCHRAMA/VONK, Dutch Report, Q 44b.
1407 See SVERDRUP/LØDRUP, Norwegian Report, Q 44 b.
1408 Art. 113 § 2 Polish Family and Guardianship Code. See MĄCZYŃSKI/MĄCZYŃSKA, Polish Report, Q 44b.
1409 Art. 1905 No. 1 Portuguese Civil Code. See DE OLIVEIRA, Portuguese Report, Q 44b.
1410 See ANTOKOLSKAIA, Russian Report, Q 44b.
1411 Art. 160 Spanish Cvil Code and Art. 135.1 Catalan Family Code. See GONZÁLEZ BEILFUSS, Spanish Report, Q 44b.
1412 See JÄNTERÄ-JAREBORG/SINGER/SÖRGJERD, Swedish Report, Q 44b.
1413 Art. 273 para. 1 Swiss Civil Code.
1414 Art. 379 French Civil Code. See FERRAND, French Report, Q 44b.
1415 See PATTI/BELLISARIO/ROSSI CARLEO, Italian Report, Q 44b.
1416 See LOWE, English Report, Q 44a, b and Q 45.
1417 Art. 70 para. 2 Bulgarian Family Code.
1418 § 27 para. 4 Czech Family Code.

GERMANY,[1419] GREECE,[1420] HUNGARY,[1421] LITHUANIA,[1422] PORTUGAL[1423] and RUSSIA[1424]). In others it is only based on existing emotional ties (AUSTRIA[1425]), a "close relationship" (THE NETHERLANDS[1426]), the child's interests (BELGIUM[1427]), the interests of the relatives (ITALY[1428]) or exceptional circumstances (SWITZERLAND[1429]). Italian law does not consider that there is such a right, but that there is an interest which is worth protecting.[1430]

Some jurisdictions have extended the right of contact to all ascendants (ancestors) (FRANCE[1431] and PORTUGAL[1432]) or relatives (RUSSIA[1433] and SPAIN[1434]) of the child. Also in Irish law "relatives" are covered, which includes persons who are related to the child by marriage or adoption as well as by blood.[1435] Under English law the issue will be determined according to the child's welfare.[1436]

Only in a minority of jurisdictions are the formal contact rights of the grandparents not recognised (DENMARK,[1437] FINLAND[1438] and POLAND[1439]) or are very restricted (NORWAY[1440] and SWEDEN[1441]). These legal systems take the view that contact with grandparents is only beneficial if it is agreed by the parents, the main parental responsibility holders. In NORWAY the right of contact is only given if the parents are no longer alive or the courts have denied a parent's right of contact.[1442] In SWEDEN proceedings requesting contact can only be initiated by the social welfare committee,

---

1419 § 1685 para. 1 German Civil Code.
1420 See KOUTSOURADIS/ZERVOGIANNI, Greek Report, Q 44c and Q 45.
1421 See WEISS/SZEIBERT, Hungarian Report, Q 44c.
1422 Art. 3.172 Lithuanian Civil Code.
1423 Art. 1887–A Portuguese Civil Code.
1424 Art. 55 Russian Family Code.
1425 § 148 para. 3 Austrian Civil Code. See ROTH, Austrian Report, Q 43 and Q 44c.
1426 Art. 1:377f Dutch Civil Code. See BOELE-WOELKI/SCHRAMA/VONK, Dutch Report, Q 44c.
1427 Art. 375bis Belgian Civil Code.
1428 See PATTI/BELLISARIO/ROSSI CARLEO, Italian Report, Q 44c.
1429 Art. 274a Swiss Civil Code. See HAUSHEER/ACHERMANN-WEBER/WOLF, Swiss Report, Q 44c.
1430 See PATTI/BELLISARIO/ROSSI CARLEO, Italian Report, Q 44 c.
1431 Art. 371–4 para. 1 French Civil Code. See FERRAND, French Report, Q 44c.
1432 Art. 1887–A Portuguese Civil Code.
1433 Art. 55 para. 1 Russian Family Code.
1434 Art. 160 Spanish Civil Code. See GONZÁLEZ BEILFUSS, Spanish Report, Q 44c.
1435 S. 9 IRISH CHILDREN ACT 1997 AS AMENDED. SEE SHANNON, IRISH REPORT, Q 44C.
1436 See LOWE, English Report, Q 44c.
1437 See LUND-ANDERSEN/JEPPESEN-DE BOER, Danish Report, Q 44c.
1438 See KURKI-SUONIO, Finnish Report, Q 44c.
1439 See MĄCZYŃSKI/MĄCZYŃSKA, Polish Report, Q 44c.
1440 § 45 Norwegian Children Act 1981. See SVERDRUP/LØDRUP, Norwegian Report, Q 44c.
1441 Ch. 6 § 15 Swedish Children and Parents Code. See JÄNTERÄ-JAREBORG/SINGER/SÖRGJERD, Swedish Report, Q 44c.
1442 See SVERDRUP/LØDRUP, Norwegian Report, Q 44c.

which rarely occurs in practice. The issue of contact rights to persons other than parents has been considered by various Danish Commissions, which concluded that contact is only in the best interests of the child if it is not opposed by the person holding parental responsibility.[1443]

The differences between the systems, however, must not be overestimated. A formal contact arrangement by the competent authority will generally only be requested if there is conflict within the family. Even where grandparents are granted an express right to have contact with the child, it is often permissible to restrict contact with grandparents if it disturbs the parent-child relationship (AUSTRIA[1444] and GERMANY[1445]). In this respect there is a tendency to give priority to the opinions of the main holders of parental responsibilities. Therefore the grandparents' right to contact will often be denied.

The right to contact with siblings is also recognized in nearly all jurisdictions (BELGIUM,[1446] BULGARIA,[1447] CZECH REPUBLIC,[1448] HUNGARY,[1449] IRELAND,[1450] ITALY,[1451] LITHUANIA,[1452] THE NETHERLANDS,[1453] PORTUGAL[1454] and RUSSIA[1455]). In some jurisdictions it has to be shown in particular that contact would be in the child's interests (AUSTRIA,[1456] ENGLAND AND WALES,[1457] FRANCE,[1458] GERMANY[1459] and SWITZERLAND[1460]). There are, however, some jurisdictions where siblings do not have such a formal right (DENMARK,[1461] FINLAND[1462] and GREECE[1463]) or where their legal position is very restricted (SWEDEN[1464]).

1443 See LUND-ANDERSEN/JEPPESEN-DE BOER, Danish Report, Q 44c.
1444 § 148 PARA. 3 AUSTRIAN CIVIL CODE.
1445 See DETHLOFF/MARTINY, German Report, Q 48b.
1446 See PINTENS/PIGNOLET, Belgian Report, Q 44c.
1447 See TODOROVA, Bulgarian Report, Q 44c.
1448 § 27 para. 4 Czech Family Code.
1449 See WEISS/SZEIBERT, Hungarian Report, Q 44c.
1450 See SHANNON, Irish Report, Q 44c.
1451 See PATTI/BELLISARIO/ROSSI CARLEO, Italian Report, Q 44c.
1452 Art. 3.172 Lithuanian Civil Code.
1453 See BOELE-WOELKI/SCHRAMA/VONK, Dutch Report, Q 44 c.
1454 Art. 1887–A Portuguese Civil Code.
1455 Art. 55 para. 1 Russian Family Code.
1456 § 148 para. 4 Austrian Civil Code. See ROTH, Austrian Report Q 44c.
1457 See LOWE, English Report, Q 44c.
1458 Art. 371–4 para. 2 French Civil Code.
1459 § 1685 para. 1 German Civil Code.
1460 Art. 274a Swiss Civil Code. See HAUSHEER/ACHERMANN-WEBER/WOLF, Swiss Report, Q 44c.
1461 See LUND-ANDERSEN/JEPPESEN-DE BOER, Danish Report, Q 44c.
1462 See KURKI-SUONIO, Finnish Report, Q 44c.
1463 See KOUTSOURADIS/ZERVOGIANNI, Greek Report, Q 44c.
1464 See JÄNTERÄ-JAREBORG/SINGER/SÖRGJERD, Swedish Report, Q 44c.

Contact between a child and third persons

A child may also be granted personal contacts with third persons who are not relatives, but to whom he or she nevertheless has significant, close emotional ties if interrupting the contact would be disadvantageous to the child (AUSTRIA[1465] and BELGIUM,[1466] FRANCE,[1467] GERMANY,[1468] IRELAND,[1469] THE NETHERLANDS[1470] and SPAIN[1471]). This group of persons includes mainly step-parents, foster-parents and a former partner of the holder of parental responsibilities. Belgian law requires that these persons prove the existence of a significant affectionate relationship with the child.[1472] In German law there is a general provision that persons with whom a "socio-familial relationship" existed have a right of contact.[1473] In THE NETHERLANDS "social parents" who had a "close personal relationship" with the child may apply for contact.[1474] In SPAIN a close relationship also gives a contact right.[1475] Similarly in IRELAND not only relatives but also persons who acted *in loco parentis* in respect of the child can be granted contact.[1476] As always, contact is subject to the welfare of the child. However, this aspect is stressed in some jurisdictions. There it has to be established why it is in the child's interests to grant a certain contact right (ENGLAND AND WALES[1477] and FRANCE[1478]). Similarly in SWISS law such a contact right is only granted under exceptional circumstances.[1479] There are also some jurisdictions where the right to contact of third persons is not recognized (BULGARIA,[1480] DENMARK,[1481] FINLAND,[1482] GREECE,[1483] HUNGARY,[1484] ITALY,[1485] LITHUANIA[1486] and RUSSIA[1487]). Sometimes third persons can be granted contact, but

1465 § 148 para. 4 Austrian Civil Code.
1466 Art. 375bis Belgian Civil Code. See PINTENS/PIGNOLET, Belgian Report, Q 45.
1467 Art. 371–4 para 2 French Civil Code.
1468 § 1685 para.2 German Civil Code.
1469 See SHANNON, Irish Report, Q 44c.
1470 Art. 1:377 a para. 1 Dutch Civil Code.
1471 See GONZÁLEZ BEILFUSS, Spanish Report, Q 44c.
1472 See PINTENS/PIGNOLET, Belgian Report, Q 44c.
1473 § 1685 para. 2 German Civil Code. See DETHLOFF/MARTINY, German Report, Q 44 .
1474 Art. 1:377 f Dutch Civil Code. See BOELE-WOELKI/SCHRAMA/VONK, Dutch Report, Q 44c and Q 45.
1475 Art. 160 Spanish Civil Code.
1476 See SHANNON, Irish Report, Q 44c.
1477 See LOWE, English Report, Q 44c.
1478 Art. 371–4 para. 2 French Civil Code. See FERRAND, French Report, Q 44c.
1479 Art. 274a Swiss Civil Code. See HAUSHEER/ACHERMANN-WEBER/WOLF, Swiss Report, Q 44c.
1480 See TODOROVA, Bulgarian Report, Q 44c.
1481 See LUND-ANDERSEN/JEPPESEN-DE BOER, Danish Report, Q 44c.
1482 See KURKI-SUONIO, Finnish Report, Q 44c.
1483 See KOUTSOURADIS/ZERVOGIANNI, Greek Report, Q 44c.
1484 See WEISS/SZEIBERT, Hungarian Report, Q 44c.
1485 See PATTI/BELLISARIO/ROSSI CARLEO, Italian Report, Q 44c.
1486 See MIKELENAS, Lithuanian Report, Q 44c.
1487 See ANTOKOLSKAIA, Russian Report, Q 44c.

they themselves do not have an independent right of contact (AUSTRIA[1488] and SWEDEN[1489]).

Right or duty to contact

The traditional view is that the right to contact is a right of the respective parent. Therefore, this right is recognized by all jurisdictions surveyed (AUSTRIA,[1490] BELGIUM,[1491] BULGARIA,[1492] CZECH REPUBLIC,[1493] DENMARK,[1494] FINLAND,[1495] FRANCE,[1496] GERMANY,[1497] GREECE,[1498] HUNGARY,[1499] ITALY,[1500] LITHUANIA,[1501] THE NETHERLANDS,[1502] NORWAY,[1503] POLAND,[1504] PORTUGAL,[1505] RUSSIA,[1506] SPAIN,[1507] SWEDEN[1508] and SWITZERLAND[1509]). In ENGLAND AND WALES[1510] and IRELAND[1511] it has been stressed that it is not the right of the parent, but the right of the child, that is at stake.

Many systems have also established that the residential parent holding parental responsibility has a duty to enable and support the exercise of the child's right to maintain personal relationships with his or her parent (AUSTRIA,[1512] BELGIUM,[1513]

1488 See ROTH, Austrian Report, Q 45.
1489 See JÄNTERÄ-JAREBORG/SINGER/SÖRGJERD, Swedish Report, Q 44c and Q 45.
1490 See ROTH, Austrian Report, Q 45.
1491 See PINTENS/PIGNOLET, Belgian Report, Q 45.
1492 See TODOROVA, Bulgarian Report, Q 45.
1493 See HRUSAKOVÁ, Czech Report, Q 45.
1494 See LUND-ANDERSEN/JEPPESEN-DE BOER, Danish Report, Q 44a.
1495 See KURKI-SUONIO, Finnish Report, Q 44a.
1496 Art. 373–2–1 French Civil Code.
1497 § 1684 para. 1 German Civil Code.
1498 See KOUTSOURADIS/ZERVOGIANNI, Greek Report, Q 45.
1499 See WEISS/SZEIBERT, Hungarian Report, Q 45.
1500 See PATTI/BELLISARIO/ROSSI CARLEO, Italian Report, Q 45.
1501 See MIKELENAS, Lithuanian Report, Q 45.
1502 See BOELE-WOELKI/SCHRAMA/VONK, Dutch Report, Q 45.
1503 See SVERDRUP/LØDRUP, Norwegian Report, Q 45.
1504 See MĄCZYŃSKI/MĄCZYŃSKA, Polish Report, Q 44a.
1505 See DE OLIVEIRA, Portuguese Report, Q 44b and Q 45.
1506 See ANTOKOLSKAIA, Russian Report, Q 45.
1507 See GONZÁLEZ BEILFUSS, Spanish Report, Q 45.
1508 See JÄNTERÄ-JAREBORG, Swedish Report, Q 45.
1509 See HAUSHEER/ACHERMANN-WEBER/WOLF, Swiss Report, Q 45.
1510 See LOWE, English Report, Q 45.
1511 See SHANNON, Irish Report, Q 45.
1512 See ROTH, Austrian Report, Q 48.
1513 See PINTENS/PIGNOLET, Belgian Report, Q 48.

BULGARIA,[1514] CZECH REPUBLIC,[1515] FINLAND,[1516] FRANCE,[1517] GERMANY,[1518] NORWAY,[1519] PORTUGAL[1520] and SWEDEN[1521]). If a parent hampers contact with the other parent, this may even lead to a change in parental responsibilities if this is compatible with the child's best interests.

In more than half of the jurisdictions surveyed the parent also has a duty to maintain personal relations with the child (AUSTRIA,[1522] FRANCE,[1523] GERMANY,[1524] HUNGARY,[1525] ITALY,[1526] LITHUANIA,[1527] PORTUGAL,[1528] RUSSIA,[1529] SPAIN,[1530] SWEDEN[1531] and SWITZERLAND[1532]). In THE NETHERLANDS there is a reform project according to which both parents will have an explicit duty to contact.[1533] In ENGLAND AND WALES such an obligation can only be assumed in theory.[1534] The contact right of the child and the corresponding duty of the parent to maintain contact are, however, difficult to enforce; see the comparative overview under Principle 3:39. In a minority of jurisdictions no such duty exists on the part of the parent (CZECH REPUBLIC,[1535] FINLAND,[1536] GREECE[1537] and NORWAY[1538]). The main argument for this position is that maintaining contact is only beneficial to a child's welfare if it is done on a voluntary basis and that forced contacts are not useful.

Where there is a contact right belonging to the grandparents, only in AUSTRIA is this also understood as a duty of these persons to take their responsibility towards the child

[1514] See TODOROVA, Bulgarian Report, Q 48.
[1515] See HRUSAKOVÁ, Czech Report, Q 48.
[1516] See KURKI-SUONIO, Finnish Report, Q 48.
[1517] Art. 373–2 para. 2 French Civil Code.
[1518] § 1684 para. 2 German Civil Code.
[1519] See SVERDRUP/LØDRUP, Norwegian Report, Q 48
[1520] See DE OLIVEIRA, Portuguese Report, Q 48.
[1521] See JÄNTERÄ-JAREBORG/SINGER/SÖRGJERD, Swedish Report, Q 48
[1522] See ROTH, Austrian Report, Q 45.
[1523] Art. 373–2 para. 2 French Civil Code. See FERRAND, French Report, Q 45.
[1524] § 1684 para. 1 German Civil Code. See DETHLOFF/MARTINY, German Report, Q 45 ("Pflichtrecht").
[1525] See WEISS/SZEIBERT, Hungarian Report, Q 45.
[1526] See PATTI/BELLISARIO/ROSSI CARLEO, Italian Report, Q 45.
[1527] See MIKELENAS, Lithuanian Report, Q 45.
[1528] See DE OLIVEIRA, Portuguese Report, Q 44b and Q 45.
[1529] See ANTOKOLSKAIA, Russian Report, Q 45.
[1530] See GONZÁLEZ BEILFUSS, Spanish Report, Q 45.
[1531] See JÄNTERÄ-JAREBORG/SINGER/SÖRGJERD, Swedish Report, Q 45.
[1532] See HAUSHEER/ACHERMANN-WEBER/WOLF, Swiss Report, Q 45.
[1533] See BOELE-WOELKI/SCHRAMA/VONK, Dutch Report, Q 45.
[1534] See LOWE, English Report, Q 45.
[1535] See HRUSAKOVÁ, Czech Report, Q 45.
[1536] See KURKI-SUONIO, Finnish Report, Q 45.
[1537] See KOUTSOURADIS/ZERVOGIANNI, Greek Report, Q 45.
[1538] See SVERDRUP/LØDRUP, Norwegian Report, Q 45.

seriously.[1539] In most legal systems only a right but not a corresponding duty exists (GERMANY,[1540] ITALY,[1541] LITHUANIA,[1542] THE NETHERLANDS,[1543] RUSSIA[1544] and SPAIN[1545]).

COMMENT

1. The maintenance of personal relationships between the child and other persons, in particular his or her parents, forms a part of parental responsibilities (see Principle 3:1). The Principles use in the heading of the chapter the broad expression "maintenance of personal relationships" to describe the relationship of the child with other persons. Such maintenance of personal relationships is established by contact. The Principles prefer contact to "access" because this term is broader and better expresses the bilateral nature of personal relationships. The objective of maintaining personal relationships is to ensure close human relations between a child and its parents, other relatives and other persons close to the child.

2. There is a common core in the jurisdictions surveyed that the child should have a right of contact with a parent holding parental responsibilities in the sense of Principles 3:2 (2)(a), 3:8 and 3:10. Therefore, according to Principle 3:25 (1), the child should have a right of contact with his or her parents. Because the maintenance of personal relationships exists mainly in the child's interests, the child should have its own right of contact.

3. The parent should have a right and a corresponding duty. There is a growing tendency in national law to recognise such an explicit duty of the parent. Principle 3:25 (1) therefore establishes expressly that contact is a right and declares implicitly that it is also a duty of the parents. As the comparative overview indicates, many national systems recognise that this duty is difficult to enforce and that it may even be detrimental to the child if not complied with voluntarily. Notwithstanding these difficulties, it seems adequate that the Principles give a clear indication that contact is also a duty of the parents. National legislators may establish sanctions if this duty is not complied with voluntarily. Paragraph 1 also establishes that parental responsibility holders are under an obligation to enable and support the child's right to maintain contact with his or her parents.

1539 See ROTH, Austrian Report, Q 45.
1540 See DETHLOFF/MARTINY, German Report, Q 45.
1541 See PATTI/BELLISARIO/ROSSI CARLEO, Italian Report, Q 45.
1542 See MIKELENAS, Lithuanian Report, Q 45.
1543 See BOELE-WOELKI/SCHRAMA/VONK, Dutch Report, Q 45.
1544 See ANTOKOLSKAIA, Russian Report, Q 45.
1545 See GONZÁLEZ BEILFUSS, Spanish Report, Q 45.

4. "Parents" are defined in Principle 3:2 (2)(a) und 3:8. Since the aim of the right of contact is to maintain and to protect the child's ties with his or her family, the maintenance of personal relationships should not depend on whether or not a parent has parental responsibilities in the sense of custody. Therefore, the child should also have a right of contact with a parent not holding parental responsibilities. A total or partial loss of the other parts of parental responsibilities does not automatically terminate the maintenance of personal relationships. This is in accordance with the majority of the jurisdictions surveyed. However, in accordance with Principle 3:3 on the protection of the child's interests and the common core of the jurisdictions surveyed the competent authority may also restrict or terminate contact according to Principle 3:28.

5. Principle 3:25 (2) states that a child should also have a right of contact with relatives other than his or her parents, insofar as these persons are holders of parental responsibilities in the sense of Principle 3:2 (2)(b). This includes mainly his or her grandparents. In these cases there exist close family ties and grandparents can fulfil an important role for the development of the child. Grandparents are not expressly mentioned despite the fact that they enjoy a privileged status according to many systems. Also with siblings, personal relationships should be maintained. However, Principle 3:25 (2) does not establish a list of such relatives. This is in accordance with Article 5 para. 1 of the *Convention on Contact Concerning Children 2003*. This right to contact should exist even against the will of the holder of parental responsibilities. The child's right to maintain relationships with persons other than a parent does create an obligation for parental responsibility holders to enable and support such contact. The establishment of contact in the sense of Principle 3:25 (2) also encompasses the maintenance of personal relationships *ex lege*.

6. However, in accordance with the majority of jurisdictions surveyed there should not be a formal duty on the part of these relatives and the best interests of the child prevail. The question of whether these persons have an actionable right allowing them to have contact even in opposition to the wishes of the parental responsibility holders is left to national law. There are good reasons for not enforcing such contact if it seriously disturbs the parent-child relationship. This is recognised by some national systems which do not grant such a right to persons other than parents or which allow more restrictions to this right than they do when the issue at stake is contact between the child and a parent.

7. Principle 3:25 (3) recognizes also that with third persons who are not relatives, close ties can exist. These persons are also holders of parental responsibilities in the sense of Principle 3:2 (2)(b). This group embraces a great variety of persons (step-parents, foster-parents). Particularly when these persons have fulfilled social family functions,

the maintenance of personal relationships is appropriate and generally in the best interests of the child. However, Principle 3:25 (3) only states that there "may" be contact; there is no automatic maintenance of personal relations. Since the factual circumstances and the degree of closeness may differ greatly, in these cases, according to Principle 3:3, there should only be a right for these persons but not an obligation. This kind of contact is also recognized by Article 5 para. 2 of the *Convention on Contact Concerning Children 2003.*

Principle 3:26 Content of contact
(1) Contact comprises the child staying for a limited period of time with or meeting a parent or person other than a parent with whom he or she is not usually living; and any form of communication between the child and such person.
(2) Such contact should be in the best interests of the child.

Principe 3:26 Contenu des relations personnelles
(1) Les relations personnelles comprennent le séjour de l'enfant pour une période limitée ou la rencontre avec le père ou la mère ou une personne autre que le père ou la mère avec laquelle l'enfant ne réside pas habituellement, ainsi que toute forme de communication entre l'enfant et une telle personne.
(2) Ces relations personnelles doivent correspondre au meilleur intérêt de l'enfant.

Prinzip 3:26 Inhalt des Umgangs
(1) Umgang umfasst den Aufenthalt des Kindes für einen begrenzten Zeitraum oder ein Treffen mit dem Elternteil oder einer anderen Person als dem Elternteil, mit dem es gewöhnlich nicht lebt; ferner jede Form der Kommunikation zwischen dem Kind und dieser Person.
(2) Ein solcher Umgang hat dem Kindeswohl zu entsprechen.

INTERNATIONAL INSTRUMENTS

Article 9 para. 3 of the *Convention on the Rights of the Child 1989* establishes that States Parties shall respect the right of the child who is separated from one or both parents to maintain personal relations and direct contact with both parents on a regular basis, except if it is contrary to the child's best interests. Article 8 of the *European Convention on Human Rights 1950* has been interpreted as attributing to the child a right to maintain contact with his or her parent after divorce; see the comparative overview under Principle 3:25. Principle 18 of the Council of Europe's *White Paper 2002* includes the maintenance of personal relationships as one of the issues included in parental responsibilities. In the *Convention on Contact Concerning Children 2003* "contact" means particularly the child staying for a limited period of time with or meeting a person mentioned in Article 4 or 5 with whom he or she is not usually living (Art. 2 (a) No. 1). The Explanatory Report states that this "first level" covers "direct" or "personal (face-to-face)" contact. The Convention also covers any other form of communication between the child and such a person (Art. 2 (a) No. 2) and the provision of information to such a person about the child or to the child about such a person (Art. 2 (a) No. 3). As in Article 3 (b) *Hague Child Protection Convention 1996* "rights of access" under the *Brussels II bis Regulation* include, in particular, the right to take a child to a place other than his or her habitual residence for a limited period of time (Art. 1 No. 10).

COMPARATIVE OVERVIEW

Concept of contact

As already stated in the comparative overview under Principle 3:25, in all the legal systems surveyed the child has a right of contact with its parents. When parental responsibilities are held jointly, but the parental responsibility holders do not live together, the non-residential parental responsibility holder has a right of contact with the child which actually enables him or her to exercise his parental responsibilities. Often national systems recognise a right of the child to maintain personal relationships with his or her parents which is independent from other kinds of parental responsibility. Contact is in many jurisdictions a general and legal term used for any form of contact. Different legal terms are used for this, such as "samvær" (DENMARK[1546]), "droit de visite et hébergement" (FRANCE[1547]), "omgang" (THE NETHERLANDS[1548]) or "Umgang" (GERMANY[1549]). The term "contact" therefore refers not only to contact between a parent and a minor but is also used for contact between the minor and other persons (e.g. GERMANY[1550] and THE NETHERLANDS[1551]).

Different forms of communication

Most jurisdictions recognise that contact encompasses any form of communication. An intensive form of communication is that the child stays for a limited period of time with the person having the right to contact, e.g. for one or several weeks during summer holidays or one day during public holidays (see e.g. CZECH REPUBLIC,[1552] GERMANY,[1553] ITALY[1554] and PORTUGAL[1555]). Another form is a meeting between the child and the respective person. This right is recognised in the form of a visiting right (e.g.

1546 See LUND-ANDERSEN/JEPPESEN-DE BOER Danish Report, Q 43.
1547 See FERRAND, French Report, Q 43.
1548 See BOELE-WOELKI/SCHRAMA/VONK, Dutch Report, Q 43.
1549 See § 1626 para. 3 and § 1684 German Civil Code. See DETHLOFF/MARTINY, German Report, Q 2b.
1550 See § 1626 para. 3, and § 1684 German Civil Code. See DETHLOFF/MARTINY, German Report, Q 2b.
1551 See BOELE-WOELKI/SCHRAMA/VONK, Dutch Report, Q 43.
1552 See HRUSAKOVÁ, Czech Report, Q 43.
1553 See DETHLOFF/MARTINY, German Report, Q 47.
1554 See PATTI/BELLISARIO/ROSSI CARLEO, Italian Report, Q 43.
1555 See DE OLIVEIRA, Portuguese Report, Q 43.

AUSTRIA[1556] and ITALY,[1557]). Generally there is case law on the frequency (often every other weekend), intensity and duration of visits (e.g. GERMANY[1558]). Case law also recognises communication by phone, fax, mail or electronic mail (e.g. ENGLAND AND WALES,[1559] HUNGARY,[1560] PORTUGAL[1561] and SPAIN[1562]).

Best interests of the child

The maintenance of personal relationships is subject to the best interests of the child. As far as parents are concerned contact is generally in the best interests of the child. Where these interests are endangered restrictions can be ordered, see the comparative overview under Principle 3:28. The situation is more complicated in respect of other relatives and third parties. As always, contact is subject to the welfare of the child. However, this aspect is stressed in some jurisdictions. There it has to be established why it is in the child's interests for certain contact to be granted (ENGLAND AND WALES[1563] and FRANCE[1564]). Similarly, in SWISS law the contact right is only granted in exceptional circumstances.[1565]

COMMENT

1. Principle 3:26 clarifies the content of the right to contact which exists according to Principle 3:25 (contact with parents and other persons). Especially the non-residential parental responsibility holder exercises his or her rights and duties through contact. When a parent does not hold parental responsibilities, there should also be contact unless the competent authority decides that contact is contrary to the child's best interests according to Principle 3:28.

2. According to Principle 3:26 (1) contact means "any form of communication". Following the purpose of maintaining personal relationships the right of contact has a broad meaning. It can take different forms under the European Contact Convention and the jurisdictions surveyed. This includes, as mentioned expressly, inviting and hosting the child. The child may stay for a limited period of time with or meet a parent

1556 See ROTH, Austrian Report, Q 2 b and 43 ("Besuchsrecht").
1557 See PATTI/BELLISARIO/ROSSI CARLEO, Italian Report, Q 2b.
1558 See DETHLOFF/MARTINY, German Report, Q 47.
1559 See LOWE, English Report, Q 43.
1560 See WEISS/SZEIBERT, Hungarian Report, Q 43.
1561 See DE OLIVEIRA, Portuguese Report, Q 43.
1562 See GONZÁLEZ BEILFUSS, Spanish Report, Q 43.
1563 See LOWE, English Report, Q 44c.
1564 Art. 371–4 para. 2 French Civil Code. See FERRAND, French Report, Q 44c.
1565 Art. 274a Swiss Civil Code. See HAUSHEER/ACHERMANN-WEBER/WOLF, Swiss Report, Q 44c.

or another person with a right of contact. Paying him or her a visit also belongs to the content of contact. The use of other forms of communication means writing to him or her, calling him or her by phone or sending him or her letters by mail, fax or electronic mail. However, contact has to be distinguished from the right to information to which Principle 3:29 applies.

3. Principle 3:26 (2) states that the guiding principle for the maintenance of personal relationships should be the best interests of the child. This is in line with the general Principle 3:3 and particularly with Principle 3:7 according to which the interests of the child should be protected whenever they may be in conflict with the interests of the holders of parental responsibilities. This means that the maintenance of personal relationships also has to respect the perspective of the child and should not harm or endanger the child. The right of the child to be informed, consulted and to express his or her views in matters of the maintenance of personal relationships shall be granted according to Principle 3:6 (see also Art. 6 *Convention on Contact Concerning Children 2003*).

Principle 3:27 Agreement
(1) Subject to the best interests of the child, the parents and the other persons identified under Principle 3:25(2) and (3) may agree on contact.
(2) The competent authority may scrutinize the agreement.

Principe 3:27 Accord
(1) Conformément au meilleur intérêt de l'enfant, les père et mère et les autres personnes mentionnées au Principe 3:25(2) et (3) peuvent conclure un accord sur les relations personnelles.
(2) L'autorité compétente peut contrôler l'accord.

Prinzip 3:27 Vereinbarung
(1) In Übereinstimmung mit dem Kindeswohl können die Eltern und die in Prinzip 3:25(2) und (3) genannten Personen eine Vereinbarung über den Umgang treffen.
(2) Die zuständige Behörde kann die Vereinbarung überprüfen.

INTERNATIONAL INSTRUMENTS

According to Article 7 (b) of the *Convention on Contact Concerning Children 2003* the judicial authorities shall encourage parents and other persons having family ties with the child to reach amicable agreements with respect to contact, in particular through the use of family mediation and other processes for resolving disputes. States Parties shall encourage parents and other persons having family ties with the child to comply with the principles laid down in Articles 4 to 7 of the Convention when making or modifying agreements on contact concerning a child (Art. 8 para. 1). These agreements should preferably be in writing. Upon request, the judicial authorities shall, except where internal law provides otherwise, confirm agreements on contact, unless it is contrary to the best interests of the child (Art. 8 para. 2). Such confirmation can give the agreement the same legal force as a court order and therefore, as the Explanatory Report states, facilitates its implementation.

COMPARATIVE OVERVIEW

Contact arrangements

In the jurisdictions surveyed it is possible and even regarded as desirable that parents make arrangements on the exercise of contact. However, it is not always clear what counts, the agreement of the parents or a decision of the competent authority, and there are different situations and contexts to be distinguished.

An agreement between the parents is often required as a precondition for a divorce based on mutual consent. This agreement will then generally be a part of the judicial and contractual arrangements in the context of divorce (BELGIUM,[1566] BULGARIA,[1567] GERMANY[1568] and HUNGARY[1569]). German law requires that there is a declaration that there will be no application as to custody or contact or that the parties agree on a judicial determination in order to have access to a divorce based on consent.[1570] In THE NETHERLANDS an obligation on the part of the parents to present a parenting plan which would include the issue of contact is part of a reform project.[1571] The agreement can generally be oral or written (e.g. BELGIUM[1572]). Only in very few jurisdictions must a binding agreement be in writing (RUSSIA[1573] and SWEDEN[1574]).

The legal nature of an agreement between the parents is not easy to determine. Sometimes it is considered to be legally binding (BELGIUM[1575] and GREECE[1576]). For RUSSIAN law the issue is debated.[1577] Sometimes it is also argued that a contact arrangement is not legally binding until is has been approved by the competent authority (AUSTRIA[1578]).

Arrangements between the parents can generally be modified by a new agreement (e.g. BELGIUM[1579]). However, where the arrangement is included in a judgment or court order specific procedural rules may apply. The agreement then has the same force as the decision of the competent authority.

There is a basic distinction between agreements between parental responsibility holders who do not live together and agreements between parental responsibility holders and other persons. As regards the former there is a growing tendency to strongly encourage agreements on contact in divorce or separation proceedings. Outside the context of

1566 See PINTENS/PIGNOLET, Belgian Report, Q 46.
1567 See TODOROVA, Bulgarian Report, Q 17, 46.
1568 See DETHLOFF/MARTINY, German Report, Q 46.
1569 See WEISS/SZEIBERT, Hungarian Report, Q 46.
1570 § 630 para. 1 No. 2 alt. 1 German Code of Civil Procedure.
1571 See BOELE-WOELKI/SCHRAMA/VONK, Dutch Report, Q 46.
1572 See PINTENS/PIGNOLET, Belgian Report, Q 46.
1573 See ANTOKOLSKAIA, Russian Report, Q 46.
1574 See JÄNTERÄ-JAREBORG/SINGER/SÖRGJERD, Swedish Report, Q 46.
1575 See PINTENS/PIGNOLET, Belgian Report, Q 46.
1576 See KOUTSOURADIS/ZERVOGIANNI, Greek Report, Q 46.
1577 See ANTOKOLSKAIA, Russian Report, Q 46.
1578 See ROTH, Austrian Report, Q 46.
1579 See PINTENS/PIGNOLET, Belgian Report, Q 46.

divorce, the law certainly encourages contact agreements. The general position is that the exercise of contact has to be agreed by the persons concerned; if there is no agreement it will be regulated by the competent authority according to the child's best interests and taking into account his or her opinions and wishes.

Scrutiny

Contractual freedom is limited by the interests of the child. Scrutiny by the competent authority often depends on the context in which the agreements on contact are made. In many jurisdictions a parental agreement on contact with the child does not necessarily require the approval of the competent authority (BELGIUM,[1580] CZECH REPUBLIC,[1581] DENMARK,[1582] FRANCE,[1583] GERMANY[1584] and NORWAY[1585]). In some systems, however, agreements are only binding if they are scrutinised. In SWEDEN an agreement is only valid if it is approved by the social welfare committee.[1586]

Scrutiny by the competent authority is often required in the case of divorce (BELGIUM,[1587] BULGARIA,[1588] FRANCE[1589] and HUNGARY[1590]). In ENGLAND AND WALES[1591] there is a general power of scrutiny in the context of divorce. Outside the framework of legal proceedings there is often no scrutiny at all.

There are limitations to the content of these agreements. In DENMARK, which does not permit an alternate residence of the child with different parental responsibility holders, an agreement allocating each parent half of the time will not be accepted as a contact arrangement.[1592] In GERMANY a total renunciation of contact is against good morals and such an agreement would be invalid unless it is in the best interests of the child.[1593] When there is an application for confirmation the competent authority is generally not bound by the arrangement of the parents but can make its own judgment or order

---

1580 See PINTENS/PIGNOLET, Belgian Report, Q 46.
1581 § 27 para. 1 Czech Family Code. See HRUSAKOVÁ, Czech Report, Q 45 and Q 46.
1582 See LUND-ANDERSEN/JEPPESEN-DE BOER, Danish Report, Q 46.
1583 See FERRAND, French Report, Q 46.
1584 See DETHLOFF/MARTINY, German Report, Q 46.
1585 See SVERDRUP/LØDRUP, Norwegian Report, Q 46.
1586 See JÄNTERÄ-JAREBORG/SINGER/SÖRGJERD, Swedish Report, Q 46.
1587 See PINTENS/PIGNOLET, Belgian Report, Q 46.
1588 See TODOROVA, Bulgarian Report, Q 17, 46.
1589 Art. 373-2-7 French Civil Code. See FERRAND, French Report, Q 46.
1590 See WEISS/SZEIBERT, Hungarian Report, Q 46.
1591 S. 41 English Matrimonial Causes Act 1973. See LOWE, English Report, Q 30 and Q 46.
1592 See LUND-ANDERSEN/JEPPESEN-DE BOER, Danish Report, Q 46.
1593 See DETHLOFF/MARTINY, German Report, Q 46.

(e.g. BELGIUM[1594] and SPAIN[1595]). The overriding criterion for the competent authority's scrutiny is the child's best interests (AUSTRIA,[1596] BELGIUM,[1597] FINLAND,[1598] IRELAND,[1599] ITALY[1600] and SWEDEN[1601]).

Enforceability of agreements

Private agreements as such are generally not directly enforceable but may only be enforced if they are contained in a judgment or court order (e.g. BELGIUM[1602] and GERMANY[1603]). For a contact arrangement to be enforced it must be approved by the competent authority (AUSTRIA,[1604] BELGIUM,[1605] FINLAND,[1606] GREECE,[1607] SPAIN[1608] and SWITZERLAND[1609]). This means that if an agreement is not complied with voluntarily the competent authority has to decide on the controversial matter and will in this context scrutinise the agreement, which can be set aside if it is contrary to the child's best interests (BELGIUM,[1610] FRANCE[1611] and SPAIN[1612]). See the COMPARATIVE OVERVIEW under Principle 3:39.

COMMENT

1. Principle 3:27 states that the parents can make agreements on the maintenance of personal relationships. This is in accordance with Article 8 of the *Convention on Contact Concerning Children 2003*. Principle 3:27 is in conformity with the general principle on the exercise of parental responsibilities (Principle 3:13) according to which the holders of joint parental responsibilities can make agreements on the exercise of

1594 See PINTENS/PIGNOLET, Belgian Report, Q 46.
1595 See GONZÁLEZ BEILFUSS, Spanish Report, Q 46.
1596 § 148 para. 1 Austrian Civil Code. See ROTH, Austrian Report, Q 46.
1597 See PINTENS/PIGNOLET, Belgian Report, Q 46.
1598 See KURKI-SUONIO, Finnish Report, Q 46.
1599 See SHANNON, Irish Report, Q 46.
1600 Art. 158 Italian Civil Code and Art. 4 para. 13 Italian Divorce Law. See PATTI/BELLISARIO/ROSSI CARLEO, Italian Report, Q 46.
1601 Ch. 6 § 15a Swedish Children and Parents Code.
1602 See PINTENS/PIGNOLET, Belgian Report, Q 58.
1603 See DETHLOFF/MARTINY, German Report, Q 58.
1604 See ROTH, Austrian Report, Q 46.
1605 See PINTENS/PIGNOLET, Belgian Report, Q 46.
1606 § 7 Finnish Child Custody and the Right of Access Act. See KURKI-SUONIO, Finnish Report, Q 46.
1607 See KOUTSOURADIS/ZERVOGIANNI, Greek Report, Q 46.
1608 See GONZÁLEZ BEILFUSS, Spanish Report, Q 17 and Q 46.
1609 See HAUSHEER/ACHERMANN-WEBER/WOLF, Swiss Report, Q 46.
1610 See PINTENS/PIGNOLET, Belgian Report, Q 58.
1611 See FERRAND, French Report, Q 46.
1612 See GONZÁLEZ BEILFUSS, Spanish Report, Q 46.

parental responsibilities. However, the scope of Principle 3:27 is narrower since it only deals with the issue of contact while, on the other hand, it is broader, because it also covers agreements with other persons.

2. The first paragraph of Principle 3:27 recalls Principles 3:11 (joint exercise) and 3:13 (agreement on exercise). When parental responsibility is held jointly the fact that parental responsibility holders do not live together does not, as such, affect parental responsibilities. But in such a case the child will often reside with one parent and have contact with the other parent. The exercise of such contact should be agreed upon by both parental responsibility holders. Disputes are deferred to the competent authority which will proceed according to Principle 3:14 (disagreement). Principle 1:6 (1) of CEFL's Divorce Principles also requires that in the case of divorce by mutual consent the spouses reach an agreement as to parental responsibility, including the residence and contact arrangements for the children.

3. In situations where a third person is a holder of parental responsibilities in addition to or instead of the parents (Principle 3:9 and Principle 3:17), such a person may also agree on contact.

4. The second paragraph of Principle 3:27 is a consequence of the respect for the best interests of the child (Principles 3:3 and 3:7) and the goal of maintaining personal relationships and contact according to Principle 3:25. Parental responsibility holders are under an obligation to enable and support the child's contact rights. This means that they should reach an agreement about the exercise of such a right. Any agreement contrary to the best interests of the child will, however, not be tolerated. Scrutiny is also an important element of Principles 1:6 (2) (a) and 1:7 (2) of the CEFL Divorce Principles. Here, the competent authority determines the consequences for the children, but takes into account any admissible agreement between the spouses insofar as it is consistent with the best interests of the child.

5. Principle 3:37 (2) only states that there "may" be scrutiny; the competent authority should have the opportunity to examine the agreement. There are several reasons for this flexible approach. The borderline between agreement and decision is often not clear, scrutiny secures that the child's best interests are guarded and preserved and scrutiny may reinforce the value of an agreement. Scrutiny generally presupposes that the agreement is in writing. There is, however, no general requirement for any special form.

Principle 3:28 Restrictions
Contact may be restricted, terminated or made subject to conditions by the competent authority if the best interests of the child so require.

Principe 3:28 Restrictions
Si le meilleur intérêt de l'enfant l'exige, l'autorité compétente peut limiter les relations personnelles, y mettre fin ou les assujettir à des conditions.

Prinzip 3:28 Beschränkungen
Der Umgang kann von der zuständigen Behörde beschränkt, beendet oder Bedingungen unterworfen werden, wenn das Kindeswohl dies verlangt.

INTERNATIONAL INSTRUMENTS

The principle of contact between parents and children is recognized by Article 9 para. 1 United Nations *Convention on the Rights of the Child 1989.* Under Article 8 of the *European Convention on Human Rights 1950* the right of contact by a non-custodial parent after divorce has been recognized, but is subject to the child's interests (see INTERNATIONAL INSTRUMENTS under Principle 3:25). Principle 18 of the Council of Europe's *White Paper 2002* mentions the maintenance of personal relationships as a part of parental responsibilities, but does not go into detail. According to the Council of Europe's *Recommendation on Parental Responsibilities 1984* the parent with whom the child does not live should have at least the possibility of maintaining personal relationships with the child unless such relationships would be seriously harmful to the interests of the child (Principle 8).

The *Convention on Contact Concerning Children 2003* deals with general principles to be applied to contact orders and with measures to promote and improve transfrontier contact. The convention specifies that contact may be restricted or excluded only where necessary in the best interests of the child (Art. 4 para. 2) and invites Member States to consider the possibility of "supervised personal contact" where it is not in the best interests of the child to maintain unsupervised contact (Art. 4 para. 3). One objective of the *Convention on Contact Concerning Children 2003* is to determine appropriate safeguards and guarantees to ensure the proper exercise of contact and the immediate return of children at the end of the period of contact (Art. 1 (b)). "Rights of access" are also part of parental responsibility in *Brussels II bis Regulation* (Art. 2 No. 7); restrictions are not mentioned separately. However, the competent authority in the Member State of enforcement can determine the practical arrangements for exercising rights of access if the necessary procedures have not been specified in the decision of the other Member State in which rights of access were granted. In determining these practical arrangements, the competent authority must at all times comply with the basic elements of the judgment conferring the right (Art. 48).

COMPARATIVE OVERVIEW

Restrictions on contact

Contact can be restricted, terminated or be subject to conditions in all systems if this is considered to be necessary in view of the best interests of the child. In all jurisdictions surveyed the competent authority may decide and intervene. The powers of this body are very wide; it may exclude or limit contact or subject it to certain conditions (e.g. AUSTRIA[1613] and GREECE[1614]). Due to the variety of situations only some guidelines can be described.

The overriding principle is the welfare or the interests of the child (e.g. BELGIUM,[1615] CZECH REPUBLIC,[1616] DENMARK,[1617] GERMANY,[1618] NORWAY[1619] and SWITZERLAND[1620]). It is considered necessary that a child has regular contact with his or her parent. A close and affectionate relationship between the child and his or her parents is generally considered to be in the best interests of the child. Therefore the exercise of contact may only be denied for serious reasons. This is done particularly in cases where there have been episodes of domestic violence (e.g. ENGLAND AND WALES[1621] and GERMANY[1622]) or where contact poses a physical or emotional danger to the child (AUSTRIA,[1623] FINLAND,[1624] GREECE,[1625] HUNGARY,[1626] ITALY,[1627] THE NETHERLANDS,[1628] PORTUGAL,[1629]

1613 § 148 para. 2 and § 178 Austrian Civil Code.
1614 Art. 1520 para. 3 Greek Civil Code.
1615 See PINTENS/PIGNOLET, Belgian Report, Q 47.
1616 § 27 para. 3 Czech Family Code.
1617 § 17 para. 3 Danish Act on Parental Authority and Contact.
1618 § 1684 German Civil Code.
1619 § 48 Norwegian Children Act 1981.
1620 Art. 274 para. 2 Swiss Civil Code.
1621 See LOWE, English Report, Q 47.
1622 See DETHLOFF/MARTINY, German Report, Q 47.
1623 See ROTH, Austrian Report, Q 47.
1624 See KURKI-SUONIO, Finnish Report, Q 47.
1625 See KOUTSOURADIS/ZERVOGIANNI, Greek Report, Q 47.
1626 See WEISS/SZEIBERT, Hungarian Report, Q 47.
1627 See PATTI/BELLISARIO/ROSSI CARLEO, Italian Report, Q 47.
1628 See BOELE-WOELKI/SCHRAMA/VONK, Dutch Report, Q 47.
1629 See DE OLIVEIRA, Portuguese Report, Q 47.

RUSSIA,[1630] SPAIN,[1631] SWEDEN[1632] and SWITZERLAND[1633]). The fact that the other parent and/or his or her new partner or spouse objects is not in itself a sufficient ground for denying contact (e.g. GERMANY[1634]). There is, however, also opposing case law (ENGLAND AND WALES[1635]).

The physical and mental well-being and development of the child must not be harmed by the contact (e.g. RUSSIA[1636]). However, a certain amount of stress caused by the contact has to be tolerated by the child and there is a vast area of discretion concerning when contact could harm the child. Most jurisdictions use general clauses to circumscribe these situations and the details are left to case law (e.g. GERMANY[1637] and PORTUGAL[1638]). There are, however, jurisdictions which have established a statutory list of grounds (THE NETHERLANDS[1639]).

The wishes of the child are an important, but often not the decisive factor. Younger children may simply not have been in contact with the other parent for a long period or have been influenced by their residential parent (e.g. GERMANY[1640]). However, even under these circumstances, according to the facts of the case, restrictions or exclusions may be ordered. The opinion of the child is important especially if he or she has attained a sufficient degree of maturity (DENMARK,[1641] ENGLAND AND WALES,[1642] GERMANY,[1643] THE NETHERLANDS,[1644] NORWAY,[1645] RUSSIA,[1646] SPAIN[1647] and SWEDEN[1648]). Sometimes the age of twelve is considered decisive. If a child older than twelve years rejects contact it will not be ordered or enforced (FINLAND,[1649] THE NETHERLANDS[1650]

1630 See ANTOKOLSKAIA, Russian Report, Q 47.
1631 See GONZÁLEZ BEILFUSS, Spanish Report, Q 47.
1632 See JÄNTERÄ-JAREBORG/SINGER/SÖRGJERD, Swedish Report, Q 47.
1633 See HAUSHEER/ACHERMANN-WEBER/WOLF, Swiss Report, Q 47.
1634 See DETHLOFF/MARTINY, German Report, Q 47.
1635 See LOWE, English Report, Q 47.
1636 Art. 66 para. 1 Russian Family Code. See ANTOKOLSKAIA, Russian Report, Q 47.
1637 See DETHLOFF/MARTINY, German Report, Q 47.
1638 See DE OLIVEIRA, Portuguese Report, Q 47.
1639 Art. 1:377a para. 3 Dutch Civil Code. See BOELE-WOELKI/SCHRAMA/VONK, Dutch Report, Q 47.
1640 See DETHLOFF/MARTINY, German Report, Q 47.
1641 See LUND-ANDERSEN/JEPPESEN-DE BOER, Danish Report, Q 47.
1642 See LOWE, English Report, Q 47.
1643 See DETHLOFF/MARTINY, German Report, Q 47.
1644 See BOELE-WOELKI/SCHRAMA/VONK, Dutch Report, Q 47.
1645 See SVERDRUP/LØDRUP, Norwegian Report, Q 47.
1646 See ANTOKOLSKAIA, Russian Report, Q 44a.
1647 See GONZÁLEZ BEILFUSS, Spanish Report, Q 47.
1648 See JÄNTERÄ-JAREBORG/SINGER/SÖRGJERD, Swedish Report, Q 47.
1649 § 2 Finnish Act of Enforcement of a decision on Child Custody and Right of Access See KURKI-SUONIO, Finnish Report, Q 59 and Q 62.
1650 See BOELE-WOELKI/SCHRAMA/VONK, Dutch Report, Q 47.

and SWEDEN[1651]). There is case law in other jurisdictions which tends to lean in the same direction (BULGARIA[1652] and NORWAY[1653]).

The conduct of the person seeking contact is of crucial importance. Alcoholism or drug addiction, violent or threatening behaviour against family members or child abuse will regularly exclude contact. These factors mean that the parent is manifestly unfit or is considered unable to have contact.

What orders should be made depend on the circumstances in question. Often the competent authority will make a temporary or an interim decision on the exercise of contact and after a test period it will make a final decision (e.g. FRANCE[1654] and THE NETHERLANDS[1655]). The competent authority often determines under which circumstances (the place, time, frequency) contact has to take place. However, also a limitation on indirect contact, for example by post, is possible (ENGLAND AND WALES[1656] and IRELAND[1657]).

If there is a risk for the child, supervised contact may take place. This means that a third person will be present. This may be a youth protection agency (social worker), a private association or even another family member. Special arrangements can be made where there is a risk that the parent seeking contact with the child will or could abduct that child abroad (FRANCE[1658], GERMANY[1659] and SWEDEN[1660]). In many countries special centres exist where the parent and the child can meet under controlled circumstances and on neutral ground (AUSTRIA,[1661] CZECH REPUBLIC,[1662] FINLAND,[1663] GERMANY[1664] and SPAIN[1665]).

1651 Ch. 21 § 5 Swedish Children and Parents Code.
1652 See TODOROVA, Bulgarian Report, Q 47.
1653 See SVERDRUP/LØDRUP, Norwegian Report, Q 47.
1654 Art. 373–2–9 para. 2 French Civil Code.
1655 See BOELE-WOELKI/SCHRAMA/VONK, Dutch Report, Q 47.
1656 See LOWE, English Report, Q 47.
1657 See SHANNON, Irish Report, Q 47.
1658 See FERRAND, French Report, Q 47.
1659 See DETHLOFF/MARTINY, German Report, Q 47.
1660 See JÄNTERÄ-JAREBORG/SINGER/SÖRGJERD, Swedish Report, Q 47.
1661 See ROTH, Austrian Report, Q 47 and Q 57.
1662 See HRUSAKOVÁ, Czech Report, Q 47.
1663 See KURKI-SUONIO, Finnish Report, Q 47.
1664 See DETHLOFF/MARTINY, German Report, Q 47.
1665 See GONZÁLEZ BEILFUSS, Spanish Report, Q 47.

In some jurisdictions a temporary exclusion or suspension of contact can be ordered (LITHUANIA,[1666] THE NETHERLANDS[1667] and PORTUGAL[1668]). In HUNGARY there exists a statutory maximum time-limit of six months.[1669] In cases of serious harm a total exclusion of contact may take place.

Disregarding the right of contact

If a holder of parental responsibilities with whom the child is living disregards the child's right to contact with the other parent, this is a violation of his or her own obligations. In the absence of an existing decision of the competent authority, this may be the occasion for an appropriate application and decision. Where there is already an order or judgment, this decision may be enforced. In the interests of the child the general approach is a flexible one. The competent authority may use reprimands and fines according to the existing methods for enforcing decisions. Alternative methods of dispute resolution, such as mediation, can also be used.

In the jurisdictions surveyed the disregard of the child's right to contact with his or her parent has no direct consequence concerning parental responsibilities. However, if other measures fail, in the case of continued obstruction of contact the parental responsibilities may be partially or even totally revoked as a last resort (AUSTRIA,[1670] BELGIUM,[1671] BULGARIA,[1672] DENMARK,[1673] FRANCE,[1674] GERMANY,[1675] GREECE,[1676] HUNGARY,[1677] IRELAND,[1678] ITALY,[1679] NORWAY,[1680] RUSSIA[1681] and SWITZERLAND[1682]). It is argued that such behaviour by the parent is against the best interests of the child and/or demonstrates that there are changed circumstances. However, this sanction is often only used as a threat. Court practice shows its limited effect because even in

---

1666 See MIKELENAS, Lithuanian Report, Q 47.
1667 See BOELE-WOELKI/SCHRAMA/VONK, Dutch Report, Q 47.
1668 See DE OLIVEIRA, Portuguese Report, Q 47.
1669 See WEISS/SZEIBERT, Hungarian Report, Q 47.
1670 See ROTH, Austrian Report, Q 48a.
1671 See PINTENS/PIGNOLET, Belgian Report, Q 48a.
1672 See TODOROVA, Bulgarian Report, Q 47, 48a and Q 58.
1673 § 12 and § 13 Danish Act on Parental Authority and Contact. See LUND-ANDERSEN/JEPPESEN-DE BOER, Danish Report, Q 48a.
1674 See FERRAND, French Report, Q 48a.
1675 See DETHLOFF/MARTINY, German Report, Q 48a and Q 58.
1676 See KOUTSOURADIS/ZERVOGIANNI, Greek Report, Q 48a.
1677 See WEISS/SZEIBERT, Hungarian Report, Q 48a.
1678 See SHANNON, Irish Report, Q 48a and Q 58.
1679 See PATTI/BELLISARIO/ROSSI CARLEO, Italian Report, Q 48a.
1680 See SVERDRUP/LØDRUP, Norwegian Report, Q 48a.
1681 See ANTOKOLSKAIA, Russian Report, Q 48a and Q 58.
1682 See HAUSHEER/ACHERMANN-WEBER/WOLF, Swiss Report, Q 48a.

this situation the paramount consideration should be the welfare of the child which may prevent him or her being placed in the other parent's care (e.g. CZECH REPUBLIC,[1683] IRELAND,[1684] THE NETHERLANDS[1685] and SWEDEN[1686]).

Insofar as other persons with a contact right are concerned, in some jurisdictions basically the same methods of enforcement are used (e.g. AUSTRIA,[1687] BELGIUM,[1688] GREECE[1689] and RUSSIA[1690]). However, conflicts do not arise very often and disregarding the right of contact with third persons is considered to be less serious than disregarding the parent-child relationship. Sometimes fines for non-compliance with a judgment (CZECH REPUBLIC[1691]) or sanctions for contempt of court can be imposed (ENGLAND AND WALES[1692] and IRELAND[1693]). In other legal systems no coercive measures can be taken (FINLAND[1694]) or only criminal sanctions may be imposed (BULGARIA[1695] and FRANCE[1696]). Sometimes, if the parents object to contact with grandparents, their view is given priority and the grandparents cannot make use of their right of contact (GERMANY[1697] and HUNGARY[1698]).

Consequences of discharging parental responsibilities

There are different solutions if there is a discharge of custody or parental responsibilities. Nearly everywhere the right to personal contact is an independent legal position. Therefore the discharged parent and/or the child retain the right to personal contact by operation of law (AUSTRIA,[1699] BULGARIA,[1700] FINLAND,[1701] GERMANY,[1702] GREECE,[1703]

1683 § 27 para. 2 Czech Family Code. See HRUSAKOVÁ, Czech Report, Q 48a.
1684 See SHANNON, Irish Report, Q 48a.
1685 See BOELE-WOELKI/SCHRAMA/VONK, Dutch Report, Q 48a.
1686 See JÄNTERÄ-JAREBORG/SINGER/SÖRGJERD, Swedish Report, Q 48a.
1687 See ROTH, Austrian Report, Q 48b.
1688 See PINTENS/PIGNOLET, Belgian Report, Q 48b.
1689 See KOUTSOURADIS/ZERVOGIANNI, Greek Report, Q 48b.
1690 See ANTOKOLSKAIA, Russian Report, Q 48b.
1691 See HRUSAKOVÁ, Czech Report, Q 48b.
1692 See LOWE, English Report, Q 48b.
1693 See SHANNON, Irish Report, Q 48b.
1694 See KURKI-SUONIO, Finnish Report, Q 48b.
1695 See TODOROVA, Bulgarian Report, Q 48b.
1696 See FERRAND, French Report, Q 48b.
1697 See DETHLOFF/MARTINY, German Report, Q 48b.
1698 See WEISS/SZEIBERT, Hungarian Report, Q 48b.
1699 § 148 para. 1 Austrian Civil Code.
1700 See TODOROVA, Bulgarian Report, Q 44b.
1701 See KURKI-SUONIO, Finnish Report, Q 53.
1702 See DETHLOFF/MARTINY, German Report, Q 53.
1703 See KOUTSOURADIS/ZERVOGIANNI, Greek Report, Q 53.

IRELAND,[1704] ITALY,[1705] LITHUANIA,[1706] THE NETHERLANDS,[1707] NORWAY,[1708] POLAND,[1709] PORTUGAL,[1710] SPAIN,[1711] SWEDEN[1712] and SWITZERLAND[1713]). Similarly, in jurisdictions where a parent is no longer a holder of parental responsibilities this parent retains the right to contact (DENMARK[1714]). Nevertheless, in all these legal systems the competent authority has to regulate the right of contact. In doing so, the reasons as to why the parent does not have custody or parental responsibilities will be of importance; often the same reasons for discharging parental responsibility will render contact contrary to the child's best interests (e.g. BULGARIA,[1715] GREECE,[1716] LITHUANIA[1717] and POLAND[1718]). Therefore, as a result, there can also be a loss of or a restriction to the right of contact if this is in the child's interests.

In other systems the right of contact is more tied to parental responsibilities. With the loss of parental responsibilities the parent also loses the right of contact. However, he or she can request a right of contact if that is in the interests of the child (BELGIUM[1719]). Similarly under CZECH law the deprival of parental responsibilities results in a prohibition of contact between the parent and the child.[1720] In FRANCE the answer primarily depends on the kind of discharge that has been ordered by the court. In the case of a total discharge, the discharged parent does not have any contact right at all. In the case of a partial discharge it is subject to judicial discretion whether there will still be a right of contact.[1721] Similarly, under HUNGARIAN law the answer depends on whether the parental responsibilities have been terminated or are only suspended. In the case of termination a right of contact is only permitted in exceptional cases.[1722] In RUSSIA parents who have been discharged of parental responsibilities lose all their rights, including the right to contact.[1723] However, the child retains the right

1704 See SHANNON, Irish Report, Q 53.
1705 See PATTI/BELLISARIO/ROSSI CARLEO, Italian Report, Q 53.
1706 See MIKELENAS, Lithuanian Report, Q 53.
1707 See BOELE-WOELKI/SCHRAMA/VONK, Dutch Report, Q 53.
1708 See SVERDRUP/LØDRUP, Norwegian Report, Q 53.
1709 See MĄCZYŃSKI/MĄCZYŃSKA, Polish Report, Q 53.
1710 See DE OLIVEIRA, Portuguese Report, Q 53.
1711 See GONZÁLEZ BEILFUSS, Spanish Report, Q 53.
1712 See JÄNTERÄ-JAREBORG/SINGER/SÖRGJERD, Swedish Report, Q 53.
1713 See HAUSHEER/ACHERMANN-WEBER/WOLF, Swiss Report, Q 53.
1714 See LUND-ANDERSEN/JEPPESEN-DE BOER, Danish Report, Q 53.
1715 See TODOROVA, Bulgarian Report, Q 53.
1716 See KOUTSOURADIS/ZERVOGIANNI, Greek Report, Q 53.
1717 See MIKELENAS, Lithuanian Report, Q 53.
1718 See MĄCZYŃSKI/MĄCZYŃSKA, Polish Report, Q 53.
1719 Art. 375bis Belgian Civil Code.
1720 See HRUSAKOVÁ, Czech Report, Q 53.
1721 Art. 379 French Civil Code. See FERRAND, French Report, Q 53.
1722 See WEISS/SZEIBERT, Hungarian Report, Q 53.
1723 Art. 71 para. 1 Russian Civil Code.

to maintain contact with such parents. Where there is a simple restriction of parental responsibilities the right of contact with the child is retained. In ENGLAND AND WALES the answer depends on whether or not there is a contact order in favour of the parent without parental responsibilities.[1724] Similarly, in IRELAND an application for access can be successful even if there was a former discharge of a custody order.[1725]

COMMENT

1. Principle 3:28 deals with restrictions. The objective of maintaining personal relationships is to ensure close human relations between a child and its parents, other relatives and other persons close to the child (see Principle 3:25). Since the guiding principle should be the best interests of the child (see Principles 3:3 and 3:7) this is also the basis for restrictions which, however, should also respect the principle of proportionality.

2. Since the aim of the right of contact is to maintain and to protect the child's ties with his or her family, the maintenance of personal relationships should not depend on whether or not a parent has parental responsibilities in the sense of care or custody. Therefore, the child should also have a right of contact with a parent not holding parental responsibilities in this sense. Effective enforcement of contact rights is of crucial importance. However, the Principles cannot go into details because the procedure is left to national law (see also Art. 9 *Convention on Contact Concerning Children 2003*).

3. A total or partial loss of the other elements of parental responsibilities does not automatically terminate the maintenance of personal relationships. This is in accordance with the majority of the jurisdictions surveyed. However, in accordance with Principle 3:3 on the protection of the child's best interests and the common core of the jurisdictions surveyed the competent authority may also, according to Principle 3:28, restrict or terminate contact.

4. According to Principle 3:28 the competent authority may restrict or terminate contact or make it subject to certain conditions when this seems necessary in order to protect the child's best interests. In cases where having contact with the parents or other holders of parental responsibilities endangers the child's physical, emotional or moral well-being due to situations such as alcohol or drug addiction, domestic violence, or sexual abuse contact should be suspended or subjected to supervision.

1724 See LOWE, English Report, Q 53.

1725 See SHANNON, Irish Report, Q 53.

There should also be a restriction on contact, especially visitation rights, if the child refuses to see his or her parents or if there is a risk of abduction. However, these situations are so manifold and complex that it is preferable to establish a general clause and to leave the matter to the competent authority's discretion. Disregarding the other parent's right of contact is not made a cogent reason for the loss of parental responsibilities because this severe sanction will often not be in the best interests of the child.

5. The restrictions should be appropriate. In some cases conditions such as supervised contact may be sufficient. In other cases a suspension or a total termination may be necessary.

Principle 3:29 Information to parents
A parent should have the right to be informed about matters concerning the personal situation of the child.

Principe 3:29 Information aux parents
Tout père ou mère a le droit d'être informé de tout ce qui concerne la situation personnelle de l'enfant.

Prinzip 3:29 Information der Eltern
Ein Elternteil hat das Recht, in Angelegenheiten, die die persönlichen Verhältnisse des Kindes betreffen, informiert zu werden.

INTERNATIONAL INSTRUMENTS

The Principle of contact between parents and children is recognized by Article 9 para. 1 United Nations *Convention on the Rights of the Child 1989*. Under Article 8 of the *European Convention on Human Rights 1950* the right of contact belonging to a non-custodial parent after divorce has been recognized, but is subject to the child's best interests. However, these instruments do not go into detail. The same is true for Principle 18 of the Council of Europe's *White Paper 2002* which mentions the maintenance of personal relationships as forming part of parental responsibilities.

According to the Council of Europe's *Recommendation on Parental Responsibilities 1984* each parent should normally be informed of the exercise of those responsibilities which have not been given to him or her, to the extent desired by him or her, and, in any event, when the essential interests of the child are affected (Principle 11).

The *European Convention on Contact Concerning Children 2003* deals with general principles to be applied to contact orders and with measures to promote and improve transfrontier contact. According to Article 2 (a) (iii) "contact" includes the providing of information to such a person about the child or to the child about such a person. "Rights of access" are also part of parental responsibility in *Brussels II bis Regulation* (Art. 2 No. 7); information is not mentioned as such.

COMPARATIVE OVERVIEW

The right to information as a separate issue

The non-custodial parent may demand information about the personal conditions relating to the child (BELGIUM,[1726] DENMARK,[1727] FRANCE,[1728] GERMANY,[1729] THE NETHERLANDS[1730] and RUSSIA[1731]). The right to information is sometimes considered to be part of the right of contact (LITHUANIA[1732]). However, in other legal systems it exists independently of the right of contact (FRANCE,[1733] GERMANY[1734] and THE NETHERLANDS[1735]). The right to information is generally subject to the child's welfare.

Matters covered

The non-custodial parent has an interest in receiving information about the child. He or she may demand information from the other parent about the personal conditions relating to the child (DENMARK,[1736] FRANCE,[1737] GERMANY,[1738] THE NETHERLANDS[1739] and RUSSIA[1740]). The matters covered are especially education and the child's state of health.

Information by third persons

Third persons, such as teachers or the medical profession, may, on account of their profession, dispose of information in respect of important facts and circumstances relating to the person of the child or the child's care and upbringing. In THE NETHERLANDS there is an express provision that these persons shall inform the parent who is not vested with parental custody, when so requested. Therefore the parent is entitled to information on the progress of his/her child. No information shall be provided if the provision of such information is against the best interests of the child.[1741]

1726 See PINTENS/PIGNOLET, Belgian Report, Q 43.
1727 § 19 para. 1 Danish Act on Parental Authority and Contact.
1728 Art. 372–2–1 para. 3 French Civil Code.
1729 § 1686 German Civil Code.
1730 Art. 1:377b and c Dutch Civil Code.
1731 Art. 66 para. 4 Russian Family Code. See ANTOKOLSKAIA , Russian Report, Q 45.
1732 See MIKELENAS, Lithuanian Report, Q 43.
1733 Art. 373–2–1 para. 2 French Civil Code.
1734 See DETHLOFF/MARTINY, German Report, Q 43.
1735 Art. 1:377b Dutch Civil Code. See BOELE-WOELKI/SCHRAMA/VONK, Dutch Report, Q 43.
1736 § 19 para. 1 Danish Act on Parental Authority and Contact.
1737 Art. 372–2–1 para. 3 French Civil Code.
1738 § 1686 German Civil Code.
1739 Art. 1:377b and c Dutch Civil Code.
1740 Art. 66 para. 4 Russian Family Code. See ANTOKOLSKAIA, Russian Report, Q 45.
1741 Art. 1:377c para. 1 Dutch Civil Code. See BOELE-WOELKI/SCHRAMA/VONK, Dutch Report, Q 43.

Consultation

In AUSTRIA it is expressly laid down that the right to be informed includes the right to express his or her opinion in matters concerning the child.[1742]

COMMENT

1. The right to information is a corollary right for the parent not residing with the child. There is a growing tendency that information to parents has to be distinguished from contact as such. On the other hand, the provision of information is often included in the issue of contact in the broad sense. Therefore Principle 3:29 treats information as part of the maintenance of personal relationships, but separately. It does not, however, treat the right to information as a separate part of the parental responsibilities listed in Principle 3:1.

2. Since the aim of the right to information is to maintain and to protect the child's ties with his or her family it should not depend on whether or not a parent has parental responsibilities in the sense of custody. Particularly when the parent is no longer actively involved, information can prove to be useful. There are, however, situations in which it is not justified that the absent parent receives information. Restrictions in a similar way as for contact under Principle 3:28 may apply in the child's best interests. The other parent may also be protected, for example a mother living at a secret address.

3. According to Principle 3:29 a parent should have the right to be informed. The claim for information is mainly directed against the other parent. The wording of the Principle does not specify whether or not the parent may be informed directly by third persons possessing the required information. Because of the links with other legal problems, this question is left to national law. Although it is not expressly mentioned, the parent should also have the right to express his or her opinion on important matters, e.g. educational or medical issues. A separate duty to provide information is laid down in Principle 3:21 on relocation.

4. The guiding principle for the right to information should be the best interests of the child (see Principle 3:3). The right of the child to be informed, consulted and to express his or her views in matters of maintaining personal relationships shall be granted according to Principle 3:6 (see also Art. 6 *Convention on Contact Concerning Children 2003*). This also applies here.

1742 § 178 para. 1 sent. 1 Austrian Civil Code. See ROTH, Austrian Report, Q 43.

CHAPTER VI: TERMINATION OF PARENTAL RESPONSIBILITIES
CHAPITRE VI : FIN DE LA RESPONSABILITÉ PARENTALE
KAPITEL VI: BEENDIGUNG DER ELTERLICHEN VERANTWORTUNG

Principle 3:30 Termination

(1) Parental responsibilities should be terminated in the case of the child:

(a) reaching majority;
(b) entering into a marriage or registered partnership;
(c) being adopted;
(d) dying.

(2) If a parent's partner adopts the child of the parent the parental responsibilities in relation to the other parent should be terminated.

Principe 3:30 Fin

(1) La responsabilité parentale prend fin lorsque l'enfant:

(a) atteint l'âge de la majorité;
(b) se marie ou conclut un partenariat enregistré;
(c) est adopté;
(d) décède.

(2) Dans le cas où le partenaire du père ou de la mère adopte l'enfant de celui-ci, la responsabilité parentale prend fin uniquement à l'égard de l'autre parent.

Prinzip 3:30 Beendigung

(1) Die elterliche Verantwortung endet kraft Gesetzes in folgenden Fällen:

(a) das Kind erreicht die Volljährigkeit;
(b) das Kind geht eine Ehe oder eine eingetragene Partnerschaft ein;
(c) Adoption des Kindes;
(d) Tod des Kindes.

(2) Adoptiert der Partner eines Elternteils das Kind des Elternteils, so endet die elterliche Verantwortung nur im Hinblick auf den anderen Elternteil.

INTERNATIONAL INSTRUMENTS

The *ex lege* termination as such is not covered by substantive international instruments. Only the death of one or both parents are included in some international instruments.[1743] In international procedural law the termination of parental responsibilities is covered by Article 2 *Hague Child Protection Convention 1996* and Article 1 para. 1(b) *Brussels II bis Regulation.*

COMPARATIVE OVERVIEW

Majority

In every surveyed legal system, the parental responsibilities are terminated *ex lege* when the child reaches the age of majority (AUSTRIA,[1744] BELGIUM,[1745] BULGARIA,[1746] CZECH REPUBLIC,[1747] DENMARK,[1748] ENGLAND AND WALES,[1749] FINLAND,[1750] FRANCE,[1751] GERMANY,[1752] GREECE,[1753] HUNGARY,[1754] IRELAND,[1755] ITALY,[1756] LITHUANIA,[1757] THE

1743 See International Instruments under Principle 3:24.
1744 See § 172 and § 21 para. 2 Austrian Civil Code. See ROTH, Austrian Report, Q 3.
1745 Art. 388 Belgian Civil Code. See PINTENS/PIGNOLET, Belgian Report, Q 3.
1746 Art. 2 Bulgarian Persons and Family Act, Art. 2 Bulgarian Child Protection Act. See TODOROVA, Bulgarian Report, Q 3.
1747 See HRUSAKOVÁ, Czech Report, Q 3.
1748 §1 Danish Act on Parental Authority and Conctact. See LUND-ANDERSEN/JEPESSEN DE BOER, Danish Report, Q 3.
1749 S. 105(1), English Children Act 1989. See LOWE, English Report, Q 3.
1750 § 3 para. 2 Finnish Child Custody and the Right of Access Act. See KURKI-SUONIO, Finnish Report, Q 3.
1751 Art. 371–1 para. 2 French Civil Code. See FERRAND, French Report, Q 3.
1752 § 1626 para. 1 sent. 1 German Civil Code. See DETHLOFF/MARTINY, German Report, Q 3.
1753 Art. 1538 Greek Civil Code. See KOUTSOURADIS/ZERVOGIANNI, Greek Report, Q 3.
1754 See WEISS/SZEIBERT, Hungarian Report, Q 3.
1755 S. 2 Irish Age of Majority Act 1985. See SHANNON, Irish Report, Q 3.
1756 Art. 316 Italian Civil Code. See PATTI/BELLISARIO/ROSSI CARLEO, Italian Report, Q 3.
1757 Art. 3.160 Lithuanian Civil Code. See MIKELENAS, Lithuanian Report, Q 3.

NETHERLANDS,[1758] NORWAY,[1759] POLAND,[1760] PORTUGAL,[1761] RUSSIA,[1762] SPAIN,[1763] SWEDEN[1764] and SWITZERLAND[1765]). The age of majority is 18 years in every reviewed legal system.[1766]

Marriage and registered partnership

A marriage *ex lege* terminates the parental responsibilities in most of the surveyed jurisdictions (AUSTRIA,[1767] BULGARIA,[1768] CZECH REPUBLIC,[1769] DENMARK,[1770] ENGLAND AND WALES,[1771] FINLAND,[1772] FRANCE,[1773] HUNGARY,[1774] ITALY,[1775] LITHUANIA,[1776] THE NETHERLANDS,[1777] POLAND,[1778] PORTUGAL,[1779] RUSSIA,[1780] SPAIN[1781] and SWEDEN[1782]), except

---

1758 Art. 1:246 Dutch Civil Code. See BOELE-WOELKI/SCHRAMA/VONK, Dutch Report, Q 3.

1759 §33 Norwegian Children Act 1981. See SVERDRUP/LØDRUP, Nowegian Report, Q 3.

1760 Art. 92 Polish Family and Guardianship Code. See MĄCZYŃSKI/MĄCZYŃSKA, Polish Report, Q 3.

1761 Art. 130, 132, 133 and 1877 Portuguese Civil Code. See DE OLIVEIRA, Portuguese Report, Q 3.

1762 Art. 61 para. 2 Russian Family Code. See ANTOKOLSKAIA, Russian Report, Q 3.

1763 Art. 158 Catalan Family Code, 169 Spanish Civil Code. See GONZÁLEZ BEILFUSS, Spanish Report, Q 3.

1764 Ch. 6 § 2 Swedish Children and Parents Code. See JÄNTERÄ-JAREBORG/SINGER/SÖRGJERD, Swedish Report, Q 3.

1765 Art. 14 Swiss Civil Code, Art. 296 para. 1 Swiss Civil Code. See HAUSHEER/ACHERMANN-WEBER/WOLF, Swiss Report, Q 3.

1766 See Resolution (72) 29 adopted by the Committee of Ministers of the Council of Europe on 19 September 1972 concerning the lowering of the age of full legal capacity.

1767 §175 Austrian Civil Code, § 1 para. 2 Austrian Marriage Act. See ROTH, Austrian Report, Q 3.

1768 Art. 12 para. 3 Bulgarian Persons and Family Act. See TODOROVA, Bulgarian Report, Q 3.

1769 § 8 para. 2 Czech Civil Code, § 13 Czech Family Code. See HRUSAKOVÁ, Czech Report, Q 3.

1770 See LUND-ANDERSEN/JEPPESEN-DE BOER, Danish Report, Q 3.

1771 See LOWE, English Report, Q 3.

1772 § 3 para. 2 Finnish Child Custody and the Right of Access Act. See KURKI-SUONIO, Finnish Report, Q 3.

1773 See FERRAND, French Report, Q 3.

1774 See WEISS/SWEIBERT, Hungarian Report, Q 3.

1775 See PATTI/BELLISARIO/ROSSI CARLEO, Italian Report, Q 3.

1776 See MIKELENAS, Lithuanian Report, Q 3.

1777 Art. 1:245 para. 1 Dutch Civil Code. See BOELE-WOELKI/SCHRAMA/VONK, Dutch Report, Q 3.

1778 Art. 10 para. 2 Polish Civil Code. See MĄCZYŃSKI/MĄCZYŃSKA, Polish Report, Q 3.

1779 See DE OLIVEIRA,Portuguese Report, Q 3.

1780 Art. 61 para. 2 Russian Family Code, Art. 21 para. 2 Russian Civil Code. See ANTOKOLSKAIA, Russian Report, Q 3.

1781 Art. 158 Catalan Family Code, 169 Spanish Civil Code. See GONZÁLEZ BEILFUSS, Spanish Report, Q 3.

1782 See Ch. 6 § 2 Swedish Children and Parents Code. See JÄNTERÄ-JAREBORG/SINGER/SORGJERD, Swedish Report, Q. 3.

for BELGIUM,[1783] GERMANY,[1784] GREECE,[1785] IRELAND,[1786] NORWAY[1787] and SWITZERLAND,[1788] where a restricted form of parental responsibilities remains applicable. In AUSTRIA, a marriage makes the child equal to an adult in his/her personal relations, but he or she cannot engage in or dispose of his/her property.[1789] In DENMARK, the permission to enter into a marriage may stipulate that the child is still subject to guardianship.[1790]

In DENMARK,[1791] THE NETHERLANDS[1792] and SWEDEN[1793] a registered partnership terminates parental responsibilities.

Adoption

In BELGIUM,[1794] THE CZECH REPUPLIC,[1795] FRANCE,[1796] ENGLAND AND WALES,[1797] GERMANY,[1798] GREECE,[1799] HUNGARY,[1800] ITALY,[1801] POLAND,[1802] PORTUGAL[1803] and SPAIN,[1804] parental responsibilities come to an end for the previous holders of parental responsibilities in the case of adoption.

1783 Art. 476 Belgian Civil Code. See PINTENS/PIGNOLET, Belgian Report, Q 3.
1784 See DETHLOFF/MARTINY, German Report, Q 3.
1785 Art. 137, 1386 and 1387 Greek Civil Code. See KOUTSOURADIS/ZERVOGIANNI, Greek Report, Q 3.
1786 See SHANNON, Irish Report, Q 3.
1787 See SVERDRUP/LØDRUP, Nowegian Report, Q 3.
1788 See HAUSHEER/ACHERMANN-WEBER/WOLF, Swiss Report, Q 3
1789 See ROTH, Austrian Report, Q 3.
1790 See LUND-ANDERSEN/JEPPESEN-DE BOER, Danish Report, Q 3.
1791 See LUND-ANDERSEN/JEPPESEN-DE BOER, Danish Report, Q 3.
1792 Art. 1:245 para. 1 Dutch Civil Code. See BOELE-WOELKI/SCHRAMA/VONK, Dutch Report, Q 3.
1793 See JÄNTERÄ-JAREBORG/SINGER/SÖRGJERD, Swedish Report, Q. 3.
1794 See PINTENS/PIGNOLET, Belgian Report, Q 3.
1795 See HRUSAKOVÁ, Czech Report, Q 3.
1796 See for the adoption simple, Art. 365 French Civil Code.
1797 See LOWE, English Report, Q 3.
1798 § 1755 German Civil Code. See DETHLOFF/MARTINY, German Report, Q 3.
1799 Art. 1561 Greek Civil Code. See KOUTSOURADIS/ZERVOGIANNI, Greek Report, Q 3.
1800 Art. 52 Hungarian Family Act.
1801 See PATTI/BELLISARIO/ROSSI CARLEO, Italian Report, Q 3.
1802 Art. 121 para. and 123 para. 1 Polish Family and Guardianship Code. See MĄCZYŃSKI/MĄCZYŃSKA, Polish Report, Q 3.
1803 Art. 1979 ff Portuguese Civil Code. See DE OLIVEIRA, Portuguese Report, Q 3.
1804 Art. 158 Catalan Family Code, 169 Spanish Civil Code. See GONZÁLEZ BEILFUSS, Spanish Report, Q 3.

Other grounds

Emancipation ends the parental responsibilities in FRANCE,[1805] ITALY,[1806] LITHUANIA,[1807] NETHERLANDS,[1808] PORTUGAL,[1809] RUSSIA[1810] and SPAIN.[1811] The child must have reached the age of 16. In FRANCE[1812] and LITHUANIA,[1813] the emancipation can be obtained on the basis of serious grounds that serve the interest of the child. The competent authority decides according to the grounds adduced. In ITALY, the only legal form of emancipation is the judicially authorized marriage of the child older than 16 years.[1814] Marriage is also a cause of emancipation in SPAIN.[1815] In RUSSIA the child can acquire full legal capacity if it has reached the age of 16 and is in rewarded employment, or, with the consent of his/her parents, is carrying out a business activity. According to DUTCH law, emancipation is restricted to a minor female with parental responsibilities. When she wishes to care for and raise her child, she may apply for emancipation at the children's court when she has reached the age of 16 before or after the birth of her child.[1816] Following the emancipation, the child acquires full legal capacity, except in SPAIN. In SPAIN the parental authority is not completely extinguished. The child will need parental authorization in order to contract a loan, or to sell or burden valuable property.[1817] ENGLISH law provides that the issue of a parental order extinguishes the parental responsibilities of existing holders and transfers them to the person(s) in whose favour the order is made.[1818] Non-parents who have responsibility by reason of a residence order and local authorities that have responsibility by reason of a care order only have responsibility for the duration of the order. In these cases responsibility automatically ends upon the termination of the residence or care order.[1819] According to BELGIAN[1820] law, parental responsibilities come to an end when the parents or the only surviving parent are continuously unable to exercise their parental responsibilities.

1805 Art. 477 and 481 French Civil Code. See FERRAND, French Report, Q 3.

1806 Art. 390 Italian Civil Code. See PATTI/BELLISARIO/ROSSI CARLEO, Italian Report, Q 3.

1807 See MIKELENAS/Lithuanian Report, Q 3.

1808 Art. 1:253ha Dutch Civil Code. See BOELE-WOELKI/SCHRAMA/VONK, Dutch Report, Q 3.

1809 Art. 130, 132, 133 and 1877 Portuguese Civil Code. See DE OLIVEIRA, Portuguese Report, Q 3.

1810 Art. 61 para. 2 Russian Family Code, Art. 27 para. 1 Russian Civil Code. See ANTOKOLSKAIA, Russian Report, Q 3.

1811 Art. 158 Catalan Family Code, 169 Spanish Civil Code. See GONZÁLEZ BEILFUSS, Spanish Report, Q 3.

1812 Art. 481 French Civil Code. See FERRAND, French Report, Q 3.

1813 See MIKELENAS/Lithuanian Report, Q 3.

1814 Art. 390 Italian Civil Code. See PATTI/BELLISARIO/ROSSI CARLEO, Italian Report, Q 3.

1815 See GONZÁLEZ BEILFUSS, Spanish Report, Q 3.

1816 See BOELE-WOELKI/SCHRAMA/VONK, Dutch Report, Q 3.

1817 See GONZÁLEZ BEILFUSS, Spanish Report, Q 3.

1818 See LOWE, English Report, Q 3.

1819 See LOWE, English Report, Q 3.

1820 Art. 32–35 Belgian Law of 8 April 1965 on Juvenile Protection. See PINTENS/PIGNOLET, Belgian Report, Q 3 and 33.

COMMENT

1. The first paragraph of the Principle states that parental responsibilities should be terminated ex lege when the child reaches the age of majority. This rule reflects an absolute common core. The second ground is entering into a marriage or a registered partnership. Although it is not in every legal system that a marriage implies the termination of parental responsibilities, but rather only a weakening thereof, the common core does seem to be termination *ex lege*. Taking into account that marriages involving minors have become rare since the lowering of the age of majority, it should be left to national law to decide whether additional protective measures are required. The Principle assimilates a registered partnership with a marriage. The termination of the parental responsibilities of the previous holder in the case of an adoption reflects the common core of the legal systems surveyed. The death of the child is a self-evident ground for termination.

2. Emancipation seems to have lost a great deal of its importance in many of the legal systems surveyed. Even in certain systems which still have emancipation as a ground for the termination of parental responsibilities, emancipation is only possible in the case of a marriage. This could be due to the fact that the age of majority has been lowered to 18 years. Therefore, it seems unnecessary to add emancipation to the grounds of termination. It should be left to national law to add supplementary grounds.

3. Principle 3:30 (2) underlines that adoption by the parent's partner only terminates the parental responsibilities in relation to the other parent. In several legal systems the consequences of such an adoption are not clear. The Principle takes a clear standpoint and follows the example of several national legislations.[1821]

[1821] E.g. § 1755 para. 2 German Civil Code.

Principle 3:31 Death of the parents

(1) If parents have joint parental responsibilities and one of them dies the parental responsibilities should belong to the surviving parent.

(2) If a parent having sole parental responsibilities dies, responsibilities should be attributed to the surviving parent or a third person upon a decision by the competent authority.

(3) On the death of both parents, of whom at least one had parental responsibilities, the competent authority should take protective measures in respect of the person and the property of the child.

Principe 3:31 Décès des parents

(1) Si les parents détiennent en commun la responsabilité parentale et que l'un d'eux décède, la responsabilité parentale appartient au parent survivant.

(2) Si un parent ayant seul la responsabilité parentale décède, l'autorité compétente attribue la responsabilité au parent survivant ou à tiers.

(3) En cas de décès des deux parents, dont un au moins détenait la responsabilité parentale, l'autorité compétente prend les mesures de protection nécessaires relatives à la personne et aux biens de l'enfant.

Prinzip 3:31 Tod der Eltern

(1) Steht beiden Elternteilen die elterliche Verantwortung gemeinsam zu und stirbt einer von ihnen, verbleibt die elterliche Verantwortung bei dem überlebenden Elternteil.

(2) Stirbt ein Elternteil, der die alleinige elterliche Verantwortung innehatte, wird diese Verantwortung aufgrund einer Entscheidung der zuständigen Behörde dem überlebenden Elternteil oder einem Dritten zuerkannt.

(3) Beim Tod beider Eltern, von denen wenigstens einer die elterliche Verantwortung innehatte, trifft die zuständige Behörde Schutzmaßnahmen für die Person und das Vermögen des Kindes.

INTERNATIONAL INSTRUMENTS

The death of the parents is not covered in international conventions containing substantive law. In international procedural law the termination of parental responsibilities and the institution of guardianship and similar institutions are covered by the *Hague Child Protection Convention 1996* (Art. 3) and the *Brussels II bis Regulation*

(Art. 1). Principle 23 of the Council of Europe's *White Paper 2002* delves deeper into the matter and distinguishes three situations:

1. Where parental responsibilities are exercised jointly by both parents and one of them dies, these responsibilities should belong to the surviving parent.

2. Upon the death of the parent who is solely entitled to exercise some or all parental responsibilities, his or her responsibilities should be exercised by the surviving parent or a third person, either by operation of law or upon a decision taken by the competent authority in the best interests of the child.

3. Where there is no longer any parent still living, the competent authority should take a decision concerning the attribution of parental responsibilities. National legislation may provide that these responsibilities may be given to a member of the family or to a step-parent or to a person designated by the surviving parent unless the interests of the child require other measures.

COMPARATIVE OVERVIEW

The death of one parent, if both parents are holders of parental responsibilities

After the death of one parent holding parental responsibilities, these responsibilities generally continue to be held by the other holder in all the surveyed legal systems (AUSTRIA,[1822] BELGIUM,[1823] BULGARIA,[1824] CZECH REPUBLIC,[1825] DENMARK,[1826] ENGLAND AND WALES,[1827], FINLAND,[1828] FRANCE,[1829] GERMANY,[1830] GREECE,[1831] HUNGARY,[1832] IRELAND,[1833]

1822 § 145 para. 1 sentence 1 and 145 para. 2 Austrian Civil Code. See ROTH, Austrian Report, Q 33.
1823 See PINTENS/PIGNOLET, Belgian Report, Q 33.
1824 See TODOROVA, Bulgarian Report, Q 33.
1825 See HRUSAKOVÁ, Czech Report, Q 33.
1826 § 14 para. 1 first sentence Danish Act on Parental Authority and Conctact. See LUND-ANDERSEN/JEPPESEN-DE BOER, Danish Report, Q 33.
1827 See LOWE, English Report, Q 33.
1828 § 14 para. 2 Finnish Child Custody and the Right of Access Act. See KURKI-SUONIO, Finnish Report, Q 33.
1829 Art. 373–1 and 373–3 French Civil Code. See FERRAND, French Report, Q 33.
1830 § 1680 para. 1 sent. 1 German Civil Code. See DETHLOFF/MARTINY, German Report, Q 33.
1831 Art. 1510 para. 2 and 1515 para. 3 Greek Civil Code. See KOUTSOURADIS-ZERVOGIANNI, Greek Report, Q 33.
1832 See WEISS/SZEIBERT, Hungarian Report, Q 33.
1833 S. 6 of the Irish Guardianship of Infants Act 1964. See SHANNON, Irish Report, Q 33.

ITALY,[1834] LITHUANIA,[1835] THE NETHERLANDS,[1836] NORWAY,[1837] POLAND,[1838] PORTUGAL,[1839] RUSSIA,[1840] SPAIN,[1841] SWEDEN[1842] and SWITZERLAND[1843]). However, the following observations must be made in order to elucidate the mentioned general rule.

In AUSTRIA a distinction is made between the situation where parental responsibilities are held jointly by both parents (at the moment of the death of one of them) or solely by one of them. In the first situation, the parental responsibilities are, by operation of law, transferred to the other surviving parent. Upon the death of a parent who held sole parental responsibilities, the competent authority has to decide whether the other parent or grandparent(s) or foster-parents and, if applicable, which grandparent(s) or foster-parent(s) are to be entrusted with parental responsibilities. If none of these persons is able to assume parental responsibilities, the court is required to entrust another suitable person.[1844] HUNGARY has a similar system. However, in the case of the death of the parent who solely exercised parental responsibilities, the surviving parent's responsibilities will revive. The surviving parent is invited by the public guardianship authority to resume his or her parental responsibilities. If another person takes care of the child when the parent dies, the authority will order this person to transfer the child to the surviving parent, who then exercises his or her own rights. In this situation a third person can be empowered with parental responsibilities.[1845]

DENMARK makes a distinction on the basis of the child's residence. If the child resides with the surviving parent, parental responsibilities remain with this parent. If the child did not reside with the surviving parent, whether or not the deceased parent had sole parental responsibilities, another person may apply for parental responsibilities.[1846] A similar system exists in NORWAY.[1847]

In GERMANY a distinction is made between three situations. If the parents held joint parental responsibilities at the moment of the death of one of them, parental

---

1834 Art. 317 para. 1 Italian Civil Code. See PATTI/BELLISARIO/ROSSI CARLEO, Italian Report, Q 33.
1835 See MIKELENAS, Lithuanian Report, Q 33.
1836 Art. 1:253f, g, Dutch Civil Code. See BOELE-WOELKI/SCHRAMA/VONK, Dutch Report, Q 33.
1837 § 38 Norwegian Children Act 1981. See SVERDRUP/ LØDRUP, Nowegian Report, Q 33.
1838 Art. 94 Polish Family and Guardianship Code. See MĄCZYŃSKI/MĄCZYŃSKA, Polish Report, Q 33.
1839 Art. 1904 Portuguese Civil Code. See DE OLIVEIRA, Portuguese Report, Q 33.
1840 See ANTOKOLSKAIA, Russian Report, Q 33.
1841 See GONZÁLEZ BEILFUSS, Spanish Report, Q 33.
1842 Ch. 6 § 9 Swedish Children and Parents Code. See JÄNTERÄ-JAREBORG/SINGER/SÖRGJERD, Swedish Report, Q. 33.
1843 See Art. 297–298 Swiss Civil Code. See HAUSHEER/ACHERMAN-WEBER/WOLF, Swiss Report, Q 33.
1844 See ROTH, Austrian Report, Q 33.
1845 See WEISS/SZEIBERT, Hungarian Report, Q 33
1846 See LUND-ANDERSEN/JEPPESEN-DE BOER, Danish Report, Q 33.
1847 See SVERDRUP/LØDRUP, Nowegian Report, Q 33.

responsibilities will be attributed to the surviving parent. If the parent who died had sole parental responsibilities, the family court must attribute the responsibilities to the surviving parent unless this would be contrary to the child's best interests. If an unmarried mother was entitled to sole parental responsibilities, the family court must attribute parental responsibilities to the father if this serves the child's best interests.[1848] In SWITZERLAND the parental responsibilities are attributed to the surviving spouse. If an unmarried parent dies, the competent authority will convey the parental responsibilities to the other parent, or it will appoint a guardian for the child, depending on its best interests.[1849]

In GREECE one exception to the general rule, namely if the child was born out of wedlock and the father had appeared as a defendant during judicial acknowledgement proceedings. In this situation, the father is not entitled to exercise parental care even after the death of the mother, unless the court, at his request, enables him to do so, taking into consideration the interests of the child. If it appears not to be in its interests, a guardian will be appointed.[1850]

According to the DUTCH system, if another person holds parental authorities at the time of the parent's death, from then on this person will exercise sole parental responsibilities or will be granted guardianship by operation of law. However, if a person other than a parent becomes a guardian, the court may at any time, upon the request of the surviving parent, attribute the surviving parent with parental responsibilities if he or she has the capacity to exercise them. If the deceased parent held sole parental responsibilities, the court will attribute parental responsibilities to the surviving parent or to a third person.[1851] In POLAND[1852] and SPAIN[1853] a guardian will be appointed if the parental responsibilities were only held by the parent who died. If parental responsibilities were held by both parents, the surviving parent will be sole holder of parental responsibilities.

The death of both parents of whom at least one was the holder of parental responsibilities

Most of the surveyed legal systems consider that parental responsibilities cannot be passed on to a person other than the parents. If both parents die, parental responsibilities come to an end and are replaced by another institution, which is mostly guardian-

1848 See DETHLOFF/MARTINY, German Report, Q 20 and Q 33.
1849 See HAUSHEER/ACHERMAN-WEBER/WOLF, Swiss Report, Q 33.
1850 See KOUTSOURADIS-ZERVOGIANNI, Greek Report, Q 31 and Q 33.
1851 See BOELE-WOELKI/SCHRAMA/VONK, Dutch Report, Q 33.
1852 See MĄCZYŃSKI/MĄCZYŃSKA, Polish Report, Q 33.
1853 See GONZÁLEZ BEILFUSS, Spanish Report, Q 33.

ship and is subject to the court's supervision (a supervision which is stricter than in the case of parental responsibilities). This is the case in BELGIUM,[1854] BULGARIA,[1855] CZECH REPUBLIC,[1856] FINLAND,[1857] FRANCE,[1858] GERMANY,[1859] GREECE,[1860] ITALY,[1861] LITHUANIA,[1862] THE NETHERLANDS,[1863] POLAND,[1864] PORTUGAL,[1865] RUSSIA,[1866] SPAIN,[1867] SWEDEN[1868] and SWITZERLAND.[1869]

Only in AUSTRIA,[1870] DENMARK,[1871] ENGLAND AND WALES,[1872] HUNGARY,[1873] IRELAND[1874] AND NORWAY[1875] can parental responsibilities be transferred to another person or institution. More precisely, in DENMARK sole parental responsibilities may be granted, upon application, to a family member or to a friend, or jointly, upon application, to a married couple who have a close personal relationship with the child. If there are no applications, the local authorities must assist in finding a suitable person or a married couple to fulfil this role.[1876] In ENGLAND AND WALES it depends on whether or not a guardian has been appointed. If there are no other holders of parental responsibilities, then in the absence of any appointment of a guardian, no one will have parental responsibilities concerning the child. There is no mechanism by which responsibilities are automatically transferred to someone else; the appointment of a guardian is thus required. In the absence of any appointment, no one will have parental responsibilities over the child.

1854 Art. 389 Belgian Civil Code. See PINTENS/PIGNOLET, Belgian Report, Q 33.
1855 See TODOROVA, Bulgarian Report, Q 33.
1856 See § 78 Czech Family Code. See HRUSAKOVÁ, Czech Report, Q 33.
1857 § 4 Finnish Guardianship Services Act.
1858 Art. 373–5 and 390 French Civil Code. See FERRAND, French Report, Q 33.
1859 § 1773 para. 1 German Civil Code. See DETHLOFF/MARTINY, German Report, Q 33.
1860 See KOUTSOURADIS/ZERVOGIANNI, Greek Report, Q 31 and Q 33.
1861 Art. 343 *et seq* Italian Civil Code. See PATTI/BELLISARIO/ROSSI CARLEO, Italian Report, Q 33.
1862 See MIKELENAS, Lithuanian Report, Q 33.
1863 Art. 1:292 para. 3 and 1:295 para. 1 Dutch Civil Code. See BOELE-WOELKI/SCHRAMA/VONK, Dutch Report, Q 33.
1864 See MĄCZYŃSKI/MĄCZYŃSKA, Polish Report, Q 33.
1865 Art. 1921 No. 1(a) Portuguese Civil Code. See DE OLIVEIRA, Portuguese Report, Q 33.
1866 Art. 124 para. 1, 137 para. 1, 145 and 151 Russian Family Code. See ANTOKOLSKAIA, Russian Report, Q 33.
1867 See GONZÁLEZ BEILFUSS, Spanish Report, Q 33.
1868 See Ch. 6 § 9 para. 1 Swedish Children and Parents Code. See JÄNTERÄ-JAREBORG/SINGER/SÖRGJERD, Swedish Report, Q 33.
1869 Art. 368 para. 1 Swiss Civil Code. See HAUSHEER/ACHERMAN-WEBER/WOLF, Swiss Report, Q 33.
1870 § 145 para. 11 sentence 2 Austrian Civil Code. See ROTH, Austrian Report, Q 33.
1871 Art. 14 para. 2 first sentence Danish Act on Parental Authority and Contact. See LUND-ANDERSEN/JEPPESEN-DE BOER, Danish Report, Q 33.
1872 See LOWE, English Report, Q 33.
1873 See WEISS/SZEIBERT, Hungarian Report, Q 33.
1874 See S. 8(1) of the Irish Guardianship of Infants Act 1964. See SHANNON, Irish Report, Q 33.
1875 See SVERDRUP/LØDRUP, Nowegian Report, Q 33.
1876 See LUND-ANDERSEN/JEPPESEN-DE BOER, Danish Report, Q 33.

In THE NETHERLANDS if upon the death of both parents one of the parents held parental responsibilities together with a non-parent, the non-parent will become the guardian. If one of the parents held sole parental responsibilities and had appointed a guardian, the appointee will become the guardian if he or she agrees to this. If no guardian had been appointed by the parent(s), the court will do this.[1877]

The parent's appointment – in the case of his or her death – of a new holder of parental responsibilities

The jurisdictions differ in their approach regarding the parents' right to transfer parental responsibilities in the case of their own death. On the one hand, we find countries where the parents do not have such a right, consisting of AUSTRIA,[1878] BULGARIA,[1879] CZECH REPUBLIC,[1880] DENMARK,[1881] FINLAND,[1882] FRANCE,[1883] LITHUANIA,[1884] NORWAY,[1885] POLAND,[1886] RUSSIA[1887] and SWEDEN.[1888] Although the wishes of a parent (in whatever form) are not legally binding they may still be taken into account by the competent authority in BULGARIA,[1889] CZECH REPUBLIC,[1890] DENMARK,[1891] FRANCE,[1892] LITHUANIA,[1893] NORWAY,[1894] POLAND,[1895] RUSSIA[1896] and SWEDEN.[1897] If, however, there is a surviving parent, then that person may be given priority at least in DENMARK and FRANCE, unless there are strong reasons which preclude this.

1877 See BOELE-WOELKI/SCHRAMA/VONK, Dutch Report, Q 33.
1878 See ROTH, Austrian Report, Q 34.
1879 See TODOROVA, Bulgarian Report, Q 34.
1880 See HRUSAKOVÁ, Czech Report, Q 34.
1881 See LUND-ANDERSEN/JEPPESEN-DE BOER, Danish Report, Q 34.
1882 See KURKI-SUONIO, Finnish Report, Q 34.
1883 Art. 373 French Civil Code. See FERRAND, French Report, Q 34.
1884 Art. 3.264–5 Lithuanian Civil Code. See MIKELENAS, Lithuanian Report, Q 34.
1885 See SVERDRUP/LØDRUP, Norwegian Report, Q 34.
1886 Art. 149 para. 1 Polish Family and Guardianship Code. See MĄCZYŃSKI/MĄCZYŃSKA, Polish Report, Q 34.
1887 See ANTOKOLSKAIA, Russian Report, Q 34.
1888 Ch. 6 § 10a, para. 4 Swedish Children and Parents Code. See JÄNTERÄ-JAREBORG/SINGER/SÖRGJERD, Swedish Report, Q 34.
1889 See TODOROVA, Bulgarian Report, Q 34.
1890 See HRUSAKOVÁ, Czech Report, Q 34.
1891 § 15 Danish Act on Parental Authority and Contact.
1892 See FERRAND, French Report, Q 34.
1893 See MIKELENAS, Lithuanian Report, Q 34.
1894 § 63.5 Norwegian Children Act 1981.
1895 Art. 149 para. 1 Polish Family and Guardianship Code. See MĄCZYŃSKI/MĄCZYŃSKA, Polish Report, Q 34.
1896 See ANTOKOLSKAIA, Russian Report, Q 34.
1897 Ch. 6 § 10a, para. 4 Swedish Children and Parents Code. See JÄNTERÄ-JAREBORG/SINGER/SÖRGJERD, Swedish Report, Q 34.

On the other hand, there are countries where the parents are, in principle, permitted to designate the holder of parental responsibilities in the case of their death. A distinction may nevertheless be made depending on whether or not the child has a surviving parent. Surviving parents who were not holders of parental responsibilities may be given priority unless this is contrary to the interests of the child. In BELGIUM,[1898] the parents may jointly designate a guardian for the child by means of a declaration before a competent authority or a notary, and this designation will take effect upon the death of both parents. Where one of the parents dies, the surviving parent may withdraw the declaration and appoint another person as a guardian by means of a will or a new declaration before a competent authority or a notary. The parents' designation of the guardian can only become effective if the person appointed agrees to this and it is not considered to be contrary to the child's interests. A similar position exists in GERMANY[1899] where the parent's designation of the new holder of parental responsibilities is to take place by means of a will or a contract of inheritance ("Erbvertrag"). In GREECE[1900] the parent's designation concerning who is to hold parental responsibilities (guardianship) after his or her death is respected if it has been made in the form of a will or declared before a competent authority or notary. If, on the other hand, the other parent is alive, that parent will automatically become the holder of parental responsibilities and any other designation is without effect. This approach basically also applies in HUNGARY,[1901] subject to the competent authority's control as to whether the appointment is in conformity with the child's interests. In ITALY[1902] such an appointment in the form of a will, public deed or authenticated private deed by the last parent holding parental responsibilities shall be respected by the court, unless it is contrary to the interests of the child. Also in THE NETHERLANDS,[1903] a parent holding parental responsibilities may appoint a new holder of parental responsibilities in the form of a will. In PORTUGAL[1904] and SPAIN,[1905] subject to confirmation by the court after the parents' death, the parents may appoint a guardian or guardians for their child if this is done by means of a will or other authentic or authenticated document . In SWITZERLAND,[1906] the parent's wishes (however they are expressed) are to be respected by the competent authority unless there are significant reasons not to do so.

1898 Art. 392 Belgian Civil Code. See PINTENS/PIGNOLET, Belgian Report, Q 34.
1899 See § 1776 and 1777 German Civil Code. See DETHLOFF/MARTINY, German Report, Q 34.
1900 Art. 1592 Greek Civil Code. See also KOUTSOURADIS/ZERVOGIANNI, Greek Report, Q 34.
1901 See WEISS/SZEIBERT, Hungarian Report, Q 34.
1902 Art. 348 Italian Civil Code.
1903 See BOELE-WOELKI/SCHRAMA/VONK, Dutch Report, Q 34.
1904 Art. 1928, 1925 Portuguese Civil Code. See DE OLIVEIRA, Portuguese Report, Q 34.
1905 Art. 223 Spanish Civil Code. See GONZÁLEZ BEILFUSS, Spanish Report, Q 34.
1906 Art. 381 Swiss Civil Code. See HAUSHEER/ACHERMANN-WEBER/WOLF, Swiss Report, Q 34.

In ENGLAND AND WALES,[1907] parents holding parental responsibilities may appoint – alone or jointly – not only one person but two or more persons to act as the child's guardian(s) in the case of the parent's or parents' death. It is sufficient that the appointment "is made in writing, is dated and is signed by the person making it". There are no restrictions or control as to who may be appointed as a guardian. For the appointment to take effect upon the death of the parent certain conditions must nevertheless be met.[1908] In IRELAND,[1909] the designation must take place in the form of a deed or a will. The person thus appointed shall act together with any other surviving guardian, unless the surviving parent protests. In that case, a court order is necessary to enable the appointed person to act as a guardian, either jointly with the surviving parent or with the latter's exclusion.

COMMENT

1. The principle deals with the consequences of the death of the parents of whom at least one parent had been attributed with parental responsibilities. The principle does not apply to the consequences of the death of third persons holding parental responsibilities. If a third person is the holder of parental responsibilities in addition to a parent, this parent will then be the sole holder of parental responsibilities according to Principle 3:8. If a third person is the holder of parental responsibilities instead of a parent, the competent authority should take protective measures. This issue is not covered by the present Principles.

2. Paragraphs 1 and 2 concern the death of one parent. Paragraph 1 concerns the case where the parents were both holders of parental responsibilities. These responsibilities belong *ex lege* to the surviving parent. Only a discharge from parental responsibilities or other protective measures prevent this parent from exercising those responsibilities. The Principle corresponds with the common core of the legal systems and is in accordance with Principle 23 n° 1 of the *White Paper 2002*.

3. Paragraph 2 concerns the case where the deceased parent was the sole holder of parental responsibilities. In this case the surviving parent will not automatically become the holder of parental responsibilities by operation of law; a decision by the competent authority will thus be necessary. This authority has to decide whether the personal responsibilities should belong to the surviving parent or to a third person. Although most legal systems do not make a distinction between the surviving parent who does

[1907] S. 5 English Children Act 1989. See LOWE, English Report, Q 34.
[1908] See LOWE, English Report, Q 34.
[1909] See SHANNON, Irish Report, Q 34.

or does not hold parental responsibilities, a better law approach seems to require that in the latter case a competent authority should be the judge of the interests of the child. Therefore, the common core of the legal systems surveyed is not followed. The Principle also deviates from the *White Paper 2002*. Article 23 n° 2 of this Paper is very broad. The CEFL Principle makes a more specific choice, based on the interests of the child and taking into account the position of e.g. a step-parent with whom the child has lived for several years.

4. Paragraph 3 of the Principle concerns the death of both parents of whom at least one parent had been attributed with parental responsibilities. In this case the competent authority should take protective measures in respect of the person and the property of the child. This part of the Principle is formulated in very general terms. This kind of measures (e.g. guardianship or the attribution of parental responsibilities to a third person or body) is currently left to national law. Only on the basis of additional information could a different principle be formulated when the CEFL moves on to guardianship and other protective measures. Although there is some valuable information on the possibility for the parent to appoint a new holder of parental responsibilities, this part is also currently left to national law.

CHAPTER VII: DISCHARGE AND RESTORATION OF PARENTAL RESPONSIBILITIES
CHAPITRE VII: RETRAIT ET RESTITUTION DE LA RESPONSABILITÉ PARENTALE
KAPITEL VII: ENTZIEHUNG UND WIEDERHERSTELLUNG DER ELTERLICHEN VERANTWORTUNG

Principle 3:32 Discharge of parental responsibilities
The competent authority should discharge the holder of parental responsibilities, wholly or in part, where his or her behaviour or neglect causes a serious risk to the person or the property of the child

Principe 3:32 Retrait de la responsabilité parentale
L'autorité compétente retire au titulaire de la responsabilité parentale tout ou partie de celle-ci si son comportement ou sa négligence cause un risque grave à la personne ou aux biens de l'enfant.

Prinzip 3:32 Entziehung der elterlichen Verantwortung
Die zuständige Behörde entzieht dem Inhaber der elterlichen Verantwortung ganz oder teilweise die elterliche Verantwortung, wenn sein Verhalten oder seine Vernachlässigung eine ernsthafte Gefahr für die Person oder das Vermögen des Kindes bedeutet.

INTERNATIONAL INSTRUMENTS

Article 9 of the *Convention on the Rights of the Child 1989* states in very general terms that exceptionally a child can be separated from his/her parents by a decision of a competent authority subject to a judicial review. Such a decision may be necessary in cases of abuse and neglect. Such a child, who is temporarily or permanently deprived of his or her family environment, shall be entitled to special protection and assistance (Art. 20). The *Hague Child Protection Convention 1996* includes within its scope certain measures to terminate or restrict parental responsibilities (Art. 3).The *Recommendation on Parental Responsibilities 1984* recommends that, when the person holding parental responsibilities exercises them in a way which is detrimental to the essential interests of the child, the competent authority should then take, of its own motion or upon request, any appropriate measures (Principle 4). A discharge from parental responsibilities is not mentioned as such, but it is clear that the broad Principle does encompass this measure. The *White Paper 2002* has considered this Principle and improved it in Principle 24:

(1) In exceptional circumstances determined by the law, the parents may, partly or totally, be deprived of parental responsibilities or of the exercise of them, upon a decision by a competent authority taken in the best interests of the child.
(2) The Member States should consider the need to establish procedures for the periodical review of such decisions even in the absence of an application to that effect by the person concerned.

The *White Paper 2002* underlines that it should not be a common occurrence to deprive parents of their responsibilities. It was therefore felt necessary to emphasize that this measure would only apply in exceptional circumstances.[1910] Such exceptional circumstances should be determined by law and may include: serious offences committed by the parent against the child (e.g. sexual or physical abuse); other circumstances when the physical and moral welfare of the child is at risk (e.g. when the parent suffers from a mental illness).[1911] The second paragraph of the Principle 24 considers the need for a periodical review of such decisions. Here the Principle takes the case law of the European Court of Human Rights into account. In many cases the Court has ruled that protective measures should be terminated as soon as there is no longer any threat to the child in question.[1912]

1910 *White Paper 2002*, n° 70.
1911 *White Paper 2002*, n° 70.
1912 E.g. European Court of Human Rights, 24.3.1988 *Olsson v. Sweden.*

COMPARATIVE OVERVIEW

Two categories

Almost all the surveyed legal systems have a possibility to discharge parents from their parental responsibilities. However, DENMARK, ENGLAND AND WALES can be considered as exceptions. In DENMARK[1913] there is no possibility to discharge parental responsibilities as such, and only measures which may diminish the powers and duties of the holders of parental responsibilities can be taken. In ENGLAND AND WALES[1914] it is not possible for the court to divest a parent of his/her parental responsibilities insofar as parental responsibility is automatically conferred on the parent at the time of the child's birth. But the exercise of these responsibilities can be restricted by a court order and transferred to someone else.

The legal systems in question can be divided into two categories. The first category has an open character. This means that they have a general clause which has to be interpreted by the courts (e.g. AUSTRIA, CZECH REPUBLIC, GERMANY, etc.) The second category has a closed character. They do not have a general clause, but rather a list of specific grounds which will give rise to a parent being discharged from exercising parental responsibilities. In most legal systems belonging to this category the list is so extensive that these systems can be compared with the first category (e.g. BELGIUM, FRANCE and RUSSIA).

Behaviour involving fault and behaviour not involving fault

Both the general clauses and the lists of specific grounds mainly consist of two general grounds for discharging a parent from his or her responsibilities: behaviour involving fault and behaviour not involving fault. Behaviour involving fault can be qualified as maltreatment, the abuse of authority, negligence or the abuse of the child, which means that the holder of parental responsibilities poses a threat to the child's interests or the behaviour of this parent harms the personality, upbringing, health or property of the child.

1913 See LUND-ANDERSEN/JEPPESEN-DE BOER, Danish Report, Q 51.

1914 See LOWE, English Report, Q 51.

Some legal systems specifically mention a conviction for a crime perpetrated against the child (e.g. BELGIUM,[1915] CZECH REPUBLIC,[1916] FRANCE,[1917] GREECE,[1918] HUNGARY,[1919] PORTUGAL[1920] and RUSSIA[1921]). BELGIUM also includes the marriage of the father or the mother with a person who has been discharged from parental responsibilities as a relevant circumstance.[1922]

AUSTRIA,[1923] BULGARIA,[1924] CZECH REPUBLIC,[1925] GERMANY,[1926] GREECE,[1927] LITHUANIA,[1928] THE NETHERLANDS,[1929] PORTUGAL,[1930] RUSSIA,[1931] SPAIN[1932] and SWITZERLAND[1933] mention behaviour which does not involve fault. This concerns acts which, although they do not directly amount to reprehensible behaviour towards the child itself, nevertheless endanger the child's safety, health or morality, such as a long mental or physical illness, the serving of a long prison term, alcoholism, and long-term separation.

Violent behaviour by a parent towards the other parent

A specific problem is the violent behaviour of a parent towards the other parent. Although in this case there is no direct interference with the relationship between the child and the parent, those systems with a general clause do accept this as a ground for depriving a parent of his/her parental rights when the interests of the child are indirectly affected. This is the case when it affects the development of the child's personality. Other open systems such as AUSTRIA cover this ground with a specific provision. Also some systems with a list of specific grounds have included a specific provision on this issue (e.g. RUSSIA). In other systems with a specific list of grounds, this form of behaviour does not amount to one of the criterions (e.g. BELGIUM).

1915 See PINTENS/PIGNOLET, Belgian Report, Q 51.
1916 See HRUSAKOVÁ, Czech Report, Q 51.
1917 See FERRAND, French Report, Q 51.
1918 See KOUTSOURADIS/ZERVOGIANNI, Greek Report, Q 51.
1919 § 88 para. 1e Hungarian Family Act. See WEISS/SZEIBERT, Hungarian Report, Q 51
1920 See DE OLIVEIRA, Portuguese Report, Q 51.
1921 See ANTOKOLSKAIA, Russian Report, Q 51.
1922 See PINTENS/PIGNOLET, Belgian Report, Q 51.
1923 See ROTH, Austrian Report, Q 51.
1924 See TODOROVA, Bulgarian Report, Q 51.
1925 See HRUSAKOVÁ, Czech Report, Q 51.
1926 See DETHLOFF/MARTINY, German Report, Q 51.
1927 See KOUTSOURADIS/ZERVOGIANNI, Greek Report, Q 51.
1928 See MIKELENAS, Lithuanian Report, Q 51.
1929 See BOELE/WOELKI/SCHRAMA/VONK, Dutch Report, Q 51.
1930 See DE OLIVEIRA, Portuguese Report, Q 51.
1931 See ANTOKOLSKAIA, Russian Report, Q 51.
1932 See GONZÁLEZ BEILFUSS, Spanish Report, Q 51.
1933 See HAUSHEER/ACHERMAN-WEBER/WOLF, Swiss Report, Q 51.

COMMENT

1. This Principle provides for the possibility to discharge the holder of parental responsibilities from exercising these responsibilities when that person is responsible for behaviour involving fault or behaviour not involving fault but which adversely affects the child. The Principle applies to parents as well as to any third person exercising parental responsibilities. The discharge can be total or partial. Although international conventions use the more general terms of deprivation and restriction, the principle has opted for the more specific term of discharge.

2. The Principle has opted for a general clause instead of a list of grounds. Although the *White Paper 2002* favours more detailed and specific grounds, a general clause is not only very much in line with the common core of the legal systems surveyed, but it is also more in accordance with the interests of the child. With a general clause the courts have the possibility to assess the behaviour in question in each specific case. With regard to behaviour involving fault, only serious actions such as maltreatment or an abuse of authority should be taken into account. The clause is sufficiently broad to cover the violent behaviour of a parent towards the other parent when this affects the child. Behaviour not involving fault can only be taken into account when it involves a risk to the child, such as the parent's long-term physical or mental illness.

Principle 3:33 Request for discharge of parental responsibilities

(1) The discharge of parental responsibilities may be requested by:

(a) any parent having parental responsibilities;

(b) the child, and

(c) any institution protecting the interests of the child.

(2) The competent authority may also order the discharge of parental responsibilities of its own motion.

Principe 3:33 Requête en retrait de la responsabilité parentale

(1) Le retrait de la responsabilité parentale peut être demandé par:

(a) un parent titulaire de la responsabilité parentale;

(b) l'enfant, ainsi que

(c) toute institution de défense des intérêts de l'enfant.

(2) L'autorité compétente peut également prononcer d'office le retrait de la responsabilité parentale.

Prinzip 3:33 Antrag auf Entziehung der elterlichen Verantwortung

(1) Die Entziehung der elterlichen Verantwortung kann beantragt werden von:

(a) einem Elternteil, der Inhaber der elterlichen Verantwortung ist;

(b) dem Kind, sowie

(c) jeder Institution, die das Wohl des Kindes schützt.

(2) Die zuständige Behörde kann die elterliche Verantwortung auch von Amts wegen entziehen.

INTERNATIONAL INSTRUMENTS

This specific issue is not covered by any international instrument.

COMPARATIVE OVERVIEW

Exclusive or general competence

The answer to the question of who is entitled to request the discharge of parental responsibilities is answered very differently in the surveyed legal systems, ranging from a very restricted group to virtually anyone at all. Some legal systems have chosen to attribute this competence exclusively to the public prosecutor (BELGIUM[1934]), the other

[1934] Art. 32 para. 3 Belgian Law on Juvenile Protection. See PINTENS/PIGNOLET, Belgian Report, Q 52.

parent (NORWAY[1935]), the child's guardian (IRELAND[1936]) or the local social authority (FINLAND[1937]). Some other countries have chosen to allow any person to bring this question to court (AUSTRIA,[1938] POLAND,[1939] GERMANY[1940] and SWITZERLAND[1941]).

Competence attributed to public and/or private actors

The remaining legal systems that have the possibility to discharge parental responsibilities (BULGARIA,[1942] CZECH REPUBLIC,[1943] FRANCE,[1944] GREECE,[1945] HUNGARY,[1946] ITALY,[1947] LITHUANIA,[1948] THE NETHERLANDS,[1949] PORTUGAL,[1950] RUSSIA,[1951] SPAIN[1952] and SWEDEN[1953]) have a more nuanced system granting this right to those legal actors who have the greatest interest in the well-being of the child. Depending on the system, this concerns a combination of private persons (the other parent or the holder of parental responsibilities, the child or other members of the family) and public actors (the public prosecutor, the court *ex officio* and the local Child Protection Administration). Only the CZECH REPUBLIC does not have a public/private combination. Only the three public actors just mentioned can take action in this legal system.[1954] In BULGARIA[1955] and in

1935 See SVEDRUP/LØDRUP, Norwegian Report, Q 52.

1936 S. 11 Irish Guardianship of Infants Act 1964 and SHANNON, Irish Report, Q 52.

1937 § 14 para. 1 Finnish Child Custody and the Rights of Access Act: Also the child's parents and custodians may submit an application to the court if it concerns child custody. The local social authority has the same power. See KURKI-SUONIO, Finnish Report, Q 52.

1938 § 176 para. 2 Austrian Civil Code. See ROTH, Austrian Report, Q 52: Persons who bring certain matters before the court but do not pertain to the group of persons authorized to file petitions (i.e. parents, grandparents, foster parents; a minor child over 14 years of age and the youth welfare agency) do not thereby gain standing as parties or to file appeals.

1939 Art. 72 para. 1 sentence 2 Polish Constitution. See MĄCZYŃSKI/MĄCZYŃSKA, Polish Report, Q 52.

1940 No formal application is necessary and any person possessing relevant facts can apply. See § 1666 German Civil Code. See DETHLOFF/MARTINY, German Report, Q 52.

1941 See HAUSHEER/ACHERMANN-WEBER/WOLF, Swiss Report, Q 52.

1942 See TODOROVA, Bulgarian Report, Q 52.

1943 See HRUSAKOVÁ, Czech Report, Q 52.

1944 See FERRAND, French Report, Q 52.

1945 See KOUTSOURADIS/ZERVOGIANNI, Greek Report, Q 52.

1946 See WEISS/SZEIBERT, Hungarian Report, Q 52.

1947 See PATTI/BELLISARIO/ROSSI CARLEO, Italian Report, Q 52.

1948 See MIKELENAS, Lithuanian Report, Q 52.

1949 See BOELE-WOELKI/SCHRAMA/VONK, Dutch Report, Q 52.

1950 See DE OLIVEIRA, Portugese Report, Q 52.

1951 See ANTOKOLSKAIA, Russian Report, Q 52.

1952 See GONZÁLEZ BEILFUSS, Spanish Report, Q 52.

1953 See JÄNTERÄ-JAREBORG/SINGER/SÖRGJERD, Swedish Report, Q 52.

1954 Czech Act No. 329/1998 Coll. On Social and Legal Protection of Children and Sec. 35 Czech Code of Civil Procedure. See HRUSAKOVÁ, Czech Report, Q 52.

1955 Art. 74 Bulgarian Family Code and the Child Protection Act. See TODOROVA, Bulgarian Report, Q 52.

GREECE[1956] a claim can be brought by the same three public actors and by the other parent. In GREECE[1957] the child's close relatives are also entitled to act.

In FRANCE[1958] and ITALY[1959] the right to request a discharge of parental responsibilities is restricted to the public prosecutor, the child's guardian or a member of the family. In HUNGARY[1960] and RUSSIA[1961] a petition to terminate parental responsibilities can be filed by the public prosecutor, the public guardianship authority and the other parent. PORTUGAL[1962] recognizes the right to act for the same actors, except for the public guardianship authority. LITHUANIA[1963], THE NETHERLANDS[1964] and SPAIN[1965] recognize the right to act for the same two public actors, for the other parent and for other members of the family and relatives. It can be mentioned that in THE NETHERLANDS also a consensual discharge can be granted upon an application by the Child Care and Protection Board or by the Public Prosecution Service.[1966]

The right of the child him or herself to request a discharge is only possible in AUSTRIA,[1967] ENGLAND AND WALES,[1968] HUNGARY,[1969] RUSSIA[1970] and SPAIN.[1971] Considering that, in a few countries, anyone is entitled to request a discharge, then it naturally

---

1956 Art. 1532 Greek Civil Code. The court may also discharge a guardian of his or her responsibilities at the request of the supervisory council: Art. 1651 Greek Civil Code. See the KOUTSOURADIS/ZERVOGIANNI, Greek Report, Q 52.

1957 Art. 1532 Greek Civil Code. The court may also discharge a guardian of his responsibilities at the request of the supervisory council: Art. 1651 Greek Civil Code. See KOUTSOURADIS/ZERVOGIANNI, Greek Report, Q 52.

1958 Art. 378–1 para. 3 French Civil Code. See FERRAND, French Report, Q 52.

1959 Art. 336 para. 1 Italian Civil Code. See PATTI/BELLISARIO/ROSSI CARLEO, Italian Report, Q 52.

1960 See WEISS/SZEIBERT, Hungarian Report, Q 52.

1961 See ANTOKOLSKAIA, Russian Report, Q 52.

1962 Art. 1915 No. 1 Portugese Civil Code and Art. 194 Portugese Child Protection Law. See DE OLIVEIRA, Portugese Report, Q 52.

1963 Part 1, Art. 3.182 Lithuanian Civil Code and MIKELENAS, Lithuanian Report, Q 52.

1964 Art. 1:270 para. 1 Dutch Civil Code. In some cases, the person who has assumed the care and upbringing of the child may also apply for a discharge: Art. 1:270 para. 2 Dutch Civil Code. See BOELE-WOELKI/SCHRAMA/VONK, Dutch Report, Q 52.

1965 Art. 134 para. 2 Catalan Family Code and Art. 158 and 176 Spanish Civil Code. See GONZÁLEZ BEILFUSS, Spanish Report, Q 52 for the criminal and matrimonial procedure.

1966 Art. 1:267 para. 1 Dutch Civil Code. In some cases, the person who has cared for and raised the child for one or more years at the time of the application may also apply for a consensual discharge: Art. 1:267 para. 2 Dutch Civil Code. See BOELE-WOELKI/SCHRAMA/VONK, Dutch Report, Q 52.

1967 § 176 para. 2 Austrian Civil Code.

1968 But this is limited to those (e.g. unmarried fathers, step-parents residence order holders) who acquire parental responsibilities subsequent to the child's birth. See also LOWE, English Report, Q 52.

1969 See WEISS/SZEIBERT, Hungarian Report, Q 52.

1970 See ANTOKOLSKAIA, Russian Report, Q 52.

1971 See GONZÁLEZ BEILFUSS, Spanish Report, Q 52.

follows that the child also will have this right. AUSTRIA,[1972] POLAND[1973] and SWITZERLAND[1974] must therefore be added to this short list. In SWEDEN the request for a discharge shall be considered by the court, upon an application by the social welfare committee or by the parent.[1975]

Legal systems not having the possibility to discharge parental responsibilities as such

In DENMARK parental authority cannot be discharged (see Principle 3:25), but a parent may apply for sole parental authority.[1976] In ENGLAND AND WALES, it is not possible for the court to divest parental responsibilities. However, in any family proceedings it is possible to limit the exercise of this responsibility. Insofar as this can be considered as a form of discharge, only private actors can apply, namely any person who has parental responsibility for the child or, with the leave of the court, the child him or herself.[1977]

COMMENT

1. The Principle provides that a request for a discharge of parental responsibilities can be made by a parent who holds parental responsibilities, the child, any institution protecting the interests of the child and the competent authority of its own motion. The Principle opts for a mixture of private and public actors and is in accordance with the common core of the legal systems. Although only in a minority of the legal systems surveyed is the child able to request a discharge, the Principle is intended to strengthen the position of the child in these extreme cases. The procedural implementation is left to national law.

2. The right to request the discharge of parental responsibilities should not be extended to other members of the family or other persons. Such solutions are exceptional and cannot always be regarded as being in line with the interest of the parties involved.

1972 See ROTH, Austrian Report, Q 52.

1973 See MĄCZYŃSKI/MĄCZYŃSKA, Polish Report, Q 52.

1974 See HAUSHEER/ACHERMANN-WEBER/WOLF, Swiss Report, Q 52.

1975 Ch. 6 § 7 para. 4 Swedish Children and Parents Code. A parent wishing to discharge the other parent of parental responsibilities may furthermore apply for sole custody Ch. 6 § 5 Swedish Children and Parents Code. See JÄNTERÄ-JAREBORG/SINGER/SÖRGJERD, Swedish Report, Q 52.

1976 § Art. 8, 12 and 13 Danish Act on Parental Authority and Contact. See LUND-ANDERSEN/JEPPESEN-DE BOER, Danish Report, Q 52.

1977 S. 4 (3), English Children Act 1989. See LOWE, English Report, Q 51 and Q 52.

Principle 3:34 Restoration of parental responsibilities
Having regard to the best interests of the child, the competent authority may restore parental responsibilities if the circumstances that led to the discharge no longer exist.

Principe 3:34 Restitution de la responsabilité parentale
Eu égard au meilleur intérêt de l'enfant, l'autorité compétente peut restituer la responsabilité parentale si les circonstances qui ont conduit au retrait ont disparu.

Prinzip 3:34 Wiederherstellung der elterlichen Verantwortung
In Übereinstimmung mit dem Kindeswohl stellt die zuständige Behörde die elterliche Verantwortung wieder her, wenn die Umstände, die zur Entziehung geführt haben, nicht mehr bestehen.

INTERNATIONAL INSTRUMENTS

This specific issue is not covered by any international instrument.

COMPARATIVE OVERVIEW

The legal systems providing grounds for discharging parental responsibilities also recognize the possibility to restore such responsibilities if the circumstances that led to the discharge of parental responsibilities no longer exist and if it is proved that this restoration appears to be in the best interests of the child (AUSTRIA,[1978] BELGIUM,[1979] BULGARIA,[1980] CZECH REPUBLIC,[1981] FINLAND,[1982] FRANCE,[1983] GERMANY,[1984] GREECE (in the case of a restricted discharge),[1985] HUNGARY,[1986] IRELAND,[1987] ITALY,[1988] LITHUANIA, (in the case of a restricted discharge),[1989] THE NETHERLANDS,[1990] NORWAY,[1991] PORTUGAL,[1992]

1978 See ROTH, Austrian Report, Q 54.
1979 See PINTENS/PIGNOLET, Belgian Report, Q 54.
1980 See TODOROVA, Bulgarian Report, Q 54.
1981 See HRUSAKOVÁ, Czech Report, Q 54.
1982 See KURKI-SUONIO, Finnish Report, Q 54.
1983 See FERRAND, French Report, Q 54.
1984 See DETHLOFF/MARTINY, German Report, Q 54.
1985 See KOUTSOURADIS/ZERVOGIANNI, Greek Report, Q 54.
1986 See WEISS/SZEIBERT, Hungarian Report, Q 54.
1987 See SHANNON, Irish Report, Q 54.
1988 See PATTI/BELLISARIO/ROSSI CARLEO, Italian Report, Q 54.
1989 See MIKELENAS, Lithuanian Report, Q 54.
1990 See BOELE-WOELKI/SCHRAMA/VONK, Dutch Report, Q 54.
1991 See SVERDRUP/LØDRUP, Norwegian Report, Q 54.
1992 See DE OLIVEIRA, Portuguese Report, Q 54.

RUSSIA[1993] and SPAIN[1994]). However, according to the law of GREECE[1995] and LITHUANIA[1996] the restoration of parental responsibilities is not possible if the discharge has been total.[1997] It has been mentioned in several reports that the restoration of parental responsibility rights and duties is a rather exceptional event (CZECH REPUBLIC[1998] and RUSSIA[1999]).

Restoring parental responsibilities requires an order by the competent authority. This order may be requested by either the discharged holder of parental responsibilities (BELGIUM,[2000] BULGARIA,[2001] ITALY,[2002] SWEDEN[2003]), the Public Prosecutor (BELGIUM,[2004] HUNGARY[2005] and PORTUGAL[2006]) or the Social Welfare Committee (FINLAND[2007] and SWEDEN[2008]), both parents (FINLAND,[2009] FRANCE[2010] and SWEDEN[2011]) or either parent (FRANCE,[2012] HUNGARY,[2013] THE NETHERLANDS,[2014] PORTUGAL,[2015] RUSSIA[2016] and SWEDEN[2017]) or the child itself (HUNGARY[2018]). In this respect a great variety of solutions exist. In BELGIUM,[2019] FRANCE,[2020] PORTUGAL[2021] and SWITZERLAND[2022] the request may only be made to the competent authority at least one year after the judgement ordering

1993 See ANTOKOLSKAIA, Russian Report, Q 54.
1994 See GONZÁLEZ BEILFUSS, Spanish Report, Q 54.
1995 See KOUTSOURADIS/ZERVOGIANNI, Greek Report, Q 54.
1996 See MIKELENAS, Lithuanian Report, Q 54.
1997 Art. 3.180 Lithuanian Civil Code.
1998 See HRUSAKOVÁ, Czech Report, Q 54.
1999 See ANTOKOLSKAIA, Russian Report, Q 54.
2000 See PINTENS/PIGNOLET, Belgian Report, Q 54.
2001 See TODOROVA, Bulgarian Report, Q 54.
2002 See PATTI/BELLISARIO/ROSSI CARLEO, Italian Report, Q 54.
2003 See JÄNTERÄ-JAREBORG/SINGER/SÖRGJERD, Swedish Report, Q 54.
2004 See PINTENS/PIGNOLET, Belgian Report, Q 54.
2005 See WEISS/SZEIBERT, Hungarian Report, Q 54.
2006 See DE OLIVEIRA, Portuguese Report, Q 54.
2007 See KURKI-SUONIO, Finnish Report, Q 54.
2008 See JÄNTERÄ-JAREBORG/SINGER/SÖRGJERD, Swedish Report, Q 54.
2009 See KURKI-SUONIO, Finnish Report, Q 54.
2010 See FERRAND, French Report, Q 54.
2011 See JÄNTERÄ-JAREBORG/SINGER/SÖRGJERD, Swedish Report, Q 54.
2012 See FERRAND, French Report, Q 54.
2013 See WEISS/SZEIBERT, Hungarian Report, Q 54.
2014 See BOELE-WOELKI/SCHRAMA/VONK, Dutch Report, Q 54.
2015 See DE OLIVEIRA, Portuguese Report, Q 54.
2016 See ANTOKOLSKAIA, Russian Report, Q 54.
2017 See JÄNTERÄ-JAREBORG/SINGER/SÖRGJERD, Swedish Report, Q 54.
2018 See WEISS/SZEIBERT, Hungarian Report, Q 54.
2019 See PINTENS/PIGNOLET, Belgian Report, Q 54.
2020 See FERRAND, French Report, Q 54.
2021 See DE OLIVEIRA, Portuguese Report, Q 54.
2022 See HAUSHEER/ACHERMANN/WOLF, Swiss Report, Q 54.

the discharge has become irrevocable. In FINLAND[2023] and NORWAY[2024] the restoration of parental responsibilities is also possible if the parents have agreed to this. In all cases – and this is of paramount and evident importance – the decision to restore the discharged holders(s) of parental responsibilities with their original status must be taken in accordance with the interests of the child.

COMMENT

1. The Principle provides for restoration of parental responsibilities if the circumstance have changed and the restoration is in the best interests of the child. The Principle follows the common core of the legal systems and is in accordance with the case law of the European Court of Human Rights prescribing that protection measures should be terminated if circumstances permit and underlining that all measures should always be consistent with the ultimate aim of possibly reuniting the family.[2025] This means that such measures are to be terminated as soon as the conditions permit.[2026] The Court strongly focuses on the biological ties between the child and his or her parents. The best interests of the child should always be taken into account.

2. The Principle does not specify who can request the restoration of parental responsibilities. The parents, the child and any institution protecting the interests of the child should have this possibility. The competent authority may also order the restoration of such responsibilities of its own motion.

2023 See KURKI-SUONIO, Finnish Report, Q 54.

2024 See SVERDRUP/LØDRUP, Norwegian Report, Q 54.

2025 E.g. European Court of Human Rights 22.6.1989 *Eriksson v. Sweden*; 25.2.1992 *Andersson v. Sweden*; 24.3.1988 *Olsson v. Sweden* – N° 1; 27.11.1992 *Olsson v. Sweden* – N° 2; 23.9.1994 *Hokkanen v. Finland*.

2026 European Court of Human Rights 24.3.1988 *Olsson v. Sweden* – N° 1. See W. PINTENS, "Europeanisation of Family Law", in: BOELE-WOELKI, K. (ed.), *Perspectives for the Unification and Harmonisation of Family Law in Europe*, 2003, pp. 3–33; J. VANDE LANOTTE/Y. HAECK (ed.), *Handboek EVRM. Deel 2. Artikelsgewijze Commentaar* (Vol. 1), 2004, pp. 752–754.

CHAPTER VIII: PROCEDURE
CHAPITRE VIII: PROCÉDURE
KAPITEL VIII: VERFAHREN

Principle 3:35 Competent authority

(1) All decisions on parental responsibilities should be taken by the competent authority which can either be a judicial or an administrative body.

(2) Where necessary, the competent authority should appoint any suitable person or body to investigate the child's circumstances.

Principe 3:35 Autorité compétente

(1) Toute décision relative à la responsabilité parentale est prise par l'autorité compétente qui peut être soit un organe judiciaire, soit un organe administratif.

(2) En cas de nécessité, l'autorité compétente désigne toute personne ou organe approprié pour enquêter sur la situation de l'enfant.

Prinzip 3:35 Zuständige Behörde

(1) Alle Entscheidungen über die elterliche Verantwortung werden von der zuständigen Behörde getroffen, die entweder ein Gericht oder eine Verwaltungsbehörde sein kann.

(2) Soweit notwendig, bestellt die zuständige Behörde eine geeignete Person oder Einrichtung, um die Verhältnisse des Kindes zu untersuchen.

INTERNATIONAL INSTRUMENTS

Most of the international instruments in question do not directly determine the authority which is competent to intervene in or to decide on parental responsibilities, the child's residence and contact arrangements. The *Convention on the Rights of the Child 1989* mentions in its Article 12 the opportunity that should be given to the child to be heard "*in any judicial or administrative proceedings* affecting the child". This implies that the Convention accepts that both kinds of authority are able to decide on issues relating to parental responsibilities.[2027]

The *Hague Child Protection Convention 1996* also only indirectly deals with the determination of the competent authority. It mentions "the *judicial or administrative authorities* of the Contracting State of the habitual residence of the child" as having jurisdiction to take measures for the protection of the child's person or property (Art. 5).

The *Convention on the Exercise of Children's Rights 1996* uses the terminology "judicial authority" but clarifies in its Article 2 that this term means "a court or an administrative body having equivalent powers". The same formulation can be found in Article 2 of the *Convention on Contact Concerning Children 2003.*

COMPARATIVE OVERVIEW

The courts have competence in most cases

In 18 out of the 22 jurisdictions surveyed the courts are competent to decide on disputes concerning parental responsibilities, the question of the child's residence or contact (AUSTRIA,[2028] where the competent authority to decide on these issues at the district court is either a judicial officer called the *Rechtspfleger* or the judge, depending on the issue to be resolved, BELGIUM,[2029] BULGARIA,[2030] CZECH REPUBLIC,[2031] ENGLAND

2027 See also Art. 3: "In all actions concerning children, whether undertaken by public or private social welfare institutions, courts of law, administrative authorities or legislation bodies, the best interests of the child shall be a primary consideration".

2028 See ROTH, Austrian Report, Q 55.

2029 See PINTENS/PIGNOLET, Belgian Report, Q 55. In BELGIUM there are a variety of competent courts, depending on the issue in question, on whether the parents are married, whether they legally cohabit or are unmarried and have not formalised their relationship: the District Court, Justice of the Peace, and in some cases the President of the Court of first instance.

2030 See TODOROVA, Bulgarian Report, Q 55: competence belongs to the District Court where the child currently resides.

2031 See HRUSAKOVÁ, Czech Report, Q 55.

AND WALES,[2032] FRANCE,[2033] GERMANY,[2034] GREECE,[2035] IRELAND,[2036] ITALY,[2037] LITHUANIA,[2038] THE NETHERLANDS,[2039] NORWAY,[2040] POLAND,[2041] PORTUGAL,[2042] RUSSIA,[2043] SPAIN[2044] and SWEDEN[2045]).

In several of these 18 countries, a variety of courts can be competent, depending on the issue to be resolved (e.g. BELGIUM,[2046] FRANCE,[2047] ITALY,[2048] THE NETHERLANDS[2049] and SPAIN[2050]) which sometimes leads to difficulties in determining the competent court in a particular case.[2051]

Kinds of proceedings: possible non-contentious proceedings

When the court is competent in issues concerning parental responsibilities, the child's residence and contact, several national laws specifically state that the proceedings to be followed are non-contentious (see e.g. AUSTRIA[2052] and CZECH REPUBLIC[2053]).

2032 See LOWE, English Report, Q 55: the possible competence of the Hight Court, the County Court or the Magistrates' Court.

2033 See FERRAND, French Report, Q 55: competence can belong to the family judge (*juge aux affaires familiales* at the *tribunal de grande instance*), the juvenile court judge (*juge des enfants* at the *tribunal de grande instance*) or the guardianship judge (*juge des tutelles* at the *tribunal d'instance*).

2034 See DETHLOFF/MARTINY, German Report, Q 55: competence of the family court (special department of the *Amtsgericht*).

2035 See KOUTSOURADIS/ZERVOGIANNI, Greek Report, Q 55: competence of the District Court either with a single judge or with a panel of three judges.

2036 See SHANNON, Irish Report, Q 55.

2037 See PATTI/BELLISARIO/ROSSI CARLEO, Italian Report, Q 55: possible competence of the family court, the ordinary court or the guardianship judge in an irrational division of parental responsibilities.

2038 See MIKELENAS, Lithuanian Report, Q 55: competence of the court of first instance, Art. 26 Lithuanian Code of Civil Procedure.

2039 See BOELE-WOELKI/SCHRAMA/VONK, Dutch Report, Q 55: District Court or in some cases the juvenile court judge.

2040 See SVERDRUP, Norwegian Report, Q 55.

2041 See MĄCZYŃSKI/MĄCZYŃSKA, Polish Report, Q 55.

2042 See DE OLIVEIRA, Portuguese Report, Q 55.

2043 See ANTOKOLSKAIA, Russian Report, Q 55: competence of the court of first instance which has general jurisdiction in civil proceedings. RUSSIA does not have special courts for juvenile or family matters.

2044 See GONZÁLEZ BEILFUSS, Spanish Report, Q 55: civil or administrative court, depending on whether or not a child protection body has intervened.

2045 See JÄNTERÄ-JAREBORG/SINGER/SÖRGJERD, Swedish Report, Q 55: District Court of the child's residence, or the divorce court if the issue is raised in conjunction with divorce proceedings.

2046 See PINTENS/PIGNOLET, Belgian Report, Q 55.

2047 See FERRAND, French Report, Q 55.

2048 See PATTI/BELLISARIO/ROSSI CARLEO, Italian Report, Q 55.

2049 See BOELE-WOELKI/SCHRAMA/VONK, Dutch Report, Q 55.

2050 See GONZÁLEZ BEILFUSS, Spanish Report, Q 55.

2051 See e.g. the critical remarks contained in PATTI/BELLISARIO/ROSSI CARLEO, Italian Report, Q 55.

2052 See ROTH, Austrian Report, Q 55.

2053 See HRUSAKOVÁ, Czech Report, Q 55.

Possible competence of an administrative authority

Among the 22 jurisdictions surveyed, four jurisdictions (DENMARK,[2054] FINLAND,[2055] HUNGARY[2056] and SWITZERLAND[2057]) grant competence either to the court or to an administrative authority, mostly depending on the issue to be resolved and/or on whether or not the case concerns a conflict. In DENMARK, the administrative authority (*Statsamt*) has exclusive competence concerning contractual matters[2058] and its decisions may be appealed to another administrative authority. As a general principle, competence in the field of parental responsibilities is split between the *Statsamt* and the ordinary courts which deal with conflict cases while the *Statsamt* resolves non-conflict cases. In FINLAND, competence can belong to the District Court of the child's residence,[2059] or to the court which is hearing the divorce proceedings. The decisions may be appealed.[2060] But FINNISH law gives competence to an administrative body (the local social authority where the child has his or her residence) to approve any parental agreements concerning child custody and/or the right to access.[2061] It seems to be taken for granted that where the parents are in agreement, there is no need for the intervention of a judicial authority (the courts) and that reviewing the agreement by an administrative authority is sufficient.

In HUNGARY[2062] the courts or a public guardianship body (an administrative authority) can be competent to decide on parental responsibilities, depending on whether the parents cohabit and on the issues to be resolved. The same applies in SWITZERLAND,[2063] the court or a guardianship authority has to decide (the criterion is whether the parents are married on not). For unmarried parents, the guardianship authority delivers rulings on personal responsibilities and contact; for married, but separated or divorced parents, either the court or the guardianship authority is competent, depending on whether or not there is a connection with the marital dispute.

2054 See LUND-ANDERSEN/JEPPESEN-DE BOER, Danish Report, Q 55.

2055 See KURKI-SUONIO, Finnish Report, Q 55.

2056 See WEISS/SZEIBERT, Hungarian Report, Q 55.

2057 See HAUSHEER/ACHERMANN-WEBER/WOLF, Swiss Report, Q 55.

2058 § 17 Danish Act on Parental Authority and Contact.See LUND-ANDERSEN/JEPPESEN-DE BOER, Danish Report, Q 55.

2059 § 13 Finnish Child Custody and the Right of Access Act. See KURKI-SUONIO, Finnish Report, Q 55.

2060 § 17 Finnish Child Protection Act.

2061 §8 Finnish Child Custody Act. See KURKI-SUONIO, Finnish Report, Q 55.

2062 See WEISS/SZEIBERT, Hungarian Report, Q 55.

2063 See HAUSHEER/ACHERMANN-WEBER/WOLF, Swiss Report, Q 55.

The power or duty to order an investigation into the child's circumstances

In almost all the jurisdictions surveyed, the competent authority has the power or even the duty to appoint a person or body in order to carry out an investigation relating to the circumstances of the child. In several countries, the competent authority is obliged to hear certain persons or bodies. In AUSTRIA[2064] for example, the youth welfare agency of the minor's domicile must be heard before the court issues any orders in proceedings concerning the care and education of the child and personal contact, or before it approves an arrangement on these issues. The same applies in BULGARIA.[2065] In GERMANY,[2066] in most matters concerning children the youth office has to be heard, but the court may also make use of expert evidence. In LITHUANIA[2067] the state institution for the protection of the rights of children has mandatory participation in all court cases involving the child's rights. In RUSSIA an investigation into the circumstances relating to the child is carried out by the Guardianship and Curatorship Department.[2068] In SWEDEN[2069] before deciding on an issue concerning custody, residence or contact, the court shall give the Social welfare committee the opportunity to submit information. In other countries, the competent authority is free to decide whether it is necessary to hear or appoint certain persons or administrative bodies like a Child protection agency. For example, in ENGLAND AND WALES[2070] the court may ask a Children and Family Court Advisory and Support Service officer or a local authority to report to the court on matters relating to the welfare of the child. The solutions are similar in IRELAND.[2071] The same possibility also belongs to the judge in FRANCE where he or she can order expert evidence to be given or a social inquiry to be undertaken.[2072] In NORWAY[2073] the court may obtain statements from the Child Welfare Office and the Social Welfare Office whenever necessary. In SWITZERLAND,[2074] the competent authority is free to consult experts or to make inquiries if necessary.

2064 See ROTH, Austrian Report, Q 55.
2065 Art. 15 para. 6 Bulgarian Child Protection Act and TODOROVA, Bulgarian Report, Q 55.
2066 See DETHLOFF/MARTINY, German Report, Q 55.
2067 See MIKELENAS, Lithuanian Report, Q 55.
2068 See ANTOKOLSKAIA, Russian Report, Q 55 and Art. 78 Russian Family Code.
2069 See JÄNTERÄ-JAREBORG/SINGER/SÖRGJERD, Swedish Report, Q 55.
2070 See LOWE, English Report, Q 55.
2071 See SHANNON, Irish Report, Q 55.
2072 See FERRAND, French Report, Q 55.
2073 See SVERDRUP/LØDRUP, Norwegian Report, Q 55.
2074 See HAUSHEER/ACHERMANN-WEBER/WOLF, Swiss Report, Q 55.

COMMENT

1. The designation of the competent authority to decide on or intervene in parental responsibilities is deliberately not precisely determined by the CEFL Principles. The common core shows that most of the jurisdictions surveyed attribute exclusive competence to a judicial court. Nevertheless, an administrative authority can also be a satisfactory solution, something which is preferred in some Nordic and Eastern countries. This is the reason why Principe 3:35 maintains both possibilities: the court or an administrative body. The same terminology is also used in the CEFL Principles regarding Divorce and Maintenance between Former Spouse,[2075] the competent authority to grant a divorce can be a judicial or an administrative body.

2. The competent authority can decide on or intervene in all matters which fall within the ambit of parental responsibilities as defined in Principle 3:1. The term "decision", as used in Principle 3:35 para. 1, covers all measures to be taken regarding parental responsibilities.

3. Depending on the circumstances of the case, the competent authority may decide ex officio or be seized by one or several persons in the case of a dispute concerning parental responsibilities or in order to approve the agreement reached by the holders of parental responsibilities.

4. The competent authority should obtain precise information on the child's circumstances. Therefore, where necessary, it should not refrain from appointing certain suitable persons or bodies (social workers, civil servants from a Child Protection authority, a psychologist etc.) in order to obtain a clear view of the child's situation before deciding on issues relating to parental responsibilities, the child's residence or contact.[2076] In some circumstances this is an obligation under national law, in others this is not the case. Principle 3:35 does not require that the competent authority should appoint a suitable person in every case, but gives the competent authority the possibility to do so if this appears to be necessary. Some national laws require such an appointment, while others do not. Principle 3:35 lays down a minimum requirement and national law can require more than this if necessary.

[2075] See Principle 1:2; Boele-Woelki/Ferrand/González Beilfuss/Jänterä-Jareborg/Lowe/Martiny/Pintens, *ibid.*, note 10, p. 20.

[2076] See Art. 6 of the *Convention on the Exercise of Children's Rights 1996*: "In proceedings affecting a child, the judicial authority, before taking a decision, shall consider whether it has sufficient information at its disposal in order to take a decision in the best interests of the child and, where necessary, it shall obtain further information, in particular from the holders of parental responsibilities".

5. The decision by the competent authority may be subsequently modified at any time if there is a change in circumstances. This is a clear common core in the jurisdictions surveyed and it is the only solution that is consistent with the duty to take into consideration the best interests of the child, which can subsequently change.

Principle 3:36 Alternative dispute resolution
In all disputes regarding parental responsibilities alternative dispute resolution mechanisms should be available.

Principe 3:36 Résolution alternative des litiges
Dans tous les conflits relatifs à la responsabilité parentale, des modes alternatifs de résolution des conflits sont mis à disposition.

Prinzip 3:36 Alternative Streitbeilegung
In allen Streitigkeiten über elterliche Verantwortung werden alternative Streitbeilegungsverfahren zur Verfügung gestellt.

INTERNATIONAL INSTRUMENTS

The Council of Europe has been remarkably active in the field of (family) mediation. *Recommendation on Family Mediation* was adopted on 21st January 1998. The governments of the Member States are recommended to introduce or promote family mediation or, where necessary, to strengthen existing family mediations. The Recommendation contains a number of Principles regarding the scope of mediation, its organisation and process, the status of mediated agreements, the relationship between mediation and proceedings before the judicial or other competent authority, the promotion of and access to mediation, and other means of resolving disputes and international matters. Additionally, on 18th September 2002 *Recommendation on Mediation in Civil Matters* was adopted by the Committee of Ministers. It contains guiding principles concerning mediation in civil matters and aims to endorse further co-operation between the Council of Europe and the European Union. Given the fact that national authorities should take into account both Recommendations as regards a regulatory framework allowing for mediation, the European Commission for the Efficiency of Justice (CEPEJ) recently assured that a preliminary experiment in the form of a pilot court-annexed mediation programme might ensure the likelihood of legislative action. To that end the CEPEJ drafted a flowchart of questions to be answered as to how to design a programme of court-annexed mediation in its report entitled "Advancing Legal and Judicial Approaches to Mediation in Civil, Family and Commercial Matters". [2077]

On 22nd October 2004 the European Commission launched a Proposal for a *Directive of the European Parliament and of the Council on Certain Aspects of Mediation in Civil*

[2077] CEPEJ (2004)14, Strasbourg 25 May 2004.

and Commercial Matters.[2078] Its objective is to facilitate access to dispute resolution by promoting the use of mediation and by ensuring a sound relationship between mediation and judicial proceedings (Art. 1 para. 1). The proposed Directive is based on Article 61 (c) and the second indent of Article 67 para. 5 *EC Treaty 1975*. Its scope has not yet been clearly delineated. If the proposed Directive only applies to cross-border situations (restricted interpretation of Article 65 *EC Treaty 1975*) this would lead to the creation of an additional parallel legal regime for internal situations. According to Article 2 under a of the proposed Directive "mediation shall mean any process, however named or referred to, where two or more parties to a dispute are assisted by a third party to reach an agreement on the settlement of the dispute, and regardless of whether the process is initiated by the parties, suggested or ordered by a court or prescribed by the national law of a Member State". This definition covers a whole range of alternative dispute resolution (ADR) mechanisms which are applied in Europe.

In addition to the envisaged communitarian instrument, the services of the European Commission, together with a group of stakeholders, have drafted a *European Code of Conduct for Mediators.*[2079] The Code sets out a number of principles to which individual mediators can voluntarily decide to commit themselves, at their own behest. It is intended to be applicable to all kinds of mediation in civil and commercial matters.

COMPARATIVE OVERVIEW

ADR in disputes concerning parental responsibilities

The question of which ADR mechanisms in disputes concerning parental responsibilities, if any, are offered in the European legal systems has been answered differently.[2080] However, in all countries the use of ADR mechanisms in family matters is gaining ground, in particular in cases where the holders of parental responsibilities disagree with regard to their children after separation, divorce or the dissolution of their personal relationship. This is the general trend.[2081] Gradually, the importance of ADR

2078 COM (2004) 718 final.

2079 http://europa.eu.int/comm/justice_home/ejn/adr/adr_ec_code_conduct_en.htm. The Code was launched at a conference in Brussels on 2nd July 2004.

2080 See MARTÍN CASALS, "Divorce Mediation in Europe: An Introductory Outline", *Electronic Journal of Comparative Law*, www.ejcl.org/92/art92-2.html.

2081 This trend has concisely been characterised by MARTÍN CASALS, *ibidem*: "First, (family mediation) is discovered with enthusiasm by professionals who deal with family conflicts; 2) next these professionals organise themselves into associations for the promotion and the practice of mediation;

mechanisms in assisting to solve family problems has been recognised. In this development judges have taken the lead to refer parties to ADR. In addition, it is increasingly accepted that both partners should reach an agreement, in particular with regard to the consequences when there is a breakdown of their personal relationship as a couple. Consequently, self-determination by the parties has been acknowledged as the basic principle.[2082] Hence, all mechanisms used and offered in the national jurisdictions surveyed are essentially aimed at achieving such an agreement between the parties. In this respect also the costs of judicial proceedings can play a significant role. If parties have not tried ADR they may in some jurisdictions be penalized with the payment of high judicial costs.

Different aspects regarding the role of ADR

Apart from these general objectives and intentions different aspects regarding the role of ADR mechanisms in parental responsibility disputes are to be distinguished. First, a distinction is to be made between the different kinds of ADR measures, such as mediation, conciliation and counselling. The dividing line between, on the one hand, mediation and, on the other, conciliation cannot easily be drawn. In general, in the case of mediation the parties make an attempt to reach an agreement on all the aspects of their dispute. This process is facilitated by a neutral and impartial third party. The mediation process, which in contrast to judicial proceedings is more flexible, should enable the parties to control the outcome of the mediation whereas the third party does not have the power to decide on the dispute. In this connection the question arises whether a judge may act as a mediator. In addition, it is questionable whether this does not run counter to the generally acknowledged idea that a mediator should be a specifically trained professional, an idea which also underpins the current project of a *European Directive Concerning Certain Aspects of Mediation in Civil and Commercial Matters*. Alternatively, although aimed at the same objective, conciliation often takes place within the judiciary. At any stage of the proceedings, it is the judge who makes an attempt to conciliate the parties. In contrast, counselling is often provided by social organisations or welfare institutions. Parties obtain advice about the different aspects of their dispute in order to better understand the strengths and weaknesses of their positions and interests and also as to how they can reach such an agreement. Secondly, the question arises whether ADR instruments are compulsory for the parties or whether they *may* make use of these measures. The national jurisdictions have chosen different

3) in a further step, the national legislature refers occasionally to mediation as a useful mechanism for the resolution of conflicts arising out of separation or divorce, a process that is considered preferable to adjudication in adversarial proceedings and 4) finally, family mediation obtains more detailed legal regulation as such or within the broader framework of rules dealing with mediation in civil and commercial matters."

2082 See Report of the CEPEJ, *ibid.*, note 2077.

solutions regarding the question of upon whose initiative ADR mechanisms are to be applied. Thirdly, are ADR mechanisms available with regard to all parental responsibility disputes, even at the stage of enforcing an agreement or decision?

ADR in family matters

In all jurisdictions the notion of ADR in family matters is recognised. In most countries references to mediation, conciliation or counselling are incorporated into the national legislation, either in the Civil Code (AUSTRIA,[2083] FRANCE,[2084] LITHUANIA[2085] and SWITZERLAND[2086]), the Code of Civil Procedure (BELGIUM[2087] and LITHUANIA[2088]), Non-Contentious Proceedings Acts (AUSTRIA[2089] and GERMANY[2090]), Children's Acts (BULGARIA,[2091] DENMARK,[2092] ENGLAND AND WALES,[2093] FINLAND,[2094] IRELAND,[2095] NORWAY[2096] and SWEDEN[2097]), Marriage (Dissolution) Acts (FINLAND,[2098] IRELAND[2099] and NORWAY[2100]), Statutes on Social Welfare and Assistance (POLAND[2101]) or Statutes on Family Mediation (BULGARIA[2102] and SPAIN, in particular CATALONIA[2103]). Legal provisions which refer to mediation, conciliation or counselling indicate that the legislator has in fact recognised the importance of ADR mechanisms in family disputes. It does not, however, say anything about how often they are used and whether they are successful. Significant answers to these questions cannot be based upon the national

2083 § 177a para. 1 and para. 2 Austrian Civil Code.
2084 Art. 373–3–10 para. 1 and 2 French Civil Code.
2085 Art. 3.54 Lithuanian Civil Code.
2086 Art. 171 Swiss Civil Code.
2087 Art. 734 *bis* – 734 *sexies* Belgian Judicial Code.
2088 Art. 231 and 376 Lithuanian Code of Civil Procedure.
2089 § 13 para. 3 and § 108 Austrian Non-contentious Proceedings Act.
2090 § 52 and § 52a para. 1 German Act on Voluntary Jurisdiction.
2091 Art. 23 para. 6 Bulgarian Child Protection Act.
2092 § 28 para. 1 Danish Act on Parental Authority and Contact.
2093 All S. 8 orders (residence, contact, specific issue or prohibited steps orders) of the Childrens Act 1989 have to be listed in a conciliation list. A conciliation appointment at the Principal Registry of the Family Division is the first hearing and an opportunity for early dispute resolution in that court.
2094 Ch. 2 Finnish Act on the Enforcement of a Decision on Child Custody and Right of Access.
2095 S. 20–24 Irish Guardianship of Infants Act 1964.
2096 § 61 Norwegian Children Act 1981.
2097 Ch. 6 Sec. 17a and 18 Swedish Children and Parents Code.
2098 § 20 para. 2 Finnish Marriage Act.
2099 S. 5 para. 2 of the Judicial Separation and Family Reform Act 1989 and S. 6 para. 4 Irish Family Law (Divorce) Act 1996.
2100 Art. 26 Norwegian Marriage Act 1991.
2101 Art. 70 Polish Social Assistance Act.
2102 Bulgarian Mediation Act 2004.
2103 Catalan Law on Family Mediation.

reports.[2104] Moreover, also in those jurisdictions which, to date, have not yet enacted legal provisions which refer to mediation, conciliation or counselling for disputes on parental responsibilities, ADR mechanisms are nonetheless used in practice (CZECH REPUBLIC,[2105] GREECE,[2106] HUNGARY,[2107] ITALY,[2108] PORTUGAL,[2109] RUSSIA[2110] and SPAIN[2111]) and in some countries even rather frequently (THE NETHERLANDS[2112]). Whether in ADR procedures sufficient attention is paid to the position of minor children is an issue which has not specifically been addressed.[2113]

When are ADR mechanisms applicable?

Various ADR mechanisms exist alongside or in addition to each other. If, outside the judicial process, a third party is involved who assists the parties in coming to an agreement, the law generally refers to mediation. If the competent authority itself has the obligation to ensure that the parties reach an amicable agreement at the beginning of or throughout the judicial process, the law often refers to either conciliation or counselling. The one does not exclude the other. Specific reference to the obligation of the administrative body or judge to conciliate between the parties is made in the laws of AUSTRIA,[2114] DENMARK,[2115] ENGLAND AND WALES,[2116] FRANCE,[2117] GERMANY,[2118]

2104 See, however, KURKI-SUONIO, Finnish Report, Q 57 who reports that according to a recent study in FINLAND which covered the years 1997–2001 in more than half of the cases where a mediator was appointed, a case was settled, recalled or otherwise terminated.

2105 See HRUSAKOVÁ, Czech Report, Q 57: an expert certified by the court may mediate.

2106 See KOUTSOURADIS/ZERVOGIANNI, Greek Report, Q 57: the judge may not proceed to hear the case before an attempt at conciliation has bee made between the parties.

2107 See WEISS/SZEIBERT, Hungarian Report, Q 57: the parties may refer to "child-welfare mediation".

2108 See PATTI/BELLISARIO/ROSSI CARLEO, Italian Report, Q 57: judges normally suggest that the parties contact the family mediation centres in disputes concerning parental responsibilities.

2109 See DE OLIVEIRA, Portuguese Report, Q 57: only in the Lisbon district does mediation take place.

2110 See ANTOKOLSKAIA, Russian Report, Q 57: the parties can apply for the services of the Guardianship and Curatorship Departments.

2111 See GONZÁLEZ BEILFUSS, Spanish Report, Q 57: mediation takes place in some autonomous communities.

2112 See BOELE-WOELKI/SCHRAMA/VONK, Dutch Report, Q 57: an evaluation of recent mediation projects demonstrated that the utilization of mediation instead of traditional judicial proceedings turned out to be a success.

2113 This issue has been dealt with in Q 59 and Q 60. All national reports refer to the traditional judicial process.

2114 § 13 para. 3 and § 108 Austrian Non-Contentious Proceedings Act and § 177a para. 1 and 2 Austrian Civil Code.

2115 § 28 para. 1 Danish Act on Parental Authority and Contact.

2116 District Court Judge's Direction – Children: Conciliation [2004] *Law Reports Family Divison High Court* 974. See LOWE, English Report Q 57.

2117 Art. 373-3-10 French Civil Code.

2118 § 52 and § 52a para.1 German Act on Voluntary Jurisdiction.

GREECE[2119] and LITHUANIA.[2120] In NORWAY[2121] mediation is compulsory for couples with children under 16 years of age, except in specific cases, such as in cases of domestic violence. The parties cannot obtain a separation decree unless they have gone through mediation; hence the court summons the parties to attempt mediation. Also in IRELAND[2122] at least the information about ADR mechanisms is obligatory. IRISH solicitors are required to furnish evidence in the form of signed certificates that ADR means have been discussed with the applicant and respondent. In FINLAND,[2123] particularly at the stage of the enforcement of custody or the right of access agreements or decisions, mediation has a mandatory character. The relevant court first appoints a mediator in these cases. In other jurisdictions the use of ADR instruments may be either initiated by the competent authority or requested by the parties themselves (*e.g.* BELGIUM,[2124] BULGARIA,[2125] HUNGARY,[2126] ITALY,[2127] THE NETHERLANDS,[2128] POLAND,[2129] RUSSIA,[2130] SPAIN,[2131] SWEDEN[2132] and SWITZERLAND[2133]).

Which disputes?

In many national reports it has been explicitly reported that ADR mechanisms may be used in all kinds of disputes regarding parental responsibilities including the child's residence and contact and even at the stage of enforcing a decision and/or an agreement (e.g. AUSTRIA,[2134] BELGIUM,[2135] ENGLAND AND WALES,[2136] GERMANY,[2137]

2119 See KOUTSOURADIS/ZERVOGIANNI, Greek Report, Q 57.

2120 Art. 3.54 Lithuanian Civil Code and Art. 231 and 376 Lithuanian Code of Civil Procedure.

2121 Art. 26 and Art. 23 Norwegian Marriage Act 1991, § 61 Norwegian Children Act 1981.

2122 S. 20–24 Irish Guardianship of Infants Act 1964 and S. 5 (2) of the Judicial Separation and Family Reform Act 1989 and S. 6 para. 4 Irish Family Law (Divorce) Act 1996. See SHANNON Irish Report, Q 57.

2123 Ch. 2 Finnish Act on the Enforcement of a Decision on Child Custody and Right of Access.

2124 If the use of ADR-mechanisms is initiated by the competent authority the parties have to agree. See PINTENS/PIGNOLET, Belgian Report, Q 57.

2125 See TODOROVA, Bulgarian Report, Q 57: also the Social Assistance Directorate may request conciliation.

2126 See WEISS/SZEIBERT, Hungarian Report, Q 57: the so-called "child-welfare mediation" may be used.

2127 See PATTI/BELLISARIO/ROSSI CARLEO, Italian Report, Q 57.

2128 See BOELE-WOELKI/SCHRAMA/VONK, Dutch Report, Q 57.

2129 Art. 70 Polish Social Assistance Act.

2130 See ANTOKOLSKAIA, Russian Report, Q 57.

2131 See GONZÁLEZ BEILFUSS, Spanish Report, Q 57.

2132 Ch. 6 § 17a and 18 Swedish Children and Parents Code: parents can receive assistance in the form of cooperative discussions with a view to reaching an agreement on parental responsibility issues.

2133 Art. 171 Swiss Civil Code: parents can turn to voluntary child protection services.

2134 See ROTH, Austrian Report, Q 57.

2135 See PINTENS/PIGNOLET, Belgian Report, Q 57: reference to mediation can be ordered by the court in order to prevent child abduction.

2136 See LOWE, English Report, Q 57.

2137 See DETHLOFF/MARTINY, German Report, Q 57.

HUNGARY,[2138] LITHUANIA[2139] and SWEDEN[2140]). In two jurisdictions contrasting solutions are proffered. In IRELAND[2141] ADR measures are not available at the stage of enforcing a decision or an agreement concerning parental responsibilities, the child's residence or contact, whereas the FINNISH legislator has since 1996 expressly codified that family mediators' services are also available to solve problems arising form the implementation of an approved agreement or a court decision on child custody or the right to access.[2142]

COMMENT

1. It is generally acknowledged that the use of ADR mechanisms in a dispute between parents regarding the future of their child(ren) after the breakdown of their relationship as a couple increases the possibility of transforming hostility and bitterness between the parties into constructive interactions. The best interests of their children require that the best possible relationship between them as the holders of parental responsibilities is established or re-established and is preserved for the future. It is essential that they stay on "speaking terms". A common core exists regarding the increased awareness that in fact the most efficient and successful way to achieve and guarantee a common understanding is that the parties have gone through the process of drafting an agreement on their own terms.[2143] ADR mechanisms provide the means to reach such an agreement on the basis of equality. The encouraging experiences with ADR projects in the national jurisdictions in Europe have directed the way forward for European organisations in the field of (family) mediation. Principle 3:36 complies with the various instruments.

2. ADR mechanisms which do not include arbitration should be available in all kinds of disputes and at all stages. Even the stage of enforcement of an agreement or a decision should be preceded by ADR. See Principle 3:39 Comment 2.

3. If the parties are holders of parental responsibilities, the breakdown of their personal relationship as a couple will not lead to an end to their relationship as parents. It is therefore desirable that ADR is not restricted to the holders of parental responsibilities but that having regard to the child's maturity and age he or she should also be informed, consulted and be able to express his or her opinion in all matters concerning

[2138] See WEISS/SZEIBERT, Hungarian Report, Q 57.
[2139] See MIKELENAS, Lithuanian Report, Q 57.
[2140] Ch. 21 § 2 Swedish Children and Parents Code.
[2141] See SHANNON, Irish Report, Q 57.
[2142] 20 para. 3 Finnish Marriage Act. See KURKI-SUONIO, Finnish Report, Q 57.
[2143] See FERRAND, "Divorce and Spousal Agreements", in: BOELE-WOELKI, *ibid.*, note 22, pp. 72–83 (81).

him or herself. The conditions laid down in Principle 3:6 are applicable. Mediators, conciliators and counsellors should ensure that the child's right to be heard is respected.

4. Should ADR be compulsory or only be used if the parties request it? The European instruments provide for different solutions. *Recommendation on Family Mediation* of the Council of Europe states that "mediation should not, in principle, be compulsory", whereas the proposal for a *Directive on Certain Aspects of Mediation in Civil and Commercial Matters is* aimed, however, without prejudice to national legislation, at "making the use of mediation compulsory or subject to incentives or sanctions, whether before or after judicial proceedings have started, provided that such legislation does not impede on the right of access to the judicial system." Apart from these diverging solutions the final answer as to whether or not ADR should be compulsory should be provided by each national system itself. At any rate, the right to have access to the courts which is guaranteed by Article 6 of the *European Convention on Human Rights* may not be violated. Moreover, it should be borne in mind that compulsory ADR does not mean that the parties have to agree to anything, but only that they have to attend an ADR session; they are not obliged to continue if they do not want to. In DENMARK,[2144] where administrative authorities must offer counselling, the parties and the child are not obliged to participate and also in NORWAY,[2145] where mediation is mandatory, it is the court that settles the dispute if the parties cannot reach an agreement.

[2144] See LUND-ANDERSEN/JEPPESEN-DE BOER, Danish Report, Q 57.

[2145] See SVERDRUP/LØDRUP, Norwegian Report, Q 57.

Principle 3:37 Hearing of the child

(1) Subject to Principle 3:6, the competent authority should hear the child in all proceedings concerning parental responsibilities but if it decides not to hear the child it should give specific reasons.
(2) The hearing of the child should take place either directly before the competent authority or indirectly before a person or body appointed by the competent authority.
(3) The child should be heard in a manner appropriate to his or her age and maturity.

Principe 3:37 Audition de l'enfant

(1) Conformément au Principe 3:6, l'autorité compétente entend l'enfant dans toutes les procédures relatives à la responsabilité parentale ; si toutefois elle décide de ne pas entendre l'enfant, elle doit invoquer des motifs spécifiques.
(2) L'audition de l'enfant a lieu soit directement devant l'autorité compétente, soit indirectement devant une personne ou un organisme désigné par l'autorité compétente.
(3) L'enfant doit être entendu d'une façon appropriée à son âge et à sa maturité.

Prinzip 3:37 Anhörung des Kindes

(1) In Übereinstimmung mit Prinzip 3:6 hört die zuständige Behörde das Kind in allen Verfahren über die elterliche Verantwortung an. Entscheidet die Behörde, das Kind nicht anzuhören, gibt sie dafür besondere Gründe an.
(2) Die Anhörung des Kindes findet unmittelbar vor der zuständigen Behörde statt oder mittelbar vor einer Person oder Einrichtung, die von der zuständigen Behörde dazu bestellt worden ist.
(3) Die Anhörung des Kindes erfolgt in einer seinem Alter und seiner Reife entsprechenden Weise.

INTERNATIONAL INSTRUMENTS

The right of the child to be heard in proceedings that concern him or her is laid down in several international instruments. The *Convention on the Rights of the Child 1989* imposes on States the obligation to assure to the child "who is capable of forming his or her own views" the right to express those views in all matters affecting him or her, "the views of the child being given due weight in accordance with the age and maturity of the child". Para. 2 of Article 12 requires, furthermore, that, for this purpose, the child shall in particular be provided with "the opportunity to be heard in any judicial and administrative proceedings affecting the child, either directly, or through a representative or an appropriate body, in a manner consistent with the procedural rules of national law".[2146]

The *Draft Treaty Establishing a Constitution for Europe 2003*, which has not yet been adopted, also contains a special provision concerning the rights of the child. Article II–84 states that "children have the right to such protection and care as necessary for their well-being. They may express their view freely. Such views shall be taken into consideration on matters which concern them in accordance with their age and maturity". The same article adds that "in all actions relating to children; whether taken by public authorities or private institutions, the child's best interests must be a primary consideration".

In 1990, the Parliamentary Assembly of the Council of Europe adopted a *Recommendation on the Rights of Children*. The Committee of Experts on Family Law (CJ-FA) then proposed the drafting of a European Convention on the Exercise of Children's Rights, which should not overlap with the United Nations Convention, but should rather be complementary. The *Convention on the Exercise of Children's Rights 1996* is very important regarding the right of the child to be heard, because its object is "in the best interests of the children, to promote their rights, to grant them procedural rights and to facilitate the exercise of these rights by ensuring that children are, themselves or through other persons or bodies, informed and allowed to participate in proceedings affecting them before a *judicial* authority".[2147] In its Chapter 2 this Convention contains several procedural rights belonging to the child: the right to be informed and to express his or her views in proceedings if the child has sufficient understanding (Art. 3),[2148] as well as the right to apply for the appointment of a special representative (Art. 4). Other procedural rights should also be considered by the States in question, in particular the right to request to be assisted by an appropriate person of the child's choice in order to help him or her to express his or her views; the right to apply himself or herself, or through other persons or bodies, for the appointment of a separate representative, in appropriate cases a lawyer; the right to appoint his or her own representative; the right to exercise some or all the rights of parties to such judicial

2146 The *Convention on the Rights of the Child 1989* also mentions, like the *Draft Treaty for a European Constitution 2003*, that in all actions concerning children, the best interests of the child shall be a "primary consideration", see Art. 3.

2147 Art. 1 and 2 of the Convention.

2148 Art. 3: "A child considered by internal law as having sufficient understanding, in the case of proceedings before a judicial authority affecting him or her, shall be granted, and shall be entitled to request the following rights:
a to receive all relevant information;
b to be consulted and express his or her views;
c to be informed on the possible consequences of compliance with these views and the possible consequences of any decision".

proceedings. The main idea which this Convention wants to promote is that children should no longer remain merely the subject of family proceedings, but that they may also participate actively therein.

The *Convention on Contact Concerning Children 2003* also lays down the rights of the child to be informed, consulted and to express his or her views (Art. 6). The only condition is that the child has sufficient understanding (like in the *Convention on the Exercise of Children's Rights 1996*) and that the exercise of this right is not manifestly contrary to his or her best interests. Due weight shall be given to the ascertainable wishes and feelings of the child. Like under the *Convention on the Exercise of Children's Rights 1996*, it is left to the States to define the criteria enabling them to evaluate whether or not children are capable of forming and expressing their own views. States can make the age of the child one of those criteria. Where national law has not determined a specific age at which children are considered to have sufficient understanding, the national judicial authority will, according to the nature of the case, determine the level of understanding which is necessary.[2149]

Indirectly, the right of the child to be heard is laid down in the *Hague Child Protection Convention* 1996. Article 23 concerning recognition and enforcement mentions in particular that the recognition of a measure taken by the authorities of a Contracting State may be refused… "if the measure was taken, except in a case of urgency, in the context of a judicial or administrative proceeding, without the child having been provided the opportunity to be heard, in violation of fundamental principles of procedure of the requested State". This ground for refusal is directly inspired by Article 12, para. 2, of the United Nations *Convention on the Rights of the Child 1989*. However, in the opinion of rapporteur P. Lagarde, this does not imply that the child ought to be heard in every case; it is not always in the child's best interest to have to give an opinion, in particular if the parents are in agreement on the measure to be taken. Only if the failure to hear the child is contrary to the fundamental principles of the law of procedure of the requested State, may recognition be refused. This possibility to deny such recognition does not apply in cases of urgency, for which the requirements of procedural due process ought to be interpreted more flexibly. In the decision-making process, the judicial authority, before taking a decision, shall "consult the child in person in appropriate cases, if necessary privately, itself or through other persons or bodies, in a manner appropriate to his or her understanding, unless this would be manifestly contrary to the best interests of the child"; the competent authority shall also "allow the child to express his or her views" and "give due weight to the views expressed by the child" (Art. 6).

2149 See Explanatory Report to the *Convention on Contact Concerning Children 2003*, No. 53.

The hearing of the child is also mentioned in the new *Brussels II bis Regulation* concerning jurisdiction and the recognition and enforcement of judgements in matrimonial matters and matters of parental responsibility. Like all the other international instruments already dealt with, the Regulation emphasises the importance of giving children the opportunity to express their views in proceedings which affect them.[2150] However, as an exception, the child may not be heard if this would be inappropriate, having regard to the child's age and maturity. The Practice Guide for the application of the *Brussels II bis Regulation* does not require a court hearing; the child's views may be obtained by "a competent authority according to national laws". It could, for example, be a social worker who hears the child and presents a report to the court indicating the wishes and feelings of the child. The Practice Guide insists upon the necessity for the judge, if the hearing takes place in court, to organise the questioning in order to take into account the nature of the case, the age of the child and the other circumstances in the case; "in any situation it is important to enable the child to express his or her views in confidence".[2151]

As an example of the importance of this right of the child to be heard, the hearing of the child is one of the requirements for the abolition of the *exequatur* procedure for access rights[2152] and decisions entailing the return of the child.[2153] It is also possible to

2150 See Art. 23, 41 and 42 of the *Brussels II bis Regulation*.

2151 See Practice Guide, IX. Hearing of the child: "When carried out properly, and with appropriate discretion, the hearing may enable the child to express his or her own wishes and to release him or her from a feeling of responsibility or guilt". The Practice Guide also stresses the necessity for the person hearing the child to receive adequate training to communicate with children and to be aware of the risk that the parents can influence the child and exert pressure on him or her.

2152 Art. 41: Rights of access
1. The rights of access, as referred to in Art. 40(1)(a), which is granted in an enforceable judgement given in a Member State shall be recognised and enforceable in another Member State without the need for a declaration of enforceability and without any possibility of opposing its recognition if the judgement has been certified in the Member State of origin in accordance with paragraph 2.
Even if national law does not provide for the enforceability, by operation of law, of a judgement granting access rights, the court of origin may declare that the judgement shall be enforceable, notwithstanding any appeal.
2. The judge of origin shall issue the certificate referred to in paragraph 1 using the standard form in Annex III (certificate concerning rights of access) only if:
...
(c) the child was given an opportunity to be heard, unless a hearing was considered inappropriate having regard to his or her age or degree of maturity.

2153 Art. 42: "The judge of origin who delivered the judgement referred to in Article 40(1)(b) shall issue the certificate referred to in paragraph 1 only if:
(a) the child was given an opportunity to be heard, unless a hearing was considered inappropriate having regard to his or her age or degree of maturity...".

refuse the recognition and enforcement of a judgement relating to parental responsibility on the basis that the child has not been given the opportunity to be heard.[2154]

The *White Paper 2002* deals with the principles relating to the legal consequences of parentage and it lays down, in Principle 21, the right of the child to express his or her own views when the holders of parental responsibilities exercise their parental rights and responsibilities.[2155] Due weight should be given to the views expressed by the child according to his or her age and maturity. Also in the case of a decision relating to parental responsibilities having to be taken by the competent authority, due weight should be given to the views expressed by the child according to his/her age and maturity (Principle 25 para. 2).

All recent international instruments emphasise the right of the child to be heard in proceedings concerning that child. This tendency, which started with the United Nations *Convention on the Rights of the Child 1989*, shows that modern law should consider the child not as an object of the proceedings but as a person who is allowed to express his or her views. Nevertheless, most international instruments require that, in order to grant this right to be heard, the child should have sufficient understanding. Sometimes, they also require that the hearing of the child should not be contrary to his/her best interests.

COMPARATIVE OVERVIEW

Children are to be consulted by the competent authority deciding upon parental responsibilities, the child's residence or contact.

Among the jurisdictions surveyed, the *Convention on the Exercise of Children's Rights 1996* is in force in the CZECH REPUBLIC, GERMANY, GREECE, ITALY and POLAND. Its ratification is expected in AUSTRIA, FINLAND, FRANCE, IRELAND, PORTUGAL, RUSSIA, SLOVAKIA, SPAIN and SWEDEN. Many European countries have therefore been influenced by this Convention with regard to the procedural rights of the child in proceedings

2154 Art. 23: Grounds of non-recognition for judgements relating to parental responsibility
A judgement relating to parental responsibility shall not be recognised:
...
(b) if it was given, except in case of urgency, without the child having been given an opportunity to be heard, in violation of fundamental principles of procedure of the Member State in which recognition is sought.

2155 Principle 21: "When exercising parental rights and responsibilities the child should have a right to express his or her views and due weight should be given to the views expressed by the child according to his or her age and maturity".

affecting that child. It is therefore becoming increasingly common for national laws to require that the child should be consulted in matters affecting him or her. Most international instruments and national laws give relevance to the age and maturity of the child[2156] in order to decide, or to allow the competent authority to decide, whether or not the child shall be heard. Some countries also make the child's right to be heard dependent on the type of proceedings concerned,[2157] or on the (non-)existence of an agreement between the holders of parental responsibilities concerning the issue affecting the child: in BULGARIA,[2158] CZECH REPUBLIC,[2159] DENMARK[2160] and FINLAND,[2161] the child is not heard if the parents have entered into an agreement concerning the issue in question, probably because the parental agreement is deemed to correspond to the child's best interests and therefore the hearing of the child would not be useful. But these restrictions on the child's right to be heard are not mentioned by the majority of the jurisdictions surveyed.

All jurisdictions surveyed generally recognise the right of the child to be heard in proceedings concerning parental responsibilities. In the great majority thereof, the right to be heard leads to a duty on the part of the court to hear the child, either in person or by delegating this task to a suitable person or body, such as a social worker or a representative of a social welfare committee. See the comparative overview under Principe 3:6. In some other countries, the court may hear the child but is not obliged

2156 But the international instruments do not mention any precise age which allows the child to be heard in proceedings affecting him or her. The child's age and maturity is in most jurisdictions considered decisive for whether the child should be heard. In almost half of the countries surveyed, the law determines a certain age at which the child shall be heard (this can be seven, ten, twelve, fourteen years etc., see the Comparative Overview under Principle 3:35 and the answers in the national reports in BOELE-WOELKI/BRAAT/CURRY-SUMNER, *ibid.*, note 23, Q 62.

2157 See the Comparative Overview under Principle 3:4.

2158 See TODOROVA, Bulgarian Report, Q 59: the Bulgarian Family Code does not provide for an opportunity of the child to be heard in the case of an agreement on parental responsibilities and a contact regime in divorce by mutual consent, but the general rule under the Child Protection Act could also apply in this case.

2159 See HRUSAKOVÁ, Czech Report, Q 59: the child is not heard by the court, but his or her opinion is investigated by a social worker.

2160 See LUND-ANDERSEN/JEPPESEN-DE BOER, Danish Report, Q 59: if the holders of parental responsibilities reach an agreement, the child is not heard because it is not "a decision".

2161 See KURKI-SUONIO, Finnish Report, Q 59: if the parents bring to the court a mutual agreement on child custody or the right of access, the child is not heard. The same applies when they request the local social authority to approve their agreement, probably because parents are supposed to take the views and wishes of their child into consideration when they enter into an agreement on matters affecting the child, like § 4 para. 2. Finnish Child Custody and Right of Access Act requires.

to do so;[2162] in some national laws, if the competent authority decides not to hear the child, it has to give specific reasons for this decision.[2163]

Relevance given to the age and maturity of the child in order to decide whether or not he or she will be heard.

All international instruments limit the child's right to be consulted to children who are capable of forming their own views, this being dependent on the child's age and maturity. Sufficient understanding on the part of the child is therefore required, but no age limit is mentioned in the international conventions and European recommendations. The national provisions of the 22 jurisdictions surveyed also mostly require this capacity to understand and for the child to be able to express his/her own views. But some countries have set an age limit over which the child must be heard by the competent authority while other jurisdictions only require that the child should be capable of understanding his or her interests and to express his or her own views. Ten of the twelve jurisdictions surveyed lay down, at least in some cases, a certain age at which the child should be heard (AUSTRIA,[2164] BELGIUM,[2165] BULGARIA,[2166] DENMARK,[2167] FINLAND,[2168] GERMANY,[2169] HUNGARY,[2170] THE NETHERLANDS,[2171] NORWAY[2172] and PORTUGAL[2173]). In NORWAY, for example, from the age of seven the general rule is that

2162 See the Comparative Overview under Principle 3:4.

2163 See, for example, BELGIAN law, PINTENS/PIGNOLET, Belgian Report, Q 59 and FRENCH law, Art. 388–1 para. 3 French Civil Code ("Lorsque le mineur en fait la demande, son audition ne peut être écartée que par une décision spécialement motivée"). See FERRAND, French Report, Q 59. For a very recent decision by the French Cour de cassation, see Cass. civ. I, 18.05.2005, *Revue Lamy droit civil* No. 18 July-August 2005, p. 47 ("Lorsque le mineur capable de discernement demande à être entendu, il peut présenter sa demande au juge en tout état de la procédure et même, pour la première fois en cause d'appel ; son audition ne peut être écartée que par une décision spécialement motivée").

2164 See ROTH, Austrian Report, Q 62.

2165 See PINTENS/PIGNOLET, Belgian Report, Q 59 and Q 62.

2166 See TODOROVA, Bulgarian Report, Q 59 and Q 62.

2167 See LUND-ANDERSEN/JEPPESEN-DE BOER, Danish Report, Q 59.

2168 See KURKI-SUONIO, Finnish Report, Q 59 and Q 62.

2169 See DETHLOFF/MARTINY, German Report, Q 59 and Q 62.

2170 See WEISS/SZEIBERT, Hungarian Report, Q 59 and Q 62.

2171 See BOELE-WOELKI/SCHRAMA/VONK, Dutch Report, Q 59 and Q 62.

2172 See SVERDRUP/LØDRUP, Norwegian Report, Q 62.

2173 See DE OLIVEIRA, Portuguese Report, Q 59 and Q 62. RUSSIA also fixes a specific age (ten years), but the child's opinion may always be taken into consideration. The child may therefore be heard even if he or she is under ten years of age ("as soon as the child is able to express an opinion"), but due weight will only be given to his or her views when the child is at least ten years old. See ANTOKOLSKAIA, Russian Report, Q 59 and Q 62. In SWEDEN, a precise age is also determined but only for the child to be able to refuse the enforcement of an order – twelve years (the enforcement may not be ordered against the child's wishes, unless the administrative county court considers the enforcement to be necessary in the best interests of the child, see JÄNTERÄ-JAREBORG/SINGER/SÖRGJERD, Swedish Report, Q 62.

the child shall be heard before decisions are taken in personal matters[2174]; in AUSTRIA the age limit is ten or fourteen years depending on the issue;[2175] in BELGIUM, depending on the issue and on the competent authority, twelve, fourteen or even fifteen years is the age limit,[2176] which leads to very complicated solutions, so that the Belgian Parliament now intends to lay down a new rule: every minor aged twelve years[2177] and over should be heard in every dispute affecting him or her. In FINLAND, different ages are fixed depending on the issue at stake (twelve or fifteen years, and no age limit in some proceedings).[2178] In GERMANY, the child must be heard when he or she is at least fourteen years old;[2179] the same applies in HUNGARY. In THE NETHERLANDS,[2180] the competent authority must hear a child of at least twelve years, unless the case is of minor importance. In the majority of these countries, a child under the required age may nevertheless be heard by the competent authority if he or she is able to reasonably appraise his or her interests, depending on his or her level of development.

However, most of the 22 jurisdictions surveyed (CZECH REPUBLIC,[2181] ENGLAND AND WALES,[2182] FRANCE,[2183] GREECE,[2184] IRELAND,[2185] ITALY,[2186] LITHUANIA,[2187] POLAND,[2188] RUSSIA,[2189] SPAIN,[2190] SWEDEN with one exception[2191] and SWITZERLAND[2192]) do not determine a precise age at which there is a duty on the part of the competent authority to hear or to consult the child. They prefer to give the competent authority the power to decide whether the hearing of the child is appropriate in each case, depending on the age and the maturity of the child. It should therefore be a specific decision in each

2174 § 31 Norwegian Children Act 1981.

2175 See ROTH, Austrian Report, Q 62: minors who are at least 14 are capable of representing themselves in proceedings regarding their care and education, residence and contact (§ 104 para. 1 *Ausserstreitgesetz*).

2176 See PINTENS/PIGNOLET, Belgian Report, Q 62.

2177 For a similar age limit, see LUND-ANDERSEN/JEPPESEN-DE BOER, Danish Report, Q 59.

2178 See KURKI-SUONIO, Finnish Report, Q 59 and Q 62.

2179 § 50 para. 2 FGG. For a similar age in proceedings relating to the exercise of parental responsibilities, see DE OLIVEIRA, Portuguese Report, Q 62.

2180 See BOELE-WOELKI/SCHRAMA/VONK, Dutch Report, Q 59 and Q 62.

2181 See HRUSAKOVÁ, Czech Report, Q 62.

2182 See LOWE, English Report, Q 62.

2183 See FERRAND, French Report, Q 62.

2184 See KOUTSOURADIS/ZERVOGIANNI, Greek Report, Q 62.

2185 See SHANNON, Irish Report, Q 62.

2186 See PATTI/BELLISARIO/ROSSI CARLEO, Italian Report, Q 62.

2187 See MIKELENAS, Lithuanian Report, Q 62.

2188 See MĄCZYŃSKI/MĄCZYŃSKA, Polish Report, Q 62.

2189 See ANTOKOLSKAIA, Russian Report, Q 62.

2190 See GONZÁLEZ-BEILFUSS, Spanish Report, Q 62.

2191 See JÄNTERÄ-JAREBORG/SINGER/SÖRGJERD, Swedish Report, Q 62.

2192 See HAUSHEER/ACHERMANN-WEBER/WOLF, Swiss Report, Q 62.

case. Logically, this decision shall be based on the specific development of the child in question.

Will the child still be heard (consulted) if the hearing would be manifestly contrary to the best interests of that child?

Some international or national provisions expressly exclude the hearing of the child if this hearing would be "manifestly contrary to the best interests of the child"[2193] or "it proves harmful to the child's interests".[2194] But most of the national provisions do not expressly mention this condition. The competent authority shall consider whether the hearing or the consultation of the child is appropriate or not; it should automatically take into account the best interests of the child, which is a primary consideration in all issues relating to parental responsibilities (see Principle 3:2).

If the competent authority decides not to hear the child, must it give special reasons for this decision?

A few countries (two are mentioned in the national reports)[2195] require the competent authority that refuses to hear the child to give special reasons for this refusal. This requirement is aimed at ensuring that the decision taken on this point by the competent authority is not arbitrary. If the competent authority is obliged to give reasons in order to explain its refusal to hear the child, it is deemed to have investigated the personal situation of the child with regard to the criteria of age, maturity and the child's best interests.

How will the child be heard? The method of consulting the child – Place of the hearing

There are two possible ways to consult and hear the child: a direct, maybe somewhat more formal way by the competent authority itself (a court or administrative authority, depending on the country in question and on the kind of issue to be resolved),[2196] or

---

2193 See Art. 6 *Convention on Contact Concerning Children 2003.*

2194 See TODOROVA, Bulgarian Report, Q 62.

2195 BELGIUM and FRANCE, see PINTENS/PIGNOLET, Belgian Report, Q 62 and FERRAND, French Report, Q 62 and Art. 388–1 French Civil Code. See also Art. 338–3 French Code of Civil Procedure.

2196 In this case, a notice to attend this hearing shall be transmitted to the minor, e.g. by recorded letter in conjunction with an ordinary letter to that effect. See as an example Art. 338–5 French Code of Civil Procedure (the notice shall inform him or her of his/her right to testify alone, or in the presence of an *avocat* or a person of his choice. On the same day, the clerk's office registry shall inform the legal representatives of the parties by ordinary memorandum and, in default thereof, the parties themselves by recorded letter of the decision ordering the the child to testify). However, the judge can be requested to consider the evidence in the presence of the parties and the minor ; in this case, the testimony hearing may sometimes take place immediately (see e.g. Art. 338–6 French Code of Civil Procedure).

an indirect, more informal method in which the competent authority delegates this task to a specially appointed person (e.g. a social worker, psychologist) or an administrative body. Most of the 22 jurisdictions surveyed allow the child to be heard in both ways (AUSTRIA,[2197] BELGIUM,[2198] depending on the proceedings and the competent court, CZECH REPUBLIC[2199] and ENGLAND AND WALES[2200] but with clear preference being given to a report made by a local authority for the court, FINLAND[2201] but the court only hears the child in special circumstances in child custody cases and right of access disputes, FRANCE,[2202] GREECE,[2203] IRELAND[2204] but children are rarely heard directly by the court unless they are of sufficient age and understanding, NORWAY,[2205] PORTUGAL,[2206] RUSSIA,[2207] SPAIN[2208] and SWEDEN[2209] but the hearing of the child in court is only possible if there are special reasons and if it will not harm the child and SWITZERLAND[2210]), which seems to be a reasonable way to ensure that the child's consultation will take place under the best and most appropriate circumstances concerning the child's best interests. Only a few countries oblige the court or any other

---

2197 See ROTH, Austrian Report, Q 60.

2198 See PINTENS/PIGNOLET, Belgian Report, Q 59 and Q 60.

2199 See HRUSAKOVÁ, Czech Report, Q 60.

2200 See LOWE, English Report, Q 60: the judge may interview the child in private, but, in practice, this does not seem to be done very often.

2201 See KIRKI-SUONIO, Finnish Report, Q 60: but in enforcement disputes, the child has to be heard by the mediator appointed to the dispute, see § 7 Finnish Act on the Enforcement of a Decision on Child Custody and Right of Access.

2202 See FERRAND, French Report, Q 60: when a panel of judges is competent to decide on the case, the hearing can take place either before this panel or before one member of this panel, Art. 338–9 French Code of Civil Procedure.

2203 See KOUTSOURADIS/ZERVOGIANNI, Greek Report, Q 60: the child seems to be heard by both a social worker and the court, Art. 681 c Greek Code of Civil Procedure.

2204 See SHANNON, Irish Report, Q 60.

2205 See SVERDRUP/LØDRUP, Norwegian Report, Q 60: the general method is to be directly heard by the competent authority in closed session, but it is also possible to appoint an expert or another suitable person.

2206 See DE OLIVEIRA, Portuguese Report, Q 60: the law does not provide any guidance, so that case law has decided that the child can be heard either directly by the court or by the social services or experts.

2207 See ANTOKOLSKAIA, Russian Report, Q 60: the court is, however, not obliged to hear the child if that child does not request to be heard. In practice, the courts seldom hear the child. The child is mostly heard by an inspector from the Department of Guardianship and Curatorship.

2208 See GONZÁLEZ-BEILFUSS, Spanish Report, Q 60.

2209 See JÄNTERÄ-JAREBORG/SINGER/SÖRGJERD, Swedish Report, Q 60: the hearing of the child in court should be restrictively applied.

2210 See HAUSHEER/ACHERMANN-WEBER/WOLF, Swiss Report, Q 60: the Federal Supreme Court, however, has decided that the pertinent rule is that the child should normally be heard by the court itself and that it may only delegate this task in exceptional circumstances.

competent authority in charge of the dispute to hear the child directly (BULGARIA,[2211] DENMARK,[2212] GERMANY[2213] in one case, LITHUANIA[2214] and POLAND[2215]).

Some national provisions provide guidance on the procedure for and the place of the hearing: For example, in DENMARK,[2216] the hearing before the judge takes the form of a conversation; in ENGLAND AND WALES,[2217] the judge may interview the child in private, but this is seldom done; in BELGIUM,[2218] the hearing shall take place in a suitable location. In LITHUANIA[2219] the court hears the child directly, but normally in closed session. The same applies in NORWAY,[2220] in THE NETHERLANDS where the judge shall not be robed while interviewing the child and in SPAIN[2221] where the hearing is often not in open court. The other national reports do not mention this point, but it can be safely assumed that also in other countries the hearing of the child will take place in Chambers or in closed session.

The presence or absence of the parents or other parties in the proceedings

Some national reports deal with the question of whether the child should be heard in the presence of his/her parents or of other parties in the proceedings. In BELGIUM,[2222] for example, neither the parties, their lawyers nor the Public Prosecutor can be present at the child's hearing, an aspect which has led to criticism because this is a violation of Article 6 para. 1 of the *European Convention on Human Rights 1950*.[2223] In HUNGARY,[2224] both the court and the public guardianship authority (depending on the

2211 See TODOROVA, Bulgarian Report, Q 60: the child is heard directly by the court if he or she is at least ten years old, but in the presence of a social worker.

2212 See LUND-ANDERSEN/JEPPESEN-DE BOER, Danish Report, Q 60: the hearing of the child by the judge or the case worker of the competent administrative authority takes the form of a conversation; in complicated cases, the judge or the case worker can be assisted by a social worker or an appointed expert.

2213 See DETHLOFF/MARTINY, German Report, Q 60: in the case of § 50 b para. 1, 2 sent. 1, 2 FGG, the child must be heard directly by the court.

2214 See MIKELENAS, Lithuanian Report, Q 60: direct hearing by the court, but the court may allow the child's teachers or a psychologist to take part in the hearing.

2215 See MĄCZYŃSKI/MĄCZYŃSKA, Polish Report, Q 60.

2216 See LUND-ANDERSEN/JEPPESEN-DE BOER, Danish Report, Q 60.

2217 See LOWE, English Report, Q 60.

2218 See PINTENS/PIGNOLET, Belgian Report, Q 60.

2219 See MIKELENAS, Lithuanian Report, Q 60.

2220 See SVERDRUP/LØDRUP, Norwegian Report, Q 60.

2221 See GONZÁLEZ BEILFUSS, Spanish Report, Q 60.

2222 See PINTENS/PIGNOLET, Belgian Report, Q 60.

2223 For this reason, the competent authority that hears the child must make a written record of the hearing in order to respect the parties' rights of defence, thereby ensuring that they have the ability to respond to the hearing.

2224 See WEISS/SZEIBERT, Hungarian Report, Q 60.

issue to be resolved) can order that the child has to be heard in the absence of the parents. More generally, some national laws require that the child should be consulted in a manner which is appropriate to his or her understanding and in a manner that does not harm the child.[2225]

Should due weight be given to the views expressed by the child?

Some international instruments[2226] require that due weight should be given to the views expressed by the child. A few jurisdictions surveyed also recognise the importance of the child's opinion. In FINLAND,[2227] for example, an enforcement order may not be implemented against the child's will if the child is 12 years of age or has reached such a level of maturity that its will can be taken into consideration. The same applies in SWEDEN[2228] unless the administrative court considers the enforcement to be necessary in the best interests of the child. In POLAND,[2229] the Constitution requires that the child should be heard in matters affecting him or her and, to the extent possible, the child's opinion should be taken into consideration.

COMMENT

1. Principe 3:6 of the CEFL Principles on Parental Responsibilities lays down the general right of the child to be informed, consulted and to express his or her opinion in all matters concerning him or her. Due weight shall be given to the views expressed by the child. Therefore, the aim and object of Principle 3:37 is to provide more details about the realisation of the child's right to be heard. It is a procedural provision which is aimed at ensuring that the hearing or consultation of the child will take place in an appropriate manner and place. This provision should also ensure that if the competent authority decides not to hear the child, a reasoned explanation for this decision must be given. With regard to the hearing of the child, no difference should be made between a dispute relating to parental responsibilities and an agreement reached by the holders of parental responsibilities concerning which they want to obtain the approval of the competent authority.

2225 See e.g. BULGARIA, Article 15 of the Child Protection Act: (4) The hearing and the consultation of the child shall by all means take place in appropriate surrounding.

2226 See e.g. Art. 12 of the *Convention on the Rights of the Child 1989*, Art. II–84 of the *Draft Treaty for a European Constitution 2003*, Art. 6 of the *Convention on Contact Concerning Children 2003*.

2227 § 2 Finnish Act on the Enforcement of a Decision on Child Custody and Right of Access. See also KURKI-SUONIO, Finnish Report, Q 59.

2228 See JÄNTERÄ-JAREBORG/SINGER/SÖRGJERD, Swedish Report, Q 59.

2229 See MĄCZYŃSKI/MĄCZYŃSKA, Polish Report, Q 59.

2. The hearing should take place *ex officio*. The competent authority, should however take into account the special circumstances of the case, the age, maturity and development of the child in order to decide whether or not the child should be heard.

3. If the competent authority, with regard to the criteria mentioned in Principles 3:6 and 3:37 (1), decides not to hear the child, its decision must contain specific reasons for this refusal, otherwise no control could be exercised concerning this point.[2230] Requiring a reasoned explanation is therefore aimed at ensuring the child's right to be heard and to avoid arbitrary refusals based on the discretion of the competent authority. Specific reasons are detailed, concrete reasons relating to the child's age and maturity.

4. Principle 3:37 (2) allows the child's hearing before the competent authority as well as before a person or body appointed by the competent authority. Nevertheless, there can be goods reasons to prefer the direct hearing of the child by the competent authority, especially when the competent authority is a specialised judge who only deals with family matters. If the competent authority appoints a person or body to hear the child, this person or body should investigate the child's opinion and wishes and should communicate them to the competent authority in a manner which is consistent with the national procedural law.

5. The manner in which the child should be consulted should be appropriate to the child's understanding. This also includes the place where the hearing should take place: it is also important not to exert any undue influence on the child and to try to avoid making him or her reticent in expressing his or her own views. The method and place of the hearing are left to national law. If the child is heard by a court, it is recommended that the hearing should take place in closed session in order to permit the child to express his or her views more easily and freely.

6. Principle 3:37 says nothing about the stage of the proceedings at which the child should be heard. This is left to national law. When the hearing takes place before a court or other competent authority, a wide degree of flexibility is to be recommended and a hearing at any stage of the proceedings (even during appellate proceedings, for example) should be allowed.[2231]

[2230] See a recent decision by the French Cour de cassation, Cass. civ. I, 18.05.2005, *Revue Lamy de droit civil* No. 18, July–August 2005, p. 47.

[2231] In favour of this solution, see a recent decision by the French Cour de cassation, *ibid.*, note 2162, p. 47 ("Lorsque le mineur capable de discernement demande à être entendu, il peut présenter sa demande au juge en tout état de la procédure, et même pour la première fois en cause d'appel"). Art. 338–2 French Code of Civil Procedure ("La demande est présentée sans forme au juge par l'intéressé. Elle peut l'être en tout état de la procédure et même pour la première fois en cause d'appel").

7. The child should not be influenced during the hearing by the presence of close relatives or other parties to the proceedings who could exert undue influence. Therefore, it is recommended that the person in charge of the hearing should talk to the child alone. The parents or other concerned persons should not be present at the hearing. Nevertheless, even if the child is generally not a party to the proceedings on parental responsibilities, it seems useful that a record of the child's opinion should be kept so as to ensure the principle of fair trial laid down in Article 6 para. 1 of the *European Convention on Human Rights 1950*. As under BELGIAN law,[2232] it would be useful that the record could be consulted by the parents or other parties who in this way would have the ability to respond if appropriate. This issue is left to national law which can decide that only excerpts of the hearing should be recorded.

[2232] See PINTENS/PIGNOLET, Belgian Report, Q 60.

Principle 3:38 Appointment of a special representative for the child
In proceedings concerning parental responsibilities in which there could either be a serious conflict of interests between the child and the holders of parental responsibilities or in which the welfare of the child is otherwise at risk, the competent authority should appoint a special representative for the child.

Principe 3:38 Désignation d'un représentant *ad hoc* pour l'enfant
Dans les procédures concernant la responsabilité parentale dans lesquelles un conflit sérieux d'intérêts pourrait exister entre l'enfant et les titulaires de la responsabilité parentale ou dans lesquelles le bien-être de l'enfant est de quelque autre façon menacé, l'autorité compétente désigne un représentant *ad hoc* pour l'enfant.

Principe 3:38 Bestellung eines besonderen Vertreters für das Kind
In Verfahren über die elterliche Verantwortung, in denen ein Interessenkonflikt zwischen dem Kind und den Inhabern der elterlichen Verantwortung bestehen könnte oder in denen das Kindeswohl in anderer Weise gefährdet ist, bestellt die zuständige Behörde einen besonderen Vertreter für das Kind.

INTERNATIONAL INSTRUMENTS

Some international instruments deal with the issue of the representation of the child in proceedings concerning him or her. The *Convention on the Rights of the Child 1989*, after stating the right of the child to express his or her views in all matters affecting him or her, adds that, for this purpose, the child "should be provided with the opportunity to be heard, either directly *or through a representative* or an appropriate body".

However, the most detailed international instrument on this issue is the *Convention on the Exercise of Children's Rights 1996* that ensures the right of the child to apply for the appointment of a special representative, in person or through other persons or bodies, in proceedings before a judicial authority[2233] affecting the child where internal law precludes the holders of parental responsibilities from representing the child as a result of a conflict of interest with the latter (Art. 4 paragraph 1). This provision contains a restriction allowing the contracting states to limit paragraph 1 to children who are considered by internal law to have sufficient understanding. The same Convention states further in its Article 9 that "In proceedings affecting a child where, by internal law, the holders of personal responsibilities are precluded from representing

[2233] For the meaning of this term, see Art. 2 of the Convention ("judicial authority means a court or an administrative authority having equivalent powers").

the child as a result of a conflict of interests between them and the child, the judicial authority shall have the power to appoint a special representative for the child in those proceedings. Parties shall consider providing that, in proceedings affecting a child, the judicial authority shall have the power to appoint a separate representative, in appropriate cases a lawyer, to represent the child". The term "*representative*" is defined in Article 2. It means "a person, such as a lawyer, or a body appointed to act before a judicial authority on behalf of a child". The role of a representative, pursuant to Article 10 of the Convention, is a) to provide all relevant information to the child (subject to the condition that the child is considered by national law to have sufficient understanding); b) to provide (subject to the same condition) an explanation to the child concerning the possible consequences of compliance with his or her views and the possible consequences of any action by the representative; c) to determine the child's views and to present those views to the judicial authority. The special representative shall do all this, unless this would be manifestly contrary to the best interests of the child. The typical situation in which a special representative should be appointed for the child is when a conflict of interest exists between the child and the holders of parental responsibilities. In such a case, the Convention gives the child the right to apply for the appointment of a special representative either personally or through other persons or bodies (Art. 4); the judicial authority is also empowered to appoint *ex officio* a representative for the child (Art. 9). When the child applies for such an appointment, the contracting states may require from the child that he or she has sufficient understanding, while this condition is not required when the judicial authority appoints such a representative *ex officio* as a result of a conflict of interest between the child and the holders of parental responsibilities. Article 9 para. 2 invites the contracting states to give the judicial authority also the power to appoint, for the purpose of the proceedings, a separate representative for the child (i.e. different from the representative of the holders of parental responsibilities) even if there is no conflict of interest, when the proceedings affect the child.

COMPARATIVE OVERVIEW

General rules

Generally, the minor child is represented in civil proceedings by the holders of parental responsibilities (see e.g. AUSTRIA,[2234] FRANCE,[2235] LITHUANIA,[2236] THE NETHERLANDS,[2237]

[2234] See ROTH, Austrian Report, Q 61: generally, the parent who takes the first procedural step will be the child's representative.

[2235] See FERRAND, French Report, Q 61.

[2236] See MIKELENAS, Lithuanian Report, Q 61.

[2237] See BOELE-WOELKI/SCHRAMA/VONK, Dutch Report, Q 61.

POLAND[2238] and RUSSIA[2239]). But the issue to be resolved can result in a conflict of interests between the child and the parents (or between the child and one parent). In such situations, it could be useful to give the child – if he or she has sufficient understanding – or the competent authority the power to appoint a special representative for the child in the proceedings.

However, this special representation of the child in proceedings affecting his or her interests is not accepted by many of the 22 jurisdictions surveyed, unless a conflict of interest exists or may appear between the child and the holders of parental responsibilities. In DENMARK[2240], for example, the child has no other legal representation than the general one belonging to the holders of parental responsibilities. In ITALY,[2241] no legal provision allows a competent authority to appoint a representative for the child or the child him or herself to apply for such a representative. In BELGIUM,[2242] even if the child has the right to be heard, he or she does not become a party to the proceedings[2243] and is only represented by the Public Prosecutor who has to defend the child's best interests.[2244] Only where there is a conflict of interest between the child and the parents does BELGIAN law[2245] provide that an *ad hoc* guardian shall be appointed by the competent authority. The same applies in FRANCE[2246] (where, in such a case, the guardianship court judge or the judge who will decide on the issue raised in the proceedings shall appoint an *ad hoc* administrator who will be entitled to represent the child and to appoint a lawyer to defend the child's interests),[2247] in GREECE,[2248] in

2238 See MĄCZYŃSKI/MĄCZYŃSKA, Polish Report, Q 61.

2239 See ANTOKOLSKAIA, Russian Report, Q 61.

2240 See LUND-ANDERSEN/JEPPESEN-DE BOER, Danish Report, Q 61.

2241 See PATTI/BELLISARIO/ROSSI CARLEO, Italian Report, Q 61.

2242 See PINTENS/PIGNOLET, Belgian Report, Q 61.

2243 Art. 931 para. 7 Belgian Judicial Code.

2244 The same applies in PORTUGAL, see DE OLIVEIRA, Portuguese Report, Q 61 and in SPAIN, see GONZÁLEZ BEILFUSS, Spanish Report, Q 61.

2245 Art. 378 Belgian Civil Code.

2246 See FERRAND, French Report, Q 61.

2247 However, the French Code of Civil Procedure states more generally (Art. 338–7) that where the minor appears alone with a view to giving evidence, the judge shall notify him of his right to give evidence in the presence of an *avocat* or a person of his choice. Where the minor shall exercise such a right, the testimony hearing shall be postponed to a later date. The *avocat* retained by the minor shall inform the judge of this. Where the minor requests to give evidence in the presence of an *avocat* and where he does not choose one himself, the judge shall direct the Chairman of the Bar to appoint an *avocat*.

2248 See KOUTSOURADIS/ZERVOGIANNI, Greek Report, Q 61: if there is a conflict of interest between the child and the holders of parental responsibilities, a special guardian is appointed by the court, whose task will be to represent the child in the particular dispute.

LITHUANIA,[2249] in THE NETHERLANDS[2250] and in SPAIN.[2251] In BULGARIA,[2252] where parental rights are concerned (after a divorce or parental separation), the child is not allowed to have a special representative. In some limited cases, the Social Assistance Directorate may represent the child, but the legal provision which lays this down is not yet in force. In GERMANY,[2253] the child is not a party in custody proceedings, but may nevertheless lodge an appeal without the help of a legal representative.[2254] In 1997, German law introduced the notion of a curator for the child ("Verfahrenspfleger")[2255] who will legally represent that child in proceedings relating to issues with regard to parental responsibilities concerning the person of the child, if this is necessary to safeguard the child's interests, e.g. because of a conflict of interest between the child and the legal representative. In IRELAND,[2256] the child is rarely legally represented in disputes concerning the exercise of parental responsibilities.[2257] In NORWAY,[2258] in some cases, the court may appoint a lawyer or another representative to protect the child's interests. In RUSSIA, too, a guardian may be appointed.[2259] In SWITZERLAND,[2260] a special representative of the child may be appointed in divorce proceedings when there are just causes.[2261]

The child as a party to the proceedings?

In some of the jurisdictions surveyed, the right of the child to have a special representative depends on whether the child is considered to be a party to the proceedings or not. In ENGLAND AND WALES,[2262] for example, the solution varies depending on whether or not the child has been made a party to the proceedings on the exercise of parental responsibilities. Only if the child has been made a party will he or she be represented by a guardian *ad litem*.

2249 See MIKELENAS, Lithuanian Report, Q 61.

2250 Art. 1:250 Dutch Civil Code. See BOELE-WOELKI/SCHRAMA/VONK, Dutch Report, Q 61.

2251 See GONZÁLEZ BEILFUSS, Spanish Report, Q 61: the notion of a conflict of interest only refers to the child's property.

2252 See TODOROVA, Bulgarian Report, Q 61.

2253 See DETHLOFF/MARTINY, German Report, Q 61.

2254 § 59 para. 1, 3 German Act on Voluntary Jurisdiction, FGG. The same applies in THE NETHERLANDS when the child is placed in a closed institution. He or she has a right to lodge an appeal, see BOELE-WOELKI/SCHRAMA/VONK, Dutch Report, Q 61.

2255 § 50 German FGG.

2256 See SHANNON, Irish Report, Q 61.

2257 If the child is represented, it is mostly by a solicitor or a barrister, see SHANNON, Irish Report, Q 61.

2258 See SVERDRUP/LØDRUP, Norwegian Report, Q 61.

2259 Art. 70 para. 1 Russian Family Code.

2260 See HAUSHEER/ACHERMANN-WEBER/WOLF, Swiss Report, Q 61.

2261 Art. 146 Swiss Civil Code. It is mandatory to order legal representation for the child who has sufficient understanding if he or she makes a request to this effect.

2262 See LOWE, English Report, Q 61.

In FINLAND,[2263] for instance, the child can be a party to the proceedings, depending on the kind of dispute: he or she is not a party in custody and right of access disputes nor in enforcement disputes, while the child is a party in public law care proceedings if he or she is at least 15 years of age. In such a case, the local social authority may make an application for a special guardian to be appointed for the child, if there is a conflict of interest between the child and the custodian. In contrast, one European country requires that the child shall always be a party to the proceedings which affect him or her (CZECH REPUBLIC,[2264] where the child – who lacks capacity to sue or to be sued – must be represented by a custodian *ad litem* who will defend the child's interests in the proceedings[2265]).

Relevance of the child's sufficient understanding

Some of the jurisdictions surveyed also give children the right to take legal action or to speak on their own when they have sufficient understanding and have reached a certain age. In AUSTRIA, for example, a minor child over 14 years of age may take legal action on his or her own in proceedings concerning care, education, residence or the right of contact, but not concerning the administration of the child's property.[2266] This child who is capable of representing him or herself in court proceedings may also select a representative (mostly, in practice, this will be the youth welfare agency). In SWEDEN,[2267] in proceedings governed by the Social Services Act and the Care of Young Persons Act, children who have reached the age of 15 years are entitled to speak on their own in the proceedings, and younger children have the right to a special representative who replaces the custodian as a representative.

None of the 22 surveyed jurisdictions seem to strictly apply the United Nations *Convention on the Rights of the Child 1989* which provides that the child should be heard either directly or "*through a representative* or an appropriate body". The appointment of a special representative for the child is not yet a common rule. Most of the time, only in cases of a conflict of interest between the child and the holders of parental responsibilities does the competent authority decide to appoint such a special representative. In most of the jurisdictions surveyed, the competent authority decides *ex officio* whether a special representative should be appointed to safeguard the child's interests; the child is normally not allowed to apply for such an appointment, although

2263 See KURKI-SUONIO, Finnish Report, Q 61.

2264 See HRUSAKOVÁ, Czech Report, Q 61.

2265 § 37 Czech Family Code.

2266 § 104 para. 1 Non-Contentious Proceedings Act (*Ausserstreitgesetz*) and ROTH, Austrian Report, Q 55 and Q 61.

2267 See JÄNTERÄ-JAREBORG/SINGER/SÖRGJERD, Swedish Report, Q 61.

the European *Convention on the Exercise of Children's Rights 1996* guarantees this right to the child "in person or through other persons or bodies".

COMMENT

1. The right of the child to have a special representative appointed should at least be guaranteed in all cases in which the child's interests could be in conflict with those of the holders (or of one holder) of parental responsibilities who normally represent the minor child. This is the common core in the majority of the 22 jurisdictions surveyed. The appointment of a special representative may also be required when the welfare of the child is otherwise at risk, even if this does not seem to be the common core in the jurisdictions surveyed. National laws may also provide that a special representative can be appointed by the competent authority in all proceedings affecting the child, as Article 9 para. 2 of the *Convention on the Exercise of Children's Rights 1996* invites the contracting states to do.

2. The appointment should take place ex officio by an order of the competent authority or a request to this effect may be made by the child subject to the condition that he or she has sufficient understanding. The competent authority may act of its own motion in all cases in which it appears necessary or useful for the child to be represented by a special representative. Sufficient understanding on the part of the child should only be required when the child applies for such an appointment him or herself.

3. The task of the special representative should be to represent the child in the current proceedings and therefore to act before the competent authority on behalf of that child. With regard to the maturity of the child and his or her best interests, the special representative should provide all relevant information to the child, he or she should provide an explanation concerning the possible consequences of compliance with his or her views and the possible consequences of any action by the representative, and the representative must also determine the child's views and present those views to the competent authority. This formulation is based on Article 10 of the *Convention on the Exercise of Children's Rights 1996.*

Principle 3:39 Enforcement
(1) Failing voluntary compliance, a decision by the competent authority and an enforceable agreement concerning parental responsibilities should be enforced without delay.
(2) Enforcement should not take place if it is manifestly contrary to the best interests of the child.

Principe 3:39 Exécution
(1) En l'absence d'exécution volontaire, la décision de l'autorité compétente ou l'accord exécutoire relatif à la responsabilité parentale, donne lieu à exécution forcée sans délai.
(2) L'exécution n'a pas lieu dans le cas où elle est manifestement contraire au meilleur intérêt de l'enfant.

Prinzip 3:39 Vollstreckung
(1) Mangels freiwilliger Befolgung wird eine Entscheidung der zuständigen Behörde und eine vollstreckbare Vereinbarung zur elterlichen Verantwortung ohne Verzögerung vollstreckt.
(2) Eine Vollstreckung findet nicht statt, wenn sie offensichtlich dem Kindeswohl widerspricht.

INTERNATIONAL INSTRUMENTS

The *Convention on the Rights of the Child 1989* only indirectly deals with the issue of the enforcement of decisions relating to the child. Article 9 provides the possibility for the child who is separated from one or both parents to maintain personal relations and direct contact with both parents on a regular basis, except if it is contrary to the child's best interests. Article 4 requires States parties to undertake all appropriate legislative, administrative and other measures for the implementation of the rights recognised in the Convention. This formulation seems to favour, indirectly, the enforcement of decisions or agreements on contact, but with an important restriction: the child's best interests, which are the paramount consideration. The same applies to the *Draft Treaty Establishing a Constitution for Europe 2003* that does not directly deal with the issue of enforcement, but lays down the right of the child to maintain, on a regular basis, a personal relationship and direct contact with both his or her parents, unless that is contrary to his or her interests.

The *European Convention on Human Rights 1950* contains two provisions which can apply in the context of the enforcement of decisions or arrangements concerning parental responsibilities, the child's residence and contact. Article 8 provides the right to have one's family life respected. The European Court of Human Rights has held in several cases that the non-enforcement of judicial decisions concerning parental rights and responsibilities may constitute a violation of this right. The States have a margin of appreciation in this context and the Court controls whether the measures taken by the competent authority were adequate and sufficient to ensure the enforcement of the applicant's right to have his or her family life respected.[2268] With regard to Article 6 para. 1 *European Convention on Human Rights 1950* and the length of the proceedings, the Court has held that judicial proceedings concerning relations between the children and their parents, including enforcement proceedings that are an integral part of the hearing within the meaning of Article 6 para. 1, must be conducted with "exceptional diligence".[2269]

The *Convention on the Exercise of Children's Rights 1996* contains an article which deals with the issue of the enforcement of decisions affecting a child. Article 7 requires that the judicial authority[2270] shall act speedily in such proceedings in order to avoid unnecessary delay. This article adds that "procedures shall be available to ensure that its decisions are rapidly enforced. In urgent cases the judicial authority shall have the power, where appropriate, to take decisions which are immediately enforceable". This provision is aimed at ensuring the effective enforcement of decisions relating to children. No restriction is expressed concerning the best interests of the child in this context.

The *Hague Child Protection Convention 1996* is aimed in particular at providing for the recognition and enforcement of measures to protect the person or the property of the child (Art. 1). It lays down the principle that the measures taken by the authorities of a contracting state shall be recognised by operation of law in all other contracting states (Art. 23). However, under some conditions, the recognition or enforcement of an order concerning the exercise of parental responsibilities, the child's residence or contact may be refused, especially if such recognition would be "manifestly contrary to public policy of the requested state, taking into account the best interests of the child" (Art. 23 para. 2 d). The same applies for enforcement: the measures that have been taken in a contracting state that are enforceable and require enforcement in another contracting state, shall upon request by an interested party, be declared enforceable or registered for the purpose of enforcement in that other state.

2268 See e.g. European Court of Human Rights 27.7.2006 *Iosub Carac v. Romania* ; 26.6.2003, *Maire v. Portugal*; 25.01.2000, *Ignaccolo-Zenide v. Romania*; 23.09.1994, *Hokkanen v. Finland*.

2269 See e.g. European Court of Human Rights, 8.7.1987 *H. v. United Kingdom*; 7.08.1996 *Johansen v. Norway*.

2270 For the meaning of this terminology, see Art. 2 of the Convention: judicial authority means a court or an administrative authority having equivalent powers.

The procedure to be followed for enforcement is the one provided by the law of the state on whose territory the measure shall be enforced (Art. 26 para. 1). The declaration of enforceability or registration in the requested state should be subject to a simple and rapid procedure (Art. 26 para. 2). Article 26 para. 3 of the Convention allows the requested state to refuse the declaration of enforceability for the same reasons as for recognition. If the requested state declares the foreign decision to be enforceable, this decision shall be enforced as if it had been taken by the authorities of that state.[2271] The applicable law for the enforcement is the law of the requested state. Article 28 of the Convention states that "enforcement takes place in accordance with the law of the requested state to the extent provided by such law, taking into consideration the best interests of the child". Also in this context, the child's best interests are the paramount consideration for deciding how to enforce and whether it should be enforced.

In the special matter of contact, the *Convention on Contact Concerning Children 2003* contains several provisions dealing with enforceability and enforcement: Article 9 requires from the states parties that they shall take all appropriate measures to ensure that contact orders are given effect, because "granting contact to a parent without the possibility of properly implementing such contact does not comply with the case-law of the European Court of Human Rights".[2272] Article 14 contains rules on the recognition and enforcement of transfrontier contact orders[2273] and a provision dealing with the conditions for implementing such transfrontier contact orders. Article 15 states that the judicial authority of the state in which such an order made in another state is to be implemented may, "when recognising or declaring enforceable the contact order, or at any later time, fix or adapt the conditions for its implementation, as well as any safeguard or guarantees attaching to it, if necessary for facilitating the exercise

---

2271 See the Lagarde Report on this Convention, under Art. 28: "The reach of this provision appears for example, at the time of the enforcement of a decision concerning a child already endowed with a certain amount of maturity who opposes the enforcement of the measure, for example who refuses absolutely to go and live with the parent designated as custodian. The Special Commission rejected a text which would in this case have authorised the requested authority to refuse enforcement of the measure. It seemed, indeed, that the problem of objections by the child arose in internal situations in the same terms as in international situations and that it was preferable to leave it to the requested authority to resolve the difficulty with all of the flexibility which its internal law left it for internal situations. If, for example, the internal law of the requested State permits in such a case that a judicial or administrative decision not be enforced, this rule may likewise be applied to judicial or administrative decisions taken in another Contracting State".

2272 See Explanatory Report to the *Convention on Contact Concerning Children 2003* n°68–72. The Report mentions that the European Court of Human Rights has held that the non-enforcement of judicial decisions concerning parental rights and responsibilities, including contact, may constitute a violation of the right to respect for family like as provided by Art. 8 of the *European Convention on Human Rights 1950.*

2273 See Art. 14: State Parties shall in particular provide a procedure whereby orders relating to contact and rights of custody made in the other State Parties may be recognised and declared enforceable in advance of contact being exercised within the State addressed.

of contact, provided that the essential elements of the order are respected and taking into account, in particular, a change of circumstances and the arrangements made by the persons concerned". This possibility to fix or modify conditions for the implementation of the contact order should be understood "not as a possibility for the judicial authorities of the state party in which the order is to be implemented to limit or extend the right of contact but a way to facilitate the implementation of the right".[2274] However, in no circumstances may the foreign decision be reviewed as to its substance. This article aims to ensure the effective enforcement of the decision, but with flexibility in order to take into account a possible change of circumstances that would make an adaptation of the enforcement necessary. But the substance of the decision may not be changed.[2275] However, the Explanatory Report to the Convention[2276] makes clear that "of course, this does not rule out the possibility for the courts of a state party to refuse the enforcement of a contact order, invoking a ground of refusal available in accordance with the relevant international instruments or with the internal law of the state".

More generally, the *Brussels II bis Regulation* deals in particular with the recognition and enforcement of judgments in matrimonial matters and matters of parental responsibility (Art. 21, 23 to 39). Article 23 and Article 28 deal with the recognition and enforcement of decisions concerning parental responsibilities. Article 23 determines a list of reasons for the refusal of recognition[2277] which also apply to enforceability. However, some exceptions are applicable to access rights. Those are directly recognised and enforceable under the *Brussels II bis Regulation* in order to ensure that the child can maintain contact with all the holders of parental responsibilities after a separation, even if they live in different member states. The exercise of cross-border access rights are facilitated by the direct enforceability of the decision on such rights. The judgment on access rights is directly recognised and enforceable in another member state if it is accompanied by a certificate issued by the judge of origin who issued the judgment. The certificate is issued after the judge of origin has checked whether several procedural safeguards have been adhered to.[2278] The certificate allows the person who is entitled to exercise access rights to request that the decision shall be enforced without any intermediate procedure. To ensure that access rights can be

[2274] See Explanatory Report to the *Convention on Contact Concerning Children 2003*, n°114.

[2275] Because otherwise two contradictory orders concerning contact could be made in two different states, see Explanatory Report to the *Convention on Contact Concerning Children 2003*, n°114.

[2276] See Explanatory Report to the *Convention on Contact Concerning Children 2003*, n°113 *in fine*.

[2277] In particular if the recognition is manifestly contrary to the ordre public of the requested state with regard to the child's best interests.

[2278] Especially whether all the parties have been given the opportunity to be heard and whether the child has been given this opportunity, unless a hearing of the child was inappropriate having regard to the child's age or maturity.

enforced even if the judgment contains no sufficient information on the arrangements concerning access rights, Article 48 of the *Brussels II bis Regulation* gives the courts of the member state of enforcement the power to make the necessary practical arrangements for organising the exercise of access rights, but subject to the condition that the essential elements of the judgment must be respected. This pragmatic rule is similar to the one contained in Article 15 of the *Convention on Contact Concerning Children 2003*. Special rules[2279] also apply in the case of a child's abduction: if the court of the member state of origin decides that the child shall return, the *exequatur* (execution order) is abolished for this decision which is directly enforceable in the requested member state.

This overview of the available international instruments shows that in most cases the effective enforcement of a decision on parental responsibilities, the child's residence or contact can be ensured. Only in a limited number of exceptions may the enforceability or the enforcement be denied. The child's best interests are mentioned in some international instruments, but not directly as a reason not to enforce a decision, but more as a paramount consideration while deciding on the exercise of parental responsibilities, the child's residence or contact.

COMPARATIVE OVERVIEW

Because of the broad extent of the contents of parental responsibilities, of the great variety of possible proceedings in this field and because of the very different situations that are dealt with, it is very difficult to state general, always applicable, rules on the enforcement of decisions relating to parental responsibilities.

General rule of enforceability – A distinction between decisions by the competent authority and agreements between the holders of parental responsibilities

In all 22 jurisdictions surveyed, the general principle is that a decision on parental responsibilities, the child's residence or contact can be enforced (AUSTRIA,[2280] BELGIUM,[2281] BULGARIA,[2282] CZECH REPUBLIC,[2283] DENMARK,[2284] ENGLAND AND WALES,[2285]

[2279] See Art. 10, 11 and especially 42 of the *Brussels II bis Regulation*.

[2280] § 110 para. 2 in conjunction with § 79 para. 2 Non-Contentious Proceedings Act (*Ausserstreitgesetz*). See ROTH, Austrian Report, Q 58.

[2281] See PINTENS/PIGNOLET, Belgian Report, Q 58.

[2282] See TODOROVA, Bulgarian Report, Q 58.

[2283] See HRUSAKOVÁ, Czech Report, Q 58.

[2284] See LUND-ANDERSEN/JEPPESEN-DE BOER, Danish Report, Q 58.

[2285] See LOWE, English Report, Q 58.

FINLAND,[2286] FRANCE,[2287] GERMANY,[2288] GREECE,[2289] HUNGARY,[2290] IRELAND,[2291] ITALY,[2292] LITHUANIA,[2293] THE NETHERLANDS,[2294] NORWAY,[2295] POLAND,[2296] PORTUGAL,[2297] RUSSIA,[2298] SPAIN,[2299] SWEDEN[2300] and SWITZERLAND[2301]), where necessary with the help of various coercive measures. But many countries distinguish between a decision made by the competent authority and an agreement reached between the holders of parental responsibilities. In most of the jurisdictions surveyed (BELGIUM,[2302] CZECH REPUBLIC,[2303] ENGLAND AND WALES,[2304] FINLAND,[2305] IRELAND,[2306] ITALY,[2307] LITHUANIA,[2308] NORWAY,[2309] RUSSIA (indirectly)[2310] and SPAIN[2311]), only court orders or decisions made by other competent authorities are enforceable. An agreement between the parents is only enforceable if it has been approved by the competent authority which can be a court or the social authorities (see e.g. BELGIUM,[2312] CZECH REPUBLIC,[2313] FINLAND,[2314]

2286 See KURKI-SUONIO, Finnish Report, Q 58.
2287 See FERRAND, French Report, Q 58.
2288 See DETHLOFF/MARTINY, German Report, Q 58.
2289 See KOUTSOURADIS/ZERVOGIANNI, Greek Report, Q 58.
2290 See WEISS/SZEIBERT, Hungarian Report, Q 58.
2291 See SHANNON, Irish Report, Q 58.
2292 See PATTI/BELLISARIO/CARLEO ROSSI, Italian Report, Q 58.
2293 See MIKELENAS, Lithuanian Report, Q 58.
2294 See BOELE-WOELKI/SCHRAMA/VONK, Dutch Report, Q 58.
2295 See SVERDRUP/LØDRUP, Norwegian Report, Q 58.
2296 See MĄCZYŃSKI/MĄCZYŃSKA, Polish Report, Q 58.
2297 See DE OLIVEIRA, Portuguese Report, Q 58.
2298 See ANTOKOLSKAIA, Russian Report, Q 58.
2299 See GONZÁLEZ BEILFUSS, Spanish Report, Q 58.
2300 See JÄNTERÄ-JAREBORG/SINGER/SÖRGJERD, Swedish Report, Q 58.
2301 See HAUSHEER/ACHERMANN-WEBER/WOLF, Swiss Report, Q 58.
2302 See PINTENS/PIGNOLET, Belgian Report, Q 58.
2303 See HRUSAKOVÁ, Czech Report, Q 58.
2304 See LOWE, English Report, Q 58: the only binding agreement that can be made is a formal parental responsibility agreement under S. 4, Children Act 1989 which attributes parental responsibilities to the unmarried father, step-parents and registered partners. In all other cases, the agreement is not binding so that it cannot be enforced.
2305 See KURKI-SUONIO, Finnish Report, Q 58.
2306 See SHANNON, Irish Report, Q 58.
2307 See PATTI/BELLISARIO/CARLEO ROSSI, Italian Report, Q 58.
2308 See MIKELENAS, Lithuanian Report, Q 58.
2309 See SVERDRUP/LØDRUP, Norwegian Report, Q 58.
2310 See ANTOKOLSKAIA, Russian Report, Q 58.
2311 See GONZÁLEZ BEILFUSS, Spanish Report, Q 58.
2312 Approval by the court.
2313 Approval by the court.
2314 Approval by the local social authority. See KURKI-SUONIO, Finnish Report, Q 46 on contact agreements.

FRANCE,[2315] LITHUANIA[2316] and SWEDEN[2317]). But this general principle of enforceability, which is a classical and logical one for all kinds of court orders against which no appeal with suspensive effect is possible, is subject to restrictions related to the precise issue that has been decided upon and to possible important reasons to refuse the enforcement in a problematic matter where the child's best interests must be safeguarded.

A distinction between decisions on parental responsibilities and the child's residence, on the one hand, and decisions on contact on the other

The enforceability of judgements or orders on contact generally follows the same rules as in other matters concerning parental responsibilities, but there can be differences when the child resists contact. As far as they exist, the provisions on non-contentious proceedings are used (AUSTRIA[2318] and GERMANY[2319]). Sometimes a specific procedure for the enforcement of decisions on the upbringing of minor children is available (CZECH REPUBLIC[2320]). More common, however, is the application of general rules on the execution of judgements and orders. It is however difficult to provide a general assessment because the issue of enforceability arises in the context of different proceedings and with respect to different persons, i.e. the parent or third person obliged to contact, the other parent (the custodian, the holder of parental responsibilities) and the child. The welfare of the child may also be taken into account at the enforcement stage.

Only in some jurisdictions, where a duty exists on the part of the parent to maintain personal relationships, can the *obliged parent* be forced to perform his or her duty of contact. In GERMANY it is contested whether enforcement in these cases can be useful because it may influence the unwilling parent or there is a possibility that it will deteriorate the situation.[2321] One method of enforcement is by fines and compensation for the child (PORTUGAL[2322]). In most jurisdictions the duty to maintain personal relationships cannot be enforced (AUSTRIA,[2323] BULGARIA,[2324] ENGLAND AND WALES,[2325]

2315 Approval by the court. See FERRAND, French Report, Q 58: on contact agreements but the solution applies to all matters concerning parental responsibilities.

2316 Approval by the court. See MIKELENAS, Lithuanian Report, Q 58.

2317 See JÄNTERÄ-JAREBORG/SINGER/SÖRGJERD, Swedish Report, Q 58: court orders as well as agreements between the parents on custody, residence and contact are enforceable, but the agreement must be in writing, signed by both parents and approved by the social welfare committee.

2318 See ROTH, Austrian Report, Q 58.

2319 § 33 German Act on Voluntary Jurisdiction. See DETHLOFF/MARTINY, German Report, Q 58.

2320 § 272 and § 273a Czech Civil Procedure Code. See HRUSAKOVÁ, Czech Report, Q 58.

2321 See DETHLOFF/MARTINY, German Report, Q 58.

2322 Art. 181 No. 1 Portuguese Child Protection Law. See DE OLIVEIRA, Portuguese Report, Q 44b, 45.

2323 § 108 Austrian Act on Non-Contentious Procedure. See ROTH, Austrian Report, Q 45, 58.

2324 See TODOROVA, Bulgarian Report, Q 45.

2325 See LOWE, English Report, Q 45.

FINLAND,[2326] ITALY,[2327] NORWAY[2328] and SWITZERLAND[2329]). There may be other sanctions, however, such as the loss of the right to be informed and the right to express one's opinion (AUSTRIA[2330]), a total loss of parental responsibilities (ITALY[2331]) or additional child maintenance payments (SWITZERLAND[2332]).

The most important question is the enforcement of contact orders against the *other parent* who is obliged to make the necessary arrangements so that contact is untroubled. The current situation is that most jurisdictions use a whole range of enforcement measures. Disobedience or the frustration of contact orders is nevertheless not easy to deal with and nearly everywhere is a subject of constant debate. Often the competent authority may issue a warning or give instructions (e.g. CZECH REPUBLIC[2333] and SWITZERLAND[2334]). Forcible execution is in some jurisdictions not admissible or at least no longer used (BELGIUM,[2335] GREECE[2336] and SWITZERLAND[2337]).

One method of enforcement is the imposition of civil fines (e.g. BELGIUM,[2338] CZECH REPUBLIC,[2339] DENMARK,[2340] FRANCE,[2341] GERMANY,[2342] THE NETHERLANDS,[2343] NORWAY,[2344] PORTUGAL[2345] and RUSSIA[2346]). Also damages for the non-residential parent (BELGIUM,[2347]

2326 See KURKI-SUONIO, Finnish Report, Q 45.
2327 See PATTI/BELLISARIO/ROSSI CARLEO, Italian Report, Q 45.
2328 See SVERDRUP/LØDRUP, Norwegian Report, Q 45.
2329 See HAUSHEER/ACHERMANN-WEBER/WOLF, Swiss Report, Q 58.
2330 § 178 para. 1 and 3 Austrian Civil Code.
2331 See PATTI/BELLISARIO/ROSSI CARLEO, Italian Report, Q 45.
2332 See HAUSHEER/ACHERMANN-WEBER/WOLF, Swiss Report, Q 58.
2333 See HRUSAKOVÁ, Czech Report, Q 58.
2334 Art. 273 para. 2 Swiss Civil Code. See HAUSHEER/ACHERMANN-WEBER/WOLF, Swiss Report, Q 48a and Q 58.
2335 See PINTENS/PIGNOLET, Belgian Report, Q 48a.
2336 See KOUTSOURADIS/ZERVOGIANNI, Greek Report, Q 58.
2337 See HAUSHEER/ACHERMANN-WEBER/WOLF, Swiss Report, Q 48a.
2338 See PINTENS/PIGNOLET, Begian Report, Q 48a, 58.
2339 See HRUSAKOVÁ, Czech Report, Q 58.
2340 See LUND-ANDERSEN/JEPPESEN-DE BOER, Danish Report, Q 48a.
2341 See FERRAND, French Report, Q 58.
2342 § 33 para. 3 German Act on Voluntary Jurisdiction. See DETHLOFF/MARTINY, German Report, Q 58.
2343 See BOELE-WOELKI/SCHRAMA/VONK, Dutch Report, Q 58.
2344 See SVERDRUP/LØDRUP, Norwegian Report, Q 48a and Q 58.
2345 See DE OLIVEIRA, Portuguese Report, Q 44b.
2346 See ANTOKOLSKAIA, Russian Report, Q 48a and Q 58.
2347 See PINTENS/PIGNOLET, Belgian Report, Q 48a.

GERMANY,[2348] HUNGARY[2349] and ITALY[2350]) or compensation for the child (PORTUGAL[2351]) can be claimed.

Under several national laws criminal proceedings can be taken against a parent who disregards someone's right of contact (BELGIUM,[2352] BULGARIA[2353] and FRANCE[2354]). In some jurisdictions punishment for contempt of court (ENGLAND AND WALES[2355] and IRELAND[2356]) or non-compliance with a judicial decision (BULGARIA,[2357] SPAIN[2358] and SWITZERLAND[2359]) is possible.

Sometimes the child will resist contact, either of its own volition or after having been unduly influenced by the custodial parent. Then the question arises whether the contact right can be enforced against the will of the child. Enforcement against the child's will by way of a fetching order or other enforcement measures can take place in some jurisdictions (BULGARIA,[2360] FINLAND with some exceptions,[2361] THE NETHERLANDS[2362] and SWEDEN[2363] with some exceptions). In other jurisdictions it is excluded

---

2348 Bundesgerichtshof 19 June 2002, BGHZ 151, 155 = NJW 2002, 2566.

2349 See WEISS/SZEIBERT, Hungarian Report, Q 58.

2350 See PATTI/BELLISARIO/ROSSI CARLEO, Italian Report, Q 48.

2351 See DE OLIVEIRA, Portuguese Report, Q 44b.

2352 Art. 432 Belgian Penal Code. See PINTENS/PIGNOLET, Belgian Report, Q 48a.

2353 Art. 270 Bulgarian Penal Code.

2354 Art. L 227–5 French Penal Code. See FERRAND, French Report, Q 48a.

2355 See LOWE, English Report, Q 48a and Q 58.

2356 See SHANNON, Irish Report, Q 48a and Q 58.

2357 See TODOROVA, Bulgarian Report, Q 58.

2358 See GONZÁLEZ BEILFUSS, Spanish Report, Q 48a and Q 58.

2359 See HAUSHEER/ACHERMANN-WEBER/WOLF, Swiss Report, Q 58.

2360 See TODOROVA, Bulgarian Report, Q 58.

2361 See KURKI-SUONIO, Finnish Report, Q 48a and Q 58: but the court can refuse to issue a fetching order if the child is at least 12 and resists the enforcement. The same effect may be given to the resistance of a younger child who has reached such maturity that its will can be taken into consideration.

2362 See BOELE-WOELKI/SCHRAMA/VONK, Dutch Report, Q 58.

2363 See JÄNTERÄ-JAREBORG/SINGER/SÖRGJERD, Swedish Report, Q 58: but for orders regarding custody, residence or contact, enforcement against the will of a child who has reached the age of twelve or a corresponding level of maturity, cannot be ordered unless it is necessary with regard to the best interests of the child (Ch. 21 § 5 Swedish Children and Parents Code).

or it is not used since this would be counterproductive and against the welfare of the child (AUSTRIA,[2364] FRANCE,[2365] GERMANY,[2366] GREECE,[2367] IRELAND[2368] and RUSSIA[2369]).

Is mediation encouraged as a first step or is it even mandatory?

Several reports mention that before coercive measures may be taken, a first step shall take place, which mostly consists of a kind of mediation or at least of information given by the competent authority to the holders of parental responsibilities about the possible consequences of non-compliance with the order or (approved) agreement. In the CZECH REPUBLIC,[2370] for instance, the court first calls on the obligated parent to obey the judicial decision voluntarily or to fulfil the court-approved agreement; the court shall inform the parent about the consequences of not complying with the order on parental responsibilities. In PORTUGAL,[2371] a meeting also takes place between the judge and both parents (on the initiative of the parent who wants to have the decision enforced) and only with the parent who does not comply with the order. This meeting may be followed by a summary inquiry and any other measures that are deemed to be necessary. In SPAIN,[2372] there must be an application for enforcement before the court which will then provide a time-limit for complying with the court order.

In FIINLAND,[2373] in most cases, mediation is the first step in the enforcement proceedings; only if the efforts of the mediator are unsuccessful will the mediator deliver a report to the court. A similar situation can be observed in HUNGARY,[2374] where the first step – in the case of the enforcement of a decision on personal responsibilities or the child's residence – consists of requesting the public guardianship authority to promote voluntary performance, whereas in the case of a contact order, child welfare mediation has to be encouraged. Also in RUSSIA,[2375] the bailiff who will enforce the decision can first try to reach a settlement by allowing the Guardianship and Curatorship Department to mediate between the parents on one further occasion.

2364 See ROTH, Austrian Report, Q 45: taking delivery of the child in order to enforce the right of contact is not permissible because it is regarded as a disproportionate measure. More generally, no coercive measure may be ordered to enforce the right of contact if a minor over 14 years of age or the parent entitled to have contact refuses to exercise this contact.

2365 See FERRAND, French Report, Q 58.

2366 § 33 para. 2 German Act on Voluntary Jurisdiction.

2367 See KOUTSOURADIS/ZERVOGIANNI, Greek Report, Q 58.

2368 See SHANNON, Irish Report, Q 58.

2369 See ANTOKOLSKAIA, Russian Report, Q 44 a, 48a, 58.

2370 Sec. 272 Czech Code of Civil Procedure. See HRUSAKOVÁ, Czech Report, Q 58.

2371 The same applies e.g. in AUSTRIA, see ROTH, Austrian Report, Q 58.

2372 See GONZÁLEZ BEILFUSS, Spanish Report, Q 58.

2373 See KURKI-SUONIO, Finnish Report, Q 58.

2374 See WEISS/SZEIBERT, Hungarian Report, Q 58.

2375 See ANTOKOLSKAIA, Russian Report, Q 58.

Possible coercive measures or sanctions in the case of non-compliance with a decision on parental responsibilities, the child's residence or contact

There is a great variety of coercive measures that may be ordered in order to obtain compliance with the order or agreement on parental responsibilities, the child's residence or contact. Most of the jurisdictions surveyed have a long list of possible measures such as fines (see e.g. AUSTRIA,[2376] BELGIUM,[2377] BULGARIA,[2378] CZECH REPUBLIC,[2379] FRANCE,[2380] GERMANY,[2381] GREECE,[2382] HUNGARY,[2383] IRELAND,[2384] THE NETHERLANDS,[2385] NORWAY,[2386] RUSSIA,[2387] SPAIN,[2388] SWEDEN[2389] and SWITZERLAND[2390]), damages (e.g. BELGIUM[2391] and HUNGARY[2392]), the child's removal from the other parent (BULGARIA,[2393] CZECH REPUBLIC,[2394] DENMARK,[2395] FINLAND,[2396] THE NETHERLANDS,[2397] NORWAY,[2398] and SWEDEN[2399]), for example with the assistance of the police or a bailiff, deprivation of the exercise of parental responsibilities through a new order or a

2376 See ROTH, Austrian Report, Q 58: also compulsory appearance before the court or taking possession of important documents like a passport are possible, see § 110 para. 2 Non-Contentious Proceedings Act.

2377 See PINTENS/PIGNOLET, Belgian Report, Q 58.

2378 See TODOROVA, Bulgarian Report, Q 58.

2379 The fine may not exceed 50,000 CZK. It is received by the state. See HRUSAKOVÁ, Czech Report, Q 58.

2380 See FERRAND, French Report, Q 58.

2381 For the amount of the fine in practice. See DETHLOFF/MARTINY, German Report, Q 58: the statutory maximum penalty is € 25,000.

2382 See KOUTSOURADIS/ZERVOGIANNI, Greek Report, Q 58.

2383 See WEISS/SZEIBERT, Hungarian Report, Q 58.

2384 A fine of € 254, see SHANNON, Irish Report, Q 58.

2385 In THE NETHERLANDS, other sanctions are also possible, like a reduction or termination of partner maintenance or a temporary suspension of child maintenance. See BOELE-WOELKI/SCHRAMA/VONK, Dutch Report, Q 58.

2386 See SVERDRUP/LØDRUP, Norwegian Report, Q 58.

2387 For many details about the amount of the fine, see ANTOKOLSKAIA, Russian Report, Q 58: if the parent again disobeys , the fine ordered by the court can be doubled.

2388 See GONZÁLEZ BEILFUSS, Spanish Report, Q 58.

2389 See JÄNTERÄ-JAREBORG/SINGER/SÖRGJERD, Swedish Report, Q 58.

2390 See HAUSHEER/ACHERMANN-WEBER/WOLF, Swiss Report, Q 58.

2391 See PINTENS/PIGNOLET, Belgian Report, Q 58.

2392 See WEISS/SZEIBERT, Hungarian Report, Q 58.

2393 See TODOROVA, Bulgarian Report, Q 58.

2394 See HRUSAKOVÁ, Czech Report, Q 58.

2395 See LUND-ANDERSEN/JEPPESEN-DE BOER, Danish Report, Q 58.

2396 See KURKI-SUONIO, Finnish Report, Q 58.

2397 See BOELE-WOELKI/SCHRAMA/VONK, Dutch Report, Q 58.

2398 See SVERDRUP/LØDRUP, Norwegian Report, Q 58.

2399 See JÄNTERÄ-JAREBORG/SINGER/SÖRGJERD, Swedish Report, Q 58.

decision taken by the competent authority (BULGARIA,[2400] GERMANY[2401] and SPAIN.[2402] The same applies in FRANCE.[2403]

Criminal sanctions are also provided by several national laws (AUSTRIA,[2404] BELGIUM,[2405] FRANCE,[2406] RUSSIA[2407] and SWITZERLAND[2408]). Some allow the court to order the imprisonment of the parent who does not comply with the decision on the exercise of parental responsibilities (see e.g. ENGLAND AND WALES with the law of contempt of court before the High Court and the county courts[2409] and with S. 63 (3) Magistrates' Courts Act 1980,[2410] GERMANY,[2411] GREECE,[2412] IRELAND,[2413] THE NETHERLANDS[2414] and SWITZERLAND[2415]). Some countries give special jurisdiction to the criminal courts to decide on criminal actions that can be taken against the parent who disregards another's right of contact (see e.g. BELGIUM,[2416] BULGARIA,[2417] FRANCE,[2418] THE NETHERLANDS[2419] and SPAIN[2420]).

Possible assistance by a public welfare institution during the enforcement

Several national laws provide for the assistance of a public welfare institution for the enforcement of a decision or an (approved) agreement on the exercise of parental

2400 See TODOROVA, Bulgarian Report, Q 58.

2401 See DETHLOFF/MARTINY, German Report, Q 58.

2402 See GONZÁLEZ BEILFUSS, Spanish Report, Q 58.

2403 See FERRAND, French Report, Q 58.

2404 See ROTH, Austrian Report, Q 58.

2405 See PINTENS/PIGNOLET, Belgian Report, Q 58.

2406 See FERRAND, French Report, Q 58.

2407 See ANTOKOLSKAIA, Russian Report, Q 58.

2408 See HAUSHEER/ACHERMANN-WEBER/WOLF, Swiss Report, Q 58.

2409 See LOWE, English Report, Q 58: imprisonment for a maximum of two years.

2410 See LOWE, English Report, Q 58: imprisonment for a maximum of two months.

2411 See DETHLOFF/MARTINY, German Report, Q 58: *Zwangshaft* , but it does not seem to be used in practice.

2412 See KOUTSOURADIS/ZERVOGIANNI, Greek Report, Q 58: imprisonment for up to one year.

2413 See SHANNON, Irish Report Q 58: imprisonment for up to six months.

2414 See BOELE-WOELKI/SCHRAMA/VONK, Dutch Report, Q 58.

2415 See HAUSHEER/ACHERMANN-WEBER/WOLF, Swiss Report, Q 58.

2416 See PINTENS/PIGNOLET, Belgian Report, Q 58.

2417 Art. 270 Bulgarian Penal Code.

2418 Art. 227–5 French Penal Code: "The unlawful refusal to produce a minor child to the person who has the right to require the production of the child is punished by one year's imprisonment and a fine of _ 100,000".

2419 See BOELE-WOELKI/SCHRAMA/VONK, Dutch Report, Q 58: but the Minister of Justice has declared that criminal provisions should be regarded as an *ultimum remedium,* and are not appropriate instruments for enforcing contact.

2420 See GONZÁLEZ BEILFUSS, Spanish Report, Q 58: but there is a reluctance to resort to criminal law or to forcibly compel because this is considered not to be in the child's best interests.

responsibilities, the child's residence or contact. For example, in AUSTRIA,[2421] when enforcing an order or a parental agreement on parental responsibilities or the child's residence, the youth welfare agency or the juvenile court assistance office may be called upon to render support.[2422] In BULGARIA,[2423] the judge executive can call for assistance by the Guardianship Authority, by a police inspector or by the Child Protection Department if other means have been unsuccessful and if the child's interests require immediate enforcement. In the CZECH REPUBLIC,[2424] the removal of the child shall take place in the presence of the judge, a social worker and a judicial officer. In LITHUANIA,[2425] if the child is involved in the enforcement procedure, the bailiff must inform the state institution for the protection of the child's rights. Also in RUSSIA,[2426] there is obligatory participation by the Guardianship and Curatorship Department in the enforcement proceedings relating to children. This tendency to require the assistance of a Child Protection Department seems to be particularly clear in Eastern countries.

Possible reasons to refuse the enforcement of the decision on parental responsibilities, the child's residence or contact

All 22 jurisdictions surveyed provide some reasons for refusing to enforce a decision or an agreement on parental responsibilities, the child's residence or contact. The reasons most often mentioned are: exceptional circumstances (e.g. BULGARIA),[2427] a change of circumstances since the order or the agreement (e.g. BULGARIA,[2428] FINLAND[2429] and SWEDEN[2430]), the child's mental or physical health that would be endangered by enforcement (e.g. DENMARK,[2431] NORWAY[2432] and POLAND[2433]) the child's refusal to see the decision enforced (e.g. FINLAND if the child is at least 12 years old or has sufficient understanding; SWEDEN subject to the same condition; IRELAND, RUSSIA and SWITZERLAND. This also corresponds with the FRENCH practice), or, more generally, the fact that the enforcement would be contrary to the best interests of the child

2421 See ROTH, Austrian Report, Q 58.
2422 In particular to care for the child on a temporary basis.
2423 See TODOROVA, Bulgarian Report, Q 58.
2424 See HRUSAKOVÁ, Czech Report, Q 58.
2425 See MIKELENAS, Lithuanian Report, Q 58.
2426 Art. 79 para. 2 Russian Family Code.
2427 See TODOROVA, Bulgarian Report, Q 58.
2428 See TODOROVA, Bulgarian Report, Q 58.
2429 See KURKI-SUONIO, Finnish Report, Q 58.
2430 See JÄNTERÄ-JAREBORG/SINGER/SÖRGJERD, Swedish Report, Q 58.
2431 See LUND-ANDERSEN/JEPPESEN-DE BOER, Danish Report, Q 58.
2432 See SVERDRUP/LØDRUP, Norwegian Report, Q 58.
2433 See MĄCZYŃSKI/MĄCZYŃSKA, Polish Report, Q 58.

(AUSTRIA,[2434] BULGARIA,[2435] FINLAND,[2436] POLAND,[2437] RUSSIA[2438] and SPAIN[2439]). In NORWAY,[2440] the general criterion for a refusal to enforce the court order is that the enforcement is "impossible" (because of the child's refusal or because of the child's psychological health). In all cases it appears that the paramount consideration for the refusal of enforcement is the best interests of the child, sometimes in conjunction with his or her own wishes subject to the condition that the child has sufficient understanding or is of sufficient age to be able to express his or her own opinions. Many national reports insist upon the fact that enforcement is a problematic matter and should not take place by using force against the child who refuses to comply with the court order or with the parental agreement (AUSTRIA,[2441] BULGARIA,[2442] FINLAND,[2443] FRANCE,[2444] GERMANY,[2445] HUNGARY,[2446] IRELAND,[2447] RUSSIA,[2448] SWEDEN[2449] and SWITZERLAND[2450]). This must be seen in conjunction with the right of the child to be heard in all proceedings affecting him or her (see Principles 3:6 and 3:37). The child's opinion should be given due weight if the child has sufficient maturity to have and to express his/her own wishes. Those wishes should be considered not only before the competent authority decides on parental responsibilities (or the child's residence or contact), but also at the enforcement stage.

COMMENT

1. As in all 22 jurisdictions surveyed, the general rule is that a decision of the competent authority or a parental agreement on parental responsibilities, the child's residence or contact should be subject to enforcement if there is no voluntary compliance therewith. The decision issued by the competent authority or the agreement reached by the holders of parental responsibilities is deemed to be in the

2434 See ROTH, Austrian Report, Q 58.
2435 See TODOROVA, Bulgarian Report, Q 58.
2436 See KURKI-SUONIO, Finnish Report, Q 58.
2437 See MĄCZYŃSKI/MĄCZYŃSKA, Polish Report, Q 58.
2438 See ANTOKOLSKAIA, Russian Report, Q 58.
2439 See GONZÁLEZ BEILFUSS, Spanish Report, Q 58.
2440 See SVERDRUP/LØDRUP, Norwegian Report, Q 58.
2441 See ROTH, Austrian Report, Q 58.
2442 See TODOROVA, Bulgarian Report, Q 58.
2443 See KURKI-SUONIO, Finnish Report, Q 58.
2444 See FERRAND, French Report, Q 58.
2445 See DETHLOFF/MARTINY, German Report, Q 58.
2446 See WEISS/SZEIBERT, Hungarian Report, Q 58.
2447 See SHANNON, Irish Report Q 58.
2448 See ANTOKOLSKAIA, Russian Report, Q 58.
2449 See JÄNTERÄ-JAREBORG/SINGER/SÖRGJERD, Swedish Report, Q 58.
2450 See HAUSHEER/ACHERMANN-WEBER/WOLF, Swiss Report, Q 58.

best interests of the child and should therefore be respected. Where necessary, the enforcement should be facilitated by different kinds of coercive measures provided by national law. Nevertheless, criminal sanctions do not generally seem to be the most appropriate solution to favour enforcement.

2. Enforcement should take place without delay. This requirement is aimed at taking into consideration the case law developed by the European Court of Human Rights which has decided that the enforcement stage must also be considered in order to determine whether the length of the proceedings has been reasonable, and that proceedings concerning the relations between children and their parents as well as the enforcement proceedings that follow must be conducted with "exceptional diligence". The use of coercive measures can be a possible way to avoid lengthy enforcement proceedings. The principle of a speedy and effective enforcement of a decision or an agreement on parental responsibilities does not preclude seizing the competent authority at a later date in order to obtain a modification of the order on parental responsibilities if the circumstances have subsequently changed.

3. Even if the main rule should be the enforceability of decisions issued by the competent authority or of parental agreements (the question whether these latter agreements should be directly enforceable or only after approval by a competent authority rests with national law), such enforcement should be excluded in all cases where it would be manifestly contrary to the best interests of the child. This narrow concept that allows only restricted exceptions covers especially the child's physical or mental health and other exceptional circumstances in which enforcement would *manifestly* be incompatible with the child's best interests. The order or the agreement on parental responsibilities, the child's residence or contact should also not be subject to enforcement against the wishes of the child, subject to the condition that the child has sufficient understanding. The child's refusal should be respected because, otherwise, it would require the use of force against the child, which should be avoided.

APPENDICES

INTERNATIONAL AND EUROPEAN INSTRUMENTS IN THE FIELD OF PARENTAL RESPONSIBILITIES

Full title	Abbreviated title
UNITED NATIONS	
1924 Geneva Declaration on the Rights of the Child	Declaration on the Rights of the Child 1924
Universal Declaration of Human Rights, 10th December 1948	Universal Declaration of Human Rights 1948
Declaration on the Rights of the Child, 10th November 1959	Declaration on the Rights of the Child 1959
International Covenant on Economic, Social and Cultural Rights, 16th December 1966	International Covenant on Economic, Social and Cultural Rights 1966
International Covenant on Civil and Political Rights, 19th December 1966	International Covenant on Civil and Political Rights 1966
Convention on the Elimination of all Forms of Discrimination against Women, 18th December 1979	Convention on the Elimination of Discrimination against Women 1979
Declaration on Social and Legal Principles relating to the Protection and Welfare of Children, with special reference to Foster Placement and Adoption Nationally and Internationally, 3rd December 1986	Declaration on Social and Legal Principles relating to the Protection and Welfare of Children 1986
The Convention of 20th November 1989 on the Rights of the Child	Convention on the Rights of the Child 1989

Full title	Abbreviated title
THE HAGUE CONFERENCE ON PRIVATE INTERNATIONAL LAW	
Convention Concerning the Powers of Authorities and the Law Applicable in Respect of the Protection of Minors, 5th October 1961	Hague Child Protection Convention 1961
Convention on the Civil Aspects of International Child Abduction, 25th October 1980	Hague Child Abduction Convention 1980
Convention on Protection of Children and Co-operation in Respect of Intercountry Adoption, 29th May 1993	Hague Adoption Convention 1993
Convention on Jurisdiction, Applicable Law, Recognition, Enforcement and Cooperation in Respect of Parental Responsibility and Measures for the Protection of Children, 19th October 1996	Hague Child Protection Convention 1996
THE COUNCIL OF EUROPE	
Conventions	
European Convention on Human Rights and Fundamental Freedoms, Rome 4th November 1950	European Convention on Human Rights 1950
Convention on the Adoption of Children, 24th April 1967	Convention on the Adoption of Children 1967
Convention on Recognition and Enforcement of Decisions Concerning Custody of Children and on Restoration of Custody of Children, 20th May 1980	Convention on Recognition and Enforcement of Decisions Concerning Custody 1980
Convention on the Exercise of Children's Rights, 25th January 1996	Convention on the Exercise of Children's Rights 1996
Convention on Contact Concerning Children, 15th May 2003	Convention on Contact Concerning Children 2003

Full title	Abbreviated title
Resolutions and Recommendations	
(CM) Resolution (77)33 of 11th March 1977 on Placement of Children	Resolution on Placement of Children 1977
(PA) Recommendation 874(1979) on a European Charter on the Rights of the Child	Recommendation on a European Charter on the Rights of the Child 1979
(CM) Recommendation (79)17 of 13th September 1979 Concerning the Protection of Children Against Ill-Treatment	Recommendation Concerning the Protection of Children Against Ill-Treatment 1979
(CM) Recommendation (84)4 of 28th February 1984 on Parental Responsibilities	Recommendation on Parental Responsibilities 1984
(PA) Recommendation 1071 of 23rd March 1988 on Child Welfare – Providing Institutional Care for Infants and Children	Recommendation on Child Welfare 1988
(PA) Recommendation 1121 of 1st February 1990 on the Rights of Children	Recommendation on the Rights of Children 1990
(CM) Recommendation (95)6 of 7th February 1995 on the Application of the European Convention on Recognition and Enforcement of Decisions Concerning Custody of Children and on Restoration of Custody of Children	Recommendation on the Application of the 1980 European Convention 1995
(PA) Recommendation 1286 of 24th January 1996 on a European Strategy for Children	Recommendation on a European Strategy for Children 1996
(CM) Recommendation No. R (98)1 of 21st January 1998 on Family Mediation	Recommendation on Family Mediation 1998
(PA) Recommendation 1371 of 23rd April 1998 on Abuse and Neglect of Children	Recommendation on Abuse and Neglect of Children 1998
(CM) Recommendation (98)8 of 18th September 1998 on Children's Participation in Family and Social Life	Recommendation on Children's Participation in Family and Social Life 1998

Full title	Abbreviated title
(CM) Recommendation (99) of 23rd February 1999 on the Application of the European Convention on Recognition and Enforcement of Decisions Concerning Custody of Children and on Restoration of Custody of Children	Recommendation on the Application of the 1980 European Convention 1999
White Paper on Principles concerning the establishment and legal consequences of parentage on 15th January 2002	White Paper 2002
THE EUROPEAN UNION	
Treaty establishing the European Community, 25th March 1975	EC Treaty 1975
Charter of Fundamental Rights of the European Union, 7th December 2000	European Charter of Fundamental Rights 2000
Council Regulation (EC) No. 1347/2000 of 29th May 2000 on jurisdiction and the recognition and enforcement of judgments in matrimonial matters and in matters of parental responsibility for children of both spouses (Brussels II)	Brussels II Regulation
Council Regulation (EC) No. 2201/2003 of 27th November 2003 concerning jurisdiction and the recognition and enforcement of judgments in matrimonial matters and the matters of parental responsibility (Brussels II bis)	Brussels II bis Regulation
Draft Treaty establishing a Constitution for Europe, 30th September 2003	Draft Treaty for a European Constitution 2003

PRINCIPLES OF EUROPEAN FAMILY LAW REGARDING PARENTAL RESPONSIBILITIES

PREAMBLE

Recognising that, notwithstanding the existing diversities of national family law systems, there is nevertheless a growing convergence of laws;

Recognising that the free movement of persons within Europe is hindered by the remaining differences;

Desiring to contribute to common European values regarding the child's rights and welfare;

Desiring to contribute to the harmonisation of family law in Europe and to further facilitate the free movement of persons within Europe;

The Commission on European Family Law recommends the following Principles:

CHAPTER I: DEFINITIONS

Principle 3:1 Concept of parental responsibilities

Parental responsibilities are a collection of rights and duties aimed at promoting and safeguarding the welfare of the child. They encompass in particular:

(a) care, protection and education;

(b) maintenance of personal relationships;

(c) determination of residence;

(d) administration of property, and

(e) legal representation.

Principle 3:2 Holder of parental responsibilities

(1) A holder of parental responsibilities is any person having the rights and duties listed in Principle 3:1 either in whole or in part.

(2) Subject to the following Principles, holders of parental responsibilities are:

(a) the child's parents, as well as

(b) persons other than the child's parents having parental responsibilities in addition to or instead of the parents.

CHAPTER II: RIGHTS OF THE CHILD

Principle 3:3 Best interests of the child
In all matters concerning parental responsibilities the best interests of the child should be the primary consideration.

Principle 3:4 Autonomy of the child
The child's autonomy should be respected in accordance with the developing ability and need of the child to act independently.

Principle 3:5 Non-discrimination of the child
Children should not be discriminated on grounds such as sex, race, colour, language, religion, political or other opinion, national, ethnic or social origin, sexual orientation, disability, property, birth or other status, irrespective of whether these grounds refer to the child or to the holders of parental responsibilities.

Principle 3:6 Child's right to be heard
Having regard to the child's age and maturity, the child should have the right to be informed, consulted and to express his or her opinion in all matters concerning the child, with due weight given to the views expressed by him or her.

Principle 3:7 Conflict of interests
The interests of the child should be protected whenever they may be in conflict with the interests of the holders of parental responsibilities.

CHAPTER III: PARENTAL RESPONSIBILITIES OF PARENTS AND THIRD PERSONS

Principle 3:8 Parents
Parents, whose legal parentage has been established, should have parental responsibilities for the child.

Principle 3:9 Third persons
Parental responsibilities may in whole or in part also be attributed to a person other than a parent.

Principle 3:10 Effect of dissolution and separation
Parental responsibilities should neither be affected by the dissolution or annulment of the marriage or other formal relationship nor by the legal or factual separation between the parents.

CHAPTER IV: EXERCISE OF PARENTAL RESPONSIBILITIES

SECTION A: PARENTS

Principle 3:11 Joint exercise
Parents having parental responsibilities should have an equal right and duty to exercise such responsibilities and whenever possible they should exercise them jointly.

Principle 3:12 Daily matters, important and urgent decisions
(1) Parents having joint parental responsibilities should have the right to act alone with respect to daily matters.
(2) Important decisions concerning matters such as education, medical treatment, the child's residence, or the administration of his or her property should be taken jointly. In urgent cases a parent should have the right to act alone. The other parent should be informed without undue delay.

Principle 3:13 Agreement on exercise
(1) Subject to the best interests of the child, parents having joint parental responsibilities may agree on the exercise of parental responsibilities.
(2) The competent authority may scrutinize the agreement.

Principle 3:14 Disagreement on exercise
(1) Where parents having joint parental responsibilities cannot agree on an important matter they may apply to the competent authority.
(2) The competent authority should promote agreement between the parents.
(3) Where agreement cannot be reached the competent authority should divide the exercise of parental responsibilities between the parents or decide the dispute. Nigel: do we have to insert a comma after reached?

Principle 3:15 Sole exercise upon agreement or decision
Subject to the best interests of the child a parent may exercise parental responsibilities alone

(a) upon agreement between the parents according to Principle 3:13, or
(b) upon a decision of the competent authority.

Principle 3:16 Exercise by one parent
If only one parent has parental responsibilities he or she should exercise them alone.

SECTION B: THIRD PERSONS

Principle 3:17 Exercise in addition to or instead of the parents
A person other than a parent may exercise some or all parental responsibilities in addition to or instead of the parents.

Principle 3:18 Decisions in daily matters
The parent's partner living with the child may take part in decisions with respect to daily matters unless the other parent having parental responsibilities objects.

CHAPTER V: CONTENT OF PARENTAL RESPONSIBILITIES

SECTION A: THE CHILD'S PERSON AND PROPERTY

Principle 3:19 Care, protection and education
(1) The holders of parental responsibilities should provide the child with care, protection and education in accordance with the child's distinctive character and developmental needs.
(2) The child should not be subjected to corporal punishment or any other humiliating treatment.

Principle 3:20 Residence
(1) If parental responsibilities are exercised jointly the holders of parental responsibilities who are living apart should agree upon with whom the child resides.
(2) The child may reside on an alternate basis with the holders of parental responsibilities upon either an agreement approved by a competent authority or a decision by a competent authority. The competent authority should take into consideration factors such as:

- (a) the age and opinion of the child;
- (b) the ability and willingness of the holders of parental responsibilities to cooperate with each other in matters concerning the child, as well as their personal situation;
- (c) the distance between the residences of the holders of the parental responsibilities and to the child's school.

Principle 3:21 Relocation
(1) If parental responsibilities are exercised jointly and one of the holders of parental responsibilities wishes to change the child's residence within or outside the jurisdiction, he or she should inform the other holder of parental responsibilities thereof in advance.
(2) If the other holder of parental responsibilities objects to the change of the child's residence, each of them may apply to the competent authority for a decision.

(3) The competent authority should take into consideration factors such as:
- (a) the age and opinion of the child;
- (b) the right of the child to maintain personal relationships with the other holders of parental responsibilities;
- (c) the ability and willingness of the holders of parental responsibilities to cooperate with each other;
- (d) the personal situation of the holders of personal responsibilities;
- (e) the geographical distance and accessibility;
- (f) the free movement of persons.

Principle 3:22 Administration of the child's property

(1) The holders of parental responsibilities should administer the child's property with due care and diligence in order to preserve and where possible increase the value of the property.

(2) In administering the child's property the holders of parental responsibilities should not make gifts unless the gifts are deemed to be made under a moral obligation.

(3) The income derived from the child's property which is not needed for the proper management of the property or for the maintenance and education of the child may, where necessary, be used for the needs of the family.

Principle 3:23 Restrictions

(1) The holders of parental responsibilities should not administer property acquired by a child through a testamentary disposition or a gift, if the testator or the donor so instructed.

(2) Similarly the earnings by the child should not be administered by the holders of parental responsibilities unless the child is not of sufficient age and maturity to decide himself or herself.

(3) Where transactions can have significant financial consequences for the child the authorisation of the competent authority should be necessary.

Principle 3:24 Legal representation

(1) The holders of parental responsibilities should legally represent the child in matters concerning the child's person or property.

(2) Legal representation should not take place where there is a conflict of interest between the child and the holders of parental responsibilities.

(3) Having regard to the child's age and maturity, the child should have the right to self-representation in legal proceedings concerning himself or herself.

SECTION B: MAINTENANCE OF PERSONAL RELATIONSHIPS

Principle 3:25 Contact with parents and other persons

(1) The child and the parents should have the right to obtain and maintain regular contact with each other.
(2) Contact should be established between the child and his or her close relatives.
(3) Contact may be established between the child and persons with whom the child has close personal relations.

Principle 3:26 Content of contact

(1) Contact comprises the child staying for a limited period of time with or meeting a parent or person other than a parent with whom he or she is not usually living; and any form of communication between the child and such person.
(2) Such contact should be in the best interests of the child.

Principle 3:27 Agreement

(1) Subject to the best interests of the child, the parents and the other persons identified under Principle 3:25(2) and (3) may agree on contact.
(2) The competent authority may scrutinize the agreement.

Principle 3:28 Restrictions

Contact may be restricted, terminated or made subject to conditions by the competent authority if the best interests of the child so require.

Principle 3:29 Information to parents

A parent should have the right to be informed about matters concerning the personal situation of the child.

CHAPTER VI: TERMINATION OF PARENTAL RESPONSIBILITIES

Principle 3:30 Termination

(1) Parental responsibilities should be terminated in the case of the child:
- (a) reaching majority;
- (b) entering into a marriage or registered partnership;
- (c) being adopted;
- (d) dying.

(2) If a parent's partner adopts the child of the parent the parental responsibilities in relation to the other parent should be terminated.

Principle 3:31 Death of the parents

(1) If parents have joint parental responsibilities and one of them dies the parental responsibilities should belong to the surviving parent.

(2) If a parent having sole parental responsibilities dies, responsibilities should be attributed to the surviving parent or a third person upon a decision by the competent authority.

(3) On the death of both parents, of whom at least one parent had parental responsibilities, the competent authority should take protective measures in respect of the person and the property of the child.

CHAPTER VII: DISCHARGE AND RESTORATION OF PARENTAL RESPONSIBILITIES

Principle 3:32 Discharge of parental responsibilities

The competent authority should discharge the holder of parental responsibilities, wholly or in part, where his or her behaviour or neglect causes a serious risk to the person or the property of the child

Principle 3:33 Request for discharge of parental responsibilities

(1) The discharge of parental responsibilities may be requested by:

- (a) any parent having parental responsibilities;
- (b) the child, and
- (c) any institution protecting the interests of the child.

(2) The competent authority may also order the discharge of parental responsibilities of its own motion.

Principle 3:34 Restoration of parental responsibilities

Having regard to the best interests of the child, the competent authority may restore parental responsibilities if the circumstances that led to the discharge no longer exist.

CHAPTER VIII: PROCEDURE

Principle 3:35 Competent authority

(1) All decisions on parental responsibilities should be taken by the competent authority which can either be a judicial or an administrative body.

(2) Where necessary, the competent authority should appoint any suitable person or body to investigate the child's circumstances.

Principle 3:36 Alternative dispute resolution

In all disputes regarding parental responsibilities alternative dispute resolution mechanisms should be available.

Principle 3:37 Hearing of the child

(1) Subject to Principle 3:6, the competent authority should hear the child in all proceedings concerning parental responsibilities but if it decides not to hear the child it should give specific reasons.

(2) The hearing of the child should take place either directly before the competent authority or indirectly before a person or body appointed by the competent authority.

(3) The child should be heard in a manner appropriate to his or her age and maturity.

Principle 3:38 Appointment of a special representative for the child

In proceedings concerning parental responsibilities in which there could either be a serious conflict of interests between the child and the holders of parental responsibilities or in which the welfare of the child is otherwise at risk, the competent authority should appoint a special representative for the child.

Principle 3:39 Enforcement

(1) Failing voluntary compliance, a decision by the competent authority and an enforceable agreement concerning parental responsibilities should be enforced without delay.

(2) Enforcement should not take place if it is manifestly contrary to the best interests of the child.

PRINCIPES DE DROIT EUROPÉEN DE LA FAMILLE CONCERNANT LA RESPONSABILITÉ PARENTALE

PREAMBULE

Reconnaissant que, malgré les diversités existantes entre les systèmes nationaux de droit de la famille, la convergence entre les lois tend à s'accroître;

Reconnaissant que la libre circulation des personnes en Europe est entravée par les différences qui demeurent;

Souhaitant contribuer à des valeurs communes européennes concernant les droits et le bien être de l'enfant;

Souhaitant contribuer à l'harmonisation du droit de la famille en Europe et faciliter encore davantage la libre circulation des personnes en Europe;

La Commission pour le Droit Européen de la Famille recommande les Principes suivants:

CHAPITRE I: DÉFINITIONS

Principe 3:1 Notion de responsabilité parentale

La responsabilité parentale est un ensemble de droits et devoirs destinés à favoriser et à sauvegarder le bien-être de l'enfant. Elle comprend notamment

(a) soins, protection et éducation;
(b) maintien des relations personnelles;
(c) détermination de la résidence;
(d) administration des biens et
(e) représentation légale.

Principle 3:2 Titulaires de la responsabilité parentale

(1) Est titulaire de la responsabilité parentale toute personne ayant, en tout ou partie, les droits et devoirs mentionnés au Principe 3:1.

(2) Sous réserve des Principes suivants, les titulaires de la responsabilité parentale sont:

(a) les parents de l'enfant, ainsi que
(b) les personnes autres que les parents de l'enfant qui ont la responsabilité parentale en complément ou à la place des parents.

CHAPITRE II: DROITS DE L'ENFANT

Principe 3:3 Meilleur intérêt de l'enfant
Dans toutes les questions relatives à la responsabilité parentale, doit être pris en considération, à titre prépondérant, le meilleur intérêt de l'enfant.

Principe 3:4 Autonomie de l'enfant
L'autonomie de l'enfant est respectée en tenant compte de la capacité et du besoin croissants de l'enfant d'agir de façon indépendante.

Principe 3:5 Non-discrimination de l'enfant
Les enfants ne font l'objet d'aucune discrimination fondée notamment sur le sexe, la race, la couleur, la langue, la religion, les opinions politiques ou autres, l'origine nationale, ethnique ou sociale, l'orientation sexuelle, le handicap, le patrimoine, la naissance ou tout autre état, que ces motifs se rapportent à l'enfant ou aux titulaires de la responsabilité parentale.

Principe 3:6 Droit de l'enfant d'être entendu
Eu égard à son âge et à sa maturité, l'enfant a le droit d'être informé, consulté et d'exprimer son opinion dans tous les domaines le concernant, l'opinion exprimée par l'enfant étant dûment prise en considération.

Principe 3:7 Conflit d'intérêts
Les intérêts de l'enfant doivent être protégés dans tous les cas où ils peuvent se trouver en opposition avec ceux des titulaires de la responsabilité parentale.

CHAPITRE III: RESPONSABILITÉ PARENTALE DES PARENTS ET DE TIERS

Principe 3:8 Parents
Les personnes dont la parenté légale a été établie envers l'enfant ont la responsabilité parentale à l'égard de ce dernier.

Principe 3:9 Tiers
La responsabilité parentale peut également être attribuée en tout ou partie à une personne autre que les père ou mère.

Principe 3:10 Incidence de la dissolution et de la séparation
La responsabilité parentale n'est affectée ni par la dissolution, l'annulation du mariage ou de toute autre union formalisée, ni par la séparation légale ou la séparation de fait des parents.

CHAPITRE IV: EXERCICE DE LA RESPONSABILITÉ PARENTALE

SECTION A: LES PARENTS

Principe 3:11 Exercice en commun
Les parents détenant la responsabilité parentale ont dans l'exercice de celle-ci les mêmes droits et devoirs. Dans la mesure du possible, ils l'exercent en commun.

Principe 3:12 Actes de la vie courante, décisions importantes et urgentes
(1) Les parents titulaires en commun de la responsabilité parentale ont le droit d'accomplir seuls les actes de la vie courante.
(2) Les décisions importantes concernant des domaines tels que l'éducation de l'enfant, son traitement médical, sa résidence ou l'administration de ses biens, sont prises conjointement. En cas d'urgence, un parent a le droit d'agir seul. L'autre parent doit être informé sans retard.

Principe 3:13 Accord sur l'exercice
(1) Eu égard au meilleur intérêt de l'enfant, les parents détenant en commun la responsabilité parentale peuvent s'entendre sur l'exercice de celle-ci.
(2) L'autorité compétente peut contrôler l'accord.

Principe 3:14 Désaccord en matière d'exercice
(1) Si les parents détenant en commun la responsabilité parentale ne parviennent pas à s'entendre sur une question importante, ils peuvent saisir l'autorité compétente.
(2) L'autorité compétente s'efforce de favoriser un accord entre les parents.
(3) Si aucun accord ne peut être conclu, l'autorité compétente divise l'exercice de la responsabilité parentale entre les parents ou tranche le désaccord.

Principe 3:15 Exercice unilatéral de la responsabilité parentale en vertu d'un accord ou d'une décision
Eu égard au meilleur intérêt de l'enfant, la responsabilité parentale peut être exercée par un seul parent

(a) en vertu d'un accord entre les parents, conformément au Principe 3:13, ou
(b) en vertu d'une décision de l'autorité compétente.

Principe 3:16 Exercice par un seul parent
Si un seul parent détient la responsabilité parentale, il l'exerce seul.

SECTION B: LES TIERS

Principe 3:17 Exercice en complément ou en lieu et place des parents
Une personne autre qu'un parent peut exercer tout ou partie de la responsabilité parentale en complément ou en lieu et place des parents.

Principe 3:18 Décisions de la vie courante
Le partenaire d'un parent qui vit avec l'enfant peut prendre part aux décisions de la vie courante, sauf objection de l'autre parent détenant la responsabilité parentale.

CHAPITRE V: CONTENU DE LA RESPONSABILITÉ PARENTALE

SECTION A: PERSONNE ET BIENS DE L'ENFANT

Principe 3:19 Soins, protection et éducation
(1) Les titulaires de la responsabilité parentale assurent à l'enfant soins, protection et éducation conformément à la personnalité de l'enfant et aux besoins de son développement.
(2) L'enfant ne doit pas subir de châtiments corporels ou de tout autre traitement humiliant.

Principe 3:20 Résidence
(1) Si la responsabilité parentale est exercée en commun, ses titulaires, s'ils vivent séparés, doivent s'entendre pour déterminer avec lequel d'entre eux l'enfant résidera
(2) L'enfant peut résider alternativement chez les titulaires de la responsabilité parentale en vertu ou bien d'un accord entre les titulaires approuvé par l'autorité compétente, ou bien d'une décision de l'autorité compétente. L'autorité compétente prend notamment en considération:
- (a) l'âge et l'avis de l'enfant;
- (b) la capacité et la volonté des titulaires de la responsabilité parentale de coopérer sur toutes questions concernant l'enfant ainsi que leur situation personnelle;
- (c) la distance entre les résidences des titulaires de la responsabilité parentale ainsi que la distance avec l'école fréquentée par l'enfant.

Principe 3:21 Changement de résidence

(1) Si la responsabilité parentale est exercée en commun et un des titulaires désire modifier la résidence de l'enfant à l'intérieur ou en dehors du territoire national, il doit en informer préalablement l'autre titulaire de la responsabilité parentale.

(2) Si l'autre titulaire de la responsabilité parentale s'oppose au changement de résidence de l'enfant, chacun des titulaires peut saisir l'autorité compétente afin qu'elle statue.

(3) L'autorité compétente prend notamment en considération:

- (a) l'âge et l'avis de l'enfant;
- (b) le droit de l'enfant d'entretenir des relations personnelles avec les autres titulaires de la responsabilité parentale;
- (c) la capacité et la volonté des titulaires de la responsabilité parentale de coopérer;
- (d) la situation personnelle des titulaires de la responsabilité parentale;
- (e) la distance géographique et les facilités d'accès;
- (f) la libre circulation des personnes.

Principe 3:22 Administration des biens de l'enfant

(1) Les titulaires de la responsabilité parentale administrent les biens de l'enfant avec soin et diligence afin de préserver et dans la mesure du possible d'accroître la valeur des biens.

(2) Dans le cadre de l'administration des biens de l'enfant, les titulaires de la responsabilité parentale ne peuvent faire de donations, sauf si celles-ci sont fondées sur une obligation morale.

(3) Les revenus produits par les biens de l'enfant qui ne sont pas nécessaires à une administration adéquate des biens, ni à l'entretien ou à l'éducation de l'enfant, peuvent en cas de nécessité être employés pour les besoins de la famille.

Principe 3:23 Limitations

(1) Les titulaires de la responsabilité parentale n'administrent pas les biens acquis par l'enfant en vertu de dispositions testamentaires ou d'une donation si le testateur ou le donateur en a disposé ainsi.

(2) De même, les gains et salaires de l'enfant ne sont pas administrés par les titulaires de la responsabilité parentale, sauf dans l'hypothèse où l'enfant n'a ni l'âge ni la maturité suffisants pour prendre lui-même les décisions.

(3) Lorsque des transactions peuvent entraîner pour l'enfant des conséquences financières importantes, l'autorisation de l'autorité compétente est requise.

Principe 3:24 Représentation légale

(1) Les titulaires de la responsabilité parentale représentent légalement l'enfant dans les affaires relatives à la personne ou aux biens de l'enfant.

(2) La représentation légale est exclue dans le cas d'un conflit d'intérêts entre l'enfant et les titulaires de la responsabilité parentale.
(3) Eu égard à son âge et à sa maturité, l'enfant a le droit de se représenter lui-même dans les procédures le concernant.

SECTION B: MAINTIEN DES RELATIONS PERSONNELLES

Principe 3:25 Relations personnelles avec ses père et mère et d'autres personnes
(1) L'enfant et ses père et mère ont le droit d'obtenir et d'entretenir entre eux des relations personnelles régulières.
(2) Des relations personnelles sont établies entre l'enfant et ses parents proches.
(3) Des relations personnelles peuvent être établies entre l'enfant et les personnes avec lesquelles l'enfant entretient des relations personnelles étroites.

Principe 3:26 Contenu des relations personnelles
(1) Les relations personnelles comprennent le séjour de l'enfant pour une période limitée ou la rencontre avec le père ou la mère ou une personne autre que le père ou la mère avec laquelle l'enfant ne réside pas habituellement, ainsi que toute forme de communication entre l'enfant et une telle personne.
(2) Ces relations personnelles doivent correspondre au meilleur intérêt de l'enfant.

Principe 3:27 Accord
(1) Conformément au meilleur intérêt de l'enfant, les père et mère et les autres personnes mentionnées au Principe 3:25(2) et (3) peuvent conclure un accord sur les relations personnelles.
(2) L'autorité compétente peut contrôler l'accord.

Principe 3:28 Restrictions
Si le meilleur intérêt de l'enfant l'exige, l'autorité compétente peut limiter les relations personnelles, y mettre fin ou les assujettir à des conditions.

Principe 3:29 Information aux parents
Tout père ou mère a le droit d'être informé de tout ce qui concerne la situation personnelle de l'enfant.

CHAPITRE VI : FIN DE LA RESPONSABILITÉ PARENTALE

Principe 3:30 Fin

(1) La responsabilité parentale prend fin lorsque l'enfant:

(a) atteint l'âge de la majorité;
(b) se marie ou conclut un partenariat enregistré;
(c) est adopté;
(d) décède.

(2) Dans le cas où le partenaire du père ou de la mère adopte l'enfant de celui-ci, la responsabilité parentale prend fin uniquement à l'égard de l'autre parent.

Principe 3:31 Décès des parents

(1) Si les parents détiennent en commun la responsabilité parentale et que l'un d'eux décède, la responsabilité parentale appartient au parent survivant.
(2) Si un parent ayant seul la responsabilité parentale décède, l'autorité compétente attribue la responsabilité au parent survivant ou à un tiers.
(3) En cas de décès des deux parents, dont un au moins détenait la responsabilité parentale, l'autorité compétente prend les mesures de protection nécessaires relatives à la personne et aux biens de l'enfant.

CHAPITRE VII: RETRAIT ET RESTITUTION DE LA RESPONSABILITÉ PARENTALE

Principe 3:32 Retrait de la responsabilité parentale

L'autorité compétente retire au titulaire de la responsabilité parentale tout ou partie de celle-ci si son comportement ou sa négligence cause un risque grave à la personne ou aux biens de l'enfant.

Principe 3:33 Requête en retrait de la responsabilité parentale

(1) Le retrait de la responsabilité parentale peut être demandé par:

(a) un parent titulaire de la responsabilité parentale;
(b) l'enfant, ainsi que
(c) toute institution de défense des intérêts de l'enfant.

(2) L'autorité compétente peut également prononcer d'office le retrait de la responsabilité parentale.

Principe 3:34 Restitution de la responsabilité parentale

Eu égard au meilleur intérêt de l'enfant, l'autorité compétente peut restituer la responsabilité parentale si les circonstances qui ont conduit au retrait ont disparu.

CHAPITRE VIII: PROCÉDURE

Principe 3:35 Autorité compétente

(1) Toute décision relative à la responsabilité parentale est prise par l'autorité compétente qui peut être soit un organe judiciaire, soit un organe administratif.
(2) En cas de nécessité, l'autorité compétente désigne toute personne ou organe approprié pour enquêter sur la situation de l'enfant.

Principe 3:36 Résolution alternative des conflits

Dans tous les conflits relatifs à la responsabilité parentale, des modes alternatifs de résolution des litiges sont mis à disposition.

Principe 3:37 Audition de l'enfant

(1) Conformément au Principe 3:6, l'autorité compétente entend l'enfant dans toutes les procédures relatives à la responsabilité parentale ; si toutefois elle décide de ne pas entendre l'enfant, elle doit invoquer des motifs spécifiques.
(2) L'audition de l'enfant a lieu soit directement devant l'autorité compétente, soit indirectement devant une personne ou un organisme désigné par l'autorité compétente.
(3) L'enfant doit être entendu d'une façon appropriée à son âge et à sa maturité.

Principe 3:38 Désignation d'un représentant *ad hoc* pour l'enfant

Dans les procédures concernant la responsabilité parentale dans lesquelles un conflit sérieux d'intérêts pourrait exister entre l'enfant et les titulaires de la responsabilité parentale ou dans lesquelles le bien-être de l'enfant est de quelque autre façon menacé, l'autorité compétente désigne un représentant *ad hoc* pour l'enfant.

Principe 3:39 Exécution

(1) En l'absence d'exécution volontaire, la décision de l'autorité compétente ou l'accord exécutoire relatif à la responsabilité parentale, donne lieu à exécution forcée sans délai.
(2) L'exécution n'a pas lieu dans le cas où elle est manifestement contraire au meilleur intérêt de l'enfant.

PRINZIPIEN ZUM EUROPÄISCHEN FAMILIENRECHT BETREFFEND ELTERLICHE VERANTWORTUNG

PRÄAMBEL

In Anerkennung, dass es trotz der bestehenden Unterschiede in den nationalen Familienrechten gleichwohl eine zunehmende Übereinstimmung gibt;

In Anerkennung, dass die bestehenden Unterschiede die Freizügigkeit der Personen in Europa behindern;

In dem Wunsch zu den gemeinsamen europäischen Werten in Bezug auf die Rechte und das Wohlergehen des Kindes beizutragen;

In dem Wunsch zur Angleichung des Familienrechts in Europa beizutragen und die Freizügigkeit der Personen in Europa weiter zu erleichtern;

Empfiehlt die Kommission für Europäisches Familienrecht die folgenden Prinzipien:

KAPITEL I: BEGRIFFSBESTIMMUNGEN

Prinzip 3:1 Begriff der elterlichen Verantwortung

Elterliche Verantwortung ist ein Bündel von Rechten und Pflichten, die auf die Förderung und Sicherung des Wohles des Kindes abzielen. Sie umfasst insbesondere:

(a) Sorge, Schutz und Erziehung;
(b) Unterhalten persönlicher Beziehungen;
(c) Bestimmung des Aufenthaltes;
(d) Verwaltung des Vermögens und
(e) gesetzliche Vertretung.

Prinzip 3:2 Inhaber der elterlichen Verantwortung

(1) Inhaber der elterlichen Verantwortung ist jede Person, der die in Prinzip 3:1 genannten Rechte und Pflichten ganz oder teilweise zustehen.

(2) Vorbehaltlich der folgenden Prinzipien, sind Inhaber der elterlichen Verantwortung

(a) die Eltern des Kindes, so wie

(b) andere Personen als die Eltern des Kindes, denen elterliche Verantwortung zusätzlich mit oder statt der Eltern zusteht.

KAPITEL II: RECHTE DES KINDES

Prinzip 3:3 Kindeswohl
In allen Angelegenheiten, die die elterliche Verantwortung betreffen, ist das Kindeswohl als oberster Gesichtspunkt in Betracht zu ziehen.

Prinzip 3:4 Autonomie des Kindes
Die Autonomie des Kindes wird respektiert, wobei den Fähigkeiten und Bedürfnissen des Kindes selbständig zu handeln, Rechnung getragen wird.

Prinzip 3:5 Nichtbenachteiligung des Kindes
Kinder dürfen nicht benachteiligt werden aus Gründen wie Geschlecht, Rasse, Hautfarbe, Sprache, Religion, politische oder andere Anschauungen, nationale, ethnische oder soziale Herkunft, sexueller Ausrichtung, Behinderung, Vermögen, Geburt oder anderem Status, unabhängig davon, ob diese Gründe sich auf das Kind oder die Inhaber der elterlichen Verantwortung beziehen.

Prinzip 3:6 Das Recht des Kindes auf Gehör
Entsprechend seinem Alter und seiner Reife hat das Kind das Recht, informiert und konsultiert zu werden, und seine Meinung zu äußern in allen das Kind berührenden Angelegenheiten, wobei der vom Kind geäußerten Auffassung angemessenes Gewicht zu geben ist.

Prinzip 3:7 Interessenkonflikt
Die Belange des Kindes sind zu schützen, wann immer sie den Belangen der Inhaber der elterlichen Verantwortung widersprechen können.

KAPITEL III: ELTERLICHE VERANTWORTUNG DER ELTERN UND DRITTER

Prinzip 3:8 Eltern
Personen, deren gesetzliche Abstammung feststeht, haben die elterliche Verantwortung für das Kind.

Prinzip 3:9 Dritte
Elterliche Verantwortung kann auch einer anderen Person als einem Elternteil ganz oder teilweise zuerkannt werden.

Prinzip 3:10 Wirkungen der Auflösung und der Trennung
Die elterliche Verantwortung wird weder von der Auflösung oder Nichtigerklärung der Ehe oder einer anderen formalisierten Lebensgemeinschaft noch von der gesetzlichen oder tatsächlichen Trennung der Eltern berührt.

KAPITEL IV: AUSÜBUNG DER ELTERLICHEN VERANTWORTUNG

ABSCHNITT A: ELTERN

Prinzip 3:11 Gemeinsame Ausübung
Eltern, denen die elterliche Verantwortung zusteht, haben bei der Ausübung dieser Verantwortung die gleichen Rechte und Pflichten. Soweit möglich üben sie sie gemeinsam aus.

Prinzip 3:12 Tägliche Angelegenheiten, wichtige und dringende Entscheidungen
(1) Eltern, denen die elterliche Verantwortung gemeinsam zusteht, haben das Recht, in täglichen Angelegenheiten alleine zu handeln.
(2) Wichtige Entscheidungen bezüglich Angelegenheiten wie Erziehung, medizinische Behandlung, Aufenthalt des Kindes oder Sorge für sein Vermögen sind gemeinsam zu treffen. In dringenden Fällen hat ein Elternteil das Recht alleine zu handeln. Der andere Elternteil ist unverzüglich zu unterrichten.

Prinzip 3:13 Vereinbarung über die Ausübung
(1) In Übereinstimmung mit dem Kindeswohl können Eltern, denen die elterliche Verantwortung gemeinsam zusteht, eine Vereinbarung über die Ausübung der elterlichen Verantwortung treffen.
(2) Die zuständige Behörde kann die Vereinbarung überprüfen.

Prinzip 3:14 Meinungsverschiedenheit über die Ausübung
(1) Können Eltern, denen die elterliche Verantwortung gemeinsam zusteht, sich über wichtige Angelegenheiten nicht einigen, können sie die zuständige Behörde anrufen.
(2) Die zuständige Behörde versucht eine Einigung zwischen den Eltern zu fördern.
(3) Kann keine Einigung erzielt werden, teilt die zuständige Behörde die Ausübung der elterlichen Verantwortung unter den Eltern auf oder entscheidet die Meinungsverschiedenheit.

Prinzip 3:15 Alleinige Ausübung aufgrund Vereinbarung oder Entscheidung
Vorbehaltlich des Kindeswohls kann ein Elternteil die elterliche Verantwortung alleine ausüben

(a) aufgrund einer Vereinbarung der Eltern gemäß Prinzip 3:13, oder
(b) aufgrund einer Entscheidung der zuständigen Behörde.

Prinzip 3:16 Ausübung durch einen Elternteil
Hat nur ein Elternteil die elterliche Veranwortung, übt er sie alleine aus.

ABSCHNITT B: DRITTE

Prinzip 3:17 Zusätzliche oder an Stelle der Eltern tretende Ausübung
Eine andere Person als ein Elternteil kann zusätzlich oder an Stelle der Eltern die elterliche Verantwortung ganz oder teilweise ausüben.

Prinzip 3:18 Entscheidungen in täglichen Angelegenheiten
Der Partner des Elternteils, der mit dem Kind zusammenlebt, kann in täglichen Angelegenheiten mitentscheiden, soweit der andere Elternteil dem nicht widerspricht.

KAPITEL V: INHALT DER ELTERLICHEN VERANTWORTUNG

ABSCHNITT A: PERSON UND VERMÖGEN DES KINDES

Prinzip 3:19 Sorge, Schutz und Erziehung
(1) Die Inhaber der elterlichen Verantwortung haben für die Sorge, den Schutz und die Erziehung des Kindes gemäß seiner Persönlichkeit und den Bedürfnissen seiner Entwicklung zu sorgen.
(2) Das Kind darf keiner körperlichen Bestrafung oder anderer entwürdigenden Behandlung ausgesetzt werden.

Prinzip 3:20 Aufenthalt des Kindes
(1) Wird die elterliche Verantwortung von Personen, die getrennt leben, gemeinsam ausgeübt, so haben sie sich zu einigen, bei wem das Kind seinen Aufenthalt hat.
(2) Das Kind kann sich abwechselnd bei den Inhabern der elterlichen Verantwortung aufhalten aufgrund einer von der zuständigen Behörde genehmigten Vereinbarung oder aufgrund einer Entscheidung der zuständigen Behörde. Die zuständige Behörde berücksichtigt Umstände wie:
- (a) das Alter und die Auffassung des Kindes;
- (b) die Fähigkeit und Bereitschaft der Inhaber der elterlichen Verantwortung, in den das Kind betreffenden Angelegenheiten zu kooperieren, sowie ihre persönliche Situation;
- (c) die Entfernung zwischen den Aufenthaltsorten der Inhaber der elterlichen Verantwortung und zur Schule des Kindes.

Prinzip 3:21 Änderung des Aufenthalts
(1) Wird die elterliche Verantwortung gemeinsam ausgeübt und wünscht ein Inhaber der elterlichen Verantwortung den Aufenthalt des Kindes innerhalb oder ausserhalb

des Staates zu ändern, hat er den anderen Inhaber der elterlichen Verantwortung vorher darüber zu informieren.
(2) Sind die Inhaber der elterlichen Verantwortung nicht über die Änderung der Aufenhaltes des Kindes einig, so kann jeder Inhaber der elterlichen Verantwortung eine Entscheidung bei der zuständigen Behörde beantragen.
(3) Die zuständige Behörde berücksichtigt Umstände wie:

- (a) das Alter und die Auffassung des Kindes;
- (b) das Recht des Kindes, persönliche Beziehungen mit den Inhabern der elterlichen Verantwortung zu unterhalten;
- (c) die Fähigkeit und die Bereitschaft der Inhaber der elterlichen Verantwortung miteinander zu kooperieren;
- (d) die persönliche Situation der Inhaber der elterlichen Verantwortung;
- (e) die geographischen Entfernungen und die Erreichbarkeit;
- (f) die Freizügigkeit der Personen.

Prinzip 3:22 Vermögensverwaltung
(1) Die Inhaber der elterlichen Verantwortung verwalten das Vermögen des Kindes mit der gebotenen Sorgfalt, um das Vermögen zu erhalten und soweit wie möglich den Wert des Vermögens zu vermehren.
(2) Bei der Verwaltung des Vermögens des Kindes dürfen die Inhaber der elterlichen Verantwortung keine Geschenke machen, es sei denn, diese Geschenke entsprechen einer moralischen Verpflichtung.
(3) Aus dem Vermögen des Kindes erzieltes Einkommen, das nicht für die ordnungsgemäße Verwaltung des Vermögens sowie den Unterhalt und die Erziehung des Kindes benötigt wird, kann, soweit notwendig, für die Bedürfnisse der Familie verwendet werden.

Prinzip 3:23 Beschränkungen
(1) Die Inhaber der elterlichen Verantwortung verwalten nicht das Vermögen, das das Kind durch testamentarische Verfügung oder Schenkung erworben hat, sofern der von Todes wegen Verfügende oder Schenker dies so angeordnet hat.
(2) Der Verdienst des Kindes wird gleichfalls nicht von den Inhabern der elterlichen Verantwortung verwaltet, es sei denn, das Kind hat noch nicht das nötige Alter und die Reife, um selbst zu entscheiden.
(3) Soweit Geschäfte bedeutende wirtschaftliche Folgen für das Kind haben können, ist die Zustimmung der zuständigen Behörde notwendig.

Prinzip 3:24 Gesetzliche Vertretung
(1) Die Inhaber der elterlichen Verantwortung vertreten kraft Gesetz das Kind in allen Angelegenheiten, die seine Person und sein Vermögen betreffen.

(2) Keine gesetzliche Vertretung findet statt, wenn ein Interessenkonflikt zwischen dem Kind und den Inhabern der elterlichen Verantwortung besteht.
(3) Entsprechend seinem Alter und seiner Reife hat das Kind das Recht, sich in Verfahren, die es betrifft, selbst zu vertreten.

ABSCHNITT B: UNTERHALTEN PERSÖNLICHER BEZIEHUNGEN

Prinzip 3:25 Umgang mit Eltern und anderen Personen

(1) Das Kind und die Eltern haben das Recht, regelmäßigen Umgang miteinander zu erhalten und zu unterhalten.
(2) Umgang erfolgt zwischen dem Kind und seinen nahen Verwandten.
(3) Umgang kann auch zwischen dem Kind und Personen erfolgen, mit denen das Kind eine enge persönliche Beziehung hat.

Prinzip 3:26 Inhalt des Umgangs

(1) Umgang umfasst den Aufenthalt des Kindes für einen begrenzten Zeitraum oder ein Treffen mit dem Elternteil oder einer anderen Person als dem Elternteil, mit dem es gewöhnlich nicht lebt; ferner jede Form der Kommunikation zwischen dem Kind und dieser Person.
(2) Ein solcher Umgang hat dem Kindeswohl zu entsprechen.

Prinzip 3:27 Vereinbarung

(1) In Übereinstimmung mit dem Kindeswohl können die Eltern und die in Prinzip 3:25(2) und (3) genannten Personen eine Vereinbarung über den Umgang treffen.
(2) Die zuständige Behörde kann die Vereinbarung überprüfen.

Prinzip 3:28 Beschränkungen

Der Umgang kann von der zuständigen Behörde beschränkt, beendet oder Bedingungen unterworfen werden, wenn das Kindeswohl dies verlangt.

Prinzip 3:29 Information der Eltern

Ein Elternteil hat das Recht, in Angelegenheiten, die die persönlichen Verhältnisse des Kindes betreffen, informiert zu werden.

KAPITEL VI: BEENDIGUNG DER ELTERLICHEN VERANTWORTUNG

Prinzip 3:30 Beendigung

(1) Die elterliche Verantwortung endet in folgenden Fällen:

(a) das Kind erreicht die Volljährigkeit;
(b) das Kind geht eine Ehe oder eine eingetragene Partnerschaft ein;
(c) Adoption des Kindes;
(d) Tod des Kindes.

(2) Adoptiert der Partner eines Elternteils das Kind des Elternteils, so endet die elterliche Verantwortung nur im Hinblick auf den anderen Elternteil.

Prinzip 3:31 Tod der Eltern

(1) Steht beiden Elternteilen die elterliche Verantwortung gemeinsam zu und stirbt einer von ihnen, verbleibt die elterliche Verantwortung bei dem überlebenden Elternteil.
(2) Stirbt ein Elternteil, der die alleinige elterliche Verantwortung innehatte, wird diese Verantwortung aufgrund einer Entscheidung der zuständigen Behörde dem überlebenden Elternteil oder einem Dritten zuerkannt..
(3) Beim Tod beider Eltern, von denen wenigstens einer die elterliche Verantwortung innehatte, trifft die zuständige Behörde Schutzmaßnahmen für die Person und das Vermögen des Kindes.

KAPITEL VII: ENTZIEHUNG UND WIEDERHERSTELLUNG DER ELTERLICHEN VERANTWORTUNG

Prinzip 3:32 Entziehung der elterlichen Verantwortung

Die zuständige Behörde entzieht dem Inhaber der elterlichen Verantwortung ganz oder teilweise die elterliche Verantwortung, wenn sein Verhalten oder seine Vernachlässigung eine ernsthafte Gefahr für die Person oder das Vermögen des Kindes bedeutet.

Prinzip 3:33 Antrag auf Entziehung der elterlichen Verantwortung

(1) Die Entziehung der elterlichen Verantwortung kann beantragt werden von:

(a) einem Elternteil, der Inhaber der elterlichen Verantwortung ist;
(b) dem Kind, sowie
(c) jeder Institution, die das Wohl des Kindes schützt.

(2) Die zuständige Behörde kann die elterliche Verantwortung auch von Amts wegen entziehen.

Prinzip 3:34 Wiederherstellung der elterlichen Verantwortung
In Übereinstimmung mit dem Kindeswohl stellt die zuständige Behörde die elterliche Verantwortung wieder her, wenn die Umstände, die zur Entziehung geführt haben, nicht mehr bestehen.

KAPITEL VIII: VERFAHREN

Prinzip 3:35 Zuständige Behörde
(1) Alle Entscheidungen über die elterliche Verantwortung werden von der zuständigen Behörde getroffen, die entweder ein Gericht oder eine Verwaltungsbehörde sein kann..
(2) Soweit notwendig, bestellt die zuständige Behörde eine geeignete Person oder Einrichtung, um die Verhältnisse des Kindes zu untersuchen.

Prinzip 3:36 Alternative Streitbeilegung
In allen Streitigkeiten über elterliche Verantwortung werden alternative Streitbeilegungsverfahren zur Verfügung gestellt.

Prinzip 3:37 Anhörung des Kindes
(1) In Übereinstimmung mit Prinzip 3:6 hört die zuständige Behörde das Kind in allen Verfahren über die elterliche Verantwortung an. Entscheidet die Behörde, das Kind nicht anzuhören, gibt sie dafür besondere Gründe an.
(2) Die Anhörung des Kindes findet unmittelbar vor der zuständigen Behörde statt oder mittelbar vor einer Person oder Einrichtung, die von der zuständigen Behörde dazu bestellt worden ist.
(3) Die Anhörung des Kindes erfolgt in einer seinem Alter und seiner Reife entsprechenden Weise.

Principe 3:38 Bestellung eines besonderen Vertreters für das Kind
In Verfahren über die elterliche Verantwortung, in denen ein Interessenkonflikt zwischen dem Kind und den Inhabern der elterlichen Verantwortung bestehen könnte oder in denen das Kindeswohl in anderer Weise gefährdet ist, bestellt die zuständige Behörde einen besonderen Vertreter für das Kind.

Prinzip 3:39 Vollstreckung
(1) Mangels freiwilliger Befolgung wird eine Entscheidung der zuständigen Behörde und eine vollstreckbare Vereinbarung zur elterlichen Verantwortung ohne Verzögerung vollstreckt.
(2) Eine Vollstreckung findet nicht statt, wenn sie offensichtlich dem Kindeswohl widerspricht.

BEGINSELEN VAN EUROPEES FAMILIERECHT BETREFFENDE OUDERLIJKE VERANTWOORDELIJKHEID

PREAMBULE

Erkennende dat ondanks de bestaande verschillen in de nationale familierechten er evenwel een toenemende convergentie bestaat;

Erkennende dat de bestaande verschillen het vrij verkeer van personen in Europa beletten;

Geleid door de wens een bijdrage te leveren aan gemeenschappelijke Europese waarden met betrekking tot de rechten en het welzijn van het kind;

Geleid door de wens een bijdrage te leveren aan de harmonisatie van het familierecht in Europa en het vrij verkeer van personen in Europa verder te vergemakkelijken;

Beveelt de Commissie voor Europees Familierecht de volgende beginselen aan:

HOOFDSTUK I: DEFINITIES

Beginsel 3:1 Begrip ouderlijke verantwoordelijkheid
De ouderlijke verantwoordelijkheid is een verzameling van rechten en plichten gericht op de bevordering en bescherming van het welzijn van het kind. Zij omvat in het bijzonder:

(a) zorg, bescherming en opvoeding;
(b) onderhouden van persoonlijke relaties;
(c) bepaling van verblijfplaats;
(d) beheer over het vermogen en
(e) wettelijke vertegenwoordiging.

Beginsel 3:2 Drager van de ouderlijke verantwoordelijkheid
(1) Een drager van de ouderlijke verantwoordelijkheid is iedere persoon die de in Beginsel 3:1 genoemde rechten en plichten geheel of gedeeltelijk heeft.

(2) Onder voorbehoud van de volgende Beginselen zijn de dragers van de ouderlijke verantwoordelijkheid:

(a) de ouders van het kind, alsmede
(b) andere personen dan de ouders van het kind die naast of in plaats van de ouders de ouderlijke verantwoordelijkheid hebben.

HOOFDSTUK II: RECHTEN VAN HET KIND

Beginsel 3:3 Belang van het kind
In alle aangelegenheden die de ouderlijke verantwoordelijkheid betreffen vormt het belang van het kind de eerste overweging.

Beginsel 3:4 Autonomie van het kind
De autonomie van het kind wordt gerespecteerd rekening met in achtneming van de ontwikkelde bekwaamheid en de behoefte van het kind om zelfstandig te handelen.

Beginsel 3:5 Non-discriminatie van het kind
Kinderen mogen niet worden gediscrimineerd op gronden zoals geslacht, ras, huidskleur, taal, godsdienst, politieke of andere overtuiging, nationale, etnische of maatschappelijke afkomst, seksuele gerichtheid, handicap, vermogen, geboorte of andere status, ongeacht of deze gronden op het kind of op de dragers van de ouderlijke verantwoordelijkheid betrekking hebben.

Beginsel 3:6 Hoorrecht van het kind
In overeenstemming met zijn leeftijd en rijpheid heeft het kind het recht om geïnformeerd en geconsulteerd te worden en zijn mening kenbaar te maken in alle aangelegenheden die het kind betreffen, waarbij passend belang wordt gehecht aan zijn mening.

Beginsel 3:7 Belangenconflict
De belangen van het kind dienen te worden beschermd in alle gevallen waar zij in conflict zijn met de belangen van de dragers van de ouderlijke verantwoordelijkheid.

HOOFDSTUK III: OUDERLIJKE VERANTWOORDELIJKHEID VAN OUDERS EN DERDEN

Beginsel 3:8 Ouders
De ouders wier wettelijke afstamming is vastgesteld, hebben de ouderlijke verantwoordelijkheid voor het kind.

Beginsel 3:9 Derden
Ouderlijke verantwoordelijkheid kan ook geheel of gedeeltelijk aan een andere persoon dan de ouder toegekend worden.

Beginsel 3:10 Werking van ontbinding en scheiding
Ouderlijke verantwoordelijkheid wordt noch door de ontbinding of nietigverklaring van het huwelijk of van een andere formele relatie, noch door de juridische of feitelijke scheiding tussen de ouders beïnvloed.

HOOFDSTUK IV: UITOEFENING VAN OUDERLIJKE VERANTWOORDELIJKHEID

TITEL A: OUDERS

Beginsel 3:11 Gezamenlijke uitoefening
Ouders met ouderlijke verantwoordelijkheid hebben gelijke rechten en plichten in de uitoefening van deze verantwoordelijkheid en oefenen deze voor zover mogelijk gezamenlijk uit.

Beginsel 3:12 Dagelijkse aangelegenheden, belangrijke en dringende beslissingen
(1) Ouders met gezamenlijke ouderlijke verantwoordelijkheid hebben het recht om alleen te handelen in geval van dagelijkse aangelegenheden.
(2) Belangrijke beslissingen betreffende aangelegenheden zoals onderwijs, medische behandeling, verblijfplaats van het kind, of het beheer over zijn vermogen worden gezamenlijk genomen. In dringende gevallen heeft een ouder het recht om alleen te handelen. De andere ouder dient onverwijld te worden geïnformeerd.

Beginsel 3:13 Overeenkomst over de uitoefening
(1) In overeenstemming met het belang van het kind kunnen ouders die gezamenlijk de ouderlijke verantwoordelijkheid hebben, een overeenkomst sluiten over de uitoefening hiervan.
(2) De bevoegde autoriteit kan de overeenkomst controleren.

Beginsel 3:14 Geschil over de uitoefening
(1) Indien ouders die gezamenlijk ouderlijke verantwoordelijkheid hebben geen overeenstemming bereiken over een belangrijke aangelegenheid, kunnen zij het geschil aan de bevoegde autoriteit voorleggen.
(2) De bevoegde autoriteit bevordert de totstandkoming van een overeenkomst tussen de ouders.

(3) Indien geen overeenstemming kan worden bereikt, verdeelt de bevoegde autoriteit de uitoefening van de ouderlijke verantwoordelijkheid tussen de ouders of beslecht het geschil.

Beginsel 3:15 Exclusieve uitoefening op grond van overeenkomst of beslissing
In overeenstemming met het belang van het kind, kan een ouder de ouderlijke verantwoordelijkheid alleen uitoefenen

(a) op grond van een overeenkomst volgens Beginsel 3:13, of
(b) op grond van een beslissing van de bevoegde autoriteit.

Beginsel 3:16 Uitoefening door een ouder alleen
Indien slechts één ouder de ouderlijke verantwoordelijkheid heeft, oefent hij of zij deze alleen uit.

TITEL B: DERDEN

Beginsel 3:17 Uitoefening naast of in plaats van de ouders
Een andere persoon dan een ouder kan naast of in plaats van de ouders de ouderlijke verantwoordelijkheid geheel of gedeeltelijk uitoefenen.

Beginsel 3:18 Beslissingen in dagelijkse aangelegenheden
De partner van de ouder die samenwoont met het kind, kan mede beslissingen nemen betreffende dagelijkse aangelegenheden, tenzij de andere ouder met ouderlijke verantwoordelijkheid zich daartegen verzet.

HOOFDSTUK V: INHOUD VAN DE OUDERLIJKE VERANTWOORDELIJKHEID

TITEL A: PERSOON EN VERMOGEN VAN HET KIND

Beginsel 3:19 Verzorging, bescherming en opvoeding
(1) De dragers van de ouderlijke verantwoordelijkheid zorgen voor de verzorging, de bescherming en de opvoeding van het kind, in overeenstemming met zijn persoonlijkheid en de behoeften van zijn ontwikkeling.
(2) Het kind mag niet worden onderworpen aan lichamelijke bestraffing of andere vernederende behandeling.

Beginsel 3:20 Verblijfplaats

(1) Indien de ouderlijke verantwoordelijkheid gezamenlijk wordt uitgeoefend door personen die gescheiden leven, dan komen zij overeen bij wie van hen het kind zal verblijven.

(2) Op grond van een overeenkomst goedgekeurd door een bevoegde autoriteit of door een beslissing van een bevoegde autoriteit mag het kind afwisselend verblijven bij de dragers van de ouderlijke verantwoordelijkheid. De bevoegde autoriteit houdt in het bijzonder rekening met:

- (a) de leeftijd en de mening van het kind;
- (b) het vermogen en de bereidheid van de dragers van de ouderlijke verantwoordelijkheid om met elkaar samen te werken in aangelegenheden betreffende het kind alsook met hun persoonlijke situatie;
- (c) de afstand tussen de verblijfplaatsen van de dragers van de ouderlijke verantwoordelijkheid en met de school van het kind.

Beginsel 3:21 Verandering van verblijfplaats

(1) Indien de ouderlijke verantwoordelijkheid gezamenlijk wordt uitgeoefend en een drager van de ouderlijke verantwoordelijkheid wenst de verblijfplaats van het kind binnen of buiten het rechtsgebied te veranderen, dan informeert hij of zij vooraf de andere drager van de ouderlijke verantwoordelijkheid hierover.

(2) Indien de andere drager van de ouderlijke verantwoordelijkheid zich verzet tegen de wijziging van de verblijfplaats van het kind, kan elke drager van de ouderlijke verantwoordelijkheid het geschil aan de bevoegde autoriteit ter beslechting voorleggen.

(3) De bevoegde autoriteit houdt in het bijzonder rekening met:

- (a) de leeftijd en de mening van het kind;
- (b) het recht van het kind om persoonlijke relaties te onderhouden met de andere dragers van de ouderlijke verantwoordelijkheid;
- (c) het vermogen en de bereidheid van de dragers van de ouderlijke verantwoordelijkheid om met elkaar samen te werken;
- (d) de persoonlijke situatie van de dragers van de ouderlijke verantwoordelijkheid;
- (e) de geografische afstanden en de bereikbaarheid;
- (f) het vrije verkeer van personen.

Beginsel 3:22 Beheer over het vermogen van het kind

(1) De dragers van de ouderlijke verantwoordelijkheid voeren met de nodige zorgvuldigheid het beheer over het vermogen van het kind om dit te behouden en waar mogelijk zijn waarde te vermeerderen.

(2) In de uitvoering van het beheer mogen de dragers van de ouderlijke verantwoordelijkheid niet schenken tenzij de schenking aan een morele verplichting beantwoordt.

(3) De uit het vermogen van het kind verworven inkomsten die niet nodig zijn voor het behoorlijk beheer van het vermogen en voor het onderhoud en opvoeding van het kind, kunnen indien noodzakelijk voor de behoefte van het gezin worden gebruikt.

Beginsel 3:23 Beperkingen

(1) De dragers van de ouderlijke verantwoordelijkheid voeren geen beheer over het vermogen van het kind verkregen bij testamentaire beschikking of schenking indien de testator of schenker dit heeft bepaald.
(2) Evenmin voeren de dragers van de ouderlijke verantwoordelijkheid het beheer over het inkomen van het kind, tenzij het kind niet de leeftijd en de rijpheid heeft om zelf te beslissen.
(3) Indien rechtshandelingen betekenisvolle financiële gevolgen kunnen hebben voor het kind, is toestemming van de bevoegde autoriteit noodzakelijk.

Beginsel 3:24 Wettelijke vertegenwoordiging

(1) De dragers van de ouderlijke verantwoordelijkheid vertegenwoordigen het kind in alle aangelegenheden die de persoon en het vermogen van het kind betreffen.
(2) Wettelijke vertegenwoordiging is uitgesloten bij belangentegenstelling tussen het kind en de dragers van de ouderlijke verantwoordelijkheid.
(3) In overeenstemming met zijn leeftijd en rijpheid, heeft het kind het recht om zichzelf te vertegenwoordigen in procedures die hem zelf betreffen.

TITEL B: ONDERHOUDEN VAN PERSOONLIJKE RELATIES

Beginsel 3:25 Omgang met ouders en andere personen

(1) Het kind en de ouders hebben het recht regelmatig omgang elkaar te verkrijgen en te onderhouden.
(2) Een omgang wordt tot stand gebracht tussen het kind en zijn naaste verwanten.
(3) Een omgang kan worden tot stand gebracht tussen het kind en de personen met wie het kind een nauwe persoonlijke relatie heeft.

Beginsel 3:26 Inhoud van omgang

(1) Omgang omvat het verblijf van het kind voor een beperkte tijd bij of een ontmoeting met de ouder, of een andere persoon dan de ouder, bij wie het kind gewoonlijk niet verblijft, alsook elke vorm van communicatie tussen het kind en deze persoon.
(2) Dergelijk omgang is in overeenstemming met het belang van het kind.

Beginsel 3:27 Overeenkomst

(1) In overeenstemming met het belang van het kind kunnen de ouders en de andere personen bepaald in Beginsel 3:25 (2) en (3) een overeenkomst over de omgang sluiten.

(2) De bevoegde autoriteit kan de overeenkomst controleren.

Beginsel 3:28 Beperkingen

In het belang van het kind kan de bevoegde autoriteit de omgang beperken, beëindigen of aan voorwaarden verbinden.

Beginsel 3:29 Informatie aan de ouders

Een ouder heeft het recht om over aangelegenheden betreffende de persoonlijke situatie van het kind te worden geïnformeerd.

HOOFDSTUK VI: BEËINDIGING VAN DE OUDERLIJKE VERANTWOORDELIJKHEID

Beginsel 3:30 Beëindiging

(1) De ouderlijke verantwoordelijkheid eindigt indien het kind:

(a) meerderjarig wordt;
(b) in het huwelijk treedt of een geregistreerd partnerschap aangaat;
(c) geadopteerd wordt;
(d) overlijdt.

(2) Indien een partner van een ouder het kind van de ouder adopteert, eindigt de ouderlijke verantwoordelijkheid van de andere ouder.

Beginsel 3:31 Overlijden van de ouders

(1) Indien de ouders gezamenlijk de ouderlijke verantwoordelijkheid hebben en een van hen overlijdt, dan behoudt de overlevende ouder de ouderlijke verantwoordelijkheid.

(2) Overlijdt een ouder die alleen de ouderlijke verantwoordelijkheid heeft, dan wordt deze verantwoordelijkheid op grond van een beslissing van de bevoegde autoriteit aan de overlevende ouder of aan een derde toegekend.

(3) Indien beide ouders overlijden, terwijl minstens een van beide ouders de ouderlijke verantwoordelijkheid had, treft de bevoegde autoriteit beschermende maatregelen over de persoon en het vermogen van het kind.

HOOFDSTUK VII: ONTTREKKING EN HERSTEL VAN DE OUDERLIJKE VERANTWOORDELIJKHEID

Beginsel 3:32 Onttrekking van ouderlijke verantwoordelijkheid
De bevoegde autoriteit onttrekt de drager van de ouderlijke verantwoordelijkheid geheel of gedeeltelijk van deze ouderlijke verantwoordelijkheid indien zijn gedrag of nalatigheid een ernstig gevaar voor de persoon of het vermogen van het kind veroorzaakt.

Beginsel 3:33 Verzoek tot onttrekking van ouderlijke verantwoordelijkheid
(1) Onttrekking van ouderlijke verantwoordelijkheid kan verzocht worden door:
- (a) iedere ouder die ouderlijke verantwoordelijkheid heeft;
- (b) het kind, alsmede
- (c) elke instelling ter bescherming van de belangen van kind.

(2) De bevoegde autoriteit kan de ouderlijke verantwoordelijkheid ook van ambtswege onttrekken.

Beginsel 3:34 Herstel van ouderlijke verantwoordelijkheid
In overeenstemming met het belang van het kind, herstelt de bevoegde autoriteit de ouderlijke verantwoordelijkheid, indien de omstandigheden die tot onttrekking geleid hebben niet langer bestaan.

HOOFDSTUK VIII: PROCEDURE

Beginsel 3:35 Bevoegde autoriteit
(1) Alle beslissingen over ouderlijke verantwoordelijkheid worden door de bevoegde autoriteit genomen, die zowel een gerechtelijk als een administratief orgaan kan zijn.
(2) Indien noodzakelijk, benoemt de bevoegde autoriteit een geschikte persoon of geschikte instelling om de situatie van het kind te onderzoeken.

Beginsel 3:36 Alternatieve geschillenoplossing
In alle geschillen betreffende ouderlijke verantwoordelijkheid zijn alternatieve procedures voor geschillenbeslechting beschikbaar.

Beginsel 3:37 Horen van het kind
(1) In overeenstemming met Beginsel 3:6 hoort de bevoegde autoriteit het kind in alle procedures betreffende de ouderlijke verantwoordelijkheid. Beslist de bevoegde autoriteit het kind niet te horen dan geeft zij hiervoor bijzondere reden aan.
(2) Het horen van het kind vindt plaats door de bevoegde autoriteit zelf of indirect door een persoon of instelling door de bevoegde autoriteit aangewezen.

(3) Het kind wordt gehoord op een wijze die in overeenstemming is met zijn leeftijd en rijpheid.

Beginsel 3:38 Benoeming van een bijzondere vertegenwoordiger voor het kind
In procedures betreffende de ouderlijke verantwoordelijkheid, waarin een belangengeschil tussen het kind en de dragers van de ouderlijke verantwoordelijkheid zou kunnen bestaan, of waarin het welzijn van het kind anderszins gevaar loopt, benoemt de bevoegde autoriteit een bijzondere vertegenwoordiger voor het kind.

Beginsel 3:39 Tenuitvoerlegging
(1) Bij gebrek aan vrijwillige uitvoering wordt een beslissing van de bevoegde autoriteit en een afdwingbare overeenkomst betreffende ouderlijke verantwoordelijkheid onverwijld ten uitvoer gelegd.
(2) Tenuitvoerlegging vindt niet plaats indien zij duidelijk in strijd is met het belang van het kind.

PRINCIPIOS DE DERECHO EUROPEO DE FAMILIA RELATIVOS A LA RESPONSABILIDAD PARENTAL

PREÁMBULO

Reconociendo que, a pesar de las divergencias de los sistemas nacionales de Derecho de familia existe, no obstante, una creciente convergencia ;

Reconociendo que las diferencias que subsisten obstaculizan la libre circulación de personas ;

Deseando contribuir a los valores comunes europeos relativos a los derechos y el bienestar del niño ;

Deseando contribuir a la armonización el Derecho de familia en Europa y facilitar aún más la libre circulación de personas en Europa ;

La Comisión para el Derecho europeo de familia recomienda los siguientes Principios:

CAPÍTULO I: DEFINICIONES

Principio 3:1 Concepto de responsabilidad parental

La responsabilidad parental es un conjunto de derechos y deberes destinados a promover y salvaguardar el bienestar del niño. Comprende en particular:

(a) el cuidado, la protección y la educación;
(b) el mantenimiento de relaciones personales;
(c) la determinación de la residencia;
(d) la administración de los bienes, y
(e) la representación legal.

Prncipio 3:2 Titulares de la responsabilidad parental

(1) Es titular de la responsabilidad parental cualquier persona que tenga, en su totalidad o en parte, los derechos y deberes mencionados en el Principio 3:1 .

(2) Salvo en lo dispuesto en los Principios siguientes los titulares de la responsabilidad parental son:

(a) los padres del niños, así como
(b) otras personas distintas de los padres del niño que tengan la responsabilidad parental adicionalmente o en sustitución de los padres.

CAPÍTULO II: DERECHOS DEL NIÑO

Principio 3:3 Interés superior del niño
En todas las cuestiones relativas a la responsabilidad parental el interés superior del niño debe ser la consideración preponderante.

Principio 3:4 Autonomía del niño
La autonomía del niño ha de respetarse teniendo en cuenta su creciente capacidad y necesidad de actuar independientemente.

Principio 3:5 No-discriminación del niño
Los niños no deben ser discriminados por causa de sexo, raza, color, religión, opinión política o de otro tipo, origen nacional, étnico y social, orientación sexual, discapacidad, patrimonio, nacimiento u otro estado, tanto si esos motivos se refieren al niño o a los titulares de la responsabilidad parental.

Principio 3:6 Derecho del niño a ser oído
Teniendo en cuenta su edad y madurez el niño tiene derecho a ser informado, consultado y a expresar su opinión en todas las cuestiones que le afecten, debiéndose tener en cuenta la opinión expresada por el niño de manera adecuada.

Principio 3:7 Conflicto de intereses
Los intereses del niño deben protegerse en todos los casos de conflicto con los intereses de los titulares de la responsabilidad parental.

CAPÍTULO III: RESPONSABILIDAD PARENTAL DE PADRES Y TERCEROS

Principio 3:8 Padres
Las personas respecto a las cuales se ha establecido la filiación legal del niño tienen la responsabilidad parental sobre el niño.

Principio 3:9 Terceras personas
La responsabilidad parental puede atribuirse en todo o en parte a una persona distinta que el padre o la madre.

Principio 3:10 Incidencia de la disolución o la separación
La responsabilidad parental no se ve afectada ni por la disolución o la anulación del matrimonio u otra unión formalizada ni por la separación legal o de hecho de los padres.

CAPÍTULO IV: EJERCICIO DE LA RESPONSABILIDAD PARENTAL

SECCIÓN A: LOS PADRES

Principio 3:11 Ejercicio conjunto
Los padres que detenten la responsabilidad parental tienen en el ejercicio de la misma iguales derechos y deberes. En la medida de lo posible la ejercen conjuntamente.

Principio 3:12 Cuestiones de la vida cotidiana, decisiones importantes y urgentes
(1) Los padres titulares en común de la responsabilidad parental tienen derecho a actuar individualmente respecto a las cuestiones de la vida cotidiana.
(2) Las decisiones importantes relativas a cuestiones como la educación, los tratamientos médicos, la residencia del niño, o la administración de sus bienes deben tomarse conjuntamente. En caso de urgencia el padre o la madre tienen derecho a actuar individualmente. El otro padre debe ser informado sin dilación.

Principio 3:13 Acuerdos sobre el ejercicio de la responsabilidad parental
(1) Teniendo en cuenta el interés superior del niño, los padres que detenten conjuntamente la responsabilidad parental pueden llegar a acuerdos sobre el ejercicio de la misma.
(2) La autoridad competente puede controlar el acuerdo.

Principio 3:14 Desacuerdo sobre el ejercicio de la responsabilidad parental
(1) Si los padres que detentan conjuntamente la responsabilidad parental no llegan a un acuerdo respecto a una cuestión importante pueden acudir a la autoridad competente.
(2) La autoridad competente ha de promover el acuerdo entre los padres.
(3) Si no puede llegarse a ningún acuerdo, la autoridad competente puede dividir el ejercicio de la responsabilidad parental entre los padres o decidir la disputa.

Principio 3:15 Ejercicio unilateral de la responsabilidad parental en virtud de un acuerdo o una decisión
Teniendo en cuenta el interés superior del niño un padre puede ejercer individualmente la responsabilidad parental

(a) en virtud de un acuerdo entre los padres conforme al Principio 3:13; o
(b) en virtud de una decisión de la autoridad competente.

Principio 3:16 Ejercicio por un solo padre
Si únicamente un padre detenta la responsabilidad parental, la ejerce sólo.

SECCIÓN B: TERCERAS PERSONAS

Principio 3:17 Ejercicio adicional o en sustitución de los padres
Una persona distinta que un padre puede ejercer en todo o en parte la responsabilidad parental adicionalmente o en sustitución de los padres.

Principio 3:18 Decisiones sobre cuestiones de la vida cotidiana
La pareja del padre o la madre que viva con el niño puede tomar parte en las decisiones sobre cuestiones de la vida cotidiana salvo en caso de objeción del otro padre que detente la responsabilidad parental.

CAPÍTULO V : CONTENIDO DE LA RESPONSABILIDAD PARENTAL

SECCIÓN A: PERSONA Y BIENES DEL NIÑO

Principio 3:19 Cuidado, protección y educación
(1) Los titulares de la responsabilidad parental deben dispensar al niño cuidado, protección y educación conforme a la personalidad del niño y a sus necesidades evolutivas.
(2) El niño no debe ser objeto de castigos corporales u otros tratamientos humillantes.

Principio 3:20 Residencia
(1) Si la responsabilidad parental se ejerce de forma conjunta los titulares de la responsabilidad parental que vivan separados deben llegar a un acuerdo acerca de con quien de ellos ha de residir el niño.
(2) El niño puede residir de forma alterna con los titulares de la responsabilidad parental, bien en virtud de un acuerdo entre los titulares de la responsabilidad parental aprobado por la autoridad competente, bien en virtud de una decisión de la autoridad competente. La autoridad competente tendrá especialmente en cuenta:

(a) la edad y la opinión del niño;
(b) la capacidad y la voluntad de los titulares de la responsabilidad parental para cooperar en las cuestiones relativas al niño así como su situación personal;
(c) la distancia entre las residencias de los titulares de la responsabilidad parental así como la distancia con la escuela del niño.

Principio 3:21 Cambio de residencia
(1) Cuando la responsabilidad parental se ejerza conjuntamente y un titular de la responsabilidad parental desee cambiar la residencia del niño dentro o fuera del territorio nacional debe informar al otro titular de la responsabilidad parental con carácter previo.

(2) Si el otro titular de la responsabilidad parental se opone al cambio de residencia del niño, cualquiera de los titulares puede acudir a la autoridad competente para que ésta tome una decisión.
(3) La autoridad competente tendrá especialmente en cuenta:
- (a) la edad y la opinión del niño;
- (b) el derecho del niño a mantener relaciones personales con los otros titulares de la responsabilidad parental;
- (c) la capacidad y voluntad de los titulares de la responsabilidad parental para cooperar;
- (d) la situación personal de los titulares de la responsabilidad parental;
- (e) la distancia geográfica y las facilidades de acceso;
- (f) la libre circulación de personas.

Principio 3:22 Administración de los bienes del niño
(1) Los titulares de la responsabilidad parental deben administrar los bienes del niño con cuidado y diligencia a fin de preservar y en la medida de lo posible aumentar el valor de los bienes.
(2) Al administrar los bienes del niño los titulares de la responsabilidad parental no pueden hacer donaciones salvo si obedecen a una obligación moral.
(3) Las rentas derivadas de los bienes del niño que no sean necesarias ni para la adecuada administración de los bienes ni para los alimentos y la educación del niño pueden, en caso de necesidad, emplearse para las necesidades de la familia.

Principio 3:23 Limitaciones
(1) Los titulares de la responsabilidad parental no deben administrar bienes adquiridos por el niño en virtud de una disposición testamentaria o una donación si el testador o el donante así lo disponen.
(2) De la misma forma, las ganancias y salarios del niño no deben ser administrados por los titulares de la responsabilidad parental salvo que el niño no tenga la edad y madurez necesarias para decidir por si mismo.
(3) Cuando las transacciones puedan tener para el niño consecuencias financieras importantes será necesaria la autorización de la autoridad competente.

Principio 3:24 Representación legal
(1) Los titulares de la responsabilidad parental representan legalmente al niño en todos los asuntos relativos a la persona o a los bienes del niño.
(2) La representación legal se excluye en caso de un conflicto de intereses entre el niño y los titulares de la responsabilidad parental.
(3) Teniendo en cuenta su edad y grado de madurez el niño debe tener derecho a representarse a si mismo en los procedimientos que le conciernan.

SECCIÓN B: MANTENIMIENTO DE RELACIONES PERSONALES

Principio 3:25 Relaciones personales con los padres y otras personas
(1) El niño y sus padres tienen derecho a obtener y mantener relaciones personales de forma regular.
(2) Deben establecerse relaciones personales entre el niño y sus familiares cercanos.
(3) Pueden establecerse relaciones personales entre el niño y personas con las que el niño tiene lazos personales estrechos.

Principio 3:26 Contenido de las relaciones personales
(1) Las relaciones personales comprenden la estancia del niño durante un periodo de tiempo limitado o el encuentro con el padre o la madre u otra persona distinta del padre o la madre con la que el niño no reside habitualmente, así como toda otra forma de comunicación entre el niño y tal persona.
(2) Dichas relaciones personales deben corresponder al interés superior del niño.

Principio 3:27 Acuerdo
(1) Conforme al interés superior del niño el padre y la madre y las demás personas mencionadas en el Principio 3:25(2) y (3) pueden concluir un acuerdo sobre las relaciones personales.
(2) La autoridad competente puede controlar el acuerdo.

Principio 3:28 Restricciones
Si el interés superior del niño lo exige, la autoridad competente puede limitar, terminar o someter a condiciones las relaciones personales.

Principio 3:29 Información a los padres
El padre y la madre tienen derecho a ser informados respecto a las cuestiones que afecten a la situación personal del niño.

CAPÍTULO VI: TERMINACIÓN DE LA RESPONSABILIDAD PARENTAL

Principio 3:30 Terminación
(1) La responsabilidad parental termina cuando el niño:
- (a) llega a la mayoría de edad;
- (b) contrae matrimonio o constituye una pareja registrada;
- (c) es adoptado;
- (d) fallece.

(2) En caso de que el niño sea adoptado por la pareja del padre o la madre, la responsabilidad parental termina únicamente en relación con su otro padre.

Principio 3:31 Fallecimiento de los padres
(1) Si los padres detentan conjuntamente la responsabilidad parental y uno de ellos fallece la responsabilidad parental corresponde al padre superviviente.
(2) Si un padre tiene individualmente la responsabilidad parental y fallece, la autoridad competente atribuirá la responsabilidad parental al padre superviviente o a una tercera persona.
(3) En caso de fallecimiento de ambos padres, de los cuales al menos uno detentaba la responsabilidad parental, la autoridad competente tomará medidas de protección respecto a la persona y los bienes del niño.

CAPÍTULO VII: PRIVACIÓN Y RESTITUCIÓN DE LA RESPONSABILIDAD PARENTAL

Principio 3:32 Privación de la responsabilidad parental
La autoridad competente debe privar total o parcialmente al titular de la responsabilidad parental de la misma, si su comportamiento o negligencia causa un grave riesgo a la persona o los bienes del niño.

Principio 3:33 Solicitud de privación de la responsabilidad parental
(1) La privación de la responsabilidad parental puede ser solicitada por:
- (a) el padre o la madre titulares de la responsabilidad parental;
- (b) el niño; así como
- (c) toda institución de defensa de los intereses del niño.

(2) La autoridad competente puede ordenar de oficio la privación de la responsabilidad parental.

Principio 3:34 Restitución de la responsabilidad parental
Habida cuenta del interés superior del niño, la autoridad competente puede restituir la responsabilidad parental si han desaparecido las circunstancias que motivaron su privación.

CAPÍTULO VIII: PROCEDIMIENTO

Principio 3:35 Autoridad competente
(1) Todas las decisiones relativas a la responsabilidad parental deben ser tomadas por la autoridad competente, que puede ser un órgano judicial o administrativo.
(2) En caso de necesidad la autoridad competente puede nombrar a una persona u órgano adecuado para investigar las circunstancias del niño.

Principio 3:36 Resolución alternativa de controversias

En todas las disputas relativas a la responsabilidad parental se pondrán a disposición medios alternativos de resolución de controversias.

Principio 3:37 Audiencia del niño

(1) Conforme al Principio 3:6, la autoridad competente oirá al niño en todos los procedimientos relativos a la responsabilidad parental; si decide no oír al niño deberá motivarlo de manera específica.

(2) La audiencia del niño tendrá lugar bien directamente frente a la autoridad competente, bien indirectamente ante una persona u organismo designado por la autoridad competente.

(3) El niño debe ser oído de una forma adecuada a su edad y grado de madurez.

Principio 3:38 Designación de un representante *ad hoc* del niño

En los procedimientos relativos a la responsabilidad parental en los que pudiera haber un serio conflicto de intereses entre el niño y los titulares de la responsabilidad parental o en los cuales pudiera estar de cualquier otra forma amenazado el bienestar del niño, la autoridad competente designará un representante *ad hoc* del niño.

Principioe 3:39 Ejecución

(1) En ausencia de ejecución voluntaria, la decisión de la autoridad competente y los acuerdos con fuerza ejecutiva relativos a la responsabilidad parental se ejecutarán sin dilación.

(2) La ejecución no tendrá lugar cuando sea manifiestamente contraria al interés superior del niño.

EUROPEISKA FAMILJERÄTTSPRINCIPER RÖRANDE FÖRÄLDRAANSVAR

PREAMBEL

Med insikt om att rådande skillnader mellan de nationella regleringarna rörande familj gradvis minskar;

Med insikt om att kvarstående skillnader hindrar den fria rörligheten av personer inom Europa;

I avsikt att bidra till gemensamma europeiska värderingar rörande barnets rättigheter och välfärd;

I avsikt att bidra till harmoniseringen av familjerätten i Europa och att ytterligare underlätta den fria rörligheten av personer inom Europa;

Rekommenderar Kommissionen för den europeiska familjerätten följande principer:

KAPITEL I: DEFINITIONER

Princip 3:1 Begreppet föräldraansvar

Med föräldraansvar avses ett antal rättigheter och skyldigheter inriktade på att främja och säkerställa barnets välfärd. De gäller i synnerhet:

(a) omvårdnad, skydd, fostran och utbildning;
(b) upprätthållande av personliga relationer;
(c) bestämmande om barnets boende;
(d) förvaltning av egendom; och
(e) rättsligt företrädarskap.

Princip 3:2 Person med föräldraansvar

(1) Person med föräldraansvar är den som helt eller delvis har sådana rättigheter och skyldigheter som anges i Princip 3:1.

(2) Med beaktande av de följande principerna tillkommer föräldraansvar:

(a) barnets föräldrar, samt
(b) andra personer än barnets föräldrar som har föräldraansvar utöver eller i stället för föräldrarna.

KAPITEL II: BARNETS RÄTTIGHETER

Princip 3:3 Barnets bästa
I alla frågor rörande föräldraansvar skall barnets bästa komma i främsta rummet.

Princip 3:4 Barnets självbestämmanderätt
Barnets rätt till självbestämmande skall respekteras, med beaktande av barnets förmåga och behov av att handla självständigt.

Princip 3:5 Icke-diskriminering av barnet
Barn får inte utsättas för diskriminering på grunder såsom kön, ras, hudfärg, språk, religion, politisk eller annan åskådning, nationellt, etniskt eller socialt ursprung, sexuell läggning, handikapp, egendom, börd eller annan ställning, oavsett om dessa grunder hänför sig till barnet eller personer med föräldraansvar.

Princip 3:6 Barnets rätt att höras
Om det är rimligt med tanke på barnets ålder och mognad skall barnet ha rätt att bli informerat och tillfrågat och att uttrycka sina åsikter i alla frågor som rör barnet, varvid barnets åsikter skall tillmätas tillbörlig betydelse.

Princip 3:7 Intressekonflikt
Barnets intressen skall alltid skyddas om de kan strida mot de intressen som en person med föräldraansvar har.

KAPITEL III: FÖRÄLDRARS OCH ANDRA PERSONERS FÖRÄLDRAANSVAR

Princip 3:8 Föräldrar
Föräldrar vars rättsliga föräldraskap är fastställt skall ha föräldraansvar för barnet.

Princip 3:9 Andra personer
Även annan person än en förälder får tilldelas föräldraansvar, helt eller delvis.

Princip 3:10 Verkan av upplösning och separation
Föräldraansvaret skall inte påverkas av att föräldrarnas äktenskap eller annat formellt förhållande upplöses eller annulleras eller av föräldrarnas rättsliga eller faktiska separation.

KAPITEL IV: UTÖVANDE AV FÖRÄLDRAANSVAR

DEL A: FÖRÄLDRAR

Princip 3:11 Gemensamt utövande
Föräldrar som har föräldraansvar har lika rättigheter och skyldigheter att utöva det och skall om möjligt utöva det gemensamt.

Princip 3:12 Dagliga frågor, viktiga och brådskande beslut
(1) Föräldrar med gemensamt föräldraansvar skall ha rätt att ensam besluta i dagliga frågor.
(2) Viktiga beslut avseende frågor såsom fostran och utbildning, medicinsk behandling, barnets boende, eller förvaltning av barnets egendom skall fattas av föräldrarna gemensamt. I brådskande fall skall en förälder kunna fatta beslut ensam. Den andra föräldern skall bli informerad utan oskäligt dröjsmål.

Princip 3:13 Avtal om utövande
(1) Med förbehåll för barnets bästa får föräldrar med gemensamt föräldraansvar avtala om hur föräldraansvaret skall utövas.
(2) Behörig myndighet får granska avtalet.

Princip 3:14 Oenighet om utövande
(1) När föräldrar med gemensamt föräldraansvar inte kan komma överens i en viktig fråga, får de vända sig till behörig myndighet.
(2) Behörig myndighet skall främja överenskommelser mellan föräldrarna.
(3) När en överenskommelse inte kan uppnås skall behörig myndighet dela utövandet av föräldraansvar mellan föräldrarna eller avgöra tvisten.

Princip 3:15 Ensamt utövande på grund av avtal eller beslut
Med förbehåll för barnets bästa får en förälder ensam utöva föräldraansvar
- (a) på grund av avtal mellan föräldrarna enligt Princip 3:13, eller
- (b) på grund av beslut av behörig myndighet.

Princip 3:16 Ensamt utövande av en förälder
Om endast en förälder har föräldraansvar skall han eller hon utöva det ensam.

DEL B: ANDRA PERSONER

Princip 3:17 Utövande vid sidan av eller i stället för föräldrarna
En annan person än barnets förälder får vid sidan av eller i stället för föräldrarna utöva föräldraansvar helt eller delvis.

Princip 3:18 Beslut rörande dagliga frågor
En förälders partner som bor med barnet får besluta i dagliga frågor utom när den andra föräldern med föräldraansvar motsätter sig det.

KAPITEL V: FÖRÄLDRAANSVARETS INNEHÅLL

DEL A: BARNETS PERSON OCH EGENDOM

Princip 3:19 Omvårdnad, skydd, fostran och utbildning
(1) Personer med föräldraansvar skall sörja för barnets omvårdnad, skydd fostran och utbildning i enlighet med vad som krävs med hänsyn till barnets personlighet och utvecklingsbehov.
(2) Barnet får inte utsättas för kroppslig bestraffning eller annan kränkande behandling.

Princip 3:20 Boende
(1) Personer som lever isär men som utövar föräldraansvar gemensamt skall komma överens om med vem barnet skall bo.
(2) På grund av avtal som behörig myndighet har godkänt eller genom beslut av behörig myndighet får barnet bo växelvis med de personer som utövar föräldraansvaret. Den behöriga myndigheten skall beakta omständigheter såsom
(a) barnets ålder och synpunkter;
(b) förmågan och beredvilligheten hos de personer som delar föräldraansvaret att samarbeta med varandra i frågor rörande barnet, liksom deras personliga situation;
(c) avståndet mellan deras bostäder och barnets skola.

Princip 3:21 Flyttning
(1) När en person som har föräldraansvar önskar att ändra barnets boende inom eller utom landet skall han eller hon i förväg informera annan person som har föräldraansvar.
(2) Om denne motsätter sig ändringen av barnets boende, får båda innehavarna av föräldraansvar vända sig till behörig myndighet för beslut.
(3) Den behöriga myndigheten skall beakta omständigheter såsom:
(a) barnets ålder och synpunkter;
(b) barnets rätt att upprätthålla en personlig relation till en annan person med föräldraansvar;
(c) förmågan och beredvilligheten hos de personer som delar föräldraansvaret att samarbeta med varandra;
(d) deras personliga situation;

(e) geografiska avstånd och tillgänglighet;
(f) den fria rörligheten av personer.

Princip 3:22 Förvaltning av barnets egendom
(1) Personer som har föräldraansvar skall förvalta barnets egendom med omsorg och flit så att egendomen behåller och, om möjligt, ökar sitt värde.
(2) Vid sin förvaltning av barnets egendom får en person med föräldraansvar inte utge gåvor utom på grund av vad som måste anses vara en moralisk förpliktelse.
(3) Sådan inkomst av barnets egendom som inte behövs för tillbörlig förvaltning eller för barnets försörjning eller uppfostran får, när det behövs, användas för familjens behov.

Princip 3:23 Begränsningar
(1) Personer med föräldraansvar skall inte förvalta sådan egendom som barnet har förvärvat genom testamente eller som gåva när testatorn eller givaren så förordnat.
(2) Inte heller skall barnets inkomster förvaltas av person med föräldraansvar utom när barnet inte självt bör bestämma på grund av sin ålder eller bristande mognad.
(3) När en transaktion kan få betydande ekonomiska konsekvenser för barnet behövs tillstånd av behörig myndighet.

Princip 3:24 Rättslig företrädare
(1) Personer med föräldraansvar är barnets rättsliga företrädare i frågor rörande barnets person eller egendom.
(2) Rättsligt företrädarskap skall inte utövas om det finns en intressekonflikt mellan barnet och den som har föräldraansvar.
(3) Om det är rimligt med tanke på barnets ålder och mognad skall barnet ha rätt att företräda sig i rättsliga förfaranden som rör barnet självt.

DEL B: UPPRÄTTHÅLLANDE AV PERSONLIGA RELATIONER

Princip 3:25 Umgänge med föräldrar och andra personer
(1) Barnet och föräldrarna skall ha rätt till regelbundet umgänge med varandra.
(2) Umgänge bör även äga rum mellan barnet och nära anhöriga till barnet.
(3) Umgänge får även äga rum mellan barnet och andra personer med vilka barnet har nära personliga relationer.

Princip 3:26 Umgängets innehåll
(1) Umgänge innebär att barnet stannar en begränsad tid hos eller träffar en förälder eller annan person med vilken barnet inte varaktigt bor, liksom varje annan form av kommunikation mellan barnet och en sådan person.
(2) Sådant umgänge skall vara till barnets bästa.

Princip 3:27 Avtal

(1) Med förbehåll för barnets bästa får föräldrarna och andra personer som avses i Princip 3:25(2) och (3) komma överens om umgänge med barnet.
(2) Behörig myndighet får granska avtalet.

Princip 3:28 Begränsningar

Umgänget får av behörig myndighet begränsas, upplösas eller villkoras om det krävs av hänsyn till barnets bästa.

Princip 3:29 Information till föräldrarna

En förälder har rätt att bli informerad om frågor rörande barnets personliga situation.

KAPITEL VI: FÖRÄLDRAANSVARETS UPPHÖRANDE

Princip 3:30 Upphörande

(1) Föräldraansvaret upphör när barnet
- (a) blir myndigt;
- (b) ingår äktenskap eller registrerat partnerskap;
- (c) blir adopterat;
- (d) dör.

(2) Om en förälders partner adopterar barnet upphör föräldraansvaret i förhållande till den andra föräldern.

Princip 3:31 Föräldrarnas död

(1) Om föräldrarna har gemensamt föräldraansvar och en av dem dör, skall föräldraansvaret åvila den kvarlevande föräldern ensam.
(2) Om en förälder som ensam har föräldraansvaret dör, skall föräldraansvaret överföras till den kvarlevande föräldern eller en annan person efter beslut av behörig myndighet.
(3) Om båda föräldrarna dör och minst en av dem hade föräldraansvaret, skall behörig myndighet vidta åtgärder till skydd för barnets person och egendom.

KAPITEL VII: ENTLEDIGANDE FRÅN OCH ÅTERSTÄLLANDE AV FÖRÄLDRAANSVAR

Princip 3:32 Entledigande från föräldraansvar

Behörig myndighet skall entlediga en person från föräldraansvar, helt eller delvis, när dennes beteende eller försummelse förorsakar en allvarlig risk för barnets person eller egendom.

Princip 3:33 Begäran om entledigande från föräldraansvar
(1) Entledigande från föräldraansvar får begäras av:
- (a) en förälder med föräldraansvar;
- (b) barnet; och
- (c) en institution som skyddar barnets intressen.

(2) Behörig myndighet får även av eget initiativ entlediga en person från föräldraansvaret.

Princip 3:34 Återställande av föräldraansvar
Med beaktande av barnets bästa får behörig myndighet återställa föräldraansvaret om de omständigheter som föranledde entledigandet inte längre föreligger.

KAPITEL VIII: FÖRFARANDET

Princip 3:35 Behörig myndighet
(1) Alla beslut rörande föräldraansvar skall fattas av behörig myndighet som kan vara antingen en judiciell eller en administrativ myndighet.
(2) När det behövs skall behörig myndighet utse en lämplig person eller ett lämpligt organ för att utreda barnets situation.

Princip 3:36 Alternativ tvistlösning
I alla tvister rörande föräldraansvar skall alternativa tvistlösningsförfaranden finnas tillgängliga.

Princip 3:37 Barnets hörande
(1) Med beaktande av Princip 3:6 skall behörig myndighet höra barnet i alla förfaranden rörande föräldraansvar. Om myndigheten avstår från det skall det motiveras.
(2) Behörig myndighet skall antingen höra barnet direkt eller utse en person eller ett organ för att höra barnet.
(3) Barnet skall höras på ett sätt som är lämpligt med hänsyn till barnets ålder och mognad.

Princip 3:38 Utseende av en särskild företrädare för barnet
När det i ett förfarande rörande föräldraansvar finns risk för en allvarlig intressekonflikt mellan barnet och personerna med föräldraansvar, eller när barnets välfärd annars riskerar att äventyras, skall behörig myndighet utse en särskild företrädare för barnet.

Princip 3:39 Verkställighet

(1) Om ett beslut av behörig myndighet eller ett verkställbart avtal rörande föräldraansvar inte följs frivilligt, skall det verkställas utan dröjsmål.

(2) Verkställighet som uppenbarligen strider mot barnets bästa får inte ske.

European Family Law Series

1. *Legal Recognition of Same-Sex Couples in Europe*, K. Boele-Woelki and A. Fuchs (eds.)
2. *European Family Law in Action Volume I: Grounds for divorce*, K. Boele-Woelki, B. Braat and I. Sumner (eds.)
3. *European Family Law in Action Volume II: Maintenance Between Former Spouses*, K. Boele-Woelki, B. Braat and I. Sumner (eds.)
4. *Perspectives for the Unification and Harmonisation of Family Law in Europe*, K. Boele-Woelki (ed.)
5. *Family Law Legislation of the Netherlands*, I. Sumner and H. Warendorf
6. *Indépendance et interdépendance patrimoniales des époux dans le régime matrimonial légal des droits néerlandais, français et suisse*, B. Braat
7. *Principles of European Family Law Regarding Divorce and Maintenance Between Former Spouses*, K. Boele-Woelki, F. Ferrand, C. González Beilfuss, M. Jänterä-Jareborg, N. Lowe, D. Martiny and W. Pintens
8. *Inheritance Law Legislation of the Netherlands*, I. Sumner and H. Warendorf
9. *European Family Law in Action Volume III: Parental Responsibilities*, K. Boele-Woelki, B. Braat and I. Curry Sumner (eds.)
10. *Common Core and Better Law in European Family Law*, K. Boele-Woelki (ed.)
11. *All's well that ends registered?*, I. Curry-Sumner (ed.)
12. *Model Family Code – From a global perspective*, I. Schwenzer and M. Dimsey
13. *Harmonisation of Family Law in Europe. A Historical Perspective*, M. Antokolskaia
14. *Brussels II bis: Its Impact and Application in the Member States*, K. Boele-Woelki and C. González Beilfuss (eds.)
15. *Tensions between Legal, Biological and Social Conceptions of Parentage*, I. Schwenzer (ed.)
16. *Principles of European Family Law Regarding Parental Responsibilities*, K. Boele-Woelki, F. Ferrand, C. González Beilfuss, M. Jänterä-Jareborg, N. Lowe, D. Martiny and W. Pintens (eds.)